AF449363

The CAT:

Facts About Fantasy

The CAT:

Facts About Fantasy

By **MARY R. HAWORTH, Ph.D.**

Senior Clinical Psychologist, Children's
Service, Nebraska Psychiatric Institute;
Associate Professor of Medical Psychology,
University of Nebraska College of Medicine.

With a Foreword by LEOPOLD BELLAK, M.D.

GRUNE & STRATTON, INC.   NEW YORK AND LONDON

Library of Congress Catalog Card Number 65-24643

Printed in the U.S.A. (O-B)

Contents

Foreword, Leopold Bellak viii
Preface xi

I. The Test and Test Administration 1
History of the CAT 1
Nature and Purpose of Test 1
Description of, and Typical Responses to, Pictures 3
Evaluative Comments 6
Foreign Versions of the CAT 7
Administration 12
The Projective Test Battery 14
Examiner Influence 15
The Child's Reaction to the Test Situation 17
Summary 18

II. Projective Theories and Measurement Problems 19
Theoretical Aspects 19
Validity 21
Reliability 24
Summary 28

III. The Nature of the Stimulus 29
Realism versus Ambiguity 29
Structural and Perceptual Aspects 30
Effect of Color 32
Iconicity 32
Rationale for the Use of Animal Pictures 33
Projective Use of Animals by Children 37
Summary 39

IV. Animal versus Human Pictures 41
Studies with Normal Children 41
Studies with Clinical Groups 47
Subject and Card Comparisons 50
Summary 52

V. Developmental Aspects 53
Mental Development 53
Development of Thought and Language 56
Emotional Aspects of Development 58
Further Findings from Developmental Studies 60
Summary 61

VI. CAT Studies with Normal Children 62
General Norms in Children's Projective Material 62
Problems in Establishing Norms 66
Age Trends in the CAT 67

Sex Differences 73
Descriptive Studies 74
Norms for Specific Cards 79
Studies of Specific Sample Variables 80
Sociocultural Studies 83
Summary 88

VII. PROTOCOLS OF NORMAL CHILDREN 89

VIII. INTERPRETATION: PART ONE 107
Bases for Interpretations 107
Problems in Interpretation 116
Interpretive Outlines 122

IX. INTERPRETATION: PART TWO 152
The Interpretive Summary 152
Illustrative Examples for Each Card 161

X. DIAGNOSTIC STUDIES 182
Physical Problems 182
Articulation Problems 184
Mental Retardation 185
Cerebral Palsy 187
Childhood Schizophrenia 187
Muscular Tension 188
Emotional Disturbance 189
Parental Loss 195
Summary 197

XI. DIAGNOSTIC PROTOCOLS 198
Retardation 198
Cerebral Palsy 200
Brain Damage 205
Behavior Disorder, Acting-Out 208
Character Disorder 210
Neurotic Acting-Out 213
Psychoneurotic Reaction 216
Obsessive-Compulsive Reaction 224
Parental Loss 233
Borderline Psychotic 238
Childhood Schizophrenia 242

XII. MULTIPLE TESTING 249
Longitudinal Studies 249
Longitudinal Clinical Data 250
Comparisons of CAT with Other Projective Tests 254
Mothers' CATs versus Children's Psychological Evaluations 261
Clinical Examples of Between-Test Data 262
Summary 281

XIII. THE CAT-H (HUMAN FORM) 282
    Purpose and Description of Test 282
    Scoring and Interpretation 283
    Research 283
    Clinical Use of the CAT-H 286
    Summary 296

XIV. THE CAT SUPPLEMENT (CAT-S) 297
    Description of the Test 297
    Scoring and Interpretation 301
    Normative Research 301
    Clinical Use of the CAT-S 303
    Summary 307

REFERENCES 308
INDEX OF NAMES 317
INDEX OF SUBJECTS 319

Foreword

The History of Science is, of course, the history of people, and it is therefore full of satire and tragicomedy. Who would have thought that it would take more than two hundred years, from Bishop Berkeley's *Esse est percipe* in the early Eighteenth Century and Hume's *Nihil est in intellectu quid non antea fueris in sensibus* about the middle of that same century until well into the middle of the Twentieth Century before the insight of these two men would be experimentally investigated, modified, and integrated into a systematic theory of personality.

Yet such is the case, by and large. Freud's theory of personality was, of course, the major step in the direction of a dynamic theory of perception. While perceptual hypotheses are implicit in most of his theory, e.g., the formation of dreams, it finds its specific expression in the concept of projection. Though this concept became best known as a defense mechanism, especially operant in paranoid distortion, one need apparently remind the profession again and again that he saw briefly conceptualized projection as a broad perceptual process of general psychological significance.[1,2]

There is more tragicomedy though. The first and foremost of the tests to become known as a projective technique was developed by a Swiss psychoanalyst, Hermann Rorschach. However, his percept analysis was, fascinatingly enough, only in tangential relationship to what was then the main body of psychoanalytic theory. It really took Henry Murray and his development of the Thematic Apperception Test to relate a major psychological technique to the main body of psychoanalytic thought.

The next episode of intellectual vagaries revolved around the fact (and as a full participant in it I am in a poor position to cast aspersions) that projection was taken too literally as the ascription of drives and sentiments. Even the defensive aspect of the narrow concept of projection was almost forgotten, and much was speculated about the relationship of the latent to the manifest response. It was in connection with that problem that it first struck me that ego psychology had already played a broader role in psychoanalysis, and that the role of the ego in imaginative production in response to test stimuli would give an answer to many puzzles.[3,4]

With the Second World War clinical psychology became Big Business, projective tests flourished, grew indeed like weeds. Statisticians worried about applying the tests of reliability and validity to them which they had found useful in the study of tests of ability, achievement, and intelligence and found the projective tests so elusive that they tended to read them out of the party or admit them tentatively in the hope that they would eventually prove tractable.

The next big step is almost pure comedy. Academic psychology belatedly discovered in well-controlled laboratory experiments that personality variables and cultural attitudes affected perception of objects. With that step, perceptual distortion, or apperceptive distortion, as I prefer, became acceptable and has remained a cornerstone of the ever-enlarging and increasingly merging field of dynamic psychology of personality and clinical psychology.

Today, then, a projective technique has a good and proper place not only in the clinical armamentarium but also in the center of experimental psychology. We present a person, a patient, with certain stimuli and study the individual differences in perception, cognitive style, or perceptual distortion. We may base inferences on the comparison of one person's performance to that of many other thousands, and we may study the individual pattern, the intratest variations as part of the intrapersonal, interpersonal, cultural, developmental, semantic patterns of functioning. Content analysis, with and without electronic aids, codifying, pattern analysis are all means of lending background for individual clinical inferences.

Meanwhile, back on the clinical farm, there have been a few more changes. Today, most of the rash of tests and techniques of the immediate postwar period have virtually disappeared. With the exception of some personal predilections, the field of individual psychological testing belongs to the Rorschach, the Thematic Apperception Test, the Children's Apperception Test, the Bender Gestalt Test, Figure Drawing (and the Wechsler-Bellevue Test which is often used as much for personality appraisal as for an assay of intelligence *per se*). There are, of course, a variety of speciality tests, e.g., for organic deficits, and a host of group tests, among them, the Minnesota Multiphasic Inventory (MMPI).

The Children's Apperception Test, to which the present volume is devoted, belongs to the postwar crop but seems to have survived. In fact, if parental pride does not mislead me and false modesty not deter me, speaking of tests exclusively used for children, the CAT is apparently the single most widely used one. I know definitely from its printing history that its use has steadily increased in the 16 years of its existence.

This fact alone would make Dr. Haworth's volume a well-motivated and welcome one. As she points out, the literature concerning the CAT has been widely spread out, often hidden in university libraries in the form of master's or Ph.D. theses, not only in the United States but in many other countries. Dr. Haworth not only reviews the literature but also integrates findings, experimental as well as clinical, and points the way towards further necessary work.

Dr. Haworth brought to the tasks of the present volume many years of experience as a child psychologist, teacher of projective techniques in several universities, co-author with Rabin of a valuable text on the psychological testing of children,[5] experimenter and clinical investigator, and originator of a very useful method of analyzing CAT responses.[6]

I could not agree more with Dr. Haworth's findings and suggestions: a relative overemphasis has been placed on rather sterile investigations of minute or not especially relevant aspects of CAT responses and not enough on some very important aspects. Predicated either on the mistaken notion that the animal nature of the CAT was its sole *raison d'être,* or seizing on this issue because it presented itself relatively neatly (not so neat if one follows Dr. Haworth examining the difficulties investigators ran into), an undue proportion of work concentrated on this issue. To be sure, there may be some value for some children in having human figures to identify with; we have therefore now developed a human version of the CAT with as much care in duplicating the dynamic implications as possible. Some experimental work has suggested that different personality types might respond better to animals and others more to human figures.[7]

The major issues which need exploring, as Dr. Haworth also points out, are still in the area of developmental longitudinal studies and others: What intrapersonal changes go on in children as they grow older? Can psychoanalytic propositions concerning the vicissitudes of drives, the relationship to the parents, the transformation in the postulated latency period, and other aspects of the libidinal timetable be verified, modified, or rejected by studies of the CAT?

Can the hypothesis of Piaget be discerned and studied in the CAT? What can be learned about developmental change and cognitive style? What syndromes can be isolated in different clinical groups, the phobias, the behavior disorders, the psychotics, the children of schizophrenics and of alcoholics? As the CAT exists in an adaptation for India, published in Delhi, and a Japanese version was produced by Marui, and as the CAT is published in France, Italy, Germany, Australia, and widely used in Scandinavian countries, Israel, South Africa, Switzerland, Holland, and nearly everywhere else, it should lend itself to any number of useful cross-cultural comparisons.

Even within our own culture, subcultural aspects could be usefully looked into: How do culturally deprived children vary from others? What about the children of different ethnic and religious backgrounds, especially in the much-discussed second generation?

If knowledge is properly used, it leads to the asking of more questions. I have little doubt that Dr. Haworth's volume will lead to increased knowledge of the facts about fantasy in children and stimulate a great deal of useful further inquiry.

Larchmont, New York   LEOPOLD BELLAK, M.D.
Summer of 1965

REFERENCES

1. Bellak, L.: The Thematic Apperception Test and the Children's Apperception Test in Clinical Use. New York, Grune & Stratton, 1954.
2. Freud, S.: Totem and Taboo (1913). New York, W. W. Norton, 1952.
3. Bellak, L.: Thematic apperception: failures and the defenses. Tr. New York Acad. Sci. (series II) 12:122–126, 1950.
4. —: A study of limitations and "failures": toward an ego psychology of projective techniques. J. Proj. Tech. 18:279–292, 1954.
5. Rabin, A., and Haworth, M. (Eds): Projective Techniques with Children. New York: Grune & Stratton, 1960.
6. Haworth, M.: A schedule for the analysis of CAT responses. J. Proj. Tech. & Pers. Assess. 27:181–184, 1963.
7. Weisskopf-Joelson, E., and Foster, H.: An experimental study of the effect of stimulus variation upon projection. J. Proj. Tech. 26:366–370, 1962.

Preface

The Children's Apperception Test (more generally known as the CAT) has filled a unique place in the test battery of clinical psychologists working with children since its publication in 1949 by Sonya and Leopold Bellak. It has seemed pertinent, after 16 years, to gather together the research studies and the published clinical findings which have appeared as a result of the use of this test both in this country and abroad. Reports and papers which either have the CAT as their major focus or have used the CAT as a test instrument, now number over 100, and have been specially designated in the list of references at the end of the book.

Research with the CAT has largely been concerned with three major issues: the relative utility of animal versus human figures; normative studies; and comparisons of various diagnostic groupings. The published studies relating to the animal-human controversy have been reviewed and compared, along with some additional data secured with the use of a new human form of the CAT(the CAT-H) published by the Bellaks. Findings from the normative studies have been compiled and presented in as global a fashion as possible, with the aim of presenting general over-all summaries of results to date, rather than making study-by-study comparisons. The available diagnostic studies range over a wide variety of clinical entities, with all too few replications using similar sample populations.

Since many of the studies using the CAT have been master's theses, and they have apparently served that purpose adequately, there seemed nothing to be gained by engaging in extended criticisms of research design and related issues. The focus in this volume has rather been on those of the findings which appear to be valid, and on methods, procedures and analyses which might be of help to other investigators. Nevertheless, critical comments have been given when unwarranted conclusions have been drawn from meager evidence, where underlying theory seemed questionable, or where gross deficiencies obtained. In many instances, discussions of unpublished manuscripts, master's theses and studies from any of the 11 different foreign countries represented, have been presented in much more detail than that accorded equivalent published studies since the former materials are not as readily available to the reader.

Certain gaps in research coverage become evident after reviewing all the pertinent literature; namely, the effect of order of administration of tests in the battery, the effects of the examiner's sex and attitudes, variations in administration or of stimuli (e.g., use of colored versus achromatic cards, varying amounts and kinds of inquiry), and new and more dynamic schema for evaluation and comparison of data. Perhaps the most glaring deficit is to be found in the realm of longitudinal studies. Unfortunately, longitudinal designs do not lend themselves to a master's, or even a doctoral, program of studies. There is a need for established professional persons to design such projects and supervise systematic collection and storage of data, both in the normative and clinical areas. Longitudinal studies would be of value not only in the assessment of the projective aspects of this particular test, but also in throwing light on developmental progressions in cognitive, emotional and ego developments, the maturation of defensive structures, and the course of such emotional difficulties as may develop over time. A further type of longitudinal study would be the collection of pre-, during-, and post-therapy projective data, for evaluation of therapeutic effects.

Throughout the volume, extensive use has been made of actual protocols and clinical examples, not only to illustrate various clinical entities, but also to present "raw" data from presumably normal children. Few protocols of the latter type have previously appeared in the literature on this test.

I am indebted to the following clinicians and clinics for the use of protocols from their files: Eleanore Raff, Louise Sandler, Marion Kagan, Marilyn Kaufman, Mary Jane Keller, Ann Lantzourakis, the Psychological Clinic of Michigan State University and the Children's Service of the Nebraska Psychiatric Institute. Due to the necessity of insuring all possible anonymity to the patients and clients involved, identification of the sources of specific clinical materials cannot be made throughout the text.

Appreciation is also extended to those persons who so kindly consented to let their unpublished material be used in this book: Lois B. Murphy, Alice E. Moriarty, Louise Sandler, Ralph L. Witherspoon, Aileen Rochester and Marcia J. Lawton; also Ann Lantzourakis and Jan Gästrin from Stockholm. Sources and titles are indicated where these materials are discussed. Acknowledgment is also given to those authors and publishers who agreed to let their published materials be quoted.

Omaha, Nebraska   MARY R. HAWORTH
April, 1965

CHAPTER I

The Test and Test Administration

The Children's Apperception Test (more generally known as the CAT) was first published by the Bellaks in 1949 as a thematic picture technique specifically designed for use with young children. The ten plates which comprise the test are shown in Figure 1.1. The origins of the test, its basic purposes and discussions of each card have best been presented in the manual (Bellak and Bellak, 1961) accompanying the test cards and are reproduced below.[*]

HISTORY OF THE CAT

The original idea of the CAT was produced in a discussion between Ernst Kris and the senior author [Leopold Bellak] of the theoretical problems of projection and of the TAT. Dr. Kris pointed out how we could expect children to identify themselves much more readily with animals than with persons, a fact we have known ever since Freud wrote his story of little Hans in "The Phobia of a Five Year Old." The present authors, after thinking the whole problem over for nearly a year, specified a number of situations fundamental to children which might conceivably be expected to expose the dynamic workings of a child's problems as against the manifest material available. It seemed that the TAT, a wonderful instrument for adults, could not entirely fulfill the needs with young children, and similarly Symonds could not recommend his Picture-Story Test for use prior to adolescence. Theoretically, we had reason to assume that animals might be preferred identification figures from three years up to possibly ten, and thus, we set out to create, pictorially, situations vital to this age range.

Violet Lamont, a professional illustrator of children's books, agreed to draw the pictures according to our suggestions, adding a few of her own liking. She presented us with 18 pictures, some of somewhat anthropomorphized nature, some entirely in animal-fashion. These we had photostated, used some sets ourselves, and distributed others to a number of psychologists working with small children. The majority of these psychologists were known to the senior author in connection with his TAT courses and therefore had an acquaintance with projective procedures and their use. They were good enough to use the original pictures of the CAT and to send us protocols with additional information about subjects' background, etc., as well as their own impressions of the problems of the test.

On the above basis, and on the basis of our own experience with records, we reduced the number of cards from 18 to the ten most useful ones, and developed the data described herein.

NATURE AND PURPOSE OF TEST

The CAT consists of ten pictures depicting animals in various situations. It is to be used with children of both sexes primarily between the ages of three and ten for maximal usefulness. . . .

---

[*]Reproduced from the manual with permission of the authors.

1

The CAT is a projective method or, as we prefer to call it, an apperceptive method: *a method of investigating personality by studying the dynamic meaningfulness of the individual differences in perception of standard stimuli.*

The test is a direct descendant of the Henry Murray Thematic Apperception Test. It does not compete with the TAT nor substitute for it. Unsurpassed as we believe the TAT is for adult personality investigation, it is nevertheless relatively unsuited for young children to the same degree that CAT is unsuited for adults. Ideally, we should like to see the CAT used for children from three to ten; Symonds Picture-Story Test, for adolescents; and the TAT for adolescents and adults.

The CAT was designed to facilitate understanding of a child's relationship to his most important figures and drives. The pictures were designed to elicit responses to feeding problems specifically, and oral problems generally; to investigate problems of sibling rivalry; to illuminate the attitude toward parental figures and the way in which these figures are apperceived; to learn about the child's relationship to the parents as a couple—technically spoken of as the oedipal complex and its culmination in the primal scene: namely, the child's fantasies about seeing the parents in bed together. Related to this, we wish to elicit the child's fantasies about aggression; about acceptance by the adult world, and his fear of being lonely at night with a possible relation to masturbation, toilet behavior and the parents' response to it. We wish to learn about the child's structure and his dynamic method of reacting to—and handling—his problems of growth.

This test, like the TAT, is primarily concerned with the *content* of production. An analysis of apperceptive behavior is usually concerned with *what* one sees and thinks in distinction to an examination of expressive behavior, which is concerned with *how* one sees and thinks. We have discussed this relationship of adaptive, expressive, and apperceptive aspects of psychological productions in a previous publication (Bellak, 1944) in which we pointed out that the Rorschach is primarily a study of the formal organization of expressive factors. As such, it is better qualified to facilitate diagnosis if this term is taken to mean identifying a given person with a nosological entity as set forth in an official manual on diagnosis. On the other hand, the CAT, like the TAT, is better able to reveal the dynamics of interpersonal relationships, of drive constellations, and the nature of defenses against them.

Thus, we believe that the CAT may be clinically useful in determining what dynamic factors might be related to a child's reaction in a group, in school or kindergarten, or to events at home. The CAT may be profitable in the hands of the psychoanalyst, the psychiatrist, the psychologist, the social worker, and the teachers as well as the psychologically trained pediatrician. It may be used directly in therapy as a play technique. After the original responses have been given, one may wish to go over them with the child in the form of play and make appropriate interpretations.

Furthermore, the CAT should lend itself to much needed longitudinal research studies on child development: if the CAT were administered to children at half-year intervals from the third year, we might learn much about the developmental fate of a number of psychological problems thus far studied only in psychoanalytic investigation or other cross-sectional studies. These latter are by necessity reconstructions and inferences which need further confirmation and/or elaboration. In research studies and clinical use alike it should be helpful that the CAT is relatively culture-free. Since we deal with animal pictures, it is used equally well with white, Negro children, and other groups as well except, of course, those groups which might not be familiar with some of the inanimate objects such as bicycles, etc.

Lack of familiarity with the animals depicted does not seem to constitute a problem, since the children simply substitute animals they are familiar with.

DESCRIPTION OF, AND TYPICAL RESPONSES TO, PICTURES

Below, we present typical themes seen as responses to the various pictures.

Picture #1: Chicks seated around a table on which is a large bowl of food. Off to one side is a large chicken, dimly outlined.

Responses revolve around eating, being or not being sufficiently fed by either parent. Themes of sibling rivalry enter in around who gets more, who is well-behaved and not, etc. Food may be seen as a reward or, inversely, its withholding seen as punishment; general problems of orality are dealt with: satisfaction or frustration, feeding problems *per se*.

Picture #2: One bear pulling a rope on one side while another bear and a baby bear pull on the other side.

It is interesting to observe whether the baby here identifies the figure with whom he cooperates (if at all) as the father or the mother. It may be seen as a serious fight with accompanying fear of aggression, fulfillment of the child's own aggression or autonomy. More benignly, this picture may be seen as a game (tug-of-war, for example). Sometimes the rope itself may be a source of concern, i.e., breakage of the rope as a toy and fear of subsequent punishment; or again, purely as a symbol concerning masturbation with the rope-breaking representing castration fears.

Picture #3: A lion with pipe and cane, sitting in a chair; in the lower right corner a little mouse appears in a hole.

This is usually seen as a father figure equipped with such symbols as pipe and cane. The latter may be seen either as an instrument of aggression or may be used to turn this paternal figure into an old, helpless one of whom one need not be afraid. This is usually a defensive process. If the lion is seen as a strong paternal figure, it will be important to note whether he is a benign or a dangerous power.

The mouse is seen by the great majority of children, and often taken as the identification figure. In such a case—by tricks and circumstance—the mouse may be turned into the more powerful one. On the other hand, it may be totally in the power of the lion. Some children identify themselves with the lion and there will be subjects who will switch identification one or more times, giving evidence of confusion about role, conflict between compliance and autonomy, etc.

Picture #4: A kangaroo with a bonnet on her head, carrying a basket with a milk bottle; in her pouch is a baby kangaroo with a balloon; on a bicycle, a larger kangaroo child.

This usually elicits themes of sibling rivalry, or some concern with the origin of babies. In both cases, the relation to the mother is often an important feature. Sometimes a child who is an older sibling will identify himself with the pouch baby, thus indicating a wish to regress in order to be nearer to the mother. On the other hand, a child who is in the reality situation the younger one, may identify himself with the older one, thus signifying his wish for independence and mastery. The basket may give rise to themes of feeding. A theme of flight from danger may also occasionally be introduced. Our experience thus far suggests that

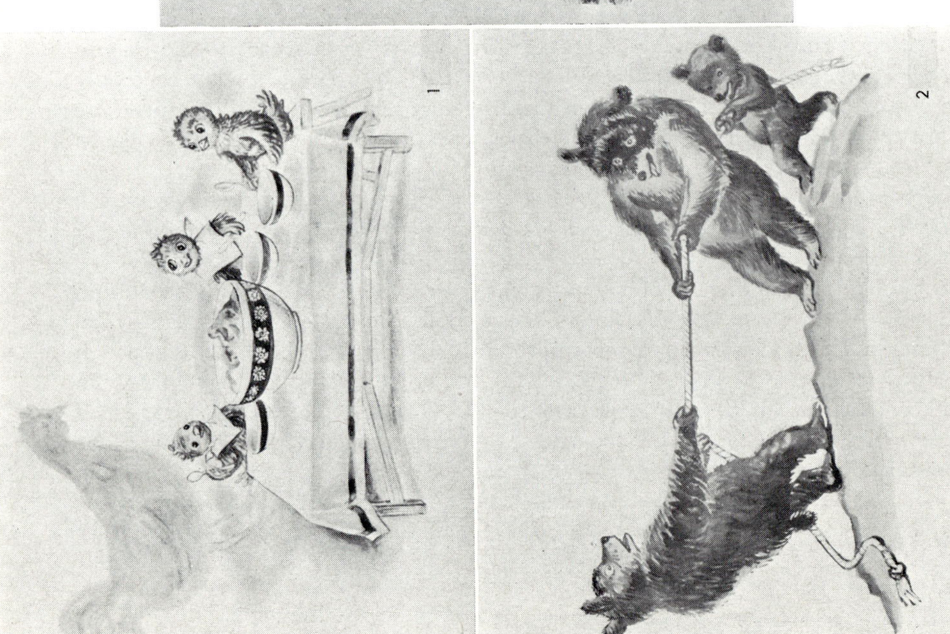

Figure 1.1. The CAT pictures (see also facing page). (The card numbers in Figures 1.1, 1.2, 1.3, 13.1 and 14.1 have been inserted for identification here, and do not appear in the actual test pictures.) (Reproduced with permission of L. Bellak.)

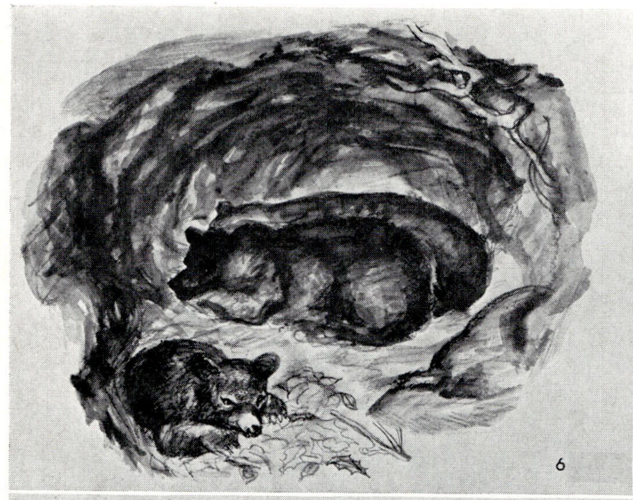

6

9

8

7

10

this can be related to unconscious fear in the area of father-mother relationship, sex, pregnancy, etc.

Picture #5: A darkened room with a large bed in the background; a crib in the foreground in which are two baby bears.

Productions concerning primal scene in all variations are common here; the child is concerned with what goes on between the parents in bed. These stories reflect a good deal of conjecture, observation, confusion, and emotional involvement on the part of the children. The two children in the crib lend themselves to themes of mutual manipulation and exploration between children.

Picture #6: A darkened cave with two dimly outlined bear figures in the background; a baby bear lying in the foreground.

This again is a picture eliciting primarily stories concerning primal scene. It is used in addition to #5 since practical experience has shown that #6 will enlarge frequently and greatly upon whatever was held back in response to the previous picture. Plain jealousy in this triangle situation will at times be reflected. Problems of masturbation at bedtime may appear in response to either #5 or #6.

Picture #7: A tiger with bared fangs and claws, leaping at a monkey which is also leaping through the air.

Fears of aggression and manners of dealing with them are here exposed. The degree of anxiety in the child often becomes apparent. It may be so great as to lead to rejection of the picture, or, the defenses may be good enough (or unrealistic enough) to turn it into an innocuous story. The monkey may even outsmart the tiger. The tails of the animals lend themselves easily to the projection of fears or wishes of castration.

Picture #8: Two adult monkeys sitting on a sofa drinking from tea cups. One adult monkey in foreground sitting on a hassock talking to a baby monkey.

Here one often sees the role in which the child places himself within the family constellation. His interpretation of the dominant (foreground) monkey as either a father or mother figure becomes significant in relation to his perception of it as a benign monkey or as an admonishing, inhibiting one. The tea cups will, on occasion, give rise to themes of orality again.

Picture #9: A darkened room seen through an open door from a lighted room. In the darkened one there is a child's bed in which a rabbit sits up looking through the door.

Themes of fear of darkness, of being left alone, desertion by parents, significant curiosity as to what goes on in the next room, are all common responses to this picture.

Picture #10: A baby dog lying across the knees of an adult dog; both figures with a minimum of expressive features. The figures are set in the foreground of a bathroom.

This leads to stories of "crime and punishment," revealing something about the child's moral conceptions. There are frequent stories about toilet training as well as masturbation. Regressive trends will be more clearly revealed in this picture than in some others.

EVALUATIVE COMMENTS

As Bellak has pointed out in the manual (see above) both the CAT and the Rorschach are useful instruments in the diagnostic appraisal of children and each fulfills a unique function. The Rorschach furnishes information relative to basic personality factors, expressive and affective modes, and defensive structures, while the symbolic imagery of the percepts lends itself to dynamic interpretations. In contrast, the CAT, like the TAT, provides a more structured stimulus. The situations portrayed in the pictures elicit responses which reflect interpersonal relationships, social interactions and identificaton patterns. Defense mechanisms are also revealed in the thematic tests, as well as some clues as to the sources and/or objects of fear, aggression and affection.

Various workers have offered criticisms and evaluations of the test in general terms. (Specific issues, such as animal vs. human figures, will be discussed in later chapters.)

Bolgar (1956) has analyzed the CAT as follows: "The CAT . . . is a narrowly circumscribed task demanding organized cognitive and verbal performance, while at the same time it is designed to arouse considerable affect and painful conflict. The conflicts which are stimulated must be solved in a realistic interpersonal setting, and the infantile impulses must be translated not into symbolic images, as in the Rorschach or into symbolic acts as in the MLT [Miniature Life Toys], but they must be integrated in a cognitive field. Parenthetically, I believe that the CAT is the most difficult projective technique for a child and that he faces in this test very much the same problem that we see in the resistance of the adult psychotic patient to the TAT."

Stone (1953) cautions against interpreting the child's responses to a particular card only in terms of the dynamics presumed by the authors to be revealed by that card. He also suggests that many other aspects of children's activities and personalities may not be tapped by any of the cards. (But this fault can be found with all of the thematic tests.) Stone also challenges the authors' claim for the culture-free aspects of the pictures by pointing out that seven of the ten cards depict objects and items (flowered hats, smoking pipe, plumbing) that are not only peculiar to western cultures but definitely middle-class as well. He also feels the animals are characterized according to the stereotypes of personality traits assigned to various animals in the American culture.

Kenny (1959) points to the need for more research on the reliability and validity aspects of the instrument and for more normative data. He cautions against making clinical inferences from the test responses and points out that ". . . the interpretation of CAT stories is on shifting grounds because practically nothing is known about how much of the story content reflects the deep underlying structure of the child and how much of it mirrors the conditions immediately antecedent to the testing, the atmosphere created by the test administration, and the pictures themselves" (pp. 126-127). He sees the test's greatest usefulness as a source of hypotheses to be checked against other clinical procedures.

FOREIGN VERSIONS OF THE CAT

The CAT cards have been adapted for the Japanese culture by Samiko Marui, as shown in Figure 1.2. In 1960, Uma Chowdhury (assisted by B. S. Guha and L. Bellak) modified the test for use in India. The Indian version is shown in Figure 1.3.

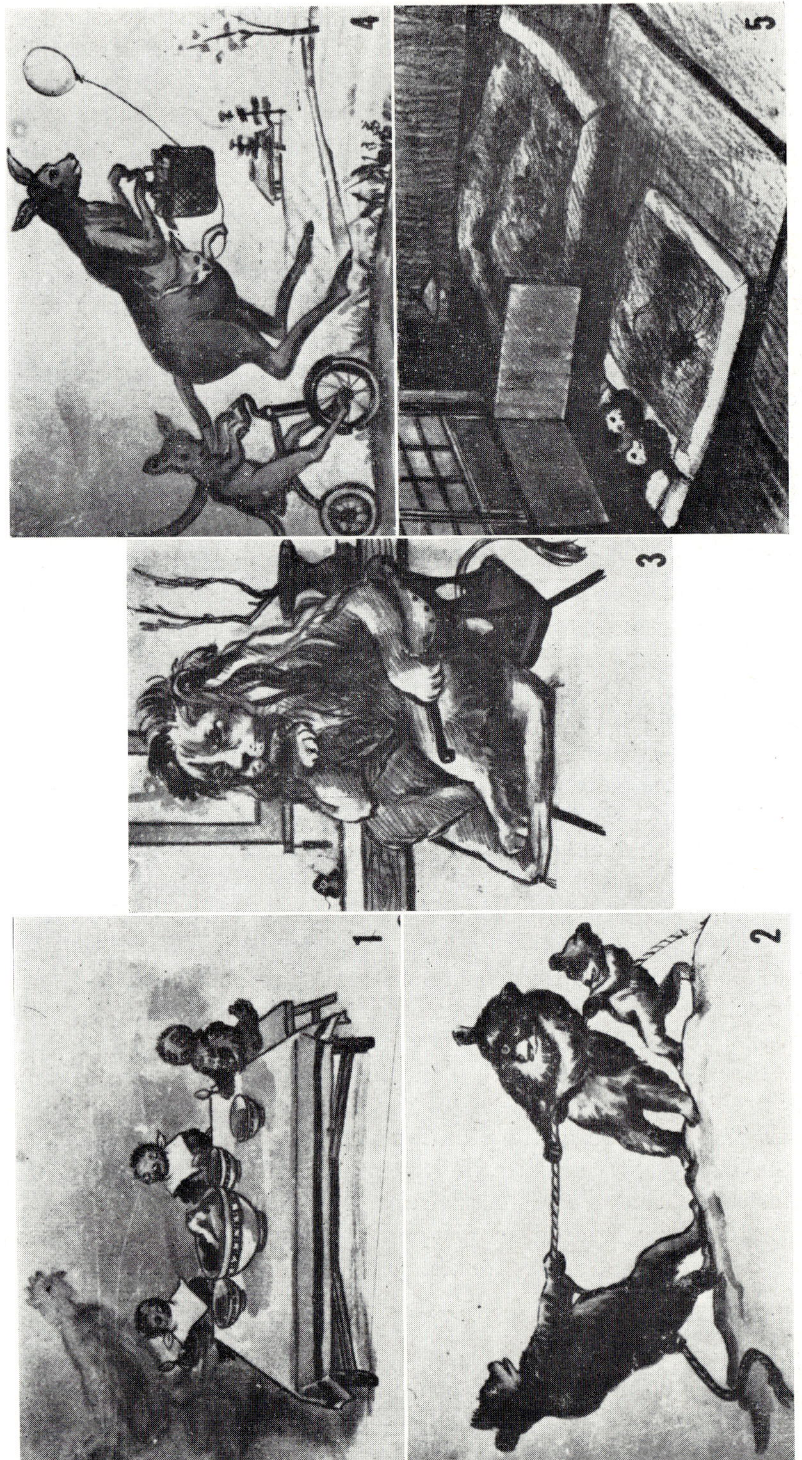

Figure 1.2. Japanese adaptation of the CAT (see also facing page) by Samiko Marui.

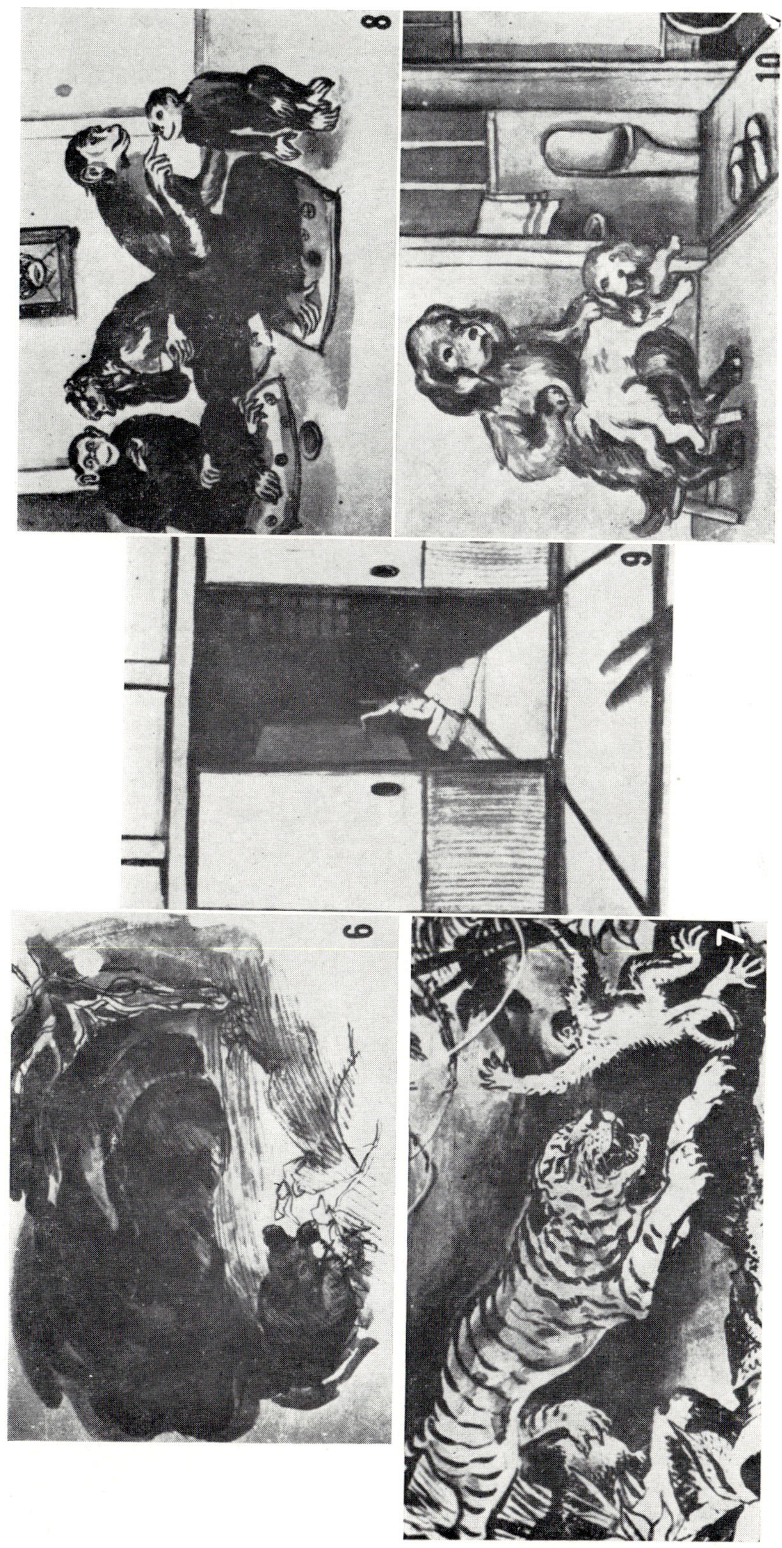

Figure 1.3. Indian adaptation of the CAT (see also facing page) by Uma Chowdhury (assisted by B. S. Guha and L. Bellak). (Reproduced with permission.)

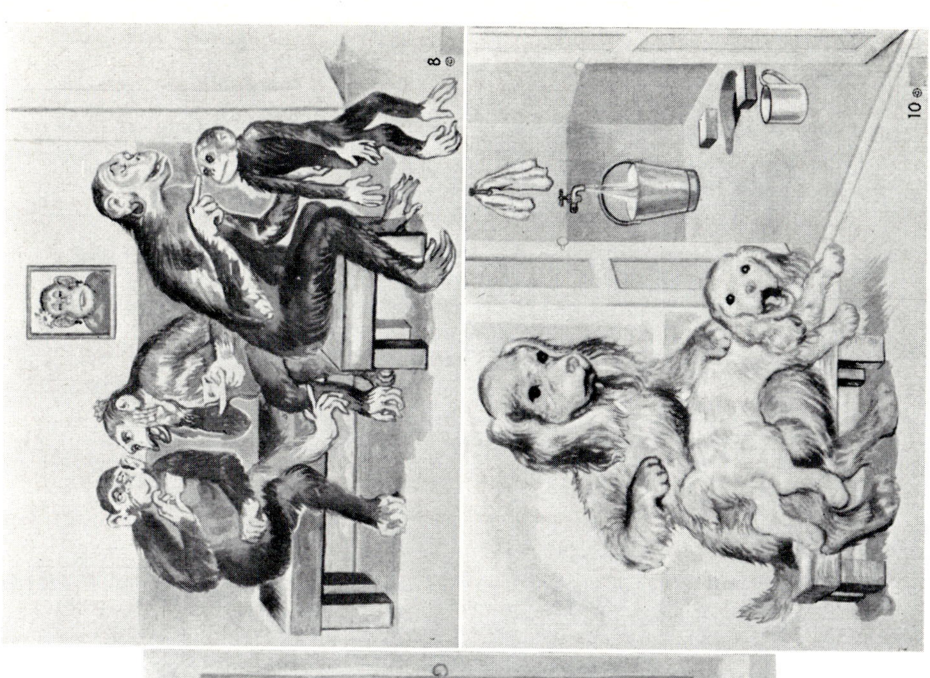

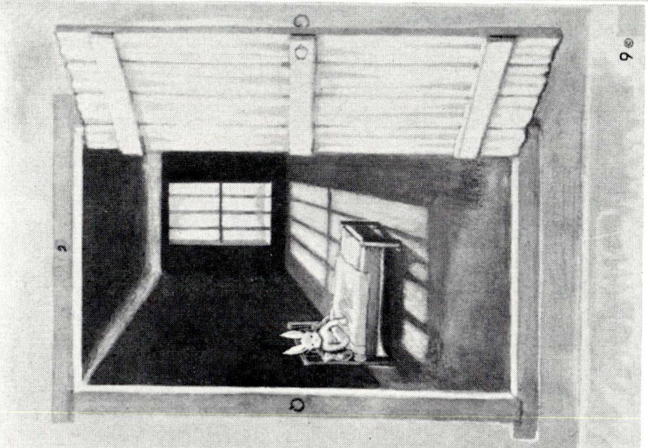

The test has also been published, with appropriate manuals, in French, Italian, German and Spanish.

ADMINISTRATION

It is assumed that the clinician giving this test will already be familiar with the basic tenets of projective testing and have acquired some understanding of the special difficulties involved in administering projective instruments to children. Briefly, the essential prerequisites to securing clinical data from children include an understanding of the developmental aspects of growth in cognitive and emotional areas; the ability to adjust one's verbalizations, instructions and expectations to the individual child; and the capacity to establish the rapport necessary for a working relationship in the test situation.

The child must first be made to feel physically and psychologically comfortable and at ease. For this particular test the question of adequate lighting is very important so that there is no glare on the cards and no shadows to blot out portions of the pictures. The specific task of telling stories to the pictures needs to be structured in such a way that there is no element of bribery or forcing, and no undue instigation to let the imagination "run wild."

After rapport seems assured, the cards are presented one at a time. The anxious child may need to be told that there are no right or wrong answers. If he is unduly cautious, one should explore his concerns that this is a "test" that may subsequently be used against him before proceeding. Knowledge of how the child's initial orientation to the clinic has been structured would be of great help in alerting the examiner to any fears which may need to be alleviated.

The child is asked to tell a story about each picture. The goal in the CAT is fundamentally the same as for the TAT, i.e., securing perceptions of what is happening in the picture, what happened before, what will happen next, and some description of the feelings of the various characters. The younger the child the less can be expected by way of keeping these goals in mind, and the more the examiner will need to take cues from the given responses in order to probe for further elaboration in the above areas. Obviously expectations of a full report of all these dimensions for each card is unrealistic for the younger children. The older, and the highly intelligent, subjects soon "catch on" and need little or no reminder of the points to be incorporated into their stories.

The cards should be presented in their numbered, sequential order, since the authors had a theoretical rationale for the specific placement in the series; e.g., Card 6 often elicits material that may have been suppressed on Card 5. To avoid distractions, the cards should be kept face down before and after presentation so that the child can concentrate on the picture at hand.

In so far as possible all remarks of the child should be recorded. Slips of the tongue, side comments and false starts are important if they occur frequently for any specific child. Word-finding or slightly aphasic difficulties can sometimes be picked up on a projective task where they may go unnoticed (or unrecorded?) in the more straightforward question and answer problems of the intelligence test. Blatt, Engel and Mirmow (1961) discuss problems in the administration of the Rorschach to young children but most of their points are equally applicable to the CAT or any other verbal projective technique used with children. They suggest close attention to physical activity, gestures, facial expressions or posturing accompanying the responses, and see this "elaboration of the response" as somewhat equivalent to the verbal productions of the adult.

Protocols can be recorded either mechanically or by hand. For many children, the presence of a tape recorder may prove too disturbing or distracting or it may stimulate them to wilder flights of fantasy than would otherwise be the case. If recording by hand, the examiner needs to develop his own shorthand system. The author has adopted a method whereby no more than a phrase or short sentence is written on each line. In addition to increasing writing-speed by eliminating wide-ranging hand and arm movements, the resulting product seems much easier to read and to interpret as compared to the usual paragraph format. All illustrative protocol material in the present volume is presented in this new "extended" manner.

Variations in Administration

Various authors have suggested additional questions or procedures which they have found fruitful when using the CAT in the clinical setting. Obviously, the standard procedure should be followed for research purposes or when it may be necessary to readminister the test (or a similar thematic instrument) after a relatively short interval of time.

Bellak, in the manual (1961) suggests going back after all the stories have been given to ask for elaboration on specific points, such as the source of the proper names used, why certain ages were assigned, or clarification of the outcomes described. He also suggests that if time is limited, if the child is particularly restive or hyperactive, or if one has prior information as to areas most likely to be basic to the child's problems, then certain cards can be selected for use. In such cases of abbreviated testing one is of necessity delimiting the range of responses and may be losing valuable opportunities to learn about other problem areas which may also be pertinent.

Cain (1961) has reported on a "dream technique" for use on Cards 5, 6 and 9 particularly, where characters are often described as being asleep. In such instances the examiner's final question is, "What did X dream?" On cards 5 and 6 the dreams of each of the characters are asked for. Cain reports that in approximately 80 per cent of a wide range of cases dreams were offered when requested. Borderline and dull normal subjects responded as readily to this technique as did the average or bright child. Cain feels that the additional "disguise and partial release from the card stimulus" enables the child to be freer in his fantasies, thus revealing more unconscious material. "The dreams, in brief, have been found to contain a wide sampling of psychic contents: pure wishes (conscious and unconscious), specific fears and vague apprehensions, particular impulse-defense constellations, major reality concerns, sexual identity confusions, fantasies of omnipotence, unconscious perceptions of parents, reflections of parental handling and attitudes, superego accusations and actual events. . . . The material elicited corresponds most closely in impulse and imagery to that produced on the Rorschach, though the story form necessarily meant greater secondary elaboration" (Cain, 1961, p. 182).

DeSousa (1952) has suggested another approach for further inquiry when the character has been "put to sleep" by the child-reporter. For example, if on Card 6 the bears are described as sleeping, the examiner will say, "The baby bear wakes up and------?" Often the child will then proceed to elaborate a longer and possibly more affect-laden story.

Booth (1953) recommends going back through all the cards after the stories have been obtained to determine the number and gender of the figures. Also, to Card 1 the child can be asked what kind of food is in the bowl; to Card 2, "Did the baby win or lose?" etc. Booth also asked each child to select, from the ten cards, the one he liked best and to tell why. Other researchers have asked the child to sort the cards into two piles, those liked most and least.

Other possible variations could incorporate procedures that have been suggested for use with other projective tests. For instance, "limits" can be tested by asking specific questions after the stories have been given. If the child did not mention the adult figure on Card 1, the mouse on Card 3, or the toilet or tub on Card 10, he could be questioned on these details; he can be asked the identity of the figures in the tug-of-war scene (Card 2) or whose picture is on the wall in Card 8.

Jones' Negation TAT (1956) could be adapted by asking the child, after the standard administration, to tell the silliest story, or the most awful story that he can think of for each card or for selected cards. Jones' theory is that this approach provides an avenue to ego-alien drives and impulses by unwittingly penetrating the defenses and thus reaching underlying primary process material.

No blank card is included in the CAT. This could be added, or an all black card, or a card which is half black and half white. The author, in experimenting with the half-and-half card, has found that it has served to uncover quite strong racial feelings in Negro children.

Further suggestions in the literature (Holt, 1951) have included presenting the pictures by means of a 35 mm. viewer or projecting them on a small screen (particularly recommended for retarded subjects). Finally, Sidler (1956) has experimented with role-playing techniques. She found that children with behavior and character disorders did not respond well to instructions to tell stories to the pictures but did enter readily into group enactment of the various role relationships suggested by the cards.

THE PROJECTIVE TEST BATTERY

Too little attention has been given, both in actual clinical practice and in research, to the effect on responses of the sequence in which the projective tests have been administered. On a theoretical basis it would seem advisable to present the least structured tasks first, i.e., the Rorschach before the CAT, and the CAT before story completions or sentence completions. Otherwise, response sets from previous tasks or specific story content may influence projective productions on subsequent tests.

Only two published studies on the effect of the ordering of projective tests in the battery could be located and both of these used adult subjects. Gibby, Stotsky and Miller (1954) were interested in the possible effects on subsequent Rorschach responses of prior administrations of either an intelligence test (Wechsler-Bellevue), a thematic test (TAT), the Goldstein-Scheerer color-form test, or a drawing test (Bender-Gestalt). Controls were given no test before the Rorschach. None of the Rorschach variables under investigation yielded significant differences for any prior test.

A more recent study by Van de Castle (1964) reports comparative data on administrations of Rorschach first, versus TAT and DAP first, to two groups of graduate students. The author was specifically interested in determining whether more human content would appear on the Rorschach when administered after the TAT and DAP which both emphasize the human category. The results confirmed his hypothesis, with significantly more human content in the Rorschachs presented after TAT and DAP as compared to initial Rorschachs.

The author has gathered some unpublished data on the number of duplicated concepts appearing in children's Rorschachs when administered after the CAT. The actual incidence was found to be infinitesimal when the total number of possibilities for duplication are considered, and would not appear to substantially alter the basic personality data.

EXAMINER INFLUENCE

While considerable attention has been given to the effect of the examiner's sex and personality characteristics on the projective responses of adult subjects,[*] very few experimenters have explored similar variables as they may affect a child subject. Lyles (1958) has made the only systematic study of the effect of examiner's attitudes on children's apperceptive responses—using both the CAT and the Rorschach with 48 normal Ss from eight-and-one-half to ten-and-one-half years of age. The examiners were trained to assume each of three roles: positive, negative and neutral. Each child was administered the tests under each of the three conditions with the same examiner and with intervals of 45 days between test sessions. Only the findings on the effect of examiner attitudes on the CAT responses will be reviewed. Themes were analyzed for length, content level, tension states and nature of outcomes. Lyles' hypotheses were confirmed insofar as positive attitudes elicited increased productiveness and an increased inclination to adaptation (defined as the consistent maintenance of a basic satisfying adaptive pattern). Negative attitudes on the part of the examiners led to an increase in anxiety, aggression and oppositional tendencies. Examiner attitudes were not found to influence freedom of emotional expression or efforts to maintain emotional and intellectual control.

Engel (1960, p. 594) points to the "mutually created uniqueness" of the

---

[*]See Masling (1960) for a review of research studies on the influence of the method of administration, the testing situation, and various attributes of the subject and the examiner on projective results with adult subjects.

testing session and states, "The relating is the warp and woof of the evaluation; test responses and interpretations are the pattern on the cloth of the two-person situation." She goes on to discuss factors, other than the actual test scores, which affect the final diagnostic assessment of the child, such as the issue of control (e.g., the child's perception that control is vested in the adult and his subsequent efforts to achieve it for himself); the levels and modalities of communication (silences, nonverbal communication, etc.); the regressive pull inherent in the situation; and the effect of time and space considerations in the transaction.

In a discussion of testing in general, but more specifically of personality evaluations, Leventhal, Slepian, Gluck and Rosenblatt (1962) advocate the establishment of a patient-helper relationship in which the examiner is no longer a passive observer but actively endeavors to elicit the patient's feelings and fears about testing, to uncover resistances and explore defenses, and to present himself to the patient as a "trusted helper." In this way not only is the patient's ego actively engaged in the diagnostic process but also the transition into therapy is often more smoothly effected. They state ". . . there has been a growing recognition that not just the tests, but the personality characteristics (e.g., needs, defenses) of the examiner as well as of the patient may play a profound role in the patient's perception of and reaction to the whole process of being diagnostically tested" (p. 68). The authors suggest using test responses during the session as opportunities for observing the patient's resistances and defenses, as clues for further elucidating problems, or as a means of enabling the examiner to focus on areas only alluded to; e.g., if a child subject speaks of lonely animals on the Rorschach or CAT, the examiner can later ask the child if he, himself, has ever felt a similar loneliness.

Blatt, Engel and Mirmow (1961) point out that the inquiry request for the Rorschach (and a similar situation obtains with the CAT) may remind the child of a distasteful aspect of parent-child relationships, in that his original response is not accepted whole-heartedly but, rather, serves as a springboard for the adult to ask further questions requiring difficult (for the child) verbal explanations. "The expectations and distortions which the child or adult brings (as well as those of the examiner) are likely to weave their way in and out of the relationship throughout the administration of the diagnostic battery" (p. 36).

These authors, also hint at the countertransference aspects of testing and further point to the examiner's frustration and, possibly, impatience when children fail to respond to his efforts to draw out an expanded inquiry. Bolgar (1956) also has called attention to the possible effects of the examiner's countertransference reactions to the child subject, i.e., his own interpretation of, and response to, the child's behavior—with the resulting effect on the child's subsequent reactions and responses.

Sex of the Examiner

Very little, if any, attention has been paid to this variable in experimental work employing projective techniques with children. Studies, with children, of the effect of sex of examiner in other somewhat related tasks have yielded varying results. In a study of attention seeking of four to five-and-one-half year olds while easel painting, Gewirtz (1954) found that boys approached women significantly more often than men. Girls directed more responses to men than to women but not to a significant extent. Stevenson (1961), using a task requiring the child to drop marbles in a hole under the influence of the examiner's continued verbal encouragement, found that women examiners had a greater effect than male examiners on both boys and girls at the three to four year level. In the six to seven year span, female examiners had more effect on boys than on girls, and there was some tendency at this age for girls tested by men to do better than boys tested by men, thus confirming Gewirtz' findings at approximately the same age level. But by the nine to ten year level, neither sex of examiner nor sex of subject yielded significant differences.

Borstelman (1961), in an experimental situation coming closest to that of projective testing, asked boys and girls of nursery school age to make sex-typed responses or choices. He found no differences due to sex of examiner or for either same- or opposite-sex examiner with respect to the sex of the child.

Multiple Examiners

Bolgar (1956) has suggested that in clinical practice with children the most valid picture may possibly be obtained when more than one examiner sees the child on the theory that the young child may react differently in response to personality differences in the various examiners (even those of the same sex) or to male versus female examiners. She specifically points out that the CAT, designed as it is to probe possible conflict areas centering on orality, rivalry, oedipal themes, etc., may be handled quite differently by a child depending on the reinforcement value of the examiner in terms of similarity to one or the other parent.

Certainly, if a child refuses to respond with one examiner, it would be well to attempt a second session with an examiner of the opposite sex. If a child is known to have had a particularly unpleasant or frightening relationship with one parent, an examiner of the same sex as the disliked or feared parent may well trigger off emotional associations and transference reactions which would impede collection of projective data. On the other hand, if the effect has not been too immobilizing, it is, of course, possible that the projective material may be richer and more dynamic as a result of the accompanying emotional reactions.

THE CHILD'S REACTION TO THE TEST SITUATION

Moriarty and Murphy (1960b)* point out that the child has not asked to come to the testing session and even though he may not object verbally or physically he still may have little need or desire to respond. His approach to this new situation and to the unfamiliar adults will depend on previously

---

*Appreciation is extended to these authors for permission to report on findings from their unpublished manuscript.

established reactions in other strange situations. In evaluating the CAT records of 20 preschool children who participated in the Coping Project of the Menninger Foundation, the authors noted consistent individual differences in perceptual style which appeared to be related to the child's reactions in the test situation. Various devices used in coping with the demands of the CAT task were observed as follows: reduction in the level of participation; resistance to further inquiry; positive efforts at problem solving; restructuring or reversing roles with the examiner; using a familiar story as a prop; being overprecise in small areas of the picture; the use of fantasy or magical processes; employing laughter and humor; releasing tension through motor expressiveness, sound effects or other forms of orality; appealing for help from the examiner; and employing defensive maneuvers such as regression (to infantile speech or dependent behavior), denial or avoidance (omissions, passivity), projection, and sublimation.

Individual children were found to react with coping patterns which were fairly consistent from one test experience to another; e.g., a child who was constricted and restrained in the CAT situation would show similar reactions in the intelligence test session.

SUMMARY

The background of the CAT and the history of its development have been reviewed as well as typical responses to each card. The discussion of the administration of the test has included suggestions for variations in presentation and inquiry procedures.

The consideration of studies relating to the sequence of tests in the battery, the effects of the examiner's sex and attitudes, transference and countertransference phenomena, and the use of multiple examiners serves to highlight huge gaps in present research coverage and to suggest challenging areas for further investigation. In order to adequately interpret test responses of young children, we need to make further efforts to delineate the environmental and interpersonal variables that may affect the results.

CHAPTER II

Projective Theories and Measurement Problems

THEORETICAL ASPECTS

Since Frank (1948) first applied the term "projective methods" to procedures for assessing the individual and characteristic aspects of personality, various authors have attempted either to reconcile this concept of "projection" with Freud's original use of the term as a defense mechanism, or to point out the many differences in connotations of the two concepts. Frank (1948) stated that: "The personality process involves a selective awareness of all situations, as patterned by the prior experience of the individual . . . so that he sees, hears and otherwise perceives what has become relevant and meaningful to him and ignores or rejects all else" (p. 42). He goes on to say that, "Every action and every spoken word of the individual becomes meaningful for understanding that individual when and as interpreted according to the significance which the individual himself gives them" (p. 45).

Murstein and Pryer (1959) and Murstein (1963) have singled out four different types of projection — classical, attributive, autistic and rationalized — which can be illustrated as follows: "The testee, in telling a thematic story . . . may assume that the central character would act just as he himself would act (attributive projection), or he may see the hero as acting out his own unacknowledged negative traits (classical projection). If the subject is hungry, he may perceive the hero as also hungry (autistic projection), or he may offer mitigating circumstances to explain away the hero's expression of aggression (rationalized projection)" (Murstein, 1963, p. 2).

Bellak (1954) has suggested the term "apperceptive distortion" to describe the process of projection based on the assumption that memory traces of past experiences and perceptions will influence present perceptions. Furthermore, "every person distorts apperceptively, the distortions differing only in degree" (p. 15). As an example of the influence of past perceptions, Bellak points out that when a subject is presented with a TAT card depicting a father figure, the response will reflect attitudes toward father figures based on the subject's previous experience and perception of his own father.

Thus, if a CAT card contains elements reminiscent of the child's previous experience or emotions, he will tend to be "bound" to the card by virtue of this similarity to his own past and can be expected to incorporate such "familiar" elements into his story. In terms of specific CAT cards, we would predict that the bathroom scene (Card 10) will elicit the child's own feelings associated with toileting or washing processes and with the possible scoldings or spankings he may have received for infractions of parental standards. Similarly, Card 1 should exert a pull on the child's past experienced oral needs, deprivations or gratifications.

Presumably the larger the experiential mass the subject has to draw upon, the more rich and varied would be the resulting apperceptions. We could reasonably expect a child's stories to be less complicated and more straightforward than those of an adult. For instance, the child's views of adult figures would be more clearly related to the original parents since there would be less overlay of characteristics and perceptions of the additional adult figures encountered throughout the life experiences of older subjects. Similarly, the younger the child, the more the "other" child figures in his stories may represent siblings rather than peers. Thus, when fewer "percept memories"* have accumulated, records will be less complex and less symbolic.

Lindzey (1953), in discussing assumptions underlying projective testing, has pointed out that the subject reveals his own impulses, needs and conflicts when required to add structure to an ambiguous situation. Persistent themes, appearing in several stories, are more apt to reflect the experiences and emotions of the subject, than single, isolated themes. While creating a "story" the subject will identify with one character whose conflicts and interests will, in turn, reflect those of the storyteller. Story material that can be directly traced to elements in the presented stimulus is less apt to be significant than that which has been added to, or indirectly suggested by, the content of the stimulus.

Vuyk (1953) has commented on projective mechanisms revealed in children's responses to the CAT, e.g., the child will project onto the stimulus figures only those needs, desires and thoughts which are related to a conflict. She also raises the question whether certain aspects of the cards may not in fact elicit negative responses since most of the larger figures are shown in scolding or punishing attitudes or as not paying attention to the younger figure. The CAT was administered to 65 children from the Netherlands, ages four to ten, some normal and some neurotic. In general she found that the child S ascribes to the child-animal figures those tendencies, emotions and wishes which are acceptable to himself. Those aspects of the parents which are acceptable to the S are ascribed to the parent-animal figures. Finally, the unacceptable tendencies of *both* child and parent, especially if these have been the cause of conflict between the two, are ascribed to figures which are introduced into the story.

Both Bellak (1954) and Henry (1956) discuss the role the ego is called upon to play when formulating projective responses. It must be able to relax controls enough to produce an imaginative story, yet retain enough intactness to avoid losing contact with reality. Bellak further points out that an analysis of the equilibrium between impulses and controls achieved by the individual subject is a useful aspect of the interpretive process.

Henry (1956) calls attention to the fact that the subject who is asked to respond to a projective task has at his disposal only verbal symbols which carry generally accepted meanings, consequently, "The irregularities, the distortions of emphasis, the imputing of motive, the introduction of figures not present in the pictures, all these represent the subject's effort to speak in terms of conventional symbols and ideas, while still conveying his personal feelings and motives" (p. 10).

---

*See Bellak, 1954, p. 14.

Levels of Response

Some consideration has been given, in the literature, to the various levels of personality structure that may be tapped by projective instruments. For instance, does a particular story represent aspects of the child's actual experiences or relationships on a manifest level, or does the story result from the operation of defense mechanisms and thus reflect repressed drives and impulses that would be unacceptable on a conscious level? Bellak (1954) points out the role of the ego in mediating between the latent and manifest levels, and emphasizes the necessity for some knowledge of the real-life situation of the subject when evaluating projective test data. He cautions that protocols may reveal emotional trends and fantasies which are in opposition to the general attitudes or actual behavior of the child, or the child's fantasies may represent wish fulfillment rather than a reflection of the actual life situation.

VALIDITY

No attempt will be made to review the many studies and discussions of the problems involved in determining both reliability and validity as applied to projective techniques in general. Only those aspects that may throw additional light on the problems as they relate to children's protocols will be considered. Much of the difficulty surrounding the validation of projective tests revolves around the assumptions underlying the techniques and the selection of appropriate criteria. Macfarlane and Tuddenham (1951) point out the dangers inherent in using isolated variables in scoring or validation studies, since the interrelationships of these variables contribute most to the real meaning of the protocols. They conclude that it is still necessary to depend largely on clinicians' judgments in the absence of more scientific measures. Frank (1948) emphasizes the fact that statistical evaluations of reliability and validity were developed for the standardization of psychometric tests on groups of subjects. "Reliability and validity, therefore, have been for *groups,* not individuals, each of whom is measured according to deviation from those *group* norms" (p. 61). In contrast, projective methods attempt to study "identified individuals" and must be reliable and valid in terms of revealing the unique personality. Frank further suggests the development of new "criteria of credibility" to fit the new projective procedures. In retrospect, over the intervening years since Frank first made these proposals, very little progress has been made in resolving the scientific versus the clinical dilemma.

In similar vein Bellak (1961), in the manual to the CAT, states that ". . . we believe that a projective test does not need validation and the establishment of norms in the sense in which such operations are necessary for intelligence tests. In an intelligence test, any datum has meaning only in relation to the frame of reference of its sample population. In projective techniques, provided one accepts the basic hypothesis of projective — or apperceptive — phenomena, the individual case can stand by itself. In projective techniques the data of manifest behavior are compared with those of the unconscious tendencies of the same individual" (p. 13). Clinically, Bellak has found that the CAT pictures have elicited problems also found in the historical material and that the responses have thrown additional light on underlying dynamics.

Construct Validity

Several CAT studies have attempted demonstration of the construct validity of the instrument by consideration of the extent to which the various cards do elicit the dynamics originally postulated for them. Byrd and Witherspoon (1954), using preschool subjects, concluded that the dynamic aspects of the stories agreed highly with the areas each picture was designed to investigate. Themes of orality were found with high frequency and intensity not only on the cards designed to measure this variable (Cards 1, 4 and 8) but also on Cards 3, 6 and 9 as well. Themes of aggression were expected to be typical on Cards 2, 3 and 7 and were found to be most often given to these cards. Fear responses were found most frequently to the two cards showing darkened rooms, Cards 5 and 9. Pictures 1 and 4 were designed to tap sibling rivalry, but only responses to Card 4 were high on this dimension. As would be expected, themes of toileting and/or cleanliness were highest on Card 10. Evidence of feelings of acceptance by an adult were predicted for Cards 3, 9 and 10. Card 9 yielded very little in this respect but the other two cards were uniformly high in themes of this kind. Oedipal situations were high on Card 5, which was consistent with expectations, although Card 6 was also postulated to elicit such themes. Very few stories contained themes of sexuality although they were expected for Cards 4, 5, 6 and 9.

Employing another projective technique as a criterion for the validity of the CAT may only raise more questions rather than solving validity problems. Nevertheless, if sufficient studies should result in satisfactory concordance, some measure of validation would be demonstrated.

Magnusson (1960) administered a test battery consisting of the Rorschach, CAT, Bender Gestalt and DAM to 12 pairs of identical twins. Different judges rank ordered the Rorschach protocols and the CAT protocols with regard to "general adjustment," resulting in a coefficient of .35 between the two tests. Bender Gestalt scores (Pascal-Suttell) correlated .38 with the general adjustment measure of the CAT, while the corresponding coefficient for the DAM and CAT was only .03. Seven specific variables common to both the Rorschach and CAT were rated by two different judges for each of the two tests. The mean correlations between comparisons of all combinations of judges' ratings on the two tests were far from encouraging with a range from —.01 for dependency to highs of .38 for reality adjustment, and .44 for inner conflicts. Mean correlations of .19 were secured for both aggression and intelligence, .21 for insecurity, and .22 for emotional maturity.

A validity study employing several projective techniques has been reported by Haworth (1962) in which the CAT, Rorschach, Despert Fables and DAP were administered to two groups of school children selected on the basis of deviant and nondeviant responses to a group projective film administered 8 to 12 months previously. The chief purpose of the study was to determine if a group projective test would yield data comparable to in-

Table 2.1. Frequency of High Scores on CAT Defensive
and Identification Measures*

| | Experimental | | | Control | |
	OBS (N = 6)	G-A (N = 9)	Total (N = 15)	Total (N = 15)	p
1. Reaction, undoing	5	4	9	1	.005
2. Isolation	6	5	11	2	<.005
3. Deception	3	4	7	4	ns
4. Denial, repression	5	3	8	4	ns
5. Guilt, fear, anxiety	4	2	6	2	ns
6. Projection, introjection	4	3	7	3	ns
7. Symbolism	2	4	6	1	.05
8. Regression	1	1	2	0	ns
9. Weak controls	3	1	4	0	.05
10. Confused identification	4	7	11	2	<.005

*Reproduced, with the permission of the publisher, from the *Journal of Projective Techniques.* 26: 47–60, 1962.

dividual projectives. Protocols were judged for evidences of disturbance in either the Obsessive or Guilt-Anxiety dimensions, areas on which the deviant film responses had also been based. It was found that significantly more of those children who had scored deviantly on the film test also scored high on the measures used in the analysis of their CAT and Rorschach protocols. Nine of the 15 experimental cases were selected by each of two judges as giving deviant responses on both the CAT and Rorschach; three more cases were rated high on both tests by one judge and on one test by the second judge.

It was predicted that the experimental Ss would show more high scores than the controls on each of the ten categories used in evaluating the CAT responses* and that, within the experimental group, the six obsessive children (on the basis of film scores) would score higher on the Reaction Formation, Undoing, and Isolation measures while the Guilt-Anxiety group would show higher scores toward the Guilt, Projection and Regression end of the continuum.

Table 2.1 shows the the experimental group did exceed the controls to a significant extent in the areas of Reaction-Undoing, Isolation, Symbolism, Weak Controls and Confused Identification. All six Obsessive (OBS) cases scored high on Isolation and five of the six scored high on Reaction-Undoing and Denial-Repression. There was no distinct patterning for the Guilt-Anxiety (G-A) subgroup.

Concurrent Validity

There have been two main approaches to the study of concurrent validity with the CAT: (1) Comparing responses of known groups, e.g., clinical versus normal, well-adjusted versus behavior problems; and (2) comparing the responses of an individual child with case history material or manifest behavior.

*Haworth's (1963) Analysis Schedule was used.

The difficulty immediately encountered in group comparisons is that of establishing adequate criteria for the selection of the groups. What is meant by "normal?" What criteria should be used for "disturbed," "neurotic" or "psychotic" as applied to children? The use of rating scales as the basis for criterion groups is a questionable practice; the researcher is oftentimes in effect accepting the subjective judgments of relatively naive raters as the basis for determining the validity of the instrument. Group comparisons, using the CAT, have utilized childhood schizophrenics (Gurevitz and Klapper, 1951); cerebral palsied (Holden, 1956); children with speech problems (Kagan and Kaufman, 1954; FitzSimons, 1958); those with emotional disturbances (Raff, 1951; DeSousa, 1952; Simon, 1954; Boulanger-Balleyguier, 1960; Haworth, 1963); and children separated from their parents (Stevenson, 1952; Haworth, 1964). These studies are reviewed in detail in Chapter X. The findings generally differentiated these special groups from their respective controls.

Validation of the individual case against real-life data has not been employed in large scale studies. There is perhaps a need for this kind of approach, i.e., to attempt to correlate dynamics and patterns of responses on projective material with known facts from the life histories of a random selection of clinic referrals. In actual practice it is the unusually dramatic case, or the one with interesting dynamic implications, which is selected for any lengthy discussion and publication. In a series of two papers, Ainsworth and Boston (1952) and Wheeler (1955-56) have presented an extensive longitudinal case history report of a child who had to be separated from his parents periodically for treatment in a sanatorium. Rorschachs and CATs were administered over a span of four years. The authors emphasize that congruence was found between behavioral and case history data, theoretical inferences (as to projective expectations on the basis of the early deprivation), and the interpretive hypotheses from the actual projective material obtained. They make a plea for more such studies whereby hypotheses concerning dynamic processes underlying behavior are checked against the dynamic hypotheses derived from projective material.

RELIABILITY

Jensen (1959), in a thorough review of the problems encountered in assessing the reliability of projective instruments, says: "It is important to realize that a test always has some degree of reliability . . . whether it is formally estimated or not. Some amount of error variance exists in all test scores, and this error, even if it were impossible to estimate it statistically, would enter into any use made of the test. . . . An estimate of reliability is one index of the degree to which the test can discriminate, and is thereby also a measure of the test's *potential* effectiveness. The test's *actual* effectiveness depends, of course, upon its validity, that is, the degree to which it measures what it purports to measure" (p. 109). Jensen then discusses certain reliability problems specific to projective techniques, namely: (1) the lack of standardized methods of administration, scoring and interpretation; (2) the fact that projective techniques usually have not been validated for the purposes claimed for them; (3) "subjective" scoring; and (4) the qualitative process involved in the interpretation. He also presents a sobering delineation of the extra-test factors which may affect reliability: different examiners may elicit quite different responses even though the test can be demonstrated to be reliable when used by one examiner; the extent of agreement between two judges may be no indication of the agreement between another pair of judges; the composition of the sample on which the reliability estimate was obtained may not be replicated due to the "range of talent" (i.e., heterogeneous versus homogeneous populations); reliability in disturbed groups can be expected to be lower than with normals. The length of the protocol is also an important variable, e.g., the reliability of a short protocol may differ considerably from that of a longer one.

Split-half reliabilities would appear to be meaningless in a thematic test such as the CAT, since the cards were specifically designed to measure different psychodynamic dimensions. For example, Nolan (1959) evaluated CAT stories for three of Murray's needs and found the cards differed markedly in their "pull" for specific motives. In view of this evidence, he cautions against the use of split-half reliability measures on the CAT and similar projective instruments.

Test-Retest Reliability

Test-retest measures also present difficulties in work with children. If the test is re-administered with only a short interval of elapsed time, the bright child may remember his previous responses. With a reasonably long interval, one could expect developmental and growth factors to affect the child's current status; the relative "push" or strength of impulses may have altered; quite conceivably new conflicts, fears or anxieties may have arisen or defenses may have consolidated and strengthened in the meantime. In contrast to adults, the child is not in all ways the same child at subsequent stages in his maturation. In this connection Tomkins (1947) has commented: "Childhood and adolescence represent the period of maximal plasticity of the individual — the organism is never again so malleable. We would therefore expect successive administrations of the TAT during this period to yield the lowest repeat reliability" (p. 7). Frank (1948) has pointed out that differences in responses to the same test at different times tell us a great deal about the subject's dynamic processes and the relative persistence of patterns.

In commenting on their longitudinal findings from repeated administrations of the Rorschach and the CAT to a young child, Ainsworth and Boston (1952) point out similar problems relative to continuity versus change over time. They speculate whether the changes noted on retests represent real changes in personality, or the result of intervening events in the life of the subject, or the reflection of developmental and maturational processes. Further variables which they considered include the unavoidable differences in each test situation and the possibility that the different samplings tapped different facets of the personality. On the other hand, the authors feel that the repetitions of similar content which did occur aided in the interpretation of the meaning attached to those particular concepts. Since they found no evidence that the child remembered responses given previously, they concluded: "Therefore the continuity of concepts, particularly of those which are not commonly evoked by the stimulus material with other subjects, points to significant 'constants' which [the child] himself brings to his perceptions of his world" (Ainsworth and Boston, 1952, p. 189).

Byrd and Witherspoon (1954) readministered Card 2 of the CAT to preschool children after an interval of two weeks. They postulated that the child's choice of parent with the small bear would be an indication of the child's identification with that parent, and they were interested in determining how consistent over time such a choice would be. They found that only 50 per cent of the children named the same parent on the second administration. Consequently, they caution against placing undue importance on any one aspect of figure identification in the protocols. Rather, the complete set of responses should be considered before interpretations are made.

Koch (1955) used the CAT as one of the instruments in a study of the influence of ordinal position on children's attitudes toward adults. She reports test-retest (two-month interval) reliability measures for the number of times in which the mother figure was seen as acting pleasantly toward the child or the child as acting pleasantly toward the mother. Similar counts were made for unpleasant reactions, and for both situations with fathers as well as mothers. For the mother figure, reliability coefficients were .55 for pleasant reactions and .54 for unpleasant ones; for father figures the corresponding coefficients were .44 and .13. Koch accounts for the lower reliabilities in the latter case on the basis of low counts in these dimensions.

Nolan (1959) reports data on five yearly administrations of the CAT which indicate a relatively consistent pattern of development for the group as a whole although, for the individual child, scores often differed from one year level to the next.

Muller (1958) readministered the CAT after a six-month interval to 14 French children, eight years of age. Protocols were scored for numerous needs and press, environmental aspects, outcomes, and defense mechanisms. These variables were then grouped into 12 categories for statistical comparisons. Normative scores for each category had been established for his entire sample of 40 protocols (secured from these 14 Ss and 12 others who received single administrations). To correct for similar responses on retest that would be largely descriptions of the cards or the result of memory of the story told previously, the normative score for each category was subtracted from each child's individual score for that category. Thus a measure was derived of the extent to which the child's score exceeded, or was less than, the normative response for each category. The over-all mean correlations between first and second administrations were .345 for boys and .316 for girls. Muller discusses his results in the context of expectations that personality changes should, in fact, be expected to take place during this particular age span. Maturational changes were further confirmed by additional data from the larger series of protocols, in which aggressive responses had moved from the active, physical types in the Ss tested at age eight toward more passive and verbal forms of expression in the Ss tested at age eight and one-half.

A study of test-retest reliability by Granick and Scheflin (1958) with the

Blacky Test suggests reasonable approaches to the study of reliability in children's projective responses. Using a sample of children aged six to 11 years, they recognized that the actual responses could not be expected to remain stable over time (three to 20 months between tests) but reasoned that if personality is assumed to have a basic underlying organization then a consideration of clinical and dynamic aspects of the responses should yield information on reliability. They employed three types of reliability measurements: (1) judges' agreement in rating (as "strong" or "weak") specific emotional and personality dimensions elicited by each card; (2) judges' matching of initial and subsequent protocols by using cues such as language, story content or emotional patterning; (3) the presentation of three stories for one card (two given by one subject on two different occasions, the third by a second child) and asking the judge to select those given by the same child using manifest, rather than implied, content as guides. Consistency of the children's choices was assessed by asking them to indicate the most liked and disliked cards after each administration. Any of the methods used in this study could as easily be applied to studies of reliability with the CAT.

Scoring Reliability

Intrascorer Reliability. A few studies utilizing the CAT have reported reliability figures for repeat scorings by the same judge. Biersdorf and Marcuse (1953) found one examiner achieved 95 per cent agreement after a two-week interval on the "number of ideas present." Weisskopf-Joelson and Lynn (1953) report a reliability coefficient for one judge of .98 using the Transcendence Index. Butler (1961) reports 97 per cent agreement after one month when scoring the number of stories with expressions of feeling, number of expressions of conflict and number of definite outcomes. Haworth (1963) rescored 30 protocols after a one-year interval, using her CAT Analysis Schedule, which resulted in a reliability coefficient of .96.

Interscorer Reliability. Weisskopf-Joelson and Lynn (1953) used the former's Transcendence Index as a measure of projection for a series of CAT-type pictures of varying completeness of contours. Interjudge reliabilities ranged from .86 to .94 for three judges for stories told to completely traced pictures, and from .44 to .90 for the incompletely traced pictures.

Light (1954) found that two psychologists achieved a reliability figure of .88 when evaluating 100 CAT and TAT stories on six criteria. Jackson (1955) found an average agreement of 75 per cent for judges scoring Murray's needs and items from Bellak's Analysis Sheet. Agreements ranged from a low of 64 per cent for needs to 86 per cent for conflicts. Ginsparg (1957) asked four judges to rate 120 CAT stories for various needs and emotions. A correlation of .71 was achieved when the nonoccurrence of these variables was included in the judgments. When only those instances were used where the categories did occur, the interjudge reliability was reduced to .045. When agreements of any two or more (of the four judges) were examined, they were found to agree on 41 per cent of needs and emotions, on 80 per cent of judgments of thematic level and endings and on 67 per cent of ratings on a psychosexual measure.

Rosenblatt (1958) asked two judges to score 89 CAT stories for dimensions organized into nine major categories. Agreements for each of the ten cards ranged from approximately 92 to 99 per cent. The least agreement was found on Card 5 and the highest on Card 10. Nolan (1959) asked two judges to score CAT stories for three of Murray's needs, resulting in rank order correlations of .87 for achievement, .85 for affiliation, and .91 for power. Budoff (1960) reports the following coefficients for two judges scoring 36 protocols: word count, .95; story level, .91; transcendence scores, .82.

Magnusson (1960) administered CATs to each member of 12 pairs of twins. Two judges rated the stories on 11 dimensions, yielding interrater reliabilities ranging from lows of .17 for dependency and .25 for sexual problems to highs of .67 for aggression and .72 for reality adjustment. The intermediate order of coefficients were as follows: relations to mother, .33; emotional maturity, .41; relations to siblings, .45; intelligence, .50; inner conflicts, .51; insecurity, .51; relations to father, .52.

Haworth (1963) reports a coefficient of .88 for two judges scoring 30 protocols according to her Analysis Schedule for the CAT. Using the same schedule, Lawton (unpublished) reports 80 per cent agreement between two judges when scoring 20 protocols for the ten categories.

SUMMARY

Brief consideration has been given to some of the past and current thinking with respect to the meaning of projection, definitions of the term, assumptions underlying projective testing, and the relationship of levels of response to ego control.

Studies of the validity of children's projective responses have approached the problem through consideration of the extent to which the cards measure what they were designed to measure, by comparisons with responses to other projective techniques, by comparisons of known groups, and by the use of case history material. Samples, in most of these studies, have been woefully small and the results often not very impressive. Much of the ambiguity of the results doubtless reflects still imprecise methods of evaluation.

Reliability studies of children's records present specific problems in that changes over time are to be anticipated along with normal maturation and development. Nevertheless, test-retest studies have been attempted with varying degrees of success. Scoring reliability estimates have been reported in many of the CAT studies, with intrascorer results appearing to be spuriously high in all instances, probably reflecting only that the author of a scoring scheme can (and should!) be consistent in its application. Difficulties readily appear when attempts are made to convey these methods to a second judge, resulting in generally and progressively lower correlations as the scoring dimensions become less objective and/or specific.

CHAPTER III

The Nature of the Stimulus

Some consideration has been given in both the theoretical and the research literature to the nature of the pictorial stimulus presented to the subject and to the effects of the variations of the stimulus on the projective responses elicited. Kagan (1960) has called attention to the necessity for knowing the content of the stimulus before attempting to interpret the response; the same statement (such as "people are fighting") may have quite different dynamic implications and meanings depending on whether the response was given to the Rorschach or to a picture-story test.

REALISM VERSUS AMBIGUITY

One area of study has been the nature of the scenes portrayed and the degree of clarity or ambiguity in the cards. Lindzey (1953) has suggested that those story elements which can be directly traced to aspects depicted in the projective stimuli are not as significant as those themes which do not show any direct connection to the original stimuli. Kagan (1956) used pictures varying in degrees of ambiguity with respect to aggression, and found that overtly aggressive boys gave more aggressive themes to the pictures portraying fighting than did the nonaggressive boys. He attributes this finding to a greater lack of anxiety over aggressive impulses in the outwardly aggressive boys and, conversely, more anxiety about, and reluctance to express, aggression by the boys who had kept their aggressive impulses under control. Kagan's findings are consistent with Lindzey's theories, in that the nonaggressive stories told to aggressive pictures by the nonaggressive boys would demonstrate little connection to the original stimulus, and should be more meaningful than aggressive stories told to an aggressive picture by the overtly aggressive boys.

In a subsequent review of research findings on ambiguous versus non-ambiguous pictures, Kagan (1959) concludes: "... when a fantasy stimulus suggests a content which is associated with anxiety, the S tends to inhibit a theme which includes the anxious material. . . . One implication of these studies is that a fantasy response to a stimulus which suggests a conflictful motive may be a more sensitive indicator of anxiety or conflict than the response to a stimulus which is ambiguous for that content. . . . However, there has been a long-standing tendency to use projective tests which contained ambiguous stimuli because they were assumed to elicit the primary preoccupations of the S. With the recent emphasis on the importance of the defensive organization of the individual and the ways in which he can repress, deny and distort anxiety arousing motives it seems profitable to use interpretations of nonambiguous stimuli as indices of conflict and associated defensive responses" (p. 270).

Translated to CAT terms, the lack of an aggressive story to Card 7 (tiger chasing a monkey), or the omission of any reference to bathing or toileting on Card 10 (bathroom scene) would be seen as demonstrations of ego defensiveness in the presence of potentially anxiety arousing situations, and so should give more meaningful data than would a story describing events closely tied to the picture content.

Wirt (1965) has compared the CAT unfavorably to the TAT, in that the situations depicted in the CAT cards are quite structured, thus leading to "popular" responses. But to follow along Kagan's line of reasoning, those responses that do deviate from the popular would then be quite important projectively.

Weisskopf-Joelson and Lynn (1953) used the CAT in approaching one aspect of ambiguous representation of pictures. Two sets of cards were traced from the originals: one set consisting of complete line drawings, while in the other, portions of the outlines were omitted to increase the ambiguity. The incomplete set was administered to 50 nine-year-old children, followed in two weeks by the completely traced set. The extent of projection elicited was measured by the Transcendence Index (Weisskopf, 1950); i.e., the mean number of comments that exceed pure description. The authors found that the completely traced (less ambiguous) cards yielded significantly higher transcendence scores than the ambiguous pictures, not only in terms of the pictures taken as a whole but also for the individual comparisons for eight of the ten pictures.

The results of this study have only a very limited application to the general problem of the amount of structure or ambiguity in pictures. By the very nature of the drawings used, the ambiguous set resembled a picture-completion task and, conceivably, this aspect would become the most important to the child. Once he had "guessed" what the lines and curves represented, he would not be likely, in view of the initial instructions to "tell all about the picture," to proceed to elaborate or to project. In contrast, the same instructions for the complete drawings, would be more likely to carry the child one step beyond mere description. The authors seem to concur in this conclusion when they point out that, in ambiguous pictures of the type they were using, one gains some insight into what the S makes of the configurations but loses a significant amount of transcendent material. They do not suggest that any inferences can or should be made from this type of ambiguity to the more common interpretation of ambiguity; i.e., indefiniteness in the portrayal of features or activities of the characters in the pictures.

STRUCTURAL AND PERCEPTUAL ASPECTS

A careful analysis of the structural aspects of the CAT cards has been made by Boulanger-Balleyguier (1957a). She was interested in the extent to which the child's descriptions of situations and figures in the cards are influenced by the composition of the drawings rather than by emotional tendencies of the child. She analyzed the responses of 105 French children of normal intelligence between the ages of three and seven years, with approximately ten boys and ten girls at each age level. In the course of determining normative responses, sex differences, and age changes, it was also possible to examine certain shifts in common reactions and in omissions and additions which may be due to stimulus ambiguity, perceptual dfficulties with small details, lack of familiarity with situations portrayed, or indirect suggestions from elements in the cards.

On Card 3, smoking was found to be a popular response only after age six, which suggests that the pipe is not recognized sufficiently by younger children to be mentioned. Only after age six do themes of conflict between the lion and mouse appear with any frequency. In fact, the mouse was frequently omitted before this age and certainly no conflict can be described if figures are not seen. The author raises the question of perceptual accuracy in young children with respect to small details and points out that this card cannot be used as a basis for inferences about father-child relationships until both figures are perceived.

On Card 4 it was found that children under six do not recognize the animals as kangaroos and do not appear to be aware of the pouch. If they are unfamiliar with this species they will not know about the use of the pouch. In addition, the baby figure itself is frequently omitted below age six. Consequently this card appears to be poorly chosen for the study of sibling rivalry or birth themes as suggested by Bellak.

The common response to Card 7 is one of conflict, usually involving eating, but Boulanger-Balleyguier remarks that of all the cards this one allows the least freedom for the child's imagination; the situation, manner of action (eating), and conclusion are all clearly suggested by the drawing. She, too, points out that the nonperception of conflict on this card would certainly be a significant response for interpretive purposes.

One of the small bears, and one of the big bears, are frequently omitted on Cards 5 and 6, respectively. Yet on Card 8, which contains the most animals of any card, the number of omissions is very low, especially beyond age four.

On the basis of the high incidence of certain omissions and their regular decrease with age, the author suggests that the younger children are not actually perceiving these figures. Those most frequently omitted are either blurred or vague (the hen on Card 1, the bear on Card 6) or very small (the mouse on Card 3, the baby on Card 4). When all the animals are large and clearly drawn there are fewer omissions, even on cards with the most animals.*

Additions were also found to be related to stimulus properties of the cards. For example, the most additions were given to Card 9 which is the only card to represent a single animal. When the number of additions to this card were compared to those for Card 8 (with the most animals) the difference was significant at the .01 level.

With respect to the elements of the cards which suggest certain responses, Boulanger-Balleyguier wonders whether the fact that mothers are mentioned more frequently than fathers is due to the prominence of mothers' roles at

---

*Millar (1952) presents figures for omissions in her sample of American children three to five years of age. Averaging figures given by Boulanger-Balleyguier for these same three age levels shows her results to be higher than Millar's on two cards and equal on the third: omission of the mouse (Card 3), 64 per cent for Boulanger-Balleyguier and 44 per cent for Millar; omission of the baby kangaroo (Card 4), 56 per cent and 30 per cent, respectively; omission of one background bear (Card 6), 52 per cent in both studies.

these ages or to characteristics of the drawings which show more animals performing maternal than paternal duties. (She also points out that there are far more parental figures shown than child figures who might be used to represent brothers and sisters.) Although children have never seen either a lion or tiger eat another animal, they will report animal aggression much more often and at earlier ages to Card 7, which depicts this behavior, than to Card 3 in which it is not directly suggested in the card itself.

Boulanger-Balleyguier does not negate the possibility that omissions, additions, etc., can result from unconscious affective and/or repressive mechanisms. She does suggest a means of determining whether emotional aspects or stimulus effects are more predominant for a particular response: When the number of omissions for a given animal decreases regularly with age, this omission could be attributed to poor perception. Where the incidence is clearly different for boys and girls, or where the decline is not regular with age, then the emotional significance of the omission would appear to be greater.

EFFECT OF COLOR

Only one study has been concerned with differential effects of colored versus achromatic projective pictures for children. Weisskopf-Joelson and Foster (1962) prepared each of four selected CAT cards in four variations (noncolored and colored animals, noncolored and colored humans). These were presented to 40 Ss from five and one-half to seven years of age, and evaluated by means of the Transcendence Index. The color variable did not yield significant differences for the entire group. When the 11 Ss with the highest scores were compared to the 11 Ss with the lowest scores, there was a trend for the high-scoring Ss to respond more to chromatic pictures, while the achromatic pictures elicited more meaningful responses in the low-scoring Ss. The authors interpret this color finding in terms of the dynamics similarly seen in Rorschach responses; i.e., that the high-scoring Ss are more responsive to color as a consequence of their freedom to express their emotions and fantasies, while the low-scoring Ss are more guarded and repressive. It would be interesting to test this hypothesis by administering the Rorschach along with colored versions of a picture-story test.

ICONICITY

In addition to the ambiguity of scenes or characters, and the issue of chromatic versus achromatic pictures, a third major area of research on the nature of the stimulus has been concerned with iconicity, or the extent of resemblance of the characters to the S with respect to sex, age and/or species.

The basic theoretical problem involved in iconicity has been summed up by Cook (1953). He points out that projective stimuli must achieve a fine balance between a pull toward identification and the counteraction of ego defensiveness. The pictures must induce enough identification between subject and pictorial character to elicit material from his personal experience and yet be dissimilar to such an extent that otherwise unacceptable impulses and attitudes can be brought to the surface without alarming the ego.

After reviewing studies of the effect of similarity or dissimilarity between subject (adults) and stimulus figure, Murstein (1959) concludes that ". . . similarity of the central character to the S is not only noneffectual in furthering projection but actually may be detrimental. . . . It seems clear that similarity to the point of idiosyncratic identification promotes ego defensiveness and a reduction in the degree of projection" (p. 9).

The remainder of this chapter will be devoted to the controversy that has arisen concerning the relative utility of animal or human characters in picture-story tests for children. Bellak has maintained that the choice of animal characters for the CAT cards was based not only on the hypothesized ease of relating and projecting to dissimilar stimuli but also on the theory of the universality of interest in animals as demonstrated by children and found in the myths and folklore of primitive, and more child-like, peoples throughout the ages.

RATIONALE FOR THE USE OF ANIMAL PICTURES

While questions have been raised concerning use of animals in a children's test, it is curious that no one seems to have challenged Blum's (1949) use of a dog family in a test specifically designed for use with adults. Blum's rationale for his use of animals in the Blacky Pictures reflects his view of the greater ease in projecting onto animal figures when he states: "Why dogs? Why the names 'Blacky' and 'Tippy'? The characters were relegated to dogdom in order to facilitate freedom of personal expression in situations where human figures might provoke an unduly inhibiting resistance—in other words, might be 'too close to home.' While, on the one hand, minimizing the dangers of resistance, the canine medium, thanks to Disney cartoons and comic strips, still preserves sufficient reality so that subjects can identify themselves quite fully with the cartoon figures and project their innermost feelings" (p. 16-17). In further discussion of the same phenomenon, Blum and Hunt (1952) conclude, "It seems almost as if the animal cartoons appeal directly to the residues of childish, pre-logical thinking in adults . . ." (p. 239).

On the other hand, Budoff (1963) suggests that ". . . the CAT may be more difficult for young children since these pictures are hardly animal pictures, rather, they are animal figures placed in a human context. The most dramatic example is the picture in which monkeys are sitting on a sofa and drinking a beverage. Might not this confabulation make the task even more difficult for the young, verbally backward child. . . ?" (p. 249). Budoff proposes that, if animal figures are used, they should be portrayed in typically animal situations.

Bellak (1960) has explained the reasons for his selection of animal characters for the CAT as follows:

On the basis of experience with children, it was expected that they would more readily relate to animals than to human figures. This assumption was predicated on the fact that the animals which children know are usually smaller than adult humans, or at any rate, are usually thought of as "under-dogs" like children, and even below children, in our pecking order.

Animals play a prominent role in children's fantasies and phobias, and they become identification figures in children's dreams; on a conscious level, they figure importantly as children's friends, in stories and in reality. The primitivity of animal drives also increases their symbolic proximity for children. From the vantage point of a projective test, it was assumed that animals would offer some manifest disguise. Aggressive and other negative sentiments could more easily be ascribed to a lion than to a human father figure, and the child's own unacceptable wishes could be more easily projected onto the less transparent identification figure, in a picture stimulus, than onto a human child. Animals also lend themselves more easily to the age and sex ambiguity in the stimuli, which was desired.

The Rorschach records of young children show a high per cent of animal references and a relative absence of human figures. The use of animals as identification figures by some psychotics and in primitive cultures also tended to support the expectation of a high stimulus value (p. 66).

In our culture, at least, the first toys given to infants are usually animal rather than human representations. Young children are universally interested in live animal pets. Caplan (1951) sees pets as serving as parent substitutes, thus transformed into objects which the child can direct and control.

Freud (1913) has called attention to the common use of animals as totems in ancient or primitive tribes, and emphasizes that the individual or the tribe feels a close kinship or descent from the totem animal. This identification with the totem is manifested in tribal ceremonies where participants dress in the skins of animals, wear animal masks, or tattoo the animal's picture on their bodies. Freud also discusses the significance of the totem as a representative of the loved, but dreaded, father and suggests similarities between primitive man's relations to animals and the reactions of the modern child. The implications for projection are readily apparent when he points out the suddenness with which an animal phobia may develop in a child who has hitherto shown intense interest in, almost to the point of identification with, an animal. Evidently fear of the father is displaced onto the animal; the ambivalent feelings toward the father are then felt toward the animal as well. The story of Little Hans (Freud, 1909) is an excellent example of this mechanism. In a later paper, Freud (1918) showed the similar role played by animals in the dreams and nightmares of children, with animals again serving as father surrogates, particularly in the oedipal period.

In speaking of primitive peoples, Werner (1948, p. 426) says: "Since the primitive man lives in a behavioral world where persons are conceived in terms of concrete qualities-of-action, it is no more than a logical consequence that commonly no essential differences are thought to exist between man and animal." He goes on to point out the higher regard held for certain animals by various tribes; the myths and legends in which men are identified with animals; and the primitive dances in which the dancers are regarded not as just representing an animal but as actually becoming that animal. Werner then describes similar syncretic phenomena in children in which their physiognomic view of the world produces the belief that animals can communicate in human terms.

Menninger (1951) has written a paper reviewing the remnants of totemic aspects of animals in our present culture. Jelliffe and Brink (1917) and Heiman (1956) emphasize the frequent use of animals in the dreams of psychoneurotics and point to the numerous roles, from the sublime to the incestuous, which animal symbols can fill.

Animals in Fairy Tales and Myths

Animals feature prominently in fairy tales and myths, and often their roles are closely connected with problems of identity at the earliest psychogenetic levels. One main theme is that of the interchangeability of human and animal figures. In ancient myths we find Jupiter variously assuming the form of a bull, a swan, a ram or an eagle, while his mistresses become heifers or bears. Arachne was transformed into a spider. In the legend of Lohengrin, Elsa's brother changes into a swan. In Hindu mythology, the god Vishnu has appeared in different incarnations such as a fish and a tortoise.

In fairy tales we find Prince Cherry transformed into a monster with a lion's head and the body and horns of a bull. The Frog Prince assumes both roles of his title; the Twelve Brothers are changed into ravens and subsequently restored to human form. The Enchanted Stag was first a human boy and, after the influence of the wicked stepmother is discovered, is eventually returned to the human condition.

Undoubtedly, the easy transmigration of species in tales told throughout the centuries reflects the primitive aspects of magic and omnipotence, as well as man's eternal questions about his identity in relation to other men and to supernatural powers. The universality of this theme would also account for the readiness with which children embrace such ideas in their own play, stories and games. The appeal of animal characters which can so readily change into human form and back again at the command of the storyteller should, on a theoretical basis, make them particularly suitable subjects for a projective instrument designed for use with children.

Another prominent theme in fairy tales is concerned with orality. Animals frequently are the villainous aggressor with the aggression being depicted in the most primitive form, namely oral incorporation, as in *Little Red Riding Hood, The Three Little Pigs, The Gingerbread Man,* and the tale of *Pinocchio* in which the whale incorporates most of the characters. In many of these stories, the characters are swallowed whole, and are eventually regurgitated, again attesting to the primitive, incorporative oral dynamic (which is also closely related in the young child's mind with impregnation fantasies).

These two themes in animal tales, magical transformations and orality, reflect basic dynamic mechanisms of omnipotence, identification, introjection and projection, as well as concerns about origins and survival. Their universal appeal would suggest that children could readily utilize animal stimuli as human representations and that the tales told about animal characters might well tap important dynamic aspects similar to those revealed in the "ready-made" fairy tale.

Animal Characters in Modern Children's Stories

Several studies have examined the favorite characters in children's story books and readers, with animals generally occupying a uniquely favored spot. Olney and Cushing (1935) found that three-fourths of children's picture books contained animal figures. Wilson (1943) asked kindergarten and first grade children to retell their favorite story and indicate their best-liked character. Both sexes preferred animal or boy characters above all others, while women, fairies and babies were least used. Child, Potter and Levine (1946) analyzed third-grade readers for type of hero, activities portrayed, and the consequences of behavior described. Even at this eight-year level, animals were the central characters in 17 per cent of the total thema, with only child characters surpassing them. Most of the animal characters were portrayed as the young of the species and in a dependent child-parent relationship. Spiegelman, Terwilliger and Fearing (1953) found that animals comprise 50 per cent of the characters in Sunday comic strips. Boyd and Mandler (1955) report that 74 per cent of 96 third-graders expressed a preference for animal stories.

Goldberg (1952) found animal stories to be the most satisfactory reading materials for use in tutoring schizophrenic children. In contrast, the children became very upset by the usual "Happy Family" type of story which elicited comparisons with these Ss' own situations and experiences. The author also found that sketchy pictures of humans, showing only parts of the bodies, aroused severe reactions from the children. In view of these observations animal figures would appear to be more appropriate than human for use with schizophrenic children.

In conclusion, one needs only to recall the popularity of Mickey Mouse, Donald Duck, Bugs Bunny and the Disney films such as *Bambi* and the *Lady is a Tramp* to wonder why so much controversy has arisen around the utility of employing animal characters in a picture-story test designed for use with young children.

Significance of Animal Symbols

Theoretical speculations as to the symbolic meaning of specific animals have generally been based on more or less informal clinical evaluations of projective stories and drawings. Levy and Levy (1958) and Schwartz and Rosenberg (1955) have presented extensive material on the symbolism generally and culturally associated with different animals and species. From clinical interviews with children, Caplan (1951) has come to the conclusion that animals used in children's language and thought are symbolic representations of family members — mother, father, siblings — and that the same animal may represent different family members at different times.

Some experimental work has also been reported relative to the meanings of animal symbols. Goldfarb (1945) was one of the first to explore this area, using an animal association task. Children were asked to name an animal in response to persons (man, woman, father, mother, etc.) and to characteristics of persons (kind, cruel, etc.). His findings were consistent with general expectations, i.e., cruel adults were associated with aggressive animals, kind adults with domestic animals, males with gorillas and females with cats or cows.

Buss and Durkee (1957) extended Goldfarb's procedure and applied it to adult psychiatric patients and normals. They secured animal associations to specified types of family characters (e.g., loving, dominating, cruel, neglecting, punishing mothers and fathers; and helpless, happy, timid children). They also secured specified parental associations (in categories similar to the above) to 24 different animals. Their findings revealed little relationship between specific animals and any designated type of familial figure, but they did find that aggressive animals are more closely associated with negative or punitive parental figures than with positive ones, while neutral animals showed a closer association with positive parental figures. Children were generally associated with small and neutral animals or with the young of any species.

Goldfried (1963) used the semantic differential with college students to assess the connotative meaning of animal symbols. Goldfried and Kissel (1963) extended the previous study to a younger age group (13- and 14-year olds) reasoning that animal symbols would be expected to have more intense meaning for younger Ss. Nine animals and 12 semantic scales were used. These younger subjects placed more significant evaluative meaning on animal symbols than had the adults, while the scales for activity and potency did not differ.

PROJECTIVE USE OF ANIMALS BY CHILDREN

Stories Told by Children

Pitcher and Prelinger (1963) secured free-fantasy stories from 137 nursery school and kindergarten children. About one-third of the characters were animals, with older Ss (ages four and five) using more wild or zoo animals and the younger Ss (ages two and three) using more domestic species. Sex differences were also noted, with girls using more domestic animals, naming them and treating them much like humans. When girls use wild animals they have a friendly quality and "live" in homes or barnyards. Boys, on the other hand, use more wild and zoo animals, their home is in the jungle, and they are portrayed as ferocious opponents.

The authors summarize the significance of animal characters as follows: "... in a large number of stories animals represent the main characters. As such they clearly become carriers of the child's own wishes, worries, and concerns. The choice of animals as personal representatives of the child can be interpreted in terms of projection, of displacement, or, in certain instances, of symbolization. From one point of view one might say that these three processes, inasmuch as they may be involved, represent defensive operations by means of which the actual person having wishes, worries, and concerns is disguised. From another point of view, and particularly from that of unconscious functioning, these processes are the basic ones which make the representation and expression of unconscious ideas possible, just as they do in dreams. They are the modes of representation and of organization which are characteristic of the 'primary process' and thus they combine expressive and defensive functions in a condensed form. Of course, not only characters are represented in such projected or symbolic forms; actions and happenings as well as circumstances surrounding them are all to be considered as partially symbolic also" (Pitcher and Prelinger, 1963, p. 228).

Children's Rorschachs

The prominent part played by animals in children's spontaneous fantasies is reflected in the progressive changes with age noted in Rorschach responses with respect to the proportions of animal to human content and in human versus animal movement. Three developmental studies (Thetford, Molish and Beck, 1951; Ames, Learned, Métraux and Walker, 1952; and Ledwith, 1959) concur in reporting remarkably constant A per cent from ages six or seven to puberty, while mean H (or H per cent) increases only slightly and never approaches the use of animal content. The Ames et al. and the Ledwith studies each found steady increases in M and FM, but with mean FM exceeding M at each year level.

Ames et al. (1952) examined the kinds of animals employed, and found a predominance of domestic animals at age two, a marked shift to wild ones from three to five, and prominent use of the butterfly-bird category at the later ages. Phillips and Smith (1953) report that young children (under age ten), in their Rorschach responses, use animals which are a part of their everyday experiences, such as bees, cats, ducks, chickens, horses and rabbits. All age levels make frequent use of dogs, bears, mice, rats and spiders, while only at the higher mental levels are such creatures as fish, bats, crabs and snakes used.

Children's Drawings

Bender and Rapoport (1944) examined the spontaneous animal drawings of children and found two groups of animals, aggressive and nonaggressive, with the former being drawn most frequently by those Ss with severe neuroses. They suggest that the animal becomes a father symbol and that the type of animal chosen is directly connected with the dynamic aspects of the case.

Those who advocate the use of animal drawings (e.g., Levy and Levy, 1958; Schwartz and Rosenberg, 1955) agree that deeper, and often more negative, aspects of personality are frequently tapped, since the ego becomes less defensive as the task is shifted from the human to the animal sphere. Hammer (1958) suggests that this same rationale can account for the effective use of animals in projective tests such as the CAT, Blacky Pictures and the Despert Fables.

Projection of Negative Affects onto Animals

As indicated in the discussions of fairy tales and of children's drawings, there is some theoretical basis for the hypothesis that animals may customarily serve as useful vehicles for the expression of negative feelings. Similar observations were made by Pitcher and Prelinger (1963) in their study of children's spontaneous stories. They found that boys, especially, made much use of wild animals as dangerous opponents and theorize as follows: "If we assume that friendly animals which, in the stories, so often behave in a human-like manner, may represent the child himself, then we must consider the same in relation to the wild, fierce, and ferocious animals. They may serve as a convenient representative of the child's consciously not acceptable wishes to harm and to destroy, of his anger and his resentments. The 'bad' unconscious wishes can be expressed through such indirect means since they are attributed to somebody else, and in particular to beings which are generally defined as dangerous and bad" (p. 173).

Similar attribution of negative traits to animals was noted in the survey of third-grade readers by Child, Potter and Levine (1946). They found that aggressive and acquisitive traits were only found in animals, adults and supernatural characters. Animals were generally shown as young, helpless and insubordinate, rewarded for dependent and socially conforming behavior but they were also depicted as engaging in more aggressive (especially unprovoked) behavior than the human child characters. Animals were also prominently used as vehicles for portraying disobedience to authority figures. The animals' rebellious behavior was usually punished, so that the animal characters served as outlets for the child reader's impulsive drives. Superego demands would also be satisfied when the disapproved behavior is punished.

Boyd and Mandler (1955) studied 96 third-grade children's reactions to human and animal stories and pictures. After listening to each of two stories with either animal or human characters, and with either "good" or "bad" behavior, each S was shown a picture (animal or human) and asked to write his own story. Ss were also asked to state their preference of the stories read to them. Stories were analyzed for eight variables (length, original ideas, punishments, rewards, etc.). Human stories showed significantly greater effect than animal stories on the S's subsequent original story, yet 74 per cent of Ss expressed a preference for the animal stories. Animal *pictures* had a significantly greater effect than human pictures on two of the variables under study, with a trend in favor of animal pictures on four of the remaining six variables.

Boyd and Mandler also found that themes of punishment increased in response to animal pictures following "good" stories, while punishment themes increased to human pictures following "bad" stories. Value judgments increased to animal pictures following "bad" stimulus stories.

The authors conclude: "Our results tend to support the hypothesis that animal pictures facilitate the expression of ego-involvement, particularly of negative affect. However, the overwhelming effect of human stimulus stories on the production of imaginative material fails to support a general theoretical assumption of children's primary identification with animals. . . . The expressed preference for animal stories may be related to the fact that socially disapproved behavior in animals is less anxiety-arousing than in human subjects" (p. 371).

SUMMARY

In reviewing studies of the various aspects of the stimulus cards, it would seem that responses to nonambiguous cards may tell us more than previously assumed, in that omission of content portrayed in the picture can be taken as an indication of strong defensive measures against the anxiety aroused by the card content. Few studies have dealt with the effect of color in projective tests and this area could be profitably explored in the future. With respect to iconicity, or similarity of content to *S's* characteristics, findings in general indicate that a very close similarity may be too threatening to the storyteller. Consequently, on theoretical grounds, the use of animal pictures should provide appropriate identification figures for use in children's tests.

Various rationales for the use of animal pictures have been advanced based on early developmental interests of children, the preponderance of animals and specific animal themes in myths and fairy tales, primitive totemistic behavior and childhood phobias. Attention has also been called to the high incidence of animals in children's spontaneous productions — stories, drawings and Rorschach percepts. Research was described in which attempts were made to determine the significance of specific animal figures, and the use of animals as vehicles for the projection of ego-alien drives and impulses.

From a theoretical standpoint, the use of animal stimuli appears well grounded and should provide a fruitful medium for children's projections. The following chapter will review the research studies of animal versus human characters in projective stimuli designed for use with children.

CHAPTER IV

Animal versus Human Pictures

A vigorous controversy is still taking place over the relative merits of animals as opposed to human characters in picture-story tests for children. Several researchers have set out to disprove the Bellaks' (1949) assertion that children would identify more with animals or find them easier figures on which to project. Murstein (1963, 1965) has summarized research in this area and concludes, "The results of these studies show not a single one clearly supporting the alleged supremacy of the CAT over pictures with humans. The results of some studies are indecisive or ambiguous, but the majority show a clear superiority for figures employing humans" (Murstein, 1965, p. 424). In order to clarify the issues involved, it seems important to re-examine all available data to determine the nature and extent of any alleged "superiority."

Historically, the first two studies to explore the utility of animal versus human pictures were published only shortly after the appearance of the CAT and did not use the CAT cards. Bills (1950) and Bills, Leiman and Thomas (1950) showed ten colored animal (rabbit) pictures and the first ten TAT cards to a total of 56 children from five to ten years of age. Apparently all cards were administered in one session, with half the *Ss* seeing animal pictures first, and half the TAT first. Word count tallies in Bills' (1950) sample of 48 children yielded a highly significant difference in favor of the animal cards. Bills, Leiman and Thomas (1950) gave six individual play sessions before administration of both sets of cards to eight young children. Responses and interview material were scored for Murray's needs, and yielded only five significant correlations out of a total of 24. Correlations between animal and TAT responses ranged from —.09 to .58.

With the availability of the CAT cards, comparative studies have been carried out with normal, retarded and emotionally disturbed *Ss*.

STUDIES WITH NORMAL CHILDREN

Sample Characteristics

Since 1952 there have been ten* CAT studies which have endeavored to tease out whatever differences there may be in the responses of normal children to animal and human figures. These studies represent a combined population of 435 children, with individual sample *N*s ranging from ten to 75. The estimated number of *Ss* at each age level are presented in Table 4.1. From

---

*It was not possible to secure one additional Japanese study by Ōuchi (1957). *Psychological Abstracts* (34:6042, 1960) reports it as follows: " '6 Bellak's C.A.T. cards and 6 Waseda T.A.T. cards were alternately presented to 20 children, 5–8 average age, from a kindergarten.' The main findings were: (a) no significant difference in all measures was found between the 2 tests. (b) no significant differences in scores were found between anthropomorphyzed and nonanthropomorphized cards in CAT and between cards of children and of adults only in TAT." (Reprinted by permission of the Managing Editor, American Psychological Association.)

Table 4.1. Number of Ss at Each Age Level in Studies of
Animal versus Human Cards

Study	Total N	4 yr.	5 yr.	6 yr.	7 yr.	8 yr.	9 yr.	10 yr.	12 yr.
Simson (1952)	10		1	2	1	2	3	1	
Biersdorf & Marcuse	30			15	15				
Light	75						38	37	
Armstrong	60			20	20	20			
Jackson	50			10	10	10	10	10	
Furuya	72			24				24	24
Simson (1959)	28					14	14		
Budoff	18	18							
Weisskopf-Joelson & Foster	40		20	20					
Lawton	52			24		28			
Totals	435	18	21	115	46	74	65	72	24

the information provided it was impossible to accurately determine the exact number of children at each age level in every study, but the figures presented are probably a close approximation. The six-year age level is well represented, and more than one-half the entire number were tested in the six to eight year range, the optimal appropriate ages for this particular test.

Table 4.2 highlights the methods used and the significant findings of each available research study.

Cards Used and Alterations Made

The stimuli used have varied considerably from study to study, especially with respect to the human figures employed. One study has also explored the variable of color in both forms. Some studies have used the standard TAT cards, while others have used human scenes especially designed to approach the CAT cards in appearance and content. Altogether, there have been six different pairs of animal-human CAT sets, with only two sets being used in more than one study.

The set developed at the State College of Washington (Biersdorf and Marcuse, 1953) has been used for two normative studies (and for one study each with disturbed and retarded Ss to be reviewed in later sections of this chapter). Several alterations were made in card content, not only when transposing to the human category, but also in the "copies" made of the original animal cards. In their human version, the "ambiguous" adult figure in Card 1 is obviously a female; Card 2 shows a woman and boy clearly opposite a man in the tug-of-war; and in Card 10 it is obviously a woman who has a boy over her knee. In Card 5 there is only one figure in the crib, and in Card 4 of the animal set the kangaroo baby is being carried in the mother's arms rather than in the pouch.

Weisskopf-Joelson and Foster (1962) altered four animal situations to correspond with the human ones used: all animals were shown with clothes on; the kangaroo baby was not placed in the pouch; and the mouse was omitted in Card 3. So not only was the original intent of the animal cards and characters altered but liberties were also taken with the actual dynamic situations portrayed.

In the Simson (1952, 1959) human set, the adults are obviously women on Cards 1, 2, 4, and 10; and obviously men on Cards 2 and 3. Card 2 is grossly altered in situational content in that the tug-of-war is only taking place between a man and a woman while a child figure is shown in the center of the card as if watching the struggle. On the other hand, Card 3 achieves a very adequate parallel situation by showing only a portion of a child's head peering around the doorway behind the seated adult.

Lawton (unpublished) used the Bellaks' (1965) newly developed set of human cards, the CAT-H. These are illustrated in Figure 13.1 in Chapter XIII.

In the ten studies using CAT cards as the animal stimulus, only two (Lawton, unpublished; Jackson, 1955) have used all ten cards. Budoff (1960) used nine cards (omitting Card 6); Simson (1952, 1959) used eight cards; Biersdorf and Marcuse (1953) and Furuya (1957) used the Washington set of six cards; Light (1954) and Armstrong (1954) used different selections of five cards each; while Weisskopf-Joelson and Foster (1962) used only four.

Thus in the eight studies employing fewer than the full complement of ten cards, Card 10 was the only one used in all cases. Cards 6 and 7 were only used twice and Card 9 was used four times. It should be pointed out that Cards 5, 6 and 9 were designed to tap areas of sleeping, oedipal problems and primal scene concerns, situations most likely to carry dynamic significance for the late preschool and early latency child for whom this test was mainly devised. With respect to Card 6, Bellak has specifically stated that this card (which was neglected in most of the studies) was placed to follow Card 5 in order to test for the effects of possible repression and defensiveness on the previous card. Consequently, this dynamic aspect of the original set has been completely discarded in the experimental sets under consideration.

Differences in Administration

In one of the ten studies (Light, 1954) both sets of cards were apparently administered in the same session. The rest have used one or two-week intervals between sets, and a balanced order with half the Ss receiving the animal set first and half the human set first. The two Washington studies (Biersdorf and Marcuse, 1953; Furuya, 1957) varied the order of the cards from S to S, but did use the same order for both administrations for each S. Again, we should call attention to the fact that the order of the cards is considered very important by Bellak.

Two studies using older Ss (Light, 1954; Furuya, 1957) had them write their own stories, thus introducing yet another dimension. In Light's procedure, the pictures were also projected onto a screen for group administration.

Criteria Employed

Several of the studies were mainly concerned with formal criteria such as length of story (word count), reaction time, number of characters added or omitted, etc. The quality and kinds of figures added and/or omitted would

Table 4.2. Summaries of Research Studies with Normal Children

Authors	Date	N	Ages	Stimulus Cards	Method of Presentation	Criteria	Significant Findings
Simson	1952	10	5 to 10 yrs.	Eight CAT cards (all but 7 & 8) Eight human cards of same scenes	Balanced order; two sessions, one week apart	Total words	.01 favor human
						Rate of speaking	ns (trend favor human)
						Reaction time	ns
						Total time	ns (trend favor human)
Biersdorf & Marcuse	1953	30	5–11 to 8–0	Six copies of CAT cards and six human cards in corresponding scenes, sizes and shading (Cards 1, 2, 4, 5, 8, 10)	Balanced order; two sessions, two weeks apart; order of cards varied between Ss but same order for each S on both sessions	Reaction time	ns
						Response time	ns
						Word count	ns
						Number of ideas	ns
						Characters mentioned in picture	ns
						Characters added	ns
						Promptings and rejections	ns
Light	1954	75	9–0 to 10–6	Five CAT cards (2, 3, 7, 8, 10) Five TAT cards (1, 2, 3BM, 7GF, 12M)	Group admin.; pictures projected on screen; alternated TAT & CAT cards. Stories written by Ss	Word count	ns
						Feelings—number	.01 favor TAT
						kind	.01 favor TAT
						Conflicts	.01 favor TAT
						Outcomes—number	ns
						kind	.01 favor TAT
						Themes—number	.02 favor TAT
						kind	.01 favor TAT
						Figures introduced	.01 favor TAT
Armstrong	1954	60	6–2 to 8–11 (Mean IQ's from 120–131)	Five CAT cards (1, 2, 4, 8, 10) Five human cards drawn to correspond, and ambiguous as to sex	Balanced order; two sessions, two weeks apart	Word count	ns
						Nouns & verbs	ns
						Ego-related words	ns
						Transcendence score	.01 favor human
						Reaction time	ns
Jackson	1955	50	6 to 10 yrs.	Ten CAT cards Ten TAT cards	Balanced order, one-week interval	Total needs	ns
						Total feelings	.02 favor TAT
						Concepts & figures introduced	.01 favor TAT
						Outcomes	ns
						Main themes	ns
						Conflict	ns
						Omissions	ns

Furuya	1957	72	6–4 to 7–3 9–7 to 10–4 11–6 to 12–5 (Japanese Ss)	Six CAT and six human cards (same as in Biersdorf & Marcuse)	Balanced order; two sessions, two weeks apart. Order of cards varied between Ss but same order for each S on both sessions Two older groups wrote stories, group situation, but cards presented individually	Reaction time	ns
						Response time	ns
						Word count	ns
						Characters mentioned in picture	ns
						Introduced figures	ns
						Expressions of feelings	.05 favor human (age 9) .02 favor human (age 11)
						Expressions of signif. conflict	.01 favor human (age 9)
						Stories with definite outcomes	.02 favor human (age 6)
Simson	1959	28	8 & 9 yrs. (all German girls)	Eight CAT cards (all but 7 & 8) Eight human cards of same scenes	Balanced order; two sessions, two weeks apart	Total words	.01 favor human
						Total time	.01 favor human
						Reaction time	.01 favor human
						Rate of speaking	.01 favor human
						Classification of 11 themes	.01 favor human
Budoff	1960	18	3–9 to 4–3 (All IQ's above 120)	Nine CAT cards (omit card 6) Nine human cards of same scenes	Balanced order; two sessions, two weeks apart	Word count	ns
						Story level (plots)	ns (trend favor human)
						Transcendence score	ns (trend favor human)
Weisskopf-Joelson & Foster	1962	40	5–6 to 7–0	Four CAT cards (3, 4, 9, 10) Four similar human cards Also colored versions of CAT and human sets	Only four cards to each S; one from each set and version	Transcendence Index: Animal vs. human	ns
						Color vs. noncolor	ns
						11 highest vs. 11 lowest: Animal vs. human	ns (trend for lows to favor animal))
						Color vs. noncolor	ns (trend for highs to favor color; lows, noncolor)
Lawton	(unpubl.)	52	5–7 to 8–6	Ten CAT cards Ten CAT-H cards (Bellak)	Balanced order; two sessions, two weeks apart	Analysis Schedule: Reaction-Undoing	ns
						Isolation	ns
						Repression-Denial	ns
						Deception	ns
						Symbolization	ns
						Projection-Introjection	ns (trend favor animal)
						Fear-Anxiety	ns
						Regression	ns
						Weak controls	ns
						Confused identification	ns

seem more significant than their number *per se*. There is no valid research evidence to indicate that the length of a story, or the reaction time, or total storytelling time, have any relationship to dynamic personality factors. In this connection, Toppelstein (1952) has pointed out that total time can be greatly influenced by the *E's* speed of recording and the *S's* speed of talking; total word count may merely reflect the additional inquiries used by the *E* to encourage a quiet child to continue; reaction times will also be affected by the *E's* repeated efforts to get a shy child underway.

When some dynamic criteria were attempted, in addition to, or in place of, the formal characteristics, the Transcendence Index was used three times (Armstrong, 1954; Budoff, 1960; Weisskopf-Joelson and Foster, 1962), and Haworth's Analysis Schedule once (Lawton, unpublished). At least some measures of expression of needs, feelings, number of conflicts or outcomes, and types of themes were employed in most instances.

Results

Of the ten studies reported in Table 4.2, only three (Light, 1954; Furuya, 1957; Simson, 1959) show any preponderance of significant findings favoring the human figures. (In two of these studies, the significant results were obtained with *Ss* nine years of age and older.) The remaining seven studies show a clear majority of nonsignificant findings. Thus the evidence for any superiority of human over animal figures for projective use with young children is not very impressive.

Lawton's (unpublished) data provide some clues as to reasons for the lack of significant differences. She reports that her school *Ss* did not appear disturbed enough to give responses which could be scored in dynamic categories representing various defensive mechanisms. Interestingly enough, the category of Projection-Introjection was the only one to show a definite trend in Lawton's data and in the direction of more such responses to the animal form. The items used in scoring this category refer to aggression and attack, blaming and having secrets, the addition of objects and characters, and references to magic; these are areas most relevant in the study of projection.

Conclusions from Studies with Normal Children

Three main observations seem pertinent:

(1) With a preponderance of nonsignificant findings, one cannot say that animal pictures elicit more projection than do the human ones, but neither can one say that human pictures are unqualifiedly superior. This latter fact has been overlooked in most discussions and summaries of research findings. For some inexplicable reason, the consensus of opinion seems to be that if no significant differences are found, then animal pictures have no utility and/or human pictures should be considered preferable. But the data do not warrant such a conclusion. The generally accepted intrinsic interest which animals have held for children through the ages, as well as some research evidence that more projection takes place as similarity of picture to subject decreases, would still seem to argue in favor of animal figures in projective tests for chil-

dren. Clearly, no one has demonstrated that any harm may be done to children by their use!

(2) More consideration needs to be given to the technical problems of administration and evaluation and to comparability of research designs. Certainly, if a test is to be subjected to research evaluations, all the cards should be used, they should be presented in the order specified, and the age ranges studied should be those for which the test was designed. These specifications have not been met in many of the current studies. For reliable and meaningful comparisons to be made between studies, research designs need to be comparable. Problems of adequately analyzing, coding and quantifying projective responses (while still maintaining their dynamic meanings) also need to be more thoroughly explored. Finally, there may well be, in all attempts at duplication of sets of cards, a very genuine lack of equivalence between the stimulus properties of the two forms, so that dissimilar findings should be anticipated, rather than significant or nonsignificant differences between common variables.

(3) Perhaps it is unrealistic to attempt to evaluate a projective instrument on samples of presumably normal children. Certainly, we would expect to uncover more dynamic material from a disturbed child, and, correspondingly, less from a normal child — else he too would be referred to a clinic. The less dynamic the response, the more similar, (and less idiosyncratic) will be the stories to both animal and human stimuli. Analysis of formal elements would not be expected to yield startling results to either form of the test, and there would be fewer incidents that would lend themselves to dynamic analyses. In other words, normal children should, *ipso facto*, have fewer negative feelings, phobias, fears, and hostilities to be projected, consequently their stories to either stimulus will yield little in the way of dynamic differences.

STUDIES WITH CLINICAL GROUPS

There have been very few studies using clinical samples and N*s* have been small. Table 4.3 summarizes information from the two investigations which have been carried out with disturbed children and the two with mental retardates.

Emotionally Disturbed Children

Mainard and Marcuse (1954) studied 28 Ss who were either in residential treatment or diagnosed as disturbed and awaiting treatment. The Washington set of cards was used. No significant differences were found between the animal and human pictures when the usual formal criteria were applied. When judges were asked to rate pairs of animal and human stories for "clinical usefulness" a significant difference (p= .001) was found in favor of the human stories.

Haworth (unpublished), using the Bellaks' CAT-H, evaluated animal and human stories of 22 outpatient clinic referrals and inpatient cases with a wide variety of psychiatric diagnoses. No significant differences were found on Haworth's Analysis Schedule, although there was a trend in favor of the animal form on the category of Projection-Introjection. Stories were also rated for the presence of responses representing the following dynamic themes: oral depriva-

Table 4.3. Summaries of Research Studies with Clinical Groups

Authors	Date	N	Ages	Stimulus Cards	Method of Presentation	Criteria	Significant Findings
Emotionally Disturbed:							
Mainard & Marcuse	1954	28 (21 boys, 7 girls)	5–4 to 8–5	Six CAT and six human cards; (same as Biersdorf & Marcuse)	Balanced order; two sessions, two weeks apart Order of cards varied but same order for each S on both sessions	Reaction time	ns
						Response time	ns
						Word count	ns
						Promptings & rejections	ns
						S's preferences	ns
						Judges' ratings of clinical usefulness	.001 favor human
Haworth	(unpubl.)	22 (16 boys, 6 girls)	6–3 to 10–3	Ten CAT cards Ten CAT-H cards (Bellak)	Balanced order; two sessions with 2–3 week intervals	Analysis Schedule:	
						Reaction-Undoing	ns
						Isolation	ns
						Repression-Denial	ns
						Deception	ns
						Symbolization	ns
						Projection-Introjection	ns (trend favor animal)
						Fear-Anxiety	ns
						Regression	ns
						Weak controls	ns
						Confused identification	ns

Retarded:

Butler	1961	50
		(25 boys,
		25 girls)
			CA = 9–7
			to 18–7
			MA = 3–6
			to 9–10
			IQ = 30
			to 70
				Six CAT and six
				human cards
				(same as
				Biersdorf &
				Marcuse)
					Balanced order;
					two sessions,
					three week
					interval
						S's preferences
						Rejections
						Self-references
						Reaction time
						Response time
						Word count
						Characters *not*
						  mentioned
						Characters introduced
						Expressions of feelings
						Expressions of conflict
						Stories with definite
						  outcomes
							ns
							ns
							ns
							ns
							ns
							ns
							
							ns
							ns
							ns
							ns
							
							ns

Budoff	1963	23 Exp. = 12 Control = 11	5–1 to 7–0 Mean MA = 4–5 IQ's = 70–78 Mean MA = 5–8 IQ's = 87–91	Nine CAT cards (omit Card 6) Nine human cards of same scenes	Balanced order; two sessions, two weeks apart	Word count Transcendence score	.05 favor human (exp. group) ns (controls) ns (exp. group) ns (controls)

tion, anal concerns, oedipal attachments, and oppositional tendencies. There was some tendency for the animal form to elicit more themes of oral deprivation and oedipal attachments, and for the human form to reveal more oppositional tendencies. The over-all numbers of such responses were too small to draw conclusions but the patterning of the differences suggests an area for further study.

Retarded Children

Butler (1961) administered the Washington set of cards to 50 retarded Ss whose IQ's ranged from 30 to 77, and MA's from 3-6 to 9-10 (Mean MA= 5-2). No significant differences were found between the two forms for formal criteria, expressions of feelings and conflicts, or for outcomes. Butler observed that the stories were brief and that only a small proportion of them could be scored for any of the dynamic criteria. The responses consisted largely of enumeration of picture details.

Budoff (1963) administered his previous (1960) set of nine cards to a small sample (N=12) of borderline retarded Ss with a mean MA of 4-5, and to low average controls (N=11) of similar chronological ages but mean MA of 5-8. The Transcendence Index yielded no differences between animal and human forms for either group. The retarded Ss told significantly longer stories to the human form, while there were no differences in story length for the controls.

Conclusions from Clinical Studies

Only 50 children have been used as subjects in the comparative studies of animal versus human responses of disturbed children while the two studies of retardates represent a total N of 62. In these small samples, virtually no differences between the two test forms were demonstrated. Rather than attempting to draw any inferences from such small samples, it is more pertinent to make a plea for more clinical studies with larger Ns. Samples of disturbed children should be large enough to permit subdivision into various diagnostic or behavioral categories. Grouping different types of disturbances may mask differences which may be relevant to test interpretation; e.g., it is the author's impression that children with marked behavior disorders give very meager dynamic material to either form of the test; consequently there would be little basis for making comparisons.

SUBJECT AND CARD COMPARISONS

The results which have been presented in the previous sections have been concerned with group data with respect to summations of responses to all ten cards for each set. It is also important to determine the extent to which individual Ss give similar responses to equivalent cards from the two sets. Group data on corresponding cards in each set have also been reported in a few studies.

Subject Comparisons

Both Lawton (unpublished) and Haworth (unpublished) have evaluated the instances in which a child has received critical scores (on the Analysis Schedule) on the same dimensions for each form of the test. In the first place, both studies revealed that approximately 55 per cent of the total number of scores represented similar dimensions used on both forms; thus 45 per cent of the scores represent instances where a dimension was scored for one form and not for the other.

In the school sample, Lawton found that five of the ten defense mechanisms in the scoring system were not used often enough to yield critical scores on either form for 60 per cent of the children. Isolation was used most frequently by Ss on both forms, followed by Projection-Introjection and Reaction-Undoing. The items making up the Isolation category reflect, to a large extent, basic elements of cognitive and expressive style, such as attention to details, comments about the cards, use of titles and direct quotations, concerns with "naughty" behavior. To a greater degree than is found in the other categories, the Isolation items do not represent as much specific involvement of the S with the situations and interpersonal relationships portrayed in the pictures; rather, they suggest avoidance and distancing. This may account for the similarities between forms on this dimension. Similarly for Reaction-Undoing, the items reveal basic approaches to problem situations somewhat independent of the picture content *per se*. When a subject's responses were scorable for a defense mechanism on one, but not on the other, form of the test, the most outstanding differences in use were in the direction of the animal form and for Projection-Introjection and Repression-Denial.

Haworth, with a clinical sample, found three dimensions were used most often by Ss on both forms: Projection-Introjection, Weak Controls, and Confused Identification. The latter two dimensions have consistently been found to characterize responses of clinical groups on the animal form of the CAT, and would now appear to reflect similar dynamics on both forms. In addition to the frequent use of Projection-Introjection by Ss on both forms, this dimension was given considerably more often on the animal form in those instances where dimensions could be scored for only one form of the test.

Card by Card Differences

Simson (1959) tabulated each of 11 themes (such as aggressiveness, passivity, punishment, eating) for each card. Correlations between the animal and human forms revealed high correspondence of themes in response to Cards 1, 2 and 5. The greatest difference was found for Card 6, with *r*'s for Cards 4, 3, 10 and 9 gradually rising in that order. (Cards 7 and 8 were not used in this set.)

In Lawton's (unpublished) analysis of specific card by card responses, she found considerable agreement between forms, but some notable differences as follows: There were more negative or aggressive reactions on the animal form (especially on Cards 2, 3 and 4). On Card 1, the adult was seen exclusively as a mother figure on the animal form, but as father about one-third of the time on the human form. On Card 2 of the human form, the child is seen almost always as being with a peer rather than with a parent. The adult figure on Card 3 is seen in a power role only on the animal form. On Card 8, male figures were mentioned only on the animal form. On Card 10 more themes of naughtiness relating to toileting were given to the human than to the animal form, while more responses suggesting that a lesson was learned were given to the animal form.

In general, Haworth's clinic data agree with the above findings, except that on Card 1, the adult is most often seen as a mother figure on both forms and on Card 3, the child is threatened with attack on both forms, while this occurs only on the animal form in the school sample.

SUMMARY

Comparative studies have been reviewed in which the CAT and human "equivalents" have been employed. The studies are scarcely comparable in terms of the specific cards used, the human adaptations made and the situations portrayed, procedures of administration, or evaluative criteria used. To confound the picture, some of the subjects used were beyond the applicable age range for this particular test. In addition, most of the subjects have been normal children who would not be expected to give rich projective material in any case.

In general, results have revealed very few significant differences between the two forms, so that neither form can be said to be superior to the other in eliciting meaningful projective responses from children. There was some suggestion that personality factors not influenced by specific card content tended to be revealed on the child's responses to both cards, and that differences between forms appear in responses which are closely dependent on the situations and relationships portrayed in the pictures.

Seemingly still unanswered is the question as to whether differences in responses to animal and human forms represent real differences in response to similar scenes when portrayed via different species, or the failure of the two sets to represent similar projective situations. It seems quite possible that changing species may well change the task in qualitative ways.

As Bellak has pointed out (1954) the critical issue is not really whether animal stories can be demonstrated to be better than, or equally as good as, human pictures. The important element often overlooked in the ongoing controversy is that scenes for the CAT pictures were selected with the aim of tapping areas of experience and emotional problems typical of the early childhood years. Murstein (1963) has more recently re-emphasized this point and suggested the directions for future research, when he states:

. . . The drawings of the CAT are designed to test *specific* problems, such as sibling rivalry and oral fixation. While granting the superiority of the TAT as a broad-band instrument, it is conceivable that the CAT may be superior with reference to the kind of problems the drawings are intended to tap. Future research, therefore, ought to avoid broad indices such as word count and reaction time and focus on the value of the test for the kinds of problems it was designed to measure.

As for the theoretical issue of the supremacy of animals or human beings, this issue can be tested only by employing a broader sampling of behavioral situations depicting animals than the relatively small number of 10 used in the CAT. Perhaps the kind of situation in which the animals are depicted also should be varied instead of using the "humanized" environment appearing on the CAT. In sum, there is a need for considerably more research on a much broader base than heretofore with regard to the CAT (p. 215).

CHAPTER V

Developmental Aspects

Evaluation and interpretation of a young child's projective responses must be made in the light of his particular stage of development at the time of testing. The maturational process occurs in all areas of functioning: in the physical and intellectual spheres, in the progression through psychogenetic levels, and in terms of ego development and interpersonal relationships. For any projective test designed to be used over the age range from three to ten years, as in the case of the CAT, the kinds of responses to be expected will naturally vary depending on the age of the particular child.

Various developmental theories will be reviewed in this chapter, with particular emphasis on those aspects which are relevant to an understanding of the young child's ability to handle the task of telling stories to a series of pictures. Table 5.1 summarizes the essential developmental phases in each of the theories to be reviewed. The age levels along the ordinate are meant only as rough indications of the probable times of appearance of the items in the body of the table. In each of the theories presented, developmental milestones should be viewed as significant with respect to the *sequence* of events, rather than to the specific age of occurrence. In addition, various interpreters of the theories mentioned here might disagree as to the exact age of appearance of a particular phenomenon, again reflecting the impossibility, as well as undesirability, of establishing rigid guidelines. Nevertheless, behavior toward the bottom of the table does not occur at the early ages, nor without the prior appearance of the earlier phenomena.

MENTAL DEVELOPMENT

Piaget and Werner have each proposed theories of mental and cognitive development which essentially involve differentiation of processes and their subsequent integration into higher levels of functioning. Piaget's schema (Piaget, 1936, 1962; Inhelder, 1962; Flavell, 1963) is the more specific and phase oriented. He essentially postulated four stages: (1) Sensory-motor, (2) Pre-operational, (3) Concrete Operations, (4) Formal Operations. "The states of intellectual development . . . represent a constant progression from a less to a more complete equilibrium and manifest therein the organism's steady tendency toward a dynamic integration" (Inhelder, 1962, p. 28).

Piaget's first, or Sensory-motor stage, has been divided into six substages ranging from the stereotyped reflex patterns at birth to the ability (by 18 months) to invent new means through deduction or mental combination, and involving the awareness of relationships (Piaget, 1936). Two important aspects of sensory-motor theory are *assimilation*, or the taking in of impressions and incorporating them into already existing schema, and *accomodation*, or the application and transformation of a schema to a new object or situation.

With the acquisition of language and the consequent possibility of forming

Table 5.1. Summary of Developmental Theories

Age Levels	Mental Development		Language Development			Emotional Development	Psychoanalytic Theories		
	Piaget	Werner	Experimental Research	Piaget	Werner	Bridges	Structural Organization	Libidinal Stages	Defense Mechanisms
1 yr.	Sensory-motor Assimilation Accommodation Imitation Symbolic play Concepts of: objects, space, time, causality	Global, diffuse, undifferentiated, syncretic				Undifferentiated excitement Distress Delight	Id Pleasure principle Primary process	Oral Dependency Early object relations	
2 yrs.	Pre-operational Concrete Irreversible Animistic			Egocentric Syncretistic Participation and magic	Syncretic Concrete	Fear, Anger, Joy, Affection	Ego Reality principle	Anal Aggression	Fixation Regression Introjection Projection Denial
3 yrs.			Enumeration (concrete)		Magic		Secondary process		
4 yrs.				Animism					
5 yrs.		Differentiation				Shame, Anxiety, Jealousy, Envy, Disappointment, Disgust, Elation, Hope, Filial and Parental Affec- tion	Superego	Phallic-oedipal Identification Affection	
6 yrs.			Description (use and func- tion)						Repression Reaction formation Undoing Isolation Displacement Sublimation
7 yrs.	Concrete Operations Conservation Reversibility Negation			Socialized				Latency	(No new defenses, sublimation and reaction formation are prominent)
8 yrs.	Reciprocity Logical classifi- cations								
9 yrs.		Integration Centralization Interpretation Abstraction Generalization			Abstract				
10 yrs.			Interpretation (abstraction)					Prepuberty	
11 yrs.	Formal thinking Hypotheses Deduction Abstraction Logic								Intellectualization
12 yrs.									Asceticism

mental representations, the second stage (Pre-operational*) is initiated around two years of age and continues to age seven. The capacity for imitation, symbolic play, and reconstruction of experiences ushers in this period. Thought processes in the Pre-operational stage are characterized by irreversibility. Flavell (1963) comments: "Preoperational thought, then, is static and immobile. It is a kind of thought which can focus impressionistically and sporadically on this or that momentary, static condition but cannot adequately link a whole set of successive conditions into an integrated totality . . . by taking account of the transformations which unify them and render them logically coherent" (p. 157).

The stage of Concrete Operations (from seven to 12 years of age) is characterized by conservation, reversibility and awareness of reciprocal relationships, logical classifications and serializations.

Only after ages 11 or 12 does the fourth stage of Formal Operations appear, with the ability to use hypotheses and propositions, and to think in abstract terms with deductive processes and logical constructions.

The child's progression from reflexive to reflective behaviour is summarized by Stevenson (1962) as follows: "The changes that occur as the child moves from sensory-motor to reflective intelligence are primarily changes in speed of responding, awareness of results, and increasing ability to operate at greater and more remote spatial and temporal distances" (p. 119). Applying Piaget's theory to thematic stories, we would thus expect, with increasing age and development, more facility in verbal expression, more ego involvement, more ability to separate fact from fantasy (and one's own experience from that of others), and a greater variety of themes drawn from the many sources of past experiences, exposures and observations.

Werner (1948) presents his theory of mental development in broader terms than those of Piaget, and in less well-defined stages. His is a genetic system based on observations of biologic growth, the development of the nervous system, psychopathology, mammalian behavior, and comparisons and contrasts with primitive peoples. He postulates "An increasing differentiation and refinement of mental phenomena and functions and a progressive hierarchization. . ." (Werner, 1948, p. 51). This increasing hierarchic integration, by its very nature, implies an increasing subordinaton of lower level functions in the motor, emotional and sensory fields. "Thinking as a relating and comparative activity assumes the role of a central selective function commanding sensori-motor, perceptual and imaginative data" (Werner, 1948, p. 52). Werner points out that early mental processes take place in very concrete terms, while abstract thought characterizes the higher levels of mental organization. Consequently the young child first perceives in a loose, syncretic and global manner, neglecting important details; only later does he see a succession of discrete and articulated parts (differentiation), and finally the unity of the larger whole encompassing subordinated details (integration).

Werner (1948) points out that, at very early levels, when a young child

---

*Sometimes included as the first part of the stage of Concrete Operations (*see* Inhelder, 1962).

draws a line or a circle it is, to him, "a man" or "an animal." He feels that similar "schematic" representations may characterize the child's language and thought processes as well, so that one word may stand for several objects or parts of objects. Obviously the child "knows," internally, much more about the concept than is outwardly demonstrated in his unelaborated drawing or meager verbal description.

To translate to the projective situation, whether the child is unable to elaborate, or does not realize the necessity for doing so in order to make his concept explicit and understandable to others, is less relevant to our purpose than the observation that he does act or communicate in this special form of "shorthand." Consequently, more assumptions may need to be made (along with extreme caution in so doing) when interpreting protocols from very young subjects. For example, when the five-year-old child responds to Card 7 with: "The tiger is biting the monkey's tail," he may be including his conception of the strength and ferocity of the tiger, the fear and panic of the monkey, as well as an awareness of the crunch of the tiger's teeth on the hapless tail, and the stab of pain felt by the victim of the assault. To the young child, it may not seem necessary to go into such elaborate detail; or, as is more likely, the ability to put these feelings into words has not yet developed. But we can no more assert that these feelings are not part of his "story" than we can assert that the child himself has never felt anger, fear, hunger or pain. From an older child (aged nine or ten), a story to the same card would be expected to cover several aspects of the picture, incorporating them into a coherent story, along with creative, imaginative elements, a sequential account of events, and a logical outcome.

DEVELOPMENT OF THOUGHT AND LANGUAGE

The problems of word usage and levels of verbalization have been the subject of some experimental research. Findings uniformly point to a developmental progression from early enumeration, through levels of description or explanation by means of function, to the mature forms of abstraction and interpretation. These are essentially the stages recognized in the scoring of items calling for pictorial description in the Stanford-Binet scales. Vernon (1940) found that normal children responded to TAT-type pictures with enumeration until age seven, at which time simple descriptions were noted; by age eleven the child could interpret the picture as a whole. Similar results were also reported by Balken and Vander Veer (1942), with enumerations and descriptions being common until age ten. Children beyond ten would invent persons and situations, and attempt to solve the problem situations portrayed in the pictures.

Feifel and Lorge (1950), in their analysis of the qualitative levels of vocabulary responses of 900 children, found similar stages. Papania (1954) studied the vocabulary responses of retarded children and found abstract definitions increased with age, while concrete definitions correspondingly decreased.

On the basis of the above findings, expectations for CAT stories from children under age six or seven would consist of concrete, enumerative responses such as naming characters and objects in the pictures. Between ages six or seven and eleven, more descriptions of the actions and objects should be given along with considerations of uses and functions. Only for very intelligent Ss at the upper age levels of appropriateness for the CAT could we expect real interpretations and abstract forms of generalizations to be incorporated into the stories.

Vernon (1940) also reports on the thought processes of emotionally disturbed children in his sample. Where cognitive functions were impaired, there were regressions to earlier levels of response; if reality awareness was deficient, phantasy-production was overly active. The obsessive children engaged in much overelaboration and attention to minute details, while highly repressed *Ss* gave brief, stereotyped responses.

In applying developmental theories specifically to the areas of thought and language, Piaget's views are again most pertinent, in terms of the syncretic and self-oriented aspects of thought in the young child. Piaget (1932) describes young children, up to about age seven, as thinking and acting egocentrically; their speech is not used to communicate to others so much as to serve as a monologue accompanying their own activities. Egocentric thought differs from the more mature socialized thought in that it jumps from premises to conclusions without any of the usual intervening steps of deduction.

Flavell (1963), in his discussion of Piaget's concept of egocentrism, points out that this includes the child's inability to take the role of another person, to see the point of view of another person, or to realize that there could be views other than his own. The child sees no need to justify his reasoning to others and is unaware of any contradictions that may exist in his own reasoning. Distortions occur by virtue of concentrating on one feature only, thus ignoring other aspects of the concept. According to Piaget (1932), syncretic thought is closely akin to primary process thinking and to dream imagery, with condensations, distortions, associations, and "leaps to conclusions." Piaget feels the ability to understand others and to communicate effectively and objectively does not appear until after age seven.

Translated to the CAT situation, the mechanisms of egocentrism and syncretism would lead us to expect that the preschool child will engage in confabulation and be "carried away" at times by the impact of his own inventions, to the point of leaving the field of the specific stimulus card. "Distance" between self and card will be less than at later ages. Personal references will abound. By age seven when, according to Piaget, the child is able to seek explanations and to reconstruct stories in sequential order and with some concern for objectivity and realism, we would anticipate that CAT stories would be told with coherence and meaning, with a logical sequence of events, and an appropriate outcome. In contrast to the younger child, the older child's fantasy will be organized and imaginative, and there will be an awareness that this fantasy differs from reality.

Magical Thinking

Piaget (1929) stresses the lack of differentiation between the child and his world, so that thoughts are regarded as being located in the object thought about and one's own feelings are viewed as being experienced by others. When all his needs are being met by the parents, the infant or young child regards himself as the center of the universe and cannot conceive that others do not know what he is thinking, or do not feel his pain while he himself is experiencing it. As a result of this egocentricity, the child gradually comes to believe he is responsible for the events around him or that he can control the environment. Piaget labels this phenomenon as "participation" which, in turn, leads readily to the belief in magic, and daily repetitive actions or habits take on the aspects of protective rituals. The next phase is "animism" in which the child regards inert or inanimate objects as being alive and conscious. Before ages four or five, animism is taken for granted as an integral aspect of objects. Only after this age does the child begin to ask questions concerning these concepts.

The gradual decrease in egocentricity (very marked after age seven or eight) leads to less feeling of one's own or the parents' omnipotence. This more objective viewpoint is accompanied by a decrease in animism, thinking becomes more socialized, and ties to the parent less strong. The child begins to see the logical connections between things, and he tries to find explanations in the objects themselves. "According as the child becomes clearly aware of personality in himself he refuses to allow a personality to things" (Piaget, 1929, p. 239).

Werner (1948) also discusses the child's magical ideation and its relation to the ceremonial rituals that develop around feeding, dressing, and going to sleep. Objects are personalized and there is very little separation of the world from the ego. The child develops the feeling that his own wishes contain magical powers, and reason is not viewed as sufficient to provide protection from the unknown. Werner emphasizes that all higher levels of mental activity include the capacity for the earlier, more primitive behaviors. Consequently, if a child is subjected to severe emotional stress, we could expect to find regressions to these earlier levels as evidenced in projective responses by more inappropriate fantasy, less distance, more use of magic and personal references, and a return to syncretistic modes of thinking.

EMOTIONAL ASPECTS OF DEVELOPMENT

To understand and interpret projective responses of young children we need not only an awareness of developmental levels in the areas of mental development, cognition and language, but also an understanding of the progressive unfolding of emotional factors, the sources of potential conflicts and the development of methods of coping and defending. These will be only briefly sketched here in order to round out the developmental picture.

Some 30 years ago, Bridges (1930) proposed a schema of emotional progression and differentiation from one original global state of Generalized Excitement. Distress and Delight are derivatives appearing in infancy. These three affects are the basic foundation for all subsequent differentiation and refinement of emotional nuances (see Table 5.1).

We can also observe the correspondence between the differentiation of emotional responses and the development of libidinal patterns and defense mechanisms in the psychoanalytic model.* For example, the differentiation of the ego takes place concomitantly with the refinements of emotional varia-

---

*The last three columns of Table 5.1 have been adapted from Watson (1959, pp. 138–139).

tions of the earlier themes of Distress, Excitement and Delight, while, at the same time, the child moves from oral dependency to a state of independence and self-assertion characteristic of the anal stage. Similarly, an analogy can be drawn between the global, undifferentiated mental states described by Piaget and Werner and the initial undifferentiated, pleasure-based, and primary process aspects of the id as delineated in psychoanalytic theory.

As the ego rises to the ascendency, secondary processes take over, and the further differentiation of various ego functions takes place, i.e., motility, memory, perception, reality testing, impulse control, organization and internalization. With the development and consolidation of the defense mechanisms, greater control of drives and impulses is achieved. Throughout the progressions from one psychogenetic level to the next, the ego is still in the process of becoming, and there may be many eruptions of more primitive, id-primary-process material, especially in times of situational stress. Anna Freud (1946) has emphasized the gradual emergence of the ego as follows:

"In little children the conflict between ego and id has its peculiar conditions. The demands for instinctual gratification, which spring from wishes characteristic of the oral, anal and phallic phases, are extraordinarily urgent and the affects and phantasies associated with the Oedipus complex and the castration-complex are intensely vivid; the ego which confronts them is only in process of formation and so is still weak and undeveloped" (p. 154).

Again translating into CAT terms, the stories of very young children can be expected to reflect the stronger influence of primary process thinking, with the stimulus card serving mainly as a take-off point for dream-like, dereistic fantasies, with condensations and confabulations prominent. If an older child's stories are found to contain many such elements, rather than the reality-based features to be expected for his age level, then one should suspect emotional interference with age-adequate functioning, in the absence of evidence for neurological or intellectual deficits. The development of the child's superego will be reflected in the appearance of stories of punishment, retribution, shame and guilt. The degree to which such aspects permeate the stories, or interfere with imagination and creativity, can serve as an index to the severity or moderation of the developing conscience.

By examining the stories for their relative emphasis on certain themes, the clinician is able to make an assessment of the libidinal level at which the child is currently functioning. Comparisons with age expectations permit inferences as to possibly delayed development, regressions or fixations that put the child out of step with his peers. For instance, if a nine-year-old tells stories which repeatedly emphasize food (e.g., introducing food content on cards which do not depict eating situations, and giving associated themes of dependency), then fixation or regression to the oral stage would be indicated.

The defense mechanisms commonly employed by the ego to handle affects and impulses can also roughly be ordered along a continuum from primitive to more advanced levels, with the implication that a certain stage of ego and emotional development and differentiation must take place before the more "advanced" mechanisms will be employed (see the last column of Table 5.1).

In the following excerpt, Anna Freud (1946) has offered a descriptive rationale for the chronological ordering of the defense mechanisms:

"Possibly each defense-mechanism is first evolved in order to master some specific instinctual urge and so is associated with a particular phase of infantile development. . . . Repression consists in the withholding or expulsion of an idea or affect from the conscious ego. It is meaningless to speak of repression where the ego is still merged with the id. Similarly we might suppose that projection and introjection were methods which depended on the differentiation of the ego from the outside world. . . . Sublimation, i.e., the displacement of the instinctual aim in conformity with higher social values, presupposes the acceptance or at least the knowledge of such values, that is to say, presupposes the existence of the super-ego" (pp. 55-56).

Evaluation of the defenses currently being employed by the child can be made from an inspection of the CAT stories.* Again, comparisons with expectations for age level will throw light on the process of ego development and control, or point up regressive aspects which might be the prelude to ego disorganization.

FURTHER FINDINGS FROM DEVELOPMENTAL STUDIES

In addition to the lines of development traced in our previous discussion, observations from many related fields also converge to form a picture of the child at nine or ten years of age who has achieved considerable maturity in all aspects of functioning. This period, toward the end of latency and just before the prepubertal upheaval, has been described by Gesell and Ilg (1946) as a time when the child seems to be finally meeting parental expectations for him as a person, i.e., reasonably dependable and responsible, and with an individuality which seems to be a precursor of the adult to come. Physiologically, the child's brain has long since achieved full size and weight, and all sensory apparatus are matured. EEGs are coming close to resembling those of normal adults. Mature articulation of speech sounds has been mastered; accurate grammar forms have become an automatic part of the language repertory (Templin, 1957). Visual motor skills, as represented by the Bender Gestalt, reach a fair degree of accuracy by age nine or ten (Bender, 1938) and the basic mastery of the fundamentals of reading and writing is normally achieved by age eight or nine.

Similar confirmations of developmental findings are reported from other projective tests. Research with the Rosenzweig Picture-Frustration Study (Rosenzweig and Rosenzweig, 1952) has shown the pronounced effects of the socialization process in terms of changes in superego patterns and rising scores on the Group Conformity Ratings with age. Hemmendinger (1953) has assessed developmental changes as revealed on the Rorschach with respect to W, D and Dd from ages three to eleven. He has found progressive changes which parallel the theoretical stages proposed by Werner (1948), namely, progression from global, whole responses, through increased differentiations with

---

*Specific methods for the assessment of defense mechanisms are discussed in Chapter VIII.

age, to hierarchically integrated percepts resembling those of the adult.

Finally, Halpern (1953) makes the following observations on the basis of children's Rorschach responses:

"Around eight the child achieves a reasonable integration of his personal problems and social demands. With this there goes a state of satisfaction and contentment not found at any other age. In a sense, eight may be said to be the peak of childhood, the time when the accumulated experiences are operating for the most satisfactory and satisfying adjustments. . . . His Rorschach records in many ways come closer to those of the adult at this time than at any other period. . . . The reactions typical of the eight year old may continue for a year or so, or may be cut short by the appearance of prepuberty problems" (p. 73).

SUMMARY

We have reviewed the development of the child through a variety of maturational channels, mentation and cognition, language, emotions, libidinal phases, id-ego-superego structures, and defense mechanisms along with some of the physiological, neurological and personality correlates. Through each avenue of approach and at corresponding age levels, we can discern the same general patterning: from a global, diffuse state, through phases of differentiation of structure, function or process, to a final complex but smooth functioning organization and integration of the whole organism.

Understanding of these parallel processes can serve as guidelines for expectations from projective instruments at various ages and as a means of assessing possible delays in development, fixations, or regressive states in older children. Thus, we could expect CAT stories of young children to either depart from the card in more or less unrelated flights of primary process fantasy or, if the focus remains on the stimulus, to relate what the characters are doing in descriptive and/or functional terms without regard for thoughts and feelings or the finer nuances of affective interaction between characters. Stories of the latency age child should be fairly rich, creative and imaginative, revealing the preferred defenses and with an over-all awareness of reality and of the reasonable limits within which fantasy can be allowed. Finally, there must surely come a time, as the child reaches the upper age limits of our schema (i.e., around ten to 12 years of age) when these particular pictures will cease to engage his fantasy, or will be regarded as actually "childish," since they were specifically designed to tap the main problems of early childhood — orality, cleanliness, rivalries and fears. The prepuberty child has put childish things behind him, and will probably resist the regressive pull of becoming truly engaged in a task of this kind.

CHAPTER VI

CAT Studies with Normal Children

GENERAL NORMS IN CHILDREN'S PROJECTIVE MATERIAL

The establishment of norms for projective techniques involves two main aspects: (1) the determination of the usual responses given by a particular age or group; and (2) the isolation of the unusual or deviate responses for further investigation. The common, or popular, responses indicate what may be expected from others in similar groups; the deviate items furnish insight into the inner worlds and thought processes of particular individuals in these groups.

Rosenzweig (1949), distinguishes between "appreciative norms," by which he means descriptive statements which are generally stimulus oriented and "popular," and "thematic norms," which refer to responses that involve personal needs, are subject-oriented, and often appear more than once in the sequence of the total protocol.

He states: "In the projective methods . . . a lack of agreement between a response and that which is popularly expected contributes a discriminatively positive finding. In the measure that the subject deviates from that which is expected according to the apperceptive norms, something which is potentially *characteristic* of him as a person has been revealed. . . . It is, in fact, these characteristic responses rather than the popular ones that are the primary goal of the projective method" (Rosenzweig, 1949, p. 479).

Bellak (1954) cautions that while norms may be useful as a frame of reference and as an indication of developmental trends with age, the statistical treatment of separate responses destroys their meaning as integral parts of a total universe. He maintains that norms are not essential for projective tests and that "actually, each person and each record constitutes a sample population of needs and behavioral variables" (p. 234).

While norms are desirable for comparative purposes, the problems involved, such as those indicated above, also need to be recognized. The meaning of the Gestalt is lost when each separate response is pulled out of context from the sequence of associations. Too much coding and quantifying can destroy the essence of the data. Sampling procedures present further difficulties. Due to the nature of projective material, work with large numbers is often prohibitive but, where "standardization" has been restricted to small or homogeneous groups, the applicability of the obtained norms to new and different groups is open to question.

When projective techniques are used with children, the determination of norms becomes still more complex. With adults, age categories, if used at all, can be quite broad; with children, a usual or commonplace response at one age level may border on the pathological at another level. In contrast to measurements of mental or physical growth, age progressions in projective content will not be as uniform or as consistent for the group as a whole. Individual variations can be expected to be even more marked.

Despite the attendant difficulties, normative studies have been attempted on most of the major projective tests used with children. Criterion measures have included frequencies of common themes, critical scores for designated variables, typical responses for specific test items, types of outcomes, and commonality of formal characteristics.

The previous chapter has highlighted the importance of considering developmental factors in any evaluation of children's projective responses. Consequently it is a *sine qua non* that norms for children must be concerned with assessing the typical responses for successive age levels. The possibility of sex differences, either over the entire age range or at specific ages, also needs to be investigated. Before using any set of norms the clinician must have information concerning the original population on which the norms were derived; cultural variables may make their use invalid on a different sample.

General findings for children, secured through the use of various projective media with respect to age, sex and cultural factors, will be reviewed first before turning to a discussion of work done specifically with the CAT.

Age Norms

The maturation of intellectual functions and of communication skills shows a steady progression with age (see Chapter V), while personality dynamics may be more labile at some levels and stabilized at others. Such factors will be reflected in the normative data obtained. Age trends have been noted in children's verbal protocols with respect to intellectual development and ability to express thoughts in words (Vernon, 1940; Amen, 1941; Balken and Vander Veer, 1944; Coleman, 1947; Ames et al., 1952). Investigators agree that stories not only increase in length with age but also progress from enumeration and description to more dynamic accounts of actions and feelings. There is a development from literalness to subjective interpretation, and from meagerness of content to greater productivity and imaginative elaboration. The younger the child, the more prodding needed to elicit responses and these are usually lacking in plots or causal relationships. The Michigan Picture Test (Andrew, Hartwell, Hutt and Walton, 1953) found age differences to be most significant between the third and fifth grade levels (i.e., between ages eight and ten).

Age progressions have also been noted in the dynamic and emotional aspects of children's verbal responses. Griffiths (1935) has discussed the fantasy life of the child as being most in evidence up to the latency period. In these earliest years, the child's lack of experience leads him to develop exaggerated and violent fantasies. As he matures he masks these feelings in more socialized productions. The same observed phenomena have been interpreted by the psychoanalytic school as indications of the early ascendency of primary process thinking in young children, which eventually gives way to secondary processes as the defense mechanisms are consolidated and strengthened. As noted in Chapter V, both Piaget and Werner speak of developmental progressions from magical, syncretistic thinking to processes of integration, logic and abstraction.

Sanford et al. (1943) and Balken and Vander Veer (1949) found an increasing concern with moral problems, guilt and conformity with age. They also found an increase in dynamic fantasy material. This is in contrast to the views just discussed, and these authors interpret their findings as a reflection of the fact that older children feel less free to work out their aggressive feelings in actual behavior, consequently more of it is expressed via verbal fantasy.

Research with the Rosenzweig Picture-Frustration Study with children (Rosenzweig, S., Fleming and Rosenzweig, L., 1948; Rosenzweig and Mirmow, 1950; Rosenzweig, S. and Rosenzweig, L., 1952) has demonstrated certain over-all developmental trends in both normal and problem children. Aggressive (extrapunitive) responses are more completely expressed in early childhood, but, nevertheless, predominate at each age level from four to thirteen years. Impunitive (evading) and intropunitive responses increase with age and represent indirect expressions of hostility. The progressive increase in socialization that seems to take place is revealed in superego patterns and the rising scores on the Group Conformity Ratings at successive age levels.

In a study of the spontaneous stories of two- to five-year-olds, Pitcher and Prelinger (1963) summarize their age-findings as follows:

The utilization and mastery of space increases with age as the characters more frequently go out into fantastic and abstract space. Main figures become somewhat less clearly differentiated from other characters, but their internal complexity increases with age in general. There are slight indications that increasingly complex thoughts and feelings are attributed to them. More passivity appears in the stories with increasing age, in the sense that more happenings affect the characters. Finally, there is a significant increase in the use of fantasy and imagination in the stories. A common factor in all these trends could well be a greater capacity of the children, as time goes on, to consider more alternatives, to be concerned with more than what is immediately real, and to expand in their view of the world. Expansion and differentiation, then, could be the most outstanding general processes manifesting themselves in the stories as age increases (p. 159).

These authors then present more specific findings at each age level, which may be summarized as follows:

Two-year-olds: Characters from home environment, and mostly relatives. Scene is domestic or close to the child's experience. More domestic than wild animals. "Stories which name an animal as a character at the beginning may end by assuming that the child himself is the animal" (p. 168).

Three-year-olds: Greater variety of characters, with inclusion of fantasy figures such as witches, ghosts, giants. Also move out into the community for characters, such as policeman, conductor. More zoo-type animals.

Four- and five-year-olds: Enlarge on range of occupations and include knowledge of time, seasons, planets, etc. More distinction between real and fanciful; concern about magic, pretense and disguise. More consideration of relationships between characters, cause and effect, truth and falsehood, etc.

Sex Differences

In general, sex differences have not been found to be of crucial importance in normative data secured from children (Rosenzweig, S., Fleming and Rosenzweig, L., 1948; Coleman, 1947). Some investigators have found more aggression and preoccupation with guilt and punishment in boys (Despert, 1938; Sanford et al., 1943; Symonds, 1949). Sanford et al. (1943) also found that girls told longer stories than boys and that more girls told stories with happy endings.

In the study of spontaneous stories of preschool children, Pitcher and Prelinger (1963) report:

"Sex differences are less clearly suggested. On the whole the data contain possible hints that boys intrude farther into space, attribute to their characters more activity, and are somewhat more fantastic in their stories. If one may speculate from such rather scanty data, it would seem that the boys exhibit somewhat more extensiveness and intrusiveness in their stories, while the stories of girls are perhaps somewhat more contained, stationary, and intensive" (p. 159).

In analyzing the content of the stories they found boys more concerned with transportation vehicles, machines, and elements of nature than were girls. Girls emphasize personal qualities of their characters, give proper names to people and animals, and quote direct conversations between characters. Girls use masculine characters more often than boys use feminine ones, and the sex of characters shifts back and forth more often in girls' stories.

Girls use small domestic animals more often while boys choose zoo or wild animal characters. When girls do use a wild animal, he is given a "home" in the farm or house rather than the jungle. In contrast, boys in their greater use of wild animals, put them in the role of the opponent, with much biting, devouring, and killing; the jungle is their habitat, and there is little personification, such as giving names to the animals.

"Considering all character categories combined, the boy more than the girl has a tendency to go out of bounds, to fraternize with the grandiose and unknown, and, as he identifies with people, animals, or objects having a high degree of motion or energy, he is more likely to go out and come to the object, rather than bring the object into himself. The girl more often stays close to the here and now in her main interests which are the domestic and the familiar scene" (Pitcher and Prelinger, 1963, p. 174).

Where death themes are used, (Pitcher and Prelinger, 1963) girls maintain the idea of the reversibility of death, while boys see death as final, are more concerned with the relations between birth and death and with the death of magical characters. In stories of hurts or misfortunes, girls are full of sympathy and concerned with the location and cure; boys' stories involve more activity and violence.

Girls mention more parents, especially the mother, and with more expressions of affection than do boys. When boys do mention parents, there is very little expressed interaction.

Cultural Norms

A projective technique which has been standardized on a homogeneous segment of the population may need revisions of content and/or norms for use with other groups. Types of toys, kinds of recreation, authority patterns in the home, moral standards, levels of anxiety, financial insecurities, family structure and the perception of sex roles are but a few of the variables which can operate to affect projective responses in differing social-class groupings.

Shifts to other races, nationalities or cultures would also be expected to produce differences. Even such a seemingly culture-free device as drawing a man has been shown to be affected by a culture which restricts representations of the human figure (Dennis, 1957). Obviously the more highly structured the stimulus in terms of one culture, the greater the need for suitable adaptations before using it with other groups.

PROBLEMS IN ESTABLISHING NORMS

Time Measurements

As Toppelstein (1952) has pointed out, measures of total time for a response depend not only on the child's rate of flow of speech but also on the examiner's speed of recording the child's verbal productions. (A tape recorder can be used, but this often creates additional distractions for the child.) Similarly, reaction time measurements are influenced by whether or not the examiner has to encourage and press the child to get started.

Length of Response

Again, Toppelstein (1952) suggests that the total number of words used will vary depending on the child's verbosity and also on the extent to which the examiner must urge and prod the less verbal child at first. Such additional promptings may serve to increase the total response length beyond that of an originally more verbal child.

Categorization of Statements

The incidence of "common themes" will depend on the manner in which themes are coded. The extensiveness of categories, and the number of sub-categories (and of overlapping meanings), can greatly influence normative results. For example, to report the incidence of aggression to each type of character separately will mask the true picture of total aggressiveness. Or, if one study lists separately every dire event that might happen, those results cannot be compared to a study where all types of disasters are grouped together.

A tabulation scheme for the CAT, listing a variety of possible responses for each card, has been prepared by Peters and Bellak (1954). The intent is to provide a uniform framework and checklist of normative responses, which, if used by all investigators, would allow for summation from various samples. Headings in the schema vary somewhat from card to card, depending on card content, but the basic categories include a listing of figures portrayed (with subheadings for age and sex of each, identity and other specific characteristics), objects, problems and outcomes, general feeling tone, figures or objects omitted or introduced.

One of the many problems in categorizing responses has been pointed out by Toppelstein (1952) with reference to the ambiguity between what the child said and what he probably meant to say resulting from the young child's lack of conciseness and fluency. For example, within the same story, the child may speak of a character first as a *he* and further along as *she*. Often the final decision in categorizing such statements becomes quite arbitrary.

Criteria of Commonality

Decisions must be made as to the level of common usage which will be adopted in determining a typical response. In scoring such open-ended responses as are found in CAT-TAT type stories, many investigators have considered an incidence of 20 per cent as a typical representation. In the CAT studies to be reported, Toppelstein (1952) and Millar (1952) have used 20 per cent; Ginsparg (1957), 30 per cent; Boulanger-Balleyguier (1957), 50 per cent; and Booth (1953), only 10 per cent. The size of the sample becomes an important consideration in this connection. Twenty per cent of 50 *Ss* would be only ten children; any smaller number would hardly warrant consideration as representing "typical" reactions of a sample of children.

AGE TRENDS IN THE CAT

Preschool Period

Normative studies using the CAT can be divided rather clearly into those using very young *Ss* and those using latency or school age children. Millar (1952), Byrd and Witherspoon (1954), and Lehmann (1959) used only preschool *Ss*, while Rosenblatt (1958) followed the same children through the age range from three to ten years. He has broken down his findings into a "phallic" group (ages three to five) and a "latency" group (ages six to ten); the former group will be included in this section.

Description of Samples. A total of 330 children (with approximately equal numbers of boys and girls) is represented in the four studies. Millar (1952) used 50 kindergarten children of working mothers (five were three years of age, 15 were four, and 30 were five). Byrd and Witherspoon (1954) used 80 nursery school and kindergarten subjects from two yrs. eight mos. through six yrs. five mos. who were above average in both intelligence and socioeconomic status. Lehmann (1959) used 160 kindergarteners, five yrs. six mos. to six yrs. four mos. selected from four socioeconomic levels as follows: low-intact, low-broken home, middle, and high. Rosenblatt's (1958) data are derived from repeated administrations to 36 children. There were 40 tests in the three to five year age range (four were age three, nine were age four, and 27 were age five).

Story Length. Byrd and Witherspoon (1954, p. 37) report: "In general the stories were brief and often lacked plots and formal aspects of causation and outcome that are found in older children's stories. There was a marked lack of spontaneity and much questioning was needed by the examiner to obtain responses." Millar found that stories were generally restricted, but that the older (five-year-olds) *Ss* told the longest stories, with shortest reaction times and longest total time. Lehmann also found stories to be short and concise.

Description versus Interpretation. Byrd and Witherspoon classified responses as enumerative (naming one or more objects in the picture), descriptive (de-

Table 6.1. Story Dynamics Found by Byrd and
Witherspoon (1954) and Lehmann (1959)

| | Per Cent of Total | |
Dynamic	Byrd and Witherspoon	Lehmann
Orality	10.2%	53.4%
Aggression	13.3	11.0
Fear	2.8	3.4
Toileting and cleanlines	2.8	18.1
Punishment	—	14.1
Sibling rivalry	1.2	0.0
Sexuality	.9	—
Oedipal situation	3.6	—
Acceptance by adult (lack of)	8.6	—
Identification with mother	28.0	—
Identification with father	17.3	—

scribing objective features of the picture), and apperceptive (going beyond enumeration and description, revealing psychological dynamics, or introducing objects). They found 20 per cent of responses fell in the first two categories (2 per cent enumeration, 18 per cent description), while 80 per cent were interpretive. Lehmann used the same three categories but found no enumerative responses. Thirty-three per cent were descriptive and 67 per cent were interpretive. Rosenblatt did not use the same categories but does report more object-naming in his younger group. Millar found that the stories were predominantly simple explanations of what was happening in the pictures.

Story Dynamics. Byrd and Witherspoon were interested in whether or not the stories elicited the dynamics originally postulated by Bellak and found that, in general, this was the case. Some of the same dynamic areas were also investigated by Lehmann and their comparative findings have been combined in Table 6.1.

Examination of the table reveals a marked difference in the findings with respect to orality. Bellak cites Cards 1, 4, and 8 as typically eliciting oral responses. Byrd and Witherspoon found such responses given frequently to Cards 1, 4, and 6 and fairly high on Cards 3 and 9, while Lehmann found the most instances of orality on Cards 1, 4, 7, and 8, with none on Card 9.

Aggressive responses were found most frequently by Byrd and Witherspoon on Cards 2, 3, and 7 (as also predicted by Bellak). Lehmann did not find aggression to be high on Card 3, but did concur on Cards 2 and 7, with the addition of Cards 5, 8 and 10.

Fear responses were most often found on Cards 5 and 9 by Byrd and Witherspoon and on Cards 3, 5, 7 and 9 by Lehmann. The low incidence in both studies may reflect the authors' use of only manifestly expressed fears, whereas a clinician would interpret evidences of fears in symbolic expressions, implications from the total responses and from interpretations at a deeper level.

While the two studies differ greatly in the proportion of toileting and cleanliness responses, both report the incidence as occurring largely to Card 10.

Lehmann found themes of punishment only on Card 10. Byrd and Witherspoon did not analyze for this dynamic but do report fairly high frequencies for the category "acceptance by adults" which actually implies *lack* of acceptance as represented by items such as seeing adult figures as scolding, or the child figure as feeling rejected or wanting to run away. These responses were found most on Cards 3 and 10 (as also suggsted by Bellak) but were not found on Card 9 (in contrast to Bellak's assumptions).

Bellak has proposed that both Cards 5 and 6 would elicit themes relating to oedipal fantasies, but Byrd and Witherspoon found these only in response to Card 5.

The remaining categories used frequently in Byrd and Witherspoon's analysis relate to "identification" with one of the parents. It should be pointed out that the term is used by these authors to include any mention of "mother" or "father" in the stories. Furthermore, on Cards 2, 4, 8 and 10 the child was asked to name the animal roles if he had not done so spontaneously. (Consequently a low response level of "father" was obtained on Card 3, because the child was not asked to identify the animal role!) One may well question whether this procedure gives a measure of identification in the customary usage of the term. By their standards, the authors found Cards 4, 6 and 10 to give the most responses of "mother" and Cards 6 and 8 produced comparable frequencies for "father" responses. By their method of inquiry, all cards (except Cards 3 and 7) yielded high incidences.

Byrd and Witherspoon, in summarizing the implications of all their findings, point out that themes of orality and aggression appeared with relatively high frequency, thus indicating that such needs and feelings must play an important role in the preschool child's personality development.* Consequently, they warn that the appearance of a large number of such responses in the protocol of a disturbed preschool child would need to be evaluated in the light of expectations for normal children of the same age.

Millar analyzed her protocols for story structure, defining "common" elements as those given by at least 20 per cent of Ss. In addition to brief stories with loose organization, she reports that the mood was predominantly neutral or unhappy, with a significant number of aggressive themes. She found that children appeared to identify with the character closest to them in age; many figures, but few "objects," were introduced; figures omitted were those not clearly distinguished in the picture. Stories generally centered around the family unit with parental characters often being introduced if they were not already depicted.

---

*Weisskopf-Joelson and Foster (1962) studied kindergarten children, using human and animal forms of only four cards. They found the most projection on the bedroom and lion scenes (Cards 9 and 3) in contrast to the oral (Card 4) and anal (Card 10) situations. They see this finding as related to the oedipal stage characteristic of five-year-old children and speculate that oral and anal problems have been superseded, at this age, by interest in parental relationships and nighttime concerns. They conclude that subjects ". . . are more productive when responding to pictures about the major preoccupations of their age group" (p. 369).

Rosenblatt, in contrasting his preschool and latency groups, found that the former described less interaction with threatening figures, and more frequently omitted characters exposed to danger; if such interaction was described, the stories concerned fears of being caught or orally incorporated. Figures were more often described as animals than as family members, in contrast to the older Ss. He found indications of castration anxiety in this group, as well as themes relating to the oedipal situation.

Card Summaries. Drawing from the findings of the four studies of preschool Ss the following summary presents the most outstanding responses to each card, over and above pure description.

Card 1. Themes of orality; sleeping; aggression in terms of one chicken either eating the other chickens or their food.

Card 2. Themes of tug-of-war or fighting over the rope. Often seen as a family group. Baby figure seen equally often near the mother or the father.

Card 3. Aggression or lack of acceptance by adults. Also themes of cooperation between the lion and the mouse; or both seen in relaxed, neutral attitudes. Many figures or objects introduced. The mouse was omitted 44 per cent of the time (Millar).

Card 4. Themes of orality and sibling rivalry; going somewhere and returning home. Baby kangaroo omitted by 30 per cent of Ss (Millar). Mother seen as provider and as authority figure.

Card 5. Themes of sleeping, play and nighttime activities; oedipal situation; cooperative activity between siblings; fears; aggression. Children and parents sleep separately, or child in bed with parents.

Card 6. Sleeping or hibernating; orality on waking; cooperative activities; one bear independent; bears are aggressed against. One background figure omitted 52 per cent of time (Millar).

Card 7. Aggression; orality; fears; retaliatory attack. Monkey escapes or aggresses against tiger 30 per cent of time (Millar).

Card 8. Orality; verbal interchange; punishment or threat of punishment, with mother in the authority role. Picture on wall mentioned by 44 per cent of Ss (Millar).

Card 9. Sleeping and getting up to provide for self; noises; fears; rabbit is hurt or scared. Mother is authority figure or provider. Other figures frequently introduced.

Card 10. Toileting and cleanliness; punishment; running away; "moral" is learned. Adults wash or dry the baby. Mother is punisher, father is authority figure.

Latency Period

Three studies provide the bulk of the data on the school age child: Rosenblatt's (1958) latency group (up to ten years of age); Toppelstein (1952) with Ss from five to eight years; and Ginsparg (1957) using Ss six to nine years of age. This represents a total of 314 Ss, with fairly equal distribution of boys and girls. In addition, Armstrong (1954) has reported some age data in her study comparing human and animal versions presented to children in the first three grades, and Booth (1953) has tabulated responses to individual cards by nine-year-old boys of Anglo- and Latin-American descent.

Description of Samples. Rosenblatt (1958), in his latency group, presents 138 records of children tested between the ages of six and ten. There were approximately 30 Ss at each year level. Toppelstein (1952) used seven boys and seven girls at each grade level from kindergarten through the third grade (total N=56). The children were from lower middle and upper lower socio-economic groups, and were rated by their teachers and a psychologist as being well adjusted. Ginsparg's (1957) sample of 120 Ss consisted of 15 boys and 15 girls at each age level from six through nine, selected from lower, middle and upper socioeconomic groups and evaluated as well adjusted by their teachers. An attempt was made to match Ss on WISC vocabulary scaled scores, but the youngest age group had a mean vocabulary level somewhat below the means for the other three groups. Estimated IQ's ranged from 85 to 130.

Story Length. Ginsparg found that eight- and nine-year-olds told the longest stories and that the former age range also had the longest total time. He found no age differences in reaction time. Armstrong found increased length of re sponse with age and the number of nouns used increased with age, while ego-related words (e.g., personal references) decreased with age.

Description versus Interpretation. Ginsparg's study was the only one which evaluated thematic level. He found the difference between age groups was highly significant (.001 level) for the use of enumeration and description, with six-year-olds giving the highest incidence. His Level 3 (thema with animals in clearly human type activities) was given most at eight years. He found no over-all statistical relationship between age and thematic level, but did find a correlation of .36 between WISC vocabulary score and thematic level. In essence, these findings reflect the fact that the lower levels of enumeration and description largely drop out after age six, which is consistent with other findings on language development and vocabulary level (as reported in Chapter V).

Story Dynamics. Rosenblatt's comparisons of his older versus younger groups revealed that the stories of the older Ss contained more cooperative activities, more instances of independence on the child's part, and more stories with definite outcomes. There were more identifications with family members, and the mother was seen as the authority figure, provider and punitive agent. Characters were now able to escape from threatened dangers (whereas, for the younger Ss, the threatened figure was often caught and/or eaten). Oedipal struggles were still prominent in this latency group; there were increasing evidences of superego functioning and the learning of moral lessons. Other maturational indices included new attitudes and interests and age-appropriate activities.

Ginsparg evaluated a total of 778 instances of Needs and found *n*-Dominance and *n*-Blame Avoidance increased with age from six to nine years. Needs used most frequently at all age levels included Aggression, Play-mirth, Dominance, Nurturance and Autonomy. Of the 349 instances of Emotions, those used most frequently were dislike, fearfulness, failure and discouragement. With respect to endings, eight-year-olds gave the most stories with realistic endings, while six-year-olds, as would be expected, gave the most stories with no endings. When animal or human figures were introduced, significantly more of the actions attributed to them were dangerous rather than helpful. Of the different age groups, the seven-year-olds ascribed the most dangerous activities to introduced figures. The author suggests this may be due to the strong use of projection at this age level when the ego is in the process of developing defenses against unacceptable impulses. More mother than father figures were seen as instigating negative needs and emotions; yet mothers were also seen as the most nurturant of all figures. Further findings of Ginsparg can be outlined by age levels as follows:

Six years: Stories were short, limited in content, stereotyped; largely enumeration and description; cliché responses; fairy tale themes; endings vague or absent; few Needs or Emotions expressed.

Seven years: Some interaction between characters and addition of dangerous characters; increase in story length and content; some realistic endings.

Eight years: Expansive and free use of fantasy, more rich and varied content; action focussed on interpersonal relationships; more realistic (than vague) endings; longest stories of any age level.

Nine years: Responses more curtailed than at age eight; structure of stories resembles that of six- and seven-year-olds with stereotyped and cliché responses. Stories are short, concise, clearcut, guarded. More individual variability than in the other groups.

Card Summaries: Normative findings for each card have been compiled from the studies of Toppelstein (1952), Rosenblatt (1958), Ginsparg (1957), Booth (1953), and Nolan (1959).

Card 1. Eating, sleeping, playing. Chickens' wants are satisfied, usually by mother figure. Mother also seen as the authority figure.

Card 2. Playful contest, bears differ or gain something from others with two figures on right usually succeeding. Mother most often paired with baby; few figures or objects introduced. Most *n*-Achievement responses (Nolan).

Card 3. Lion attacks or dislikes mouse; mouse trespasses on lion. Lion seen as king, or as elderly. Outcome unclear.

Card 4. Going home or to market; wants are satisfied; mishaps occur but outcome is successful. Fear of attack or disaster (by age nine). Few themes of sibling rivalry.

Card 5. Bears cannot sleep, or are dreaming. Cubs under threat from outside person or animal. Cubs are naughty, or tell jokes, etc. Figures and objects frequently introduced. Realistic endings. Parents usually seen under the covers.

Card 6. Bears watch out for, or are threatened by, animal or hunter; play or sleep is disrupted or cave made uninhabitable. Small figure independent.

Card 7. Tiger attacks monkey; monkey escapes or retaliates; tiger is injured or killed. Both figures seen as males.

Card 8. Party or verbal interchange, family grouping. Child naughty or disobeys; child disciplined (usually by mother or grandmother) and learns lesson. A quarrel or mishap occurs and is rectified. Few endings and few introduced figures or objects. Being talked about or ridiculed. Most n-Affiliation (Nolan).

Card 9. Rabbit disobeys orders, is naughty. Afraid of dark or about to be attacked; bad dream. Getting up from bed; parent figures are away from home. Eating activities, mother is provider. Figures or objects frequently introduced; realistic endings.

Card 10. Child is naughty or resistant; toilet training infractions. Child is punished by mother or father. Child cries, learns lesson, or does as told. Child runs away. Most n-Power (Nolan).

SEX DIFFERENCES

Few sex differences have been found in studies employing the CAT. Measures of total time, word count, or reaction time yielded no differences in studies by Biersdorf and Marcuse (1953) with first graders or by Ginsparg (1957) with six- to nine-year-olds. Armstrong (1954) did find that bright first-through third-grade girls tended to tell longer stories than did boys, and had longer reaction times. She also found girls to be superior to boys in number of nouns used and in the number of subjective, nondescriptive statements (as measured by the Transcendence Index). In contrast to this latter finding, Biersdorf and Marcuse found no sex differences in number of ideas expressed, or in number of characters mentioned or introduced.

In more specific dynamic areas, Ginsparg (1957) found no sex differences in psychosexual interests. Nolan (1959) found no sex differences, but a trend for boys to exceed girls on n-Achievement at each age level from five to ten years. Koch (1960) noted that five- and six-year-old boys used more themes of hostility than did girls of the same ages, but more girls described sibling figures as quarreling with each other. Rosenblatt (1959) found significant sex differences between his two age categories. In the younger (phallic) group, boys more frequently omitted the threatened figure in one of the cards, and girls named figures more often as tiger, lion, mouse or rat, etc. In his older (latency) group, boys gave more aggressive responses while girls gave more responses of the paternal figure being the winner, included the mother figure in more stories, and more often saw the mother as the punitive agent.

Muller (1958) found that eight-year-old French boys, when compared to girls, were more aggressive, more oriented toward objects, gave more responses dealing with dangers, catastrophes and death. Girls, on the other hand, showed more awareness of the motives of others, more interest in interpersonal relationships, more dependency, and gave more responses involving punishments.

Several studies have examined the sex of the larger figure paired off with the child on Card 2. Both Rosenblatt (1958) and Byrd and Witherspoon (1954) found that the younger girls more often see the larger figure as the mother, while boys are more apt to mention either parent. In the latency groupings, Ginsparg (1957) found that six- and seven-year-old boys and girls chose the mother or father with equal frequency, but eight- and nine-year-old boys more often chose the mother, while the girls of this age still split their choices between the two parents. Rosenblatt (1958) found that both sexes, in latency, more often mentioned the child as being with the mother.

Boulanger-Balleyguier (1957), working with French children ages three to eight, found that boys give more themes of playing than do girls (Cards 1, 2, and 10), while girls more often emphasize dressing (Card 9), shopping (Card 4), and receiving commands from parents (Card 8). In terms of characters introduced into the stories, girls add mother and women characters more often than do boys, and girls add fewer dangerous animals, while both sexes introduce friendly animals with equal frequency.

DESCRIPTIVE STUDIES

Several CAT studies of normal children have been less concerned with the incidence of specific responses to each card, levels of response, or length of protocols, than with the effect on the child of this particular projective task and the means at his disposal for complying or evading. The chief focus has been on the positive aspects revealed, such as sources of gratification, constructive values, healthy emotional and intrafamilial relationships. Following the above approach, Moriarty and Murphy (1960a, 1960c)* have summarized their findings on 32 preschool children who were administered the CAT as part of the Coping Project of the Menninger Foundation. Stories were analyzed to determine the relationship of the response to the particular stimulus, the nature of the affects elicited, the underlying mechanisms which were revealed, and the various ways in which anxieties and tensions were handled.

In general, these youngsters were found to be aware of, and able to focus on, the problem situations portrayed in the cards. Dependence-independence themes were common, indications of the clarity of self-images could be ascertained, and all Ss gave evidence of finding comfort as members of family groups. Punishments were expected and accepted, as was aggression from larger figures. Orality and toileting processes were also viewed in a matter-of-fact manner. More conflict was experienced in relation to mother than to father figures. While the children could conform to the test-taking requirements, they also demonstrated the capacity to protest, tease and joke, or seek help. Avoidance and denial were noted in all records to a certain extent, although some Ss used these restrictive techniques more than others.

The authors caution that, because of lack of expressive and verbal skills in such young children, the examiner must be careful to differentiate between responses reflecting such immaturity and responses which result from real emotional stress arising from the demands of the particular task. They cite instances of marked perceptual distortions, and even some bizarreness, on potentially stressful cards, while the same child might handle other cards quite

---

*Appreciation is extended to the authors for permission to make extensive use of findings from their preliminary research reports. The major details of the analysis were made by Dr. Alice E. Moriarty in consultation with Dr. Lois B. Murphy, Director of the Coping Project, supported by The Menninger Foundation and USPHS grants M-680 and M-4093. The preschool data were collected in 1953–54 and the latency data in 1957.

adequately. Tensions may also be revealed by increased articulatory difficulties, delays, hesitations, denials, or refusals to continue at all. In this connection, Cards 5 and 6 were found to be the most stressful, eliciting the most perceptual inaccuracies, evasions and unrealistic solutions. Card 4 was the next most difficult card, probably because it elicits feelings about mother in relation to other siblings in the family.

The following interesting card by card findings are reported by Moriarty and Murphy (1960a, 1960c) in terms of perceptual accuracy, affective reactions, and ways of experiencing and handling the various problem areas:

Card 1. About equal numbers of Ss saw adult figures as male and female, with as many girls as boys seeing the figure as masculine. Chickens were generally expected to eat independently, with parents seen as nurturant bystanders.

Card 2. The three figures were usually seen as a family group, with the interaction viewed as a struggle with indefinite outcome. When there was a winner, it was usually the father. Over half of the Ss were vague as to the child's allegiance, suggestive of psychosexual immaturity.

Card 3. Half of the Ss had the lion win in a power struggle, while close to half the children subjected the lion to teasing or derogation. All Ss seemed realistically aware of the aggressive potential of the larger figure and accepted the smaller animal's lesser status.

Card 4. This card elicited more stressful reactions than the first three cards, with more perceptual distortions and some bizarre responses from a few Ss. Responses generally portrayed competition with siblings for attention from the mother but also with definite and positive feelings that mother was still nurturant with the older child.

Card 5. At least half of the children did not see the animals as bears but as less aggressive animals, almost as if they were perceiving the figures as more helpless in the face of darkness, bedtime, and the potentials of the oedipal situation. This card was generally tension arousing, but this was often handled by having the child characters remain asleep (avoidance) or seek help or assert their self-sufficiency by means of cognitive or motor activity. One-fourth of the Ss revealed fearfulness related to aspects of separation from the family; such isolative aspects appeared to be generating more stress than any oedipal implications in the stimulus.

Card 6. Increased intensity of affect and free-floating anxiety were noted for this card; oedipal themes were prominent. There appeared to be a cumulative pressure from Cards 5 to 6 resulting in expressions of fearfulness and unpleasant effects such as punishments or running away.

Card 7. Most children were realistically aware of the aggressive aspects of the card and accepted this without undue anxiety. A few Ss presented themes of teasing or fighting back on the part of the intended victim.

Card 8. Three-fourths of the children interpreted the card as representing conflict between family members; nevertheless, the aggressive aspects were handled realistically and with acceptance. Children were about equally divided in designating the mother or father as the punishing agent.

Card 9. Half of the Ss avoided any fearful implications by describing the small figure as remaining passive or asleep. One-third expressed feelings of loneliness and abandonment. Dangers from external sources were related by six of the 32 Ss. Close to one-third of the group offered self-sufficient solutions. Generally, it was felt that the discomfort in relation to the bedtime aspects of this card was less intense than on Cards 5 and 6, where the oedipal implications are more in evidence.

Card 10. There was generally a realistic and natural attitude toward toileting processes. Half the children gave themes of punishments which were accepted when they seemed justified. One-fourth of the Ss gave themes of helpfulness and nurturance from the parent figure, with the child seen as dependent.

In addition to the above normative generalizations, the authors were impressed with the resources available to the individual child, and the complexity and uniqueness of his "coping maneuvers." Furthermore, there were consistent trends throughout a protocol, both in terms of affects expressed (e.g., fearfulness) and of the child's reaction patterns (e.g., evasiveness). In addition, they found that coping approaches used by children to this test proved to be similar to methods adopted by the same child in the more structured situations.

The authors conclude: "Despite the very definite threat in the situation and in the stimuli *per se*, the children were able at this level to employ a variety of coping devices which served both to *reduce stress* provoked by the competitive images and to *handle the adult demands* of the depicted situations, in ways which were both effective from the adult's viewpoint and compatible with the child's personal view of himself and his own world" (Moriarty and Murphy, 1960c).

Tentative findings on the Coping Sample as they reached latency have also been reported by Moriarty and Murphy (1960b). Many of the children showed an increased range of coping techniques, an increase in activities and in satisfaction with achievements, a wider range of affective expression along with greater capacity for timing and control. Increases were also noted in desires to conform, awareness of social needs, and ability to check against reality factors.

Boulanger-Balleyguier (1957a, 1960)* secured CATs from 105 French children of normal intelligence between the ages of three and eight years, with approximately ten boys and ten girls at each age level. Her main findings are concerned with commonly reported activities, omissions, additions, and parental-sex attributes of some of the main figures. She has presented her findings separately for each sex, and for each of the five year levels. She considered popular responses for each card as those occurring in 50 per cent of protocols and confirms previous findings in that they are largely descriptive of the activities portrayed. She does note some interesting changes with age for certain cards, e.g., on Card 2, at least one of the animals often falls in stories of children above five years of age. For Card 3, smoking becomes a popular response only by age six, while the conflict between the lion and mouse is only expli-

---

*Unless otherwise specified, the findings reported are taken from Boulanger-Balleyguier (1957a).

cated at ages six and seven. (As reported in an earlier discussion of this study, Chapter III, the mouse was not usually seen by children below age six). While animals are seen as drinking at all ages on Card 8, conversation does not become a popular response until age five; for girls, this verbal interchange often contains a command.

Card 10 yields the expected popular response of going to the toilet *only* for four-year-old girls, while washing is popular only for seven-year-old boys. Boulanger-Balleyguier suggests cultural differences may be responsible in that the bathroom is represented as typically American and so not as readily recognized by French children, and, in France, two people rarely go there together. The findings may also reflect an excess of modesty in these children who, having learned personal hygiene, no longer wish to speak of the generally forbidden theme.

Boulanger-Balleyguier (1960) presents a table listing, for each card, the specific popular responses at three different age levels. For three-year-olds, there is a total of eight responses which are frequently given; for ages four and five there are 15; and for ages six and seven there are 17, probably reflecting not only the increasing complexity of responses with age but also an increase in socialization and conformity to conventional modes of thinking. When correlated with IQ, the number of popular responses employed yielded a coefficient of .74. The author suggests that a protocol with very few popular responses would indicate the child's poor adaptation to his surroundings and autistic trends which could be quite serious if accompanied by other pathological signs. On the other hand, a very large number of popular responses in a scanty protocol would indicate a narrow, constricted personality pattern. Children who have much originality and a creative imagination may give many additions and elaborations, but they will also give a large number of normative responses showing that they do perceive reality as do their peers.

Mean omissions by age show a progressive decrease for both sexes from highs at age three of 4.3 to a low of 1.4 at age seven. Specific figures omitted most frequently are the hen (Card 1) up to age seven, and especially by five-year-old girls; the mouse (Card 3) very frequently through age five; the baby kangaroo (Card 4) through age five and also for six-year-old boys; one of the small bears (Card 5) at ages three and four; one of the big bears (Card 6) for ages three through five. In contrast, the omission of any monkey from Card 8 is very low at age three and never occurs beyond age four. Boulanger-Balleyguier concludes (as did Millar, 1952) that the figures most often omitted, particularly at the younger ages, are those which are drawn in blurred or vague manner or those which are very small. She interprets those omissions which decrease with age as being due to perceptual difficulties in these younger Ss. She also found (1960) a negative correlation of —.76 between IQ and the number of omissions on the CAT.

Additions were noted most frequently at the two extremes of the age range, following a U-shaped curve, and are explained on the basis of differing mechanisms. The young child probably pays little attention to the stimulus and can readily "leave the field" entirely. Gradually as he adapts to reality he exerts effort to remain close to the stimulus, while the somewhat older child is able to utilize imagination, but under control, to elaborate and expand his stories to include additional objects and characters. The largest number of additions were noted on Card 9, the only card to present a single animal. Other cards which elicited fairly frequent additions were Cards 5, 7, 3, 4 and 10 in descending order. Card 1 contained the fewest additions, probably due to increased vigilance and control when initially entering the storytelling situation. Characters most frequently added were mothers, with girls introducing them more often than boys, except at age five. There was no relationship between IQ and the number of additions (Boulanger-Balleyguier, 1960).

The identification of the large animal in the various cards revealed a greater description of mothers than of fathers, except, of course, for the lion in Card 3. Furthermore, mothers were mentioned more often by both sexes and especially so at ages six and seven.

Boulanger-Balleyguier suggests a genetic evolution in the development of projective responses in that the child's perception appears to become more and more clear and detailed as he matures, as evidenced by the decrease in the number of omissions with age and the increase in popular responses. The children are more aware of the stimulus in their stories and their interpretations become more conventional and better adapted to the material presented. Even the youngest children (age three) are able to project themselves into the stories; this projection grows with age, the story being enriched with elements "added" to the pictures. Descriptions of the hero and secondary characters reflect the reality situation of the child and his surroundings. Increasingly with age, the child expresses the numerous bonds which unite him to his mother and to other children, thus realizing the place which they occupy in his life. Also with age, the dominant functions of the mother are clearly affirmed, thus differentiating her from others, e.g., the child is conscious of the mother's educational role, one which seems to be essential to assure the child's normal development.

Finally, those characters in which the family environment is not reflected acquire, with age, a well-defined function, namely an avenue for the expression of aggressive tendencies. Projection of these "undifferentiated others" may represent either their rejection by the subject's self, or the beginning of the formation of conscience in its punitive form. The evolution of these different tendencies does not occur in an absolutely regular progression; the most important variation takes place between ages five and six, which corresponds to the beginning of latency and entrance into school.

Simon (1954) was interested in the child's view of the main characters and the manner in which parent-child relationships are handled. Results are reported for a mixed group of 49 normal and neurotic Austrian children from three to seven years of age. Both sexes saw mothers more often as nurturant than as non-nurturant. With respect to fathers, boys were fairly equally divided in views of nurturance while girls saw fathers more often as non-nurturant. Both sexes fantasied many aggressive actions against the parents, either separately or together. Only 25 per cent of Ss felt a positive acceptance by adults. Siblings were only mentioned infrequently and generally in negative terms.

Fears of impersonal figures (spooks, animals) and of unpleasant events (fire, thunder, darkness, falling) were found in about 10 per cent of the stories. Stories revolving around eating and oral aspects revealed somewhat more negative than positive aspects. In stories with aggressive themes, the main hero was the victim 60 per cent of the time, and parents about 20 per cent. The child was seen as the aggressor in 44 per cent of the aggressive stories, and one or the other parent in 46 per cent of the aggressive stories.

Stories of sickness and accidents were not frequent but happened most often to the main character, and eventuated about equally between dying and recovery. Ten children told a total of 35 stories of death to one or both parents. Twelve children told stories of being eaten and coming out alive; eight children told stories of dirt, defecation or exhibitionism.

Simon rated the stories for degree of fantasy versus realism, and found about 54 per cent were realistic, and only 2. 6 per cent had fantasies extreme enough to be indicative of a psychotic process.

Stories ended happily about one-third of the time; one-fourth of the stories had either unhappy endings or the conflicts remained unresolved.

Simon also compared her results with the themes suggested by Bellak for each card, and found little confirmation, in her sample, for themes relating to the oedipus complex, castration fears, masturbation, and concerns over cleanliness or sexual problems.

NORMS FOR SPECIFIC CARDS

The dynamic significance of certain responses to specific cards has been studied and reported here and there in the literature. Only some of the results can be reviewed here.

Card 1. Moriarty and Murphy (1960b) found that preschool children often omit the background figure and speculate that this may be related to unsatisfactory mother-child relations. Boulanger-Balleyguier (1957a) found that omissions for this figure were only common for girls at age five.

Card 2. Bennett and Johannsen (1954) analyzed responses to this card to determine which parent the child figure was aligned with and whether the child's side then won out in the struggle. Of their sample of 57 (diabetic) children, 37 specified the adult of the pair as being either mother or father. Of these 37 instances, 24 indicated whether the child's side won or lost. The conflict was won significantly more often when the child was allied with the opposite-sex parent, than when the child was mentioned as being with the same-sex parent. On the basis of other personality data gathered as part of a larger study, results indicated that children who allied themselves with the opposite-sex parent were more conforming, more blame-accepting, more physically active, and more passive in the presence of adults, than were the same-sex allied Ss.

Card 3. Millar (1952) found that the mouse was omitted by 44 per cent of her kindergarten Ss. Moriarty and Murphy (1960b) found the mouse to be one of the figures most frequently omitted by their preschool sample, as did Boulanger-Balleyguier (1957a) in children from ages three to five. Boulanger-Balleyguier regards this, and other omissions which occurred frequently in the preschool portions of her sample, as reflecting perceptual inefficiency in the youngest Ss (see discussion in Chapter III). Moriarty and Murphy, on the other hand, suggest that this omission is the result of denial and efforts at inhibition of aggression, rather than perceptual defects. With regard to omissions in general, they feel that the children did appear to "see" the small details, looking back and forth, checking and rechecking, so that the final response (with its omission) represented their way of handling the stress generated by the card content.

Card 4.   Ephrussi's (1955) data suggest that the child's identification with the baby animal in the kangaroo pouch is an indication of dependence on the mother. Boulanger-Balleyguier (1957a) questions the validity of these findings since it is probable (on the basis of her studies) that a large number of the children would not have seen the animal unless it was pointed out to them.

Card 7.   According to Shneidman (1953), Vuyk found that the monkey was portrayed as being caught more often by the less intelligent children. Boulanger-Balleyguier (1957a), did not find this to be the case, at least among normal Ss.

Card 8.   Several studies have reported on the incidence of male figures mentioned on this card. Data from Ginsparg's (1957) tables indicate that over 50 per cent of Ss (ages six to nine years) mention one of the figures as "father." Boulanger-Balleyguier (1957a) found that the large figure on the right was more often seen as a male by both sexes at ages three, four, and five, while a reverse trend was noted at ages six and seven. Means for all ages indicate the large figure was specified as male 34 per cent of the time and as female 25 per cent of the time. Lawton (unpublished) reports that, in a sample of 52 school children, at least one male figure was mentioned by 35 per cent of Ss. Haworth (unpublished) found a male figure was seen by 10 out of 22 clinic cases (45 per cent).

STUDIES OF SPECIFIC SAMPLE VARIABLES

This section reports specific studies, or findings from more general CAT research projects, which relate to differences in intellectual level, or to the effects of sib-order, twinships, and sociometric position.

Intellectual Level

Kaake (1951) studied the relationship between intellectual level and maturity of response among children in a nine-month span of chronological age (six years three months to seven years). Mental ages ranged from four years nine months to eight years ten months, with Ss divided into three IQ levels: slow (IQs from 72-87); average (90-108); and superior (110-129). The usual levels of verbal response were studied: enumeration, description, and interpretation, with the addition of a fourth category, identification (defined as instances of the S identifying with a character or naming a character as a person from his own experience, e.g., mother bear). Kaake found that the proportion of interpretive and identification responses increased as intelligence increased, while the proportions of enumeration and description decreased. Most of the dfferences noted occurred between the slow and average groups, while the average and superior levels were fairly similar. The effect of additional inquiry upon the level of responses was also assessed; results indicated an increase in the proportion of the two higher levels of response, with this effect being most marked in the slow group. On the basis of her findings, Kaake questions the usefulness of the CAT for the personality evaluation of young children in the slow group.

Ginsparg (1957), using WISC vocabulary raw scores of six- through nine-year-olds, found a correlation of .36 between vocabulary and thematic levels, while there was no correlation between chronological age and thematic level. The use of n-Dominance and n-Blame Avoidance correlated with vocabulary as well as with age. Ginsparg, as did Kaake, concluded that Ss of lower intelligence are limited in ability to express their ideas freely or dynamically.

Sibship Patterns

Koch (1955, 1960) has used the CAT as part of her test battery in several studies of the effects of sex and ordinal position of siblings on their attitudes and relationships to each other and to their parents. In a study of attitudes of five- and six-year-olds toward parents, Koch (1955) found that, of the first-born groupings, the girls with younger brothers told the most CAT stories which included a mother figure, and described mother-child and child-mother interactions (both positive and negative, but particularly the latter). The stories of these girls frequently contained themes of favoritism, described quarrels between siblings, or saw one character as enjoying an advantage over another. This group of girls was also rated by their teachers as the most jealous, competitive, aggressive and quarrelsome.

Boys with younger sisters (as compared with boys with younger brothers) showed more concern with mother-child, and father-child relationships. Boys with older brothers described sib activities in a highly favorable light and gave the lowest frequency of themes concerned with sib fights or favoritism. As the interval of age spacing between this younger brother and his older brother increased so did the number of stories which included a mother figure, while stories of cooperative sibling play and mentions of father figures decreased.

In presenting general findings with respect to first- and second-borns, Koch (1960) again mentions CAT data. First-borns more often gave themes of parental favoritism. When the age differential was smallest, the first-born described mother-child relations significantly more often as positive (compared to second-borns), but at the middle spacing the incidence of negative mother-child relations reached its peak. Second-born children tended to deal with sibling activities more than did first-borns but within the latter category, first-born girls mentioned sibling interactions more than did first-born boys and their stories were more positive in tone. First-born Ss with younger sisters told fewer CAT themes of sibling quarrels or parental favoritism and made fewer comparisons stressing the advantages of one person over another than did Ss with younger brothers.

Twins

In her study of 80 pairs of five- and six-year-old twins, Koch (1962) found identical twins told less imaginative CAT stories than did the singletons in her previous studies, while the stories of fraternal twins were comparable to those of the singletons with respect to accuracy, imagination, volume and syntactical accuracy. It should be noted that the mean IQ of the identical twins was also lower than that of the various fraternal sex groupings. In fraternal opposite-sex pairs, the boys mentioned mother figures more often than did the males of same-sex fraternal twin pairs. Interesting, too, is the observation that teachers rated the boys from opposite-sex pairs as more "sissyish" than singleton control boys of the same age.

In a subsequent study of twin samples, Koch (1964) reports on two levels of prematurity (severe and mild by birth weight) as compared to twins born at term. Ss were studied at the five- to six-year level and were normal enough to be attending public schools. Intellectual tests were used as well as teacher ratings, parent interviews, and speech evaluations. The CAT was the only projective instrument. Very few of the measured characteristics yielded significant group differences. Of the 14 CAT comparisons, only one reached the .05 level; namely, more pleasant father-child interactions in the stories of the mild prematures than in the term Ss. On the CAT the mild premature group generally showed trends for more mention of parent figures and more unpleasant child-parent interactions than the other two groups. They also exceeded the others in terms of higher hostility ratings, higher thematic scores, more catastrophe themes and more unpleasant themes and outcomes.

In the other measures, as well, the trend was for the mild group to be more involved with adults and to show more emotionality and intensity of reaction. Koch speculates that this group may have received more attention and stimulation than the other groups, thus leading to stronger "attachment" behavior at an earlier period in their physiological development, since the extreme group would have remained longer in the hospital and the term babies would have generated less maternal anxiety and attention.

Magnusson (1960) administered the CAT, Rorschach, Bender Gestalt and DAM to 12 pairs of identical twins in Sweden. (It should be pointed out that the Ss were ten and one-half years of age when the CAT was administered, which is beyond the upper limits of appropriateness for the test.) Two groups were formed, each containing one member of each twin pair. CAT protocols of one group were given to two examiners for ratings of 11 variables, using a seven-point scale. After the ratings, both examiners together rank-ordered the protocols with regard to "general adjustment." The same procedure was followed with the second set of protocols.

Inter-rater reliabilities ranged from .41 to .72 for eight of the variables (Aggression, Emotional maturity, Intelligence, Reality adjustment, Inner conflicts, Relations to siblings, Relations to father). Dependency, Sexual problems, and Relations to mother yielded r's of .17, .25, and .33, respectively.

When intraclass coefficients were considered, except for Intelligence (with r's of .57 and .51), respective correlations for the same variable differed markedly between examiners. In addition, the correlations for the different variables ranged from —.58 to +.70 for one examiner and from —.41 to +.61 for the other rater, suggesting marked differences between members of twin pairs in the measures under inspection. The rank ordering of general adjustment also demonstrated lack of correspondence, with a coefficient of —.22. As will be reported in Chapter XII, the Rorschach measures showed much more consistency between pair members. It is possible that the CAT variability may reflect the unsuitability of the CAT at this older age level.

Sociometric Status

Lumpkin (1952) used a sociometric device with fifth, sixth and seventh grade youngsters to select the "stars" (most often chosen and best liked) and the "isolates" (neither accepted nor rejected). The CAT was then administered to those Ss at the extremes to determine the extent to which story dimensions pertaining to relationships to parents and to the environment would reflect the interpersonal relationships demonstrated in the school assessment. After presenting descriptive interpretations of the stories of four stars and four isolates, the author concluded that the stars showed a drive for aggression and achievement, and demonstrated good interpersonal relationships with parental figures who reward the child for good behavior and punish for bad deeds. The stories of the isolates were meager in content, and showed deep-seated anxieties and other signs of maladjustment, along with hostile reactions to parent figures who were seen as threatening and punishing at all times.

SOCIOCULTURAL STUDIES

Two studies presented in this section have been concerned with the assumption that before projective responses can be adequately interpreted, the cultural, social and/or economic backgrounds of the respondents must be taken into consideration. Lehmann (1959) compared four different socioeconomic groups of Canadian children. Booth (1953) studied boys with Latin-American and Anglo-American antecedents.

The CAT was used in a unique fashion by Olim, Hess and Shipman (1965) in that stories told to a CAT card by mothers of differing socioeconomic status were used as a means of evaluating maternal language style in relation to children's abstract abilities.

In applying the CAT to children of quite different cultural backgrounds from that for which the test was designed, Chowdhury (1960) found that Indian children had difficulty with certain picture details. This subsequently led to her modifications of some of the cards. Earle's (1958) study of Maori children represents a slightly different approach, i.e., determining how the peculiar aspects of early child-rearing in that culture may be reflected in subsequent CAT responses. In the process, she has arrived at valuable normative data for this particular culture.

Other CAT studies of children in different countries (e.g., Boulanger-Balleyguier, 1957, 1957a, 1960, in France; Furuya, 1957, in Japan; Simon, 1954, in Austria, etc.) have not been included in this section, since their concern has been with general normative or diagnostic aspects of the CAT as an instrument, rather than with any cultural differences that might be revealed. Reports of such studies have been placed in chapters where their content is most relevant.

Socioeconomic Levels in Canadian Sample

Lehmann (1959) used four socioeconomic groups in his Canadian kindergarten samples: low intact, low broken home, average, and high, with 40 Ss in each grouping. He reports differences on five dynamic themes:

Aggression. No significant differences were found but the low-broken group used the fewest aggressive themes.

Fear. The high group expressed significantly more fear responses than the low-broken group, but the total incidence was small for all four groups.

Toileting and Cleanliness. The high group made the least mention of toileting and the most frequent mention of cleanliness.

Punishment. Themes were most frequently given by the high and middle groups.

Orality. Oral themes accounted for more than half of all responses. The middle group showed the most orality but there were no significant differences between groups.

Lehmann also reports that the responses of the low-broken group bordered on vulgarity at times, especially to Card 10.

Latin- versus Anglo-American Descent

Booth (1953) compared CAT responses of nine-year-old Latin-American (LA) and Anglo-American (AA) boys, using 25 Ss in each sample. In the LA group all boys were of Spanish or Spanish-Indian descent, only Spanish was spoken by the parents, and the children had spoken no English before entering school. Both groups were from low socioeconomic levels of unskilled and semi-skilled occupations. Further criteria for both groups included presence of other siblings in the home, and no gross mental, physical or behavior problems.

Although some differences were found between groups, as will be reported below, the over-all impression was that the responses were essentially similar, and that all Ss had generally identified with the child figure and saw it as a male.

The LA boys introduced more figures and objects and these were less threatening than the figures introduced by the AA group. The LA employed more themes, while the AA told longer stories and used more descriptions of objects in the pictures. The LA identified more with father figures, while the AA tended to identify more frequently with the mother figure. Of the 115 different themes employed, 91 were common to both groups. But of these 91 common themes, 11 differed significantly in frequency, with the LA giving more themes of: sleeping, cleanliness, death, destruction, obedience, attending school or the movies; the AA gave significantly more themes of: punishment, anger, being talked about, age and infirmity. Themes exclusive to the LA included parental desertion, dressing and grooming, reading in bed. Exclusive AA themes concerned subterfuge and eluding the parents, stealing food, and being worried.

To summarize apparent differences between groups: The LA boys are more dependent, engage in less scheming to get around adults, and are more acceptant of old age as a natural phenomenon. They have more clear male identification, which may be related in turn to their view of the father as the more frequent punisher. In contrast, the AA boys have less respect for adults, and do more scheming to get around them; in turn, they also feel they are being talked about. Punishments and revenge are protracted or delayed, and anger is common. Identification is less clearly male; mother is the more frequent punisher. The LA children seem to accept life and parental authority as it is and live in the immediate present, while the AA boys are more goal-directed, striving, and in conflict with parental authority.

Levels of Abstraction and Socioeconomic Status

Olim, Hess and Shipman (1965) were interested in the relationship between language styles of mothers of differing socioeconomic status and the cognitive styles of their children. If the mother uses language at an abstract level, this should facilitate abstract conceptualizing abilities in her child. Conversely, a low level of language communication between mother and child, as was anticipated for disadvantaged families, would create deficits in those cognitive skills necessary for future success in school. Mother-child pairs were drawn from three social class levels: middle, upper-lower, and lower-lower. Mothers were shown Card 3 of the CAT (the lion and mouse) and asked to tell their child a story about the card.* Mothers' language abstraction scores were obtained from the stories and compared with their children's cognitive abstraction scores secured from performance on Sigel's Cognitive Sorting Task for Children.

The mothers' abstract language scores were found to be significantly correlated with their children's cognitive abstraction scores. There was no relationship between the children's scores and either their own or their mother's IQs, although there was a significant correlation between mothers' and children's IQs. There were definite and significant social class differences between the abstraction scores of middle and lower-lower class mothers. Trends in a similar direction were found for children's abstract abilities. Thus the demonstrated relationships suggest that the mother's language abstraction style tends to facilitate the development of abstract conceptualizations in her child.

Children of India

Chowdhury (1960) was interested in assessing the extent to which the CAT was actually culture-free. She administered the test to Indian children from different parts of Calcutta, in nearby rural villages, and in the Abor tribes of the North East Frontier. She found that some of the city children from the

---

*For one other study in which the CAT was administered to mothers, see Chapter XII.

more sophisticated sections had no difficulty with the environmental details in the pictures, while the remaining groups became so concerned with the strange and "foreign" aspects of the cards that identification with the characters was hampered, and their responses failed to reflect the problem situations portrayed in the cards. For example:

Card 5.   This is a house. The house of foreigners. One man is living inside the house.
Card 9.   This is a big, strange house. . . . .
Card 10.   The mother dog is sitting with the pup. What is there I do not know.

Chowdhury (1960) describes the modifications which were necessary to more adequately reflect the Indian culture (see Fig. 1.3, in Chapter I, for illustrations of the Indian set). Only Cards 2 and 6 could be retained exactly as in the original. Except for Card 4, the animals remain unchanged, with appropriate modifications being made in accessories and background details.

Great care was exercised to preserve the symbolic significance of the original scenes. Chowdhury (1960) discusses the problems involved in adapting pictures to another culture as follows:

It should be remembered . . . that modification does not imply the mere substitution of a few environmental details or particular animal or human figures. The two basic necessities are: (1) that it should be closer to the original test so that it can be used as a substitute test for the original, and (2) that appropriate changes should be considered essential in order to fulfil the needs of the particular cultural group for whom the test is meant. In the present adaptation therefore the special features of the Indian social situations and the environmental needs which do not have counterparts in the original CAT had to be supplemented by introducing new cards to suit the requirements of its cultural milieu keeping the new drawings as close as possible to the original (p. 4).

Maori Children of Rakau

The CAT was the major personality instrument used by Earle (1958) in a study of six- to thirteen-year-old children of Rakau, a relatively isolated Maori community in New Zealand. Her study was one of a series exploring personality structure and functioning from birth through adolescence. Observations of the culture reveal that during infancy permissiveness and gratification are the rule. Then, at age two, or with the birth of a new baby, there is a sudden and sharp rejection, as the youngster is turned over to the care of older siblings, with resentment over this new arrangement flowing in both directions. The main family role for children in the middle years is that of performing household chores for which rewards are few. Punishments are frequent and inconsistent; children have no clearly established guidelines for determining what is expected behavior. They solve this dilemma by staying away from the adults as much as possible. In fact, children frequently move from one family to another and back again. (Only 66 per cent of Earle's sample were living with their real parents at the time of her study.) Families are large and adults view children as "little workers and little nuisances." It is not surprising that the peer group assumes great importance to the children as a source of support and security. There are few two-child friendships; rather, play groups are large and only loosely organized. There is much teasing and aggression and very little imagination in their games.

Earle (1958) interviewed children and their parents, collected sociometric data in the classrooms and administered the CAT and the Stewart Emotional Response Test. Her major informants were 52 children, from the ages of seven to thirteen (26 boys and 26 girls) who comprised half of the children attending the local school. All 102 children participated in the sociometric study and 21 children were given the CAT.

She found that Rakau children responded to the CAT quite differently from the reported typical responses of American children. She did not feel that the test was inappropriate for her group, but rather that the results must be interpreted in the light of Maori culture. In other words, her interest was in the modal personality of Rakau children, so she looked for personality characteristics common to most of these children, with no attempt to make comparisons with children from other cultures.

In terms of intellectual and cognitive approaches to problems, as revealed in the child's handling of the CAT task, she found evidence of good organizational abilities initially, but this would soon be disrupted by emotional factors, resulting in anxiety, confusion, and excessive attention to details. There was a lack of spontaneity and imagination in the stories.

Parents were seen as physically present but with little existence as "persons." Child-parent interactions were usually avoided except when engaging in a common activity. Parents were not portrayed as having an emotional relationship to the child, but were seen as being indifferent or actually rejecting. On the other hand, children were shown as having an underlying orientation *toward* the parents, making positive approaches toward them and reacting to rebuffs with anxiety and conflict. Children tended to identify more with the same-sex parent and to feel hostility toward the opposite-sex parent. Both parents were seen as authority-control figures and children reacted with resentment to exclusion from the parents' world.

Interpersonal involvement and affective relationships were also avoided in connection with any nonparent figures. There was very little mention of peers or siblings, but where they were seen, it was in the context of peer-play and availability for security and support. Sibling rivalry themes were noticeably absent on Card 4. Stories of aggression were frequent, especially to Card 7, and appeared to be a mechanism of release resulting from the frustration experienced in the parent-child relationship.

In considering the inner dynamics as revealed through the CAT, the author found much withdrawal and inhibition and concludes: "The anxiety which resulted from the earlier childhood 'rejection' has by the middle-years generalized to all situations of emotional involvement and thus the avoidance of such situations has become an extremely important defense" (Earle, 1958, p. 68).

No evidence was found for strong inner controls or concepts of right and wrong; instead a conscious effort to avoid unpleasantness and anxiety appeared to be the general pattern. Control thus is achieved through anxiety, rather than because of any felt guilt or shame. The author relates these findings to the real-life situation as follows: "The children do not have any basis for an internalized superego system for they are unable to predict accurately what is expected of them. They therefore have become extremely wary and have lost any spontaneity which might have been present in a more secure environment" (Earle, 1958, p. 79).

It is of interest that when the results of the CAT study of the middle years were compared with the other studies in the series, involving doll play and plasticine with five-year-olds and TAT and Rorschach responses of adolescents, high agreement was found with respect to modal personality patterns in this culture, and there was a demonstrable continuity from one age period to the next.

SUMMARY

General findings relative to age, sex and sociocultural differences in projective responses of children have been discussed, as well as problems in developing norms for data secured from children. Normative studies, using the CAT, were then reviewed with respect to age trends (generally present) and sex differences (for the most part absent).

It seems time to "call a halt" to further card-by-card tabulational studies. The normative responses turn out to be the ones that could be predicted by looking at and describing the cards; in other words, the most frequent findings simply reflect the objects and activities pictured. The clinically useful responses are, in effect, those which deviate from the stimulus, introduce figures or objects, or give unusual combinations or interpretations to the figures and activities portrayed.

A more valuable type of normative study is represented by the papers of Moriarty and Murphy (1960a, 1960c) and Boulanger-Balleyguier (1957a, 1957b, 1960). The focus of concern is with the meanings and implications of the usual responses, rather than in their number *per se*. The investigators are also interested in the child's emotional reactions to these specific stimuli and have made observations and generalizations from their findings which contribute more meaning to the particular responses.

Studies have been reviewed which have evaluated various "normal" samples by means of the CAT; variables investigated have included intelligence, sibship patterns and "twinness," and sociometric status. Sociocultural antecedents have been investigated via the CAT with respect to socioeconomic levels, different racial backgrounds, and the influence of unique cultural aspects such as those found among isolated Maori tribes. One might summarize all these studies with the observation that, although individuals and groups of children may differ in some respects, the over-all similarities between diverse groups of normal children are compellingly in evidence.

CHAPTER VII

Protocols of Normal Children

Examples of projective responses of presumably normal children rarely appear in the literature. The CAT protocols presented here were secured from children, three to eight years of age, who had never been referred to a clinic. It is readily apparent that these records are neither bland, colorless nor barren. Rather, each child has used the CAT stimuli in his own unique way, revealing idiosyncratic perceptions of family relationships, attitudes toward siblings, and methods of handling hostility and aggression. When compared to the protocols of disturbed children presented in Chapter XI, the normal Ss present more positive themes, happier and more optimistic outcomes, fewer instances of bizarre ideation and more evidences of a firm basis in the reality aspects of normal family interactions.

The records of the three-, four-, and five-year-old children are used with the permission of Eleanore Raff from her sample of "well-adjusted" nursery school children (Raff, 1951). The six-, seven-, and eight-year-old protocols are taken from the control sample of the author's (1962) study of individual projectives given to school children who had previously been administered a group projective film. The control cases had given no deviant responses to the film and, as far as could be determined, were not presenting problems at home or at school.

Following each record, those adaptive mechanisms are listed which were used frequently enough to reach the level of a "critical score" on Haworth's Analysis Schedule (1963).* Research with this scoring instrument suggests that the presence of five or more such high "scores" would indicate the need for clinical referral. Only one of the records presented here (the eight-year-old boy) reaches this level. Bellak's Short Form TAT and CAT Blank was also used for evaluating the records of the school aged children; the examiner's summary notes are presented for each of Bellak's categories.

Three-Year-Old Girl

1. They are eating
   and the rooster's there.
(What's he doing?) He's looking over
   to see if there's any food for him.

2. The bears are pulling a rope
   and growling.
(Why?) I guess maybe
   they're pulling the rope too hard.
(Who are they?) Those are the three bears,
   mommy (single) and daddy and baby.

---

*The use of the Analysis Schedule is discussed in Chapter VIII.

3. The lion's — daddy lion
   is sitting in a chair thinking.
(About what?) Maybe thinking about a mouse.
Who drew this? Who drew these?

4. About the kangaroos.
These are kangaroos, about the. . .
That's mommy and baby and the other child.
They're going on a picnic.

5. A baby sleeping in a room.
Who's in the bed?
(Who do you think?) Maybe bears or lions.
Lions sleeping in a bed
   in the room making noise (points to crib).
(Who's in the other bed?) I can't see very well.
I guess the mommy and daddy
   'cause I saw a spot (points to spot on headboard).

6. Bears sleeping in the woods,
   and I don't know what else they're doing.
They just curled up
   and went to sleep.

7.   The lion's chasing the monkey to eat
   and he's running away
   and the lion's growling to eat it up.

8.   The monkeys are talking and eating
   and the daddy monkey is talking to the little monkey.
(What's he saying?) I don't know.
(What think?) Must be telling him something.
(What?) Maybe . . . I don't know.

9.   The bunny is sleeping and sitting in bed.
What's this thing here? (Points to mirror.)
(What look like?) I don't even know.
(Why in bed?) Maybe he's sick.

10.   Oh. Puppies.
Mommy puppy is sitting on a stool
   trying to keep him
   and he's trying to go to the toilet.
(Why keeping him?) Maybe she's angry with him.
(For what?) Maybe he's done something bad.
(What's she going to do?) Maybe spank him.

   Analysis Schedule: No critical scores.

Four-Year-Old Girl

1. See they're eating, and the hen.

They're thinking that they should play
    and learn what they should learn.

Then they're thinking
    they should build a house,
    but this is their table.
They're thinking.
(Then what are they going to do?) They're going to go
    and wander in the woods.
Can I stop telling this story now?

2.   Well, they're pulling something up,
    pulling as hard as possible.
The baby bear is thinking that
    they should pull as hard as anything.
If they do, that's just fine.
They should pull as hard as hard.
If they do then they'll be through.
(Who's the daddy, etc.?) Daddy (on one side), mommy and little baby.

3.   Well, the tiger is sitting in the chair
    and the little chipmunk is right beside him in this hole.
He's thinking he should be a grandpa or a grandma.
He's thinking he should move somewhere.
If he moves then he can do anything he likes.
His mommy won't know where he is.
Do I have to tell all of these? (Looks into folder).

4.   Well, the rooster and a little baby
    and a big child and the mommy.
They were out walking
    and they came to a. . . a. . . queer tree
    and wondered what was that tree.
"Oh, somebody lives in that tree,"
    so they went on.
(Who said that?) I did.
(Who in the story?) I did. You're silly.

5.   Is this a house?
(Do you think it is?) Yes. Here's a house
    and here's a mama bear and a baby bear (in crib)
    and they're sleeping, sound asleep.
Papa bear says
    "Someone has been sleeping in my bed"
    (this said in a deep voice, laughs).
    And Goldilocks was in his bed.
Baby bear says,
    "Someone has been sleeping in my bed,"
    and he points to Goldilocks (uses a wee voice).

So away she ran
    leaving a piece of her dress
    with the bears that tried to pull her.

6.   Some bears, baby bear and mommy bear
    and, and, uh papa.
(She kept searching in the picture for papa and pointed to a couple of places
in the picture where she thought he was.)
They're sleeping, sound, sound asleep.
Papa, "I want some food.
    It's morning everyone. Get up!"
Mommy bear woke up.
    "Baby bear, wake up,
    it's breakfast time.
    Why don't you get up?"

7.   Here's a tiger.
So the tiger is chasing the monkey
    but he can't catch him
    'cause tigers can't climb trees, can they?
He's trying to get him but he can't,
    so what can he do,
    what can he do?
(What does he do?) That's the end.

8.   (Whispers) Let me think. (Looking from left to right)
Here's a papa, a mama.
Daddy monkey and little baby having a party
    so the papa says, "I want my tea."
    The daddy is talking.
(Baby): "Give me my clothes
    and dress me before the party."
"Get dressed.
    We'll go away until you get dressed.
    Are you all dressed?"
"Yes."

9.   This is a little baby rabbit
    going to go to sleep
    and he got up.
He said, "Mommy bunny, where are you?"
"I'm lost."
"Where?"
"I'm lost in the woods.
    I've got a microphone
    so someone can save me.
    I'm telling them where I am
    so they can save me.

Daddy's lost. He's home;
  he's lost too but he's home."
I'm only telling one more, O.K.

10.   Here's a mommy — doggy and baby doggy.
Mommy, "Make wee wee
  or I'll spank you."
"No."
(What happened?) So mommy spanked him.

   Analysis Schedule: Reaction-formation and Undoing
                           Isolation

Five-Year-Old Boy

1.   They are eating.
(Tell me more?) Birds and chicken.
(What's the chicken doing?) Lookin'.
(At the birds?) Yeh, lookin' at the birds.

2.   Oh, he's pulling a rope.
The daddy and mommy and baby.
Here's the mother (by baby)
  and daddy and baby.
(Why pulling?) Because they want to get it away from him.
'Cause look at the face of the mother.
  She's doing that to pull.
The only way is to pull harder and harder.

3.   That's a lion sitting down.
  He's thinking.
(What about?) . . . . Hard one to think.
I think he's thinking
  about taking a walk
  and he is 'cause he has got his pipe out.
I see his cane and pipe
  and a little mouse.
(What doing?) Lookin' up at a hole.
  Rugs, chair. . .

4.   Um. Kangaroo carrying groceries,
  Little kangaroo riding on a trike.
  Little one holding a balloon.
(Who are they?) Their names?
(If you want to give them names.)
I want one to be Karon
  and one to be little Dicky.
(What doing?) One is sitting and one is riding.
(Where going?) One's in the pocket
  and one's on a trike.

5. Daddy and mother and baby zebras.
Bed, crib, rugs, crib, curtains, lamp.
(What doing?) They're sleeping.
They're going to try and beat their beds up
   with their great big fists.

6. Looks like a baby and daddy and mother.
They're peeking
   and he's looking.
   Looking in the great big round woods.
They see a snake coming down,
   down here (points to spot on left hand wall of cave).
They're going to eat him up.

7. A monkey and tiger.
The monkey is getting scared.
He has his great big mouth open
   and he's gettin' ready to claw him.
The monkey's on the tree
   and he's jumping up.
He's going to crawl up the tree
   and eat him.

8. Um. Mother monkey (by baby).
Here and here and another picture
   and baby and grandma I guess (the one with flowers).
(What doing?) They're arguing.
(Who?) All of them.
(About what?) I don't know.
   I think about the picture.

9. There's a rabbit in a crib
   not like the other one,
   with a place to get out like a chair.
Door knobs,
   can see window and window sills
   and curtain.
(What doing?) Lookin'.
(At what?) Just lookin' at the hall, I guess.

10. There's a doggy at the toilet.
Big dog and baby dog.
Paws and tail,
   mouth open and floppy ears.
Baby's going to the toilet
   and big one is sitting on the stool.

     Analysis Schedule: Repression and Denial

Six-Year-Old Girl

1.   They want something to eat.
One needs a napkin.
Mother needs a chair.
(Q) Yes, they eat after they get everything.
(Q) Food and napkin.

2.   Playing tug-of-war
(Q) Father lion only has one on one side, so he falls.
(Q) Baby on mother's side.
(Q-Why there?) Don't know.

3.   Tiger is mad.
(Q) Mouse.
(Q) Mouse hurt the lion
   by biting him on the foot
   and then ran away.

4.   Kangaroo jumped over other baby.
(Q) Wanted to beat him to the store.
(Q) Don't know.

5.   Don't know. Don't know no story.

6.   They are sleeping,
   except one baby.
(Q) Can't go to sleep.
(Q) Monkeys outside making screetchy noise...
   No, a man is making noise.
(Q) Wants bear to come out
   so he can shoot him
   and get more meat.
(Q-Does he?) Yes.

7.   Lion wants something to eat.
(Q) He chases the monkey
   but the monkey gets away.
(Q) He jumps in a tree.
The monkey laughs
   and the lion is mad.

8.   Don't know no story.
   Can't tell no story.

9.   Don't know (refused, shook head)

10.   Little baby has to go to the bathroom.
He gets a spanking
   cause he wet in his pants.

(Q-Why did he do that?)
He didn't tell his mother he had to go.

Analysis Schedule: No critical scores.

BELLAK'S CAT BLANK

Unconscious structure and drives: Struggle between adult and child, with child sometimes winning. If child wins, he laughs or runs out of reach.
Anxieties: Anal regression.
Defenses: Refused bedtime cards (Nos. 6 and 9).
             Denial
Superego structure: Immature
Ego integration: Possible masculine identification; immature ego.

Six-Year-Old Boy

1. Chickies are eating
    and mother rooster came.
(Q) She got mad at them.
(Q) Cause she was supposed to fix the dinner.
(Q) Made them go sit in a chair.
(Q) Were sad and mad.

2. Bears pulling rope,
    mother and daddy and little bear.
(Q) Little bear with daddy
    cause in case he falls
    father can get him.
    No, so he can help father.
(Q) Mother wants the rope to play with
    and father wants it, too.

3. King lion sitting in a chair.
(Q) Don't know what he's thinking about.
(Q) He goes to the zoo.
    The zoo man picks him up and takes him.

4. Little kangaroos going home
    cause they are done shopping.
(Q) They get caught by the wind
    and it blows them far away.
(Q) They get away.

5. Little bear is sleeping in bed,
    no, playing there.
His mother and father come and spank him.
(Q) He should have gone to sleep.

6. Little bears are sleeping in their cave
    cause winter's there.

Snow falls and they get cold
  and die.

7. A tiger jumps on a monkey
  and eats him.
(Q) Eats him up
  and then goes to sleep.
(Q) Naughty tiger.

8. Little monkeys sitting on chairs.
Telling secrets,
  Everyone is telling secrets.
(Q) Secrets about being good to each other.
(Q) That's all that happens.

9. Door fell down.
Blowed baby's crib upside down
  and his blanket blew away
  and he got cold and died.
No, he hid and got warm.

10. Mother puppy is petting baby puppy.
Is giving,
  No, trying to give him a bath.
(Q) She wraps him up in a towel
  so he won't get cold.
(Q) That's all.

    Analysis Schedule: Reaction-formation and Undoing
                          Repression and Denial
                          Symbolization
                          Projection and Introjection

Bellak's CAT Blank

Unconscious structure and drives: Sequence from Cards 2 through 10 can be interpreted as preoccupation with masturbation and guilt coincident with the oedipal situation. He overreacts to father (2), then eliminates him (3), is spanked by parents for playing in bed (5), further punishment, dying of cold (6), guilt and reaction-formation in the secrets about "being good" (8), child's exposure and death are resolved by undoing (9), and finally mother covers the child's nakedness with a towel after petting him (10), thus attaining the oedipal goal in fantasy.

Relationship to others: Omits specific mention of parents in four stories where they are usually seen (Cards 4, 6, 8 and 9).

Significant conflicts: Guilt; some rebellion against mother.

Anxieties: Awful things may happen while asleep.

Defenses: Denial, repression, some reaction-formation and undoing.

Superego structure: Guilt, naughtiness, concern with wrong deeds, secrets.

Ego integration: Ambivalence and indecision, strong oedipal wishes.

Seven-Year-Old Girl

1. The little chickens are eating
    and here's the mother chicken.
(Q) They eat too slowly
    so she hurries them up.
(Q) They don't like to hurry.

2. The bears are playing tug-of-war.
Father bear is so strong
    that baby bear has to help mother out,
    it's even.
(Q) Go play something else.

3. The lion is pretending he don't see the mouse.
Then the mouse will sneak out
    and the lion will catch him by surprise.
(Q) The mouse sneaks out
    and the lion catches him
    and eats him.

4. The kangaroos are going to a picnic,
    there's the picnic basket.
(Q) Father went ahead
    to save a table.
(Q) They find father and have a picnic.

5. The bears are just getting up.
They see that mother and daddy
    are already up
So they are trying to decide
    what to wear.
(Q) Put on overalls
    and go eat.

6. The little bear is having trouble sleeping.
Mother and father bear are already hibernating,
    but he's still awake.
(Q) Guess he wonders if it will be warm all winter.
(Q) He crawls in between mother and father
    and keeps warm.
(Q) They're sleeping and don't know.

7. The monkey is being chased
    by the hungry tiger.
The tiger catches the monkey
    and eats him.
(Q) He wasn't fast enough
    so he got caught.

8. The monkeys are having coffee
    after Sunday dinner.
And the little monkey keeps interrupting,
    so his father gives him a lecture
    and says not to talk like that.
(Q) He goes out and plays
    and leaves the grownups alone.

9. The rabbit wakes up
    and is scared.
The wind blew the window open
    but he thought it might be a hunter.
(Q) His mother comes
    and tells what it was
    so he goes back to sleep OK.

10. Dog is getting spanked for being naughty.
(Q) He splashed water around the floor
    when washing.
(Q) Just wasn't paying attention.
(Q) Cries and goes to bed
    without any supper.

Analysis Schedule: Projection and Introjection

BELLAK'S CAT BLANK

Unconscious structure and drives: No real stress or severe conflicts. Describes a happy family. Some oedipal desires, wants to separate or be with parents. Wants adult's attention (Card 8) and is rebuffed by father. Mother gives comfort in danger situation.

Relationship to others: Adults may be somewhat strict but they are also seen as dependable and protective.

Significant conflicts: Some chafing under adult supervision.

Anxieties: No severe ones.

Defenses: No clear defensive structure.

Superego structure: Seems adequate, normal for age.

Ego integration: Reality oriented; trusts adults; independent and accepts punishment if justified. Normal feminine identification.

Seven-Year-Old Boy

1. The chickens are hungry.
(Q) No food in their dishes.
(Q) Mother bird just didn't put any there.
(Q) They wait for awhile
    then go out
    and see where they can get some.
(Q) Die.

2.   The bears are fighting.
(Q) Mother wants it
   and father wants it.
(Q) Baby's on father's side.
   Mother doesn't need him to help her.
(Q) Father and baby win
(Q) Play with it.

3.   The lion just ate the mouse's mother.
The little mouse is scared
   and wonders where father mouse is.
(Q) Well, the little mouse hides
   until father comes home.
   He's working.
(Q) They go out
   and find a new house.

4.   The kangaroos are going to the store,
   only the little kangaroo can't keep up.
The bike is too big for him.
(Q) He should be riding with mother kangaroo, too.
(Q) Baby gets there
   cause he's smallest.
(Q) He has trouble keeping up.
(Q) Maybe he'll be big enough
   to ride the bike good next year.

5.   Bears are awake.
It's morning
   and mother and daddy are still asleep.
(Q) They are real quiet.
(Q) Mother would spank them
   for being bad
   and waking them up early.
(Q) They're quiet until
   mother and daddy get up.

6.   Bears are hibernating.
The little bear gets up
   and goes outside
   to see if snow is still there.
(Q) He gets lost
   and can't find their cave.
(Q) When mother and daddy wake up
   they look for him.
(Q) They can't find him.
He grows up by himself.

7. The tiger gets after the monkey
     for pulling his tail.
(Q) Tiger grabs the monkey
     and shakes him and says,
     "You be good or I'll eat you."
(Q) The monkey is good from then on.

8. Monkeys are having coffee.
The little monkey is helping mother.
(Q) She's telling him to go
     to the kitchen for more cookies.
(Q) He gets them
     and then goes out to play.

9. Rabbit hears a hunter
     coming after him
So he runs away into the woods.
(Q) He hides in a hole
     until the hunter goes away.
(Q) He goes back home
     and eats breakfast.
(Q) He goes back to school.

10. The dog played in the mud
     and got all dirty.
(Q) Mother spanked him
     and washed him
     and made him go to bed
     without any supper.
(Q) He's sorry he was a bad boy.
(Q) Is good.

> *Analysis Schedule*: Repression and Denial
>   Symbolization
>   Fear and Anxiety

Bellak's CAT Blank

Unconscious structure and drives: Strong need to grow up and to be independent, yet also fears it. Mother seen as non-nurturant (Cards 1 and 2) so he eliminates her (Card 3). Then he attacks father (Card 7), resulting in castration fears (Cards 7 and 9); then he seeks restitution by being sorry, thus getting back into mother's favor. Some jealousy of siblings.

Conception of world: Restricting, retaliatory.

Relationship to others: Mother non-nurturant and must be placated by obedience. Looks to father for security, but also sees him as a rival and fears attack from him. Solution is to be good and obedient.

Significant conflicts: Guilt, castration fears.

Anxieties: Being lost, punished, orally deprived.

Defenses: Repression.

Superego structure: More severe than usual for age; strong guilt feelings and sense of right and wrong; tendency to be masochistic.

Ego integration: Overly defended, strong needs for control and to win parental approval.

Eight-Year-Old Girl

1. This rooster is always crowing
    and when he does,
     they get up
     and eat their breakfast.
(Q) After they get through, they play
    and then they come back in
    and they go to sleep.
And the rooster calls them again in the morning.

2. It looks like these bears
     are having a tug-of-war.
And whoever wins
     they get some honey.
(Q) Little bear's on mother's side
    cause father bear is stronger
    and mother needs a little help.

3. This looks like an old lion
    and he has so many mouses in his house
    he doesn't know what to do.
(Q) He just sits and thinks.
(Q) He makes a trap for them
    under his seat.
(Q) Then the mouse sees it
    and doesn't get hurt.
    He stays in his hole.

4. This looks like they're going on a picnic.
Mother has a purse
    and will buy them something
    if they're good.
She's pulling one baby
    cause she can't hold them both
    in her pouch.
(Q) She will buy one a bike
    and for the little one a balloon.
(Q) He doesn't care
    cause he wants to ride the bike,

5. This bear lives here
    and she had some babies.
It looks like they sneaked some candy to bed
    and ate it.
(Q) Then the mother and daddy heard them
    and took and put the blanket
    over their heads
    cause they thought it was ghosts.
(Q) The babies cried
    cause they heard a noise, too,
But mother didn't get up
    cause she didn't want to get captured
    by the ghost.

6. Mother and father bear are sleeping
    and baby bear is trying to sneak out
    to get something to eat.
Baby bear gets out
    and mother bear
    and father bear wake up.
They put on winter coats
    and get him.
And they don't let him
    play with his friends in the summer
    since he didn't obey his mother and father.

7. This monkey wants to get
    to the other branch.
The lion likes monkeys to eat.
(Q) The lion chases him
    when he's swinging on the rope.
The lion knocks him down
    and eats him all up.

8. This is a monkey family.
Big sister and little boy are talking
    cause he spilled the cocoa.
And his sister is warning him
    not to do it.
(Q) Mother and dad are going to buy
    a new house pretty soon
    and are whispering
    so the kids won't hear.

9. This looks like this little girl
    didn't take her nap
    like her mother said.

She opened her door cause the TV was on
  and she wanted to hear.
(Q) Her mother shut the door
  so she crept out
  and saw a movie.
(Q) Mother caught her
  and gave her a spanking.

10. This looks like this mother told her baby
  to have a nap,
  and she didn't do it.
(Q) She played with her toys.
(Q) Her mother caught her
  and turned her over
  and spanked her.

> *Analysis Schedule*: Deception
>   Projection and Introjection
>   Regression

BELLAK'S CAT BLANK

Unconscious structure and drives: General picture of normal family life. Child persists in mild forms of disobedience, expecting and accepting punishments. No strong guilt or severe superego reactions. Identifies with females, rivalry with mother. Defies parents in areas of eating and sleeping.

Conception of world: Normal to somewhat restrictive. Child recognizes existence of rules but does not always obey them.

Relationship to others: Parents are not very understanding or sympathetic, put their own interests first. No sibling rivalry.

Significant conflicts: Self-assertion versus obedience.

Anxieties: No severe ones.

Defenses: Immature, not well-developed considering age of child.

Superego structure: Normal for age.

Ego integration: Fairly adequate for age. Strong feminine identification.

Eight-Year-Old Boy

1. They're eating.
That chicken (big one) is going
  to get those little chickens.
(Q) Eat them.
(Q) Because they're eating his food.

2. He's trying to get the rope,
  No, those guys are trying
  to get it away from him.
Even the little guy is pulling.
Those guys want the rope
  and he won't give it to them.

(Q) Maybe he wants it to tie something up.
(Q-What tie up?) Like maybe a fox
  or his little bear.
(Q) They fight and fight
  and these guys win.

3.   He's sitting smoking a pipe
  and this mouse is going to come
  out of his hole
  and sneak up in back of him.
He bites the lion.
(Q) He gets mad at the mouse
  and kills him.

4.   This little kangaroo is riding his bike
  and hitting his dad on the back.
(Q) Maybe he wants to get mad
  so he'll spank him.
(Q) Don't know why.
(Q-What happens?) He turns around hits him.

5.   There's two little baby bears in there
  and there ain't nobody in there (big bed).
These guys are all alone
  and their mother and daddy
  ain't in bed.
(Q) They get sad and cry
  then their mother and daddy come
  and spank them, I think.

6.   These bears are sleeping
  in a tunnel at night.
No, it's winter and they're hibernating.
They get killed or something.
(Q) Someone's out hunting
  and shoots them.

7.   This lion's after this monkey
  cause he's going to eat him.
That lion eats him
  after he finishes chasing him.
(Q) He was hungry.

8.   This lady monkey
  is telling her little boy
  to go to bed.
These other ladies
  are talking and drinking tea.
(Q) They want to talk together
  and she don't want him to hear.

(Q) Might be special business
  like going to court or something.
(Q) He stole a watch or something.
(Q) Maybe they'll talk about
  who will drive to court.
(Q) He stole it cause he wanted it.

9. This baby rabbit is in bed
  and a bear comes in
  and eats him
  cause the door was open
  and he just walks in.
(Q) When her mother comes home
  she won't be there.
(Q) Will call the police.

10. That's a mother dog
  and he's, she's spanking the baby
  cause she wants to give him a bath
  and he wouldn't come.
(Q) Then she closes the door,
  and he sneaks out the window.
(Q) Doesn't want to take a bath
  cause then he has to go to bed.
(Q) She goes out and looks for him
  and spanks him.

> *Analysis Schedule*: Reaction-formation and Undoing
>   Deception
>   Symbolization
>   Projection and Introjection
>   Confused Identification

BELLAK'S CAT BLANK

Unconscious structure and drives: Child attacks, and is attacked by, his elders; gets no comfort or affection; must be destroyed to be missed. Sneaks and provokes attack to secure punishment and attention; steals to be noticed; rebels. Probably an acting-out child.

Conception of world: Overwhelming, devouring, defeating.

Relationship to others: Is always beaten and overpowered.

Significant conflicts: Must fight to survive; an eye for an eye; castration fears, no guilt.

Anxieties: Is spanked, unloved, devoured.

Defenses: Projection, submit or escape.

Superego structure: Primitive level with little guilt; get what you can and you can't keep it for long.

Ego integration: Child is small, weak, sad, sneaking and acting-out. Little rebellions are not always successful but worth trying. Confused, feminine identification.

CHAPTER VIII

Interpretation: Part One

It is not the intent of this chapter to cover all the ramifications of the interpretive process, but rather to point to some of the general issues that seem particularly relevant when testing children. Consideration will be given to various schedules which have been proposed for use in evaluating picture-story protocols, including three which have been specifically developed for use with the CAT.

BASES FOR INTERPRETATIONS

Recurrent Themes

At best, we have only ten stories from which to derive assumptions and speculations about the personality organization of the child under study. As noted in previous chapters, the youngest children may give quite brief stories which would limit the data even more. Consequently, more confidence can be put in themes which recur in several stories (possibly in somewhat different guises) than in an isolated deviant response. Recurrent responses may be of two kinds: (1) Perseverative repetition of the same phrases or of specific objects, persons or events (especially important if not shown in the cards, e.g., ghosts, tornadoes, hunters); or (2) employment of the same affect or attitude but expressed in different situations (e.g., themes of success but in different pursuits; a persistently depriving or punishing mother figure; or rebellion and disobedience in a variety of circumstances). As Bellak (1954) has pointed out, the recurrence of a theme can be viewed as a form of reliability and of validity for that subject since it indicates that this response has particular meaning for him. We would certainly not wish to suggest disregarding those particularly deviant and atypical responses which occur but once in a record. Rather, the emphasis is on careful consideration of all possible clues and indicators.

Sequence Analysis

It is easy to become engrossed in the content of individual stories or in themes which stand out because of their recurrent nature. But evaluation also needs to be made of the sequence of themes throughout the protocol. Is a rebellious story succeeded by one of obedience? Is expressed aggression toward a father figure followed by a story of restitution to another father figure or by incidents of hurt or injury to the child character? One may also get a delayed response to a story which has been upsetting, with the sequel not appearing until two or three stories later.

In the first of the following sequence of two stories told by a nine-year-old boy,* mothers are seen as somewhat sarcastic and disgusted with their children

---

*For the complete protocol of this child, the reader is referred to the section on Obsessive-Compulsive Reactions in Chapter XI.

yet also as feeling helpless to do anything about their behavior. In the second story, the S attempts to gloss over the negative aspects of the mother by emphasis on her "niceness," and attempts to rectify his implied naughtiness by careful compliance with standards of proper and expected getting-up activities.

8.   Looks like a bunch of monkeys (smiles).
Probably having a coffee break.
Looks like one of the monkeys has children,
   telling them to sit down.
Two sit on the davenport
   talking to each other.
On the wall is a grandma ape.
One monkey's telling the other,
   "What a mean kid you've got!"
The other one says,
   "Don't you think I know it."
One said "he's nice."
   One said "he's mean."
   The other says "I know."
It keeps on until one comes up and says,
   "Is that all you can say. . .
   'Don't I know it'?"

9.   Looks like a rabbit sitting up in bed,
   probably thinking about something.
Probably thinking about
   what a nice mother he has.
Probably dreaming,
   has a window in there.
It's probably morning,
   he gets up,
   puts clothes on,
   brushes teeth,
   washes,
   puts his shoes and sox on.
Then he gets breakfast,
   and plays, if it's Saturday. . . .

If the character traits of mother, father, and the child "hero" are consistent throughout the stories one can postulate that stable and predictable relationships have been established. Where the personalities and attitudes of the various figures fluctuate from card to card, ambivalence and insecurity are suggested. For example, the mother figure may be represented in Card 1 as very solicitous of the children and as eager to satisfy their oral needs, while on Card 4 she scolds the child on the tricycle and threatens not to give him any of the food she is carrying. Does this child see his mother as sometimes nurturant and sometimes denying and punitive? Bellak (1961) has found that responses to Card 6 will often elaborate on Card 5, or that the S may "open up" to Card 6 after seemingly repressing strong feelings on the previous card.

Another sequential pattern has been noted by Haworth (1962) from Card 6 to Card 9. Although neither card portrays aggression (both suggest sleep) she found that an equal number of neurotic and control *Ss* in a school sample gave themes of attack to one or both cards. The neurotic *Ss* all told attack stories to *both* cards, with stories to Card 6 usually expressing fears that an attack was imminent, while *all* stories to Card 9 described an actual attack as taking place, usually from ghosts, hunters or wild animals. Also, the attack theme on Card 9 was usually a fulfillment of the specific fear previously expressed on Card 6. On the other hand, only one of the control *Ss* using attack themes did so on both cards, and only rarely was an attack theme given to Card 6. Furthermore, the fantasy attacks described to Card 9 did not actually take place; they were either feared or dreamed of, but did not occur. Such a story often included reassuring comments to the effect that the child character realized it was "just a dream" or he hid until the danger was past.

These findings suggest examination of the stories told to these two cards as possible indicators of phobic, panic reactions and especially if attack themes are given to both cards. In contrast, healthy, realistic adjustment to stress can be inferred when attack themes occur on only one of these cards and if the event does not actually take place but is rationalized or handled in some constructive manner.

Evidences of increasing anxiety as testing progresses may be reflected at the point where the child suddenly starts giving titles to his stories as if to better contain his fantasies within a predetermined framework. He may count the number of cards still left in the pile, or complain of being too tired to continue. Rejected cards should be evaluated in terms of the content of the particular picture and its relation to the story, or build-up of stories, just preceding it. Also, one should note the quality of recovery when storytelling is resumed. Some examiners record initial reaction times for each story as a basis for an analysis of those cards whose content may be threatening or for interpretations relative to repression, suppression and inhibitions.

Use of Case History Information

It is important that the clinician have a knowledge of the child's home situation, know the names of the siblings, and any recent or impending crisis events as well as the presenting problems. There is little virtue in making blind interpretations of clinical data. Rather, it should be the psychologist's function to integrate and interpret, on the basis of all the facts and findings, in such a manner as to be of most help to those persons closely involved with the child.

One would hardly expect a physician to diagnose a child's physical illness over the phone, knowing only the location of the pain, degree of fever, and amount of lost sleep. Instead, he will insist on seeing the patient, giving his own examination, and gathering additional information concerning the present and past complaints and symptoms, the previous health history, general functioning level and all other possibly relevant factors. Similarly, a psychological evaluation should represent careful integration of every aspect of the case and involve generalizations made on the basis of all the information and test results. The clinician needs to go beyond the test data to a consideration of their meaning in the total Gestalt of known events.

To illustrate, suppose school authorities have referred a child because of serious incidents of acting-out behavior. It is not very helpful for them to receive a clinical report which pictures a child desperately struggling to control his aggressive impulses and which warns that he might, if put under undue stress, lose these tenuous controls and act in an antisocial manner. Surely there is nothing to be lost by looking at the intake material. If our subject is, in fact, already acting-out, then the report can confirm these tendencies as being an outstanding characteristic and can point up the child's difficulties in maintaining control despite good intentions.

Gory accounts of aggression and hostility may reflect a child's current mode of reacting, but may also represent the overly active fantasy life of a meek, quiet, intimidated child. To report both cases as indicating similar dynamics would do injustice to the facts which should be known ahead of time. In the former instance, the child's fantasies are consistent with his behavior and probably are less serious — at least more available for intervention — than the second child whose stories reflect a severe rift between his outer modes of behavior and the inner turmoil and conflict.

Wild stories of Zorro and Superman need to be evaluated with knowledge of the extent of exposure to these particular characters (including, of course, consideration as to *why* these figures present such an appeal to this particular child). Tales of ghosts and witches need to be discounted to some extent if told in the weeks just preceding or following Halloween.

Adopted Status. Dramatic illustrations of the necessity for relating test findings to family data can be found in cases of adopted children. One boy, as an infant, had experienced desertion by his mother, the death of his father, and various periods of time in an orphanage and in inadequate foster homes, before being placed for adoption at age three and one-half. Upon examination at age seven, his CAT stories were filled with reciprocal aggression between adult animals or between hunters and animals. More specifically, on Card 2 an alligator attacks papa bear and is killed, then deer come to the house and are successfully warded off by papa bear. On Card 3 the lion eats up men, women and children and is, in turn, killed by a hunter. On Card 4 three bears eat up everybody, a gorilla eats the bears, a man kills the gorilla, then "everything is new again." A student clinician, in his attempt to be unbiased by refusing to look at the background information, initially interpreted these stories as representing the child's aggressive feelings directed toward his parents (inferring the present ones) and culminating in self-destruction to satisfy his need for punishment.

Taking a second look at the stories, in the light of the actual life events, revealed that in each case it is the "adults" who are fighting each other, while the child character is either defended by "papa" or annihilated along with everybody else. It hardly seems presumptive to speculate that this boy feels very insecure, never knowing when the overpowering adults in his world will again be arguing over, or at least reconsidering, his disposition.

Two stories seem obviously to relate back to the early home environment with his own parents rather than indicating the child's negative feelings toward his adoptive parents. In Card 2 not only is the baby protected by "papa," (see above) but also the mother is "mean;" on Card 5 father says, "It's bedtime, son," but the son tears up everything in the room, then the father comes to bed. In the morning the little bear is whipped, father and mother go to New York and leave baby bear at home, baby fixes up everything and runs away to Chicago, gets into an accident, is jailed (orphanage?), and then lives happily ever after. Certainly this child is not only reliving his negative feelings toward his natural mother, who deserted him, but also expressing warmer, closer affect toward his father and his anxiety that he (the child) may have been in some way responsible for the "breaking-up" of his home. Yet, along with so much turmoil and insecurity, one sees an optimistic attitude in several stories, probably related to his present more satisfying situation (e.g., "everything's new again" or things turn out happily in the end). There seems to be sufficient ego strength for favorable prognosis.

Death in the Family. If the death of a relative or friend has recently occurred, references to illnesses and death are logically to be expected and represent an attempt at mastery of an overwhelming event. In contrast, a preponderance of death references unrelated to an actual event may be taken as a representation of inner preoccupations which, if pronounced, can signal severe pathology.

With knowledge that a five-year-old girl had lost her father at the age of four, as the result of an auto accident, we can see in her stories, how she views the loss, and how she regards her own role in relation to her father. (It should be noted that she did not attend the funeral, but subsequently was often taken to the cemetery by her mother.) On Card 3, the lion "maybe has magic power," the fairy may turn him into the king of the beasts. (Is father now viewed as everpresent and omnipotent?) On Card 5, the floor will break and fall and all the animals will get killed and a forest fire will come (death and destruction to family and home). On Card 6, the animals are lying in a basement, they're living "under the dirt" (burial fantasy, possibly a misperception that people are buried alive). Then a mean dragon killed the little boy, and "maybe this papa killed a little boy, maybe he killed his own little boy." When asked why the papa would do that, she said, "Maybe it was a little girl." She continued the theme on Card 7 with, "The lion can kill anyone, even little children."

Had the father possibly been viewed as "mean," punishing and rejecting, so that she had, at times, wished he were gone? If so, does she now feel responsible for the event, and so fear retaliation in kind? Or is she fearful that if her father could be taken so suddenly in death, perhaps the same frightening event could happen as easily to little children?

The next example is presented to illustrate how knowledge of prior events can help the examiner understand the depth of feeling in what appears to be a rather bizarre story. This boy was evaluated when ten and one-half years of age. When four years old he was in a car accident in which his mother was killed. After a year in the homes of several relatives, he and his two younger sisters were sent to a children's home. Rather than the usual family characters on Card 6 he sees the three figures as a big brother and two little ones, a sister and a baby. His intense feeling of responsibility for his siblings is highlighted, as well as evidence of some loosening of thought processes (preceded by slips of the tongue and obsessive clinging to details) when confronted with the enormity of his position.

6.　This . . . . Once upon a time
　　there were four bears. . .
　　Three bears and they lived in a rock.
There was a big brother,
　　a sister and a baby bear.
It became very cold.
Big brother better find a cave
　　where they could stay all night.
It said on the radio
　　it will be 200 below . . . 10 below.
They will die
　　if they don't go to sleep for the winter.
"You'd better get under the leaves, baby brother.
　　Your skin will . . .
　　can thaw out better . . .
　　easier than your skin."
So they all got out.
Big brother bear went hunting.
Big brother . . .
　　a hunter shot him.
Sister and baby bear
　　were captured for a circus.

Traumatic Illness: An instructive example of the influence of events preceding referral upon the child's projective responses is seen in the case of an eight and one-half year old girl. She had been infected with pinworms and had been given strong medication for their removal, resulting in an acute toxic condition. When admitted, she was fantasying (or hallucinating?) snakes twining around her arms. Further case history material suggested that there had been much sexual exhibitionism on the part of the parents to which the child had been a frequent witness. An incident was also reported in which an adolescent male baby-sitter had once locked her in a closet and told her there were snakes in the closet.

Her responses to three CAT cards were as follows:

3.　King—queen setting in chair.
He's setting, thinking
　　about when set in chair,
　　mices get out
　　and climb all over him and tickle.

He can catch them and all that.
(Q) He'll take em and kill em,
   might even spray them with poison
   and be all rid of em.
Then he can set down and be comfortable
   without having mices run all over him.

6.   There's a great, great ole hole
   some man digged.
Mama bear, papa bear,
   cousin bear and baby bear
All sleep in a big cave.
All at once,
   something went ssss.........
It was a snake
   and they didn't know it,
   And baby bear's eyes were still open.
Snakes protect themselves by biting.
They'll not hurt us
   unless we hurt them.
If they hurt us
   we'll have to hurt them,
   because we don't want to get killed.
(Q) They ran all over the house;
Snakes are still there, sleeping.
Then a *great, big, long* one,
   tangled all around,
   had fun, laughing—
   a real nice snake.

8.   All papa bear and mama bear
   and baby and old grandma was setting, and . . .
This one lady—man,
   has feet around this lady's leg.
The baby bear is sitting (giggles)
   on grandma's hand.

On Card 3, the mice may symbolize the fantasied snakes "climbing all over." Snakes are openly talked about on Card 6, starting with their phobic aspects, then some efforts at reassurance, finally ending with massive undoing accompanied by inappropriate affect. The tangling aspects of the snake theme become merged and "condensed" on Card 8 into an unusual theme of twined legs which could be interpreted as sexual caressing, thus throwing more light on the meaning of the symptom to this particular child.

Snakes and worms figured prominently also on four of the Rorschach cards (which were presented after the CAT in this case, as part of a study to determine order effects).

Rorschach

Free Association:	Inquiry:
IV. A cow with horns and eyes and mouth and feet and legs and arms.	Big wings sticking out.
A snake (D-4). Looks like a little belly worm to me (giggles).	Way it's going—mad (gestures with tongue and lips).
V. Butterfly noodles (D-9) (giggles)	Noodles sticking out here (D-10). Doodles sticking out here (D-7).
(AE?) Yeh, wings (giggles). Looks like a picnic basket with chicken,	One big one jumped in (D-9), I'm sleepy.
Looks like a chicken basket with chicken noodles and that's all, and a bird.	
VI. Oh, looks like a snake crawling from a hole.	(D-2), (D-1 is the hole).
Ugh, long legs and the whole thing's sticking out. Ears, no ears, legs.	Because of whiskers.
VIII. A pink, wiggle worm (D-1). What you call em? (giggles)	
They're bears walking up hill.	Way they walk.

Of particular interest is the unusual and quite disorganized response (both in the free association and the inquiry) to Card V which usually elicits a banal popular response. If, as Halpern (1953) suggests, Card V represents views of one's own self and body image, we could not find a more vivid instance of bending the percept to fit the subject's current problems with respect to invasion of the self by foreign "bodies."

There is no intent to minimize the bizarreness of these responses because they can be so directly related to her symptoms. Rather, the record serves to highlight the importance of her recent experiences and to aid in understanding their traumatic effect on the child as revealed through the fusion of symbols. Without a knowledge of the actual facts, this protocol could have been readily interpreted as evidence for thought dissociation and severe pathology.

Premature Sexual Experiences. Stories replete with sexual allusions or symbols may reflect unusual preoccupations in an area of experience to which the child feels himself excluded, or they may represent the unanswered questions of a child who has been exposed, literally, to sexual scenes. In the following series of CAT stories, the theme of "peeking" on the adult's activities leaves little doubt of the sexual connotation. This five-year-old girl had, in fact, been present when her mother entertained a succession of lovers; had herself been molested; and subsequently attempted to engage other children in sex play.

3. Oh gosh (laughs).
Lion smoking a cigar.

Mouse is peeking out at the lion.
Lion turns his face
    to look at the mouse peeking.
Is that man lion
    going to get that mouse?
(E - what do you think?)
He's sitting in a chair
    with his tail down.
(Q) He's going to beat the mouse up,
    to make him so he will keep quiet.
He's a half old lion.
He looks like a mama lion
    but it's a daddy lion.

5.   Mama bear sleeping right there,
    when hears noise,
    going to say something real loud.
When said "Be quiet,"
    she be real mean.
The boy bear went to sleep.
The girl bear tried to go to sleep
    but girl bear's waking up boy bear.
    He wouldn't wake up.
(Q) She's going to try to go to sleep.
When mama—bear girl,
    when she sees her mama,
    she try to go to sleep.
When she didn't see her mama,
    she go to sleep.
The mama bear covers herself up
    so she not see or hear what going on.

6.   The daddy bear going to sleep.
He says, "Shut up."
Then that girl bear goes to sleep.

9.   When that mama said, "Lay down"
    he didn't lay down.
    He's just peeking.
Knock- knock.
"Come in, mother."
"You lay down."
She woke up and peek again,
    Sees mama gone,
    goes to see where her mama at.
    Looks all around for her mama.
(Q-does she find her mama?)
Her mama not there yet,
    she looks, just herself.

This child's Rorschach also revealed an unusual sensitivity to the fact that men and women pair off together. On three cards, figures were seen as "a man and lady" or as "Mama and Daddy."

In summary, the clinical psychologist must utilize all possible information about his subject in order to arrive at a *meaningful* interpretation of the test findings. He needs this information in order to fully understand the child and to be able to place himself in the child's frame of reference and so enter the child's figure-ground Gestalt. It subsequently becomes the psychologist's function to interpret this newly encompassed world of the child to the adults who are a significant part of his "ground."

PROBLEMS IN INTERPRETATION

Overt Versus Fantasy Behavior

The problem of determining whether specific projective responses are reflecting manifest or latent levels is one which plagues clinicians and researchers alike. As suggested earlier, when highly aggressive stories are given by both acting-out and meek, passive children, the responses *per se* throw little light on the underlying personality processes. The question becomes one of determining why similar content is given by two such different children.

As a first step in solution, Kagan (1960) has pointed out that one must know not only the content of the response but also the nature of the stimulus which elicited that response. Lindzey (1952) has suggested that story material which can be directly traced to elements in the presented stimulus is less apt to be significant than that which has been added or indirectly suggested by the stimulus content. In other words, to tell an aggressive story in which the adult figure on Card 1 attacks the children seated at table would carry quite different connotations from a story of the tiger attacking the monkey on Card 7 where the "set" for aggression is obviously built into the card. The introduction of an attacker on Card 9, where no adult figure is represented, would be a clearer instance of projection than when using adult figures already present, as in Card 1. Similarly, punishment themes to cards *other than* Card 10 would carry more weight with respect to that dimension than on Card 10 itself, where the adult is seen by most children as administering a spanking. We can also assume that themes of oral nurturance would be more meaningful if given in response to a nonoral card than when found in stories to Cards 1, 4 or 8 where food and eating are clearly the focus of portrayed activities. Nevertheless, this is not meant to imply ignoring, for example, any reference to eating on an "oral" card; rather, on such cards we will look for the S's reactions to the situation and for reflections of feelings and attitudes connected with the pictured activity.

In research on the problem of manifest versus latent levels of fantasy, Kagan (1956) presented pictures ambiguous for aggression and pictures which suggested aggressive actions to known groups of aggressive and nonaggressive boys. He found that the ambiguous pictures did not differentiate between groups, while the aggressive boys gave significantly more aggressive stories to the openly aggressive stimuli. Kagan reasoned that aggressive boys had less anxiety about telling aggressive stories to aggressive stimuli. In a study of a related nature, Lesser (1957) first determined the amount of overt aggression displayed by a group of boys and the extent to which their mothers encouraged or discouraged aggressive behavior. He then showed pictures of aggressive and nonaggressive situations. For boys whose mothers encouraged aggression, there was a positive correlation between overt and fantasy aggression, while for boys whose mothers discouraged aggression the correlation was negative. Presumably, the latter group had more anxiety over the expression of overt aggression which, in turn, led to increased use of aggression in fantasy.

Kagan (1960) concludes from the above findings that ". . . When apperceptive fantasy is used to assess conflict in a motive area, prediction of presence or absence of the corresponding behavior is better than when the fantasy is used to measure 'motive strength.' Clinicians faced with the problem of predicting overt aggression in children should attend closely to fantasy content which suggests anxiety over aggression and to distortions and abrupt changes in fantasy performance to stimuli which suggest aggressive behavior. It is also reasonable to assume that these conclusions about aggression are applicable to other conflict areas" (p. 117).

Several earlier investigators, working with children's apperceptive stories, were also concerned with relationships between fantasy themes and overt behavior. Sanford et al. (1943) found that a comparison of children's fantasy scores (using the TAT) with overt behavior scores suggested that the presence of a need in fantasy was no indication that the subject would act accordingly. Symonds (1949) found the most obvious correspondence between overt behavior and fantasy in the best-adjusted adolescents. The less well-adjusted subjects told stories which did not correspond to their character, e.g., when a shy docile child produced very hostile themes. Eiserer (1949) suggests that "... the more positive, acceptable feelings and attitudes are more readily expressed in everyday behavior and that the projective tests purport to uncover tendencies which the individual dare not or cannot reveal" (p. 266).

Translating the above findings to CAT interpretations, we should carefully evaluate, for example, responses to Card 7 which omit aggressive content, or to Card 10 which make no mention of spanking or scolding. Omissions of any reference to sleeping activities on Cards 5 and 6 should also be noted, with the view of determining sources of anxiety and stress.

Identification

The determination of the character with which the child is identifying is an important aspect of personality evaluation. Clues throughout the stories can usually be found which will throw light on the child's sex-role tendencies and attitudes toward the self. Obviously one would be concerned if a boy repeatedly identified with female characters or a girl with male. But the process of determining just which character can be assumed to be the child's identification model is a difficult one at best and apt to be subjective and unreliable.

Bellak's (1961) discussion in the CAT manual offers little real help in locating the identification figures:

Since there can be a number of people in a story, it becomes necessary to state that we speak of the figure with which our subject mainly identifies himself as the hero. We will have to specify, for this purpose, some objective criteria for differentiating the hero from other figures: The hero is the figure about whom the story is woven primarily. He resembles the subject most in age and sex and from his standpoint the events are seen. While these statements hold true most of the time, they do not always do so. There may be more than one hero and our subject may identify with both, or first with one and then with another. There may be a deviation in that a subject may identify with a hero of a different sex; it is important to note such identifications. Sometimes an identification figure secondary in importance in a story may represent more deeply repressed unconscious attitudes of the subject. Probably the interests, wishes, deficiencies, gifts and abilities with which the hero is invested are those which the subject possesses, wants to possess, or fears that he might have (p. 5).

Some of the normative CAT studies reported in Chapter VI adopted various criteria for assessing identification. For instance, Byrd and Witherspoon (1954) used any mention of a parent as an indication of identification with that parent. It is difficult to see how this procedure could be defended on theoretical grounds. To confound the data, if the child failed to "label" an adult figure on Cards 2, 4, 8 or 10 he was asked to do so, while no such inquiry was made on Cards 1 and 3 (which also contain figures often seen as parents). In fact, the authors report a low frequency for "father identification" on Card 3! In their tabulation, group data were used for each story. They report that maternal identification exceeded paternal identification on all cards except Cards 3 and 8. No cognizance is taken of the fact that an individual child may mention mother on some cards and father on others. In actual clinical practice some method must be devised which will take into account an accumulation of identification clues from all ten cards.

Even within their method of approach, Byrd and Witherspoon (1954) report discouraging reliability results. Card 2 was re-administered to 36 Ss, after a two to four week interval, to determine their choice of parent pulling the rope on the same side as the child figure. Only one-half of the Ss named the same parent on the second trial.

Kaake (1951), also working with the CAT, counted as identification those instances in which the subject named a figure as mother or father or appeared to identify himself with a character. On this basis, she found most identifications occurred on Cards 2, 4, 6, 8 and 10, although the percentage of identification responses to each card was not high. Kaake feels that these particular five cards elicit more identification since they are the most anthropomorphic, present situations from the child's life experiences, contain the most structure, and involve figures of various sizes thus suggesting family relationships. Yet Card 1 also contains a family eating situation with one larger figure; Card 3 shows a large and a small figure, and so on. Again, one can certainly question whether the mere naming of a figure is an adequate measure of identification.

In summary, reliance on the simple naming of parents as the major clue to identification does not seem adequate. Often the parent so named is the one who, in the child's experience, fulfills the particular role consistent with the activity depicted in the card, i.e., feeding, protecting, punishing. The combina-

tion of specific parent *and* role may bring us closer to some meaningful interpretation, particularly if these ascribed roles are fairly consistent throughout
the stories.

The guidelines for the assessment of identification to be presented here can
be viewed as stemming from a combination of psychoanalytic and learning
theories. In terms of the former, development of same-sex identification basically is considered to result from the oedipal situation in which the child loves
the parent of the opposite sex and wants to be like the powerful and rival same-
sex parent. Anna Freud's (1946) concept of "identification with the aggressor"
adds additional impetus to the identification process when the "aggressor" is
the parent of the same sex, while confusion in the ultimate identification can
result if the opposite-sex parent is consistently or severely punitive. Social-
learning theories (e.g., Parsons, 1955) assume that identification takes place
with the parent who provides the optimum balance between nurturance and
control. Role theory has been subjected to experimental verification by
Emmerich (1959) with nursery school Ss; Mussen and Distler (1959, 1960)
with kindergarten boys; and Mussen and Rutherford (1963) with first-grade
boys and girls. Here again, an extreme degree of punitive control from the
opposite-sex parent, especially if affection is also withheld, would seem to be
the most influential variable leading to confusion in sexual identification.

Let us suppose that a boy emphasizes the mother figures, in terms of their
affectional, nurturant qualities; this would suggest a masculine identification in
response to the oedipal attraction of the mother. The masculinity would be re-
inforced if fathers are also seen as powerful and at least moderately affectionate. Another boy, who sees mother figures as domineering and punitive and
fathers as passive, may be expressing a feminine trend. A girl who sees father
figures as kind and affectionate, and mothers more often as agents of punishment, would be demonstrating the establishment of a healthy feminine identification. In contrast, expressions of rejection by the father or of severe punishments repeatedly delivered at his hands, would indicate loosening of a girl's
feelings of worth and a tendency toward cross-sex identification.

The actual application of these principles, with respect to parent figures on
the CAT, leads to further complications, to be sure. For example, on Card 2
(tug-of-war) when a boy states that the baby bear is pulling with the mother,
is this because of inclinations toward feminine identification or is it an expression of masculine identification in the oedipal situation: either with the
desire to receive mother's affection and protection, or because of the opportunity to align himself with mother and against father? On the other hand,
would pairing of the child with the father indicate male identification or aggressive (contra-oedipal) feelings toward the mother? Of course, there are
times when the further elaboration of the story gives some clues to the affects
involved (as in the following example) but quite often any interpretation of
identification on this particular card becomes extremely subjective. The nine-
year-old boy whose story to Card 2 is given below was quite obsessively oriented and was regarded as a "sissy" by his peers.*

---

*For this child's complete protocol, see Chapter XI.

2. Looks like three bears
      having a tug-of-war.
A rope in their hands,
      on the end a knot on each side.
Looks like father bear and baby bear
      against the mother.
The rope's almost tearing.
Have black nose.
      Other one's eyes look like popped out, (single)
      Other bear's eyes look in the middle.
      Baby bear's eyes looking on the ground.
They're tugging hard
      on a hill.
(Q-win?) The two bears.
(Q) The two bears will go falling
      when she lets go of the rope.

Other cards give somewhat less difficulty. For example, on Card 10, a boy may see the spanking parent as the mother or the father, or he may see either parent as offering comfort and warmth. According to the theory under consideration, only the first instance (punishment by the mother) would suggest confusion in sex-role identification, while expecting punishment from the father or looking to either parent for nurturance would represent adequate identification and normal adjustment in this area.

In effect, we are suggesting that to decipher identification clues from child-parent situations involves not only the objective *naming* of the parent figure but also consideration of the *sex of the child* in relation to the *sex of the parent,* the *role-function* portrayed in the specific situation, and the *affects* attributed to each figure in the card.

A second major indication of identification is the sex ascribed by the subject to the child characters in his stories. Here we are probably on firmer ground when assessing identification patterns of boys as compared to girls. The rather general cultural stereotype of assigning masculine gender to figures whose sex is unclear has previously been pointed out by the author (Haworth and Rabin, 1960) when reviewing the normative studies on the IT Scale (Brown, 1956, 1957). In this test, children are asked to assign masculine or feminine activities and attributes to a supposedly neutral figure (IT). Throughout the age range studied, both boys and girls tended to ascribe masculine activities to the IT figure until the fifth grade, when girls' scores moved to the feminine end of the scale. When kindergarten children were asked to give a name to IT after the test, 85 per cent of boys assigned masculine names while only 45 per cent of girls gave feminine names. Brown has interpreted both these findings in terms of a masculine preference in girls of our culture, but the general inclination to assign masculine properties to ambiguous figures should be seriously considered.

A recent study by King and King (1964) has again questioned the validity of feminine identifications on verbal tests. They found both sexes attributed male sex to the usual dog in the Blacky Pictures and also to a supposedly more feminine series of pictures of cats. They interpret their findings in linguistic and cultural, rather than psychodynamic, terms and point out that there is a definite language dictum in our culture to use the masculine form when the sex is unspecified. They suggest caution when evaluating a response from females suggestive of cross-sex identification, while cross-sex references in males are patently in opposition to current cultural stereotypes. They go on to suggest the application of their findings to other projective tests and make these observations with respect to the CAT:

"The Children's Apperception Test contains a number of young ('child') animals with whom the child presumably identifies in telling stories. These young animals are essentially ambiguous with respect to sex. The writers would hold, then, that the responses of girls to the CAT would contain more so-called cross-sex identifications than would the boys' stories" (King and King, 1964, p. 298).

Thus, on the CAT, we might expect that girls will more readily speak of the animal characters as masculine, while it would be very unusual, and deviant, for boys to see the child characters as feminine. Regardless of origin, whether due to language usage or a basically confused sex-role identification in girls, the phenomenon itself suggests that the norm for girls is not as clear-cut as for boys. Consequently, when a girl speaks of characters as boys (or uses masculine pronouns) little light is thrown on her sex-role identification. But when a girl specifically gives a female sex to a character, this may be a rather definite indication of strong feminine (same-sex) leanings on her part. When a boy speaks of the characters as girls, this presupposes a shift away from the usually expected gender of the character, and represents an opposite-sex direction of sexual identification.

In summary, and to simplify identification questions with respect to child characters in the stories, it is suggested that attention be largely paid to any assignment of feminine qualities to the child characters, with opposite-sex identification implications when given by a boy and a definite same-sex identification when given by a girl.

One further point should be made in connection with the tendency for both boys and girls to see child characters as males. It seems wisest to interpret expressed attitudes and activities of parent figures in relation to the *actual* sex of the child subject, rather than in relation to the sex ascribed by the subject to the pictured child character. This is consistent with what is known about abstracting abilities at the age levels for which the CAT is designed. Children up to age nine or ten are still bound by the concrete and have difficulty assuming and consistently maintaining the role of another. It would seem presumptive, at best, to imagine that any but the most intelligent child could ascribe the opposite sex to a child character and then speak of the attitudes of that character to its perceived parents, or of activities of the parent toward the child, all the while keeping consistently oriented to the shift in gender. Rather, it seems more likely that the expressed attitudes toward parent figures will be a projection of the child's own attitudes to his specific parents and in relation to *his* and their respective sexes. These problems will be considered in more specific detail in a later section of this chapter.

INTERPRETIVE OUTLINES

Before discussing outlines that have been devised specifically for the CAT, mention will be made of several schemata which have been proposed for verbal projective techniques in general, or for certain tests, but which could readily be adapted for use with children's records.

Symonds (1948) presents an outline in his manual for the analysis of his Picture-Story Test devised for use with adolescents. Analysis of content includes responses relating to the hero, psychological forces (hostility, love, ambivalence, punishment, anxiety and defenses, etc.), relationships, interests and attitudes, and outcomes. Formal analysis takes into account test-taking attitudes, special comments by the S, story structure, emotional tone, language level and intra-individual consistency. Henry (1956) offers a comprehensive schema for individual case analysis organized around the following areas: mental approach, imaginative processes, family dynamics, inner adjustment, emotional reactivity, sexual adjustment, and behavioral approach. Fine (1955) has published a schema for use in evaluating verbal protocols based on scoring manifest content in three major categories: feelings (26 are listed), outcome (favorable, unfavorable, indeterminate) and interpersonal relationships. In the latter category, various combinations of "characters" are listed (such as mother-child, sibling-sibling) and three main types of interaction are checked: moving toward, moving against, and moving away from. Fine (1955) cautions against using the term "scoring system" for the analysis of projective material, and states: "What we really have is a shorthand extraction of meaningful data. Hence the scoring system, while quite useful never tells the whole story, nor can it be expected to. Rather, it is to be looked upon first as a means of high-lighting important information, and second as a framework for more detailed analysis" (p. 308).

The Transcendence Index was devised by Weisskopf (1950) and has been used by her in CAT studies (Weisskopf-Joelson and Lynn, 1953; Weisskopf-Joelson and Foster, 1962) as well as in TAT analyses for which it was originally devised. It has also been used by several other investigators in CAT studies reported in earlier chapters of this volume (Armstrong, 1954; Budoff, 1960). In essence, the Index consists of counting the number of comments which go beyond pure description, and statements which are independent of what is actually shown in the picture. It is, in effect, a measure of productivity and includes such statements as descriptions of emotions or thoughts of the characters, events which occurred before or after the scene shown, relationships between figures, direct quotations of what the characters are saying, and subjective evaluative statements about the figures in the picture or about the picture as a whole.

Bellak's TAT and CAT Blank (Short Form)

Bellak (1955) has published an analysis sheet for use with the CAT (and the TAT) which includes consideration of each of ten variables when evaluating each story. A final summary analysis can then be readily pulled together after inspection of each variable across all ten stories. The use of the blank, each of the variables and their final summation have been described as follows: *

One of the main purposes of the Blank is to permit a safe transition from concrete primary data to summary of inference and final diagnosis, with a minimal danger of contamination by the interpreter's personality. The nature of the hypothetical inferences and the detailed process of the formation of the diagnosis are reported elsewhere (Bellak, 1954).

Each story should be scrutinized with the help of the ten major categories listed in the blank, and the essential data recorded in the relevant box. The major categories and the details listed under them are used primarily as a frame of reference, a reminder to look for certain aspects. Naturally, not all aspects will be presented in every story, in which case, of course, the boxes are simply left empty. Also, occasionally, facets not mentioned in the Blank will occur and need recording.

The Main Theme

We are interested in what a child makes of the pictures and *why* he gives this particular story. Rather than judge by one story, we will be on safer interpretive ground if we can find a common denominator or trend in a number of stories. That is, if the main hero of several stories is hungry, and resorts to stealing in order to satisfy himself, it is not unreasonable to conclude that this child is preoccupied with thoughts of not getting enough—food literally, or gratification generally—and in his fantasy wishes to take it away from others. We can speak of the theme of a story or of several stories, and the theme may be more or less complex. Also, a story may have more than one theme, all of which may be complexly interrelated. In children of three and four the theme is usually very simple.

The Main Hero

A basic assumption in our reasoning thus far is that the story which our subject tells is, in essence, a reflection of himself. Since there can be a number of people in a story, it becomes necessary to state that we can speak of the hero as that figure with which our subject mainly identifies himself. We will have to specify some objective criteria for differentiating the hero from other figures. The hero is the figure about whom the story is primarily woven. He resembles the subject most in age and sex, and it is from his standpoint that the events are seen. While these statements hold true most of the time, they do not always. There may be more than one hero, and our subject may identify with both, or first with one and then with another. There may be a deviation in that a subject may identify with a hero of a different sex; it is important to note such identifications. Sometimes an identification figure secondary in importance may represent more deeply repressed unconscious attitudes of the subject. Probably the interests, wishes, deficiencies, gifts and abilities with which the hero is invested are those which the subject possesses, or wishes or fears that he might have. We will want to establish which of these is the most probable. It will be important to observe the adequacy of the

---

*From Bellak, L. and Adelman, Crusa: The Children's Apperception Test (CAT). *In* A. I. Rabin and Mary R. Haworth (Eds.): *Projective Techniques with Children.* New York: Grune & Stratton, 1960, pp. 62–94. Pages 69–75 reproduced by permission of the senior author and the publisher.

hero—the ability to deal with circumstances in a way considered adequate by the society to which he belongs. The adequacy of the hero serves as the best single measure of ego strength, or, in many ways, of the subject's own adequacy. An exception is, of course, the case of the story which is a blatant compensatory wish fulfillment. Careful scrutiny will show the real inadequacy, in such cases.

Self Image. By self image we mean the conception which the subject has of his body and of his entire self and social role. Schilder first described body image as the picture of one's own body in one's mind. The separation of the self from the outside world, and from the mother particularly, takes place slowly. Federn particularly contributed valuable ideas with his concept of ego boundaries and its defects in psychoses. The self image has found little systematic discussion so far, except for the concept of "role playing." Nevertheless it is most important, and may be revealed in the CAT, e.g., by the hero thinking of himself as dangerous, dirty, defective, etc.

Main Needs of the Hero

Behavioral Needs of the Hero (as in the Story). The story behavior of the hero may have one of a variety of relationships to the storyteller. The needs expressed may correspond directly to the needs of the child. These needs may be, at least in part, expressed behaviorally in real life, or they may be the direct opposite of real life expression and constitute the fantasy complement. In other words, very aggressive stories may be told sometimes by a very aggressive child, or by a rather meek, passive-aggressive one, who has fantasies of aggression. At least to a certain extent the needs of the hero may not reflect so much the needs of the storyteller as they do the drive quality which the child perceives in other people. He may be describing the aggression feared from various objects, or referring to idealized expectations, such as brilliance and fortitude, ascribed to significant figures in his life and only in part internalized in himself. In short, the behavioral needs of the hero expressed in the story have to be examined and understood in the light of all the varieties and vicissitudes of drive modification as subsumed under the broader concepts of projection or apperceptive distortion.

It is the difficult task of the interpreter to determine to what extent the manifest needs of the hero correspond to various constituents of the storyteller's personality and what the relationship is to the narrator's manifest behavior. It is here that comparison with the actual clinical history is most useful and entirely appropriate under clinical circumstances (as distinct from a research setting). If a child is reported to be particularly shy, passive and withdrawn and the CAT stories overflow with aggression, the compensatory nature of the fantasy material is obvious. Of course, it must remain a goal of psychological science to develop further criteria which will make for increasingly valid predictions from the fantasy material to behavior. The study of ego functions is particularly useful in this respect. The relationship of drives expressed to their vicissitudes within the story may often serve as one clue; that is, if the sequence of the story shows an initial response with aggression which becomes entirely controlled by the end of the story, the chances are that this is a person who does not translate the fantasy or latent need into reality. There are other criteria helpful in attempting predictions about what one might call "acting-out." The high degree of detail and realism in the description of needs may suggest the likelihood of the expression in reality. Vaguely structured needs of the hero are less likely to be related to reality.

Figures, Objects or Circumstances Introduced. A subject who introduces weapons of some type or another in a number of stories (even without using them) or frequently refers to food (even without its being eaten) may be tentatively judged, on such evidence, as having a need for aggression or oral gratification, respectively. Similarly, the introduction of such figures as punisher, pursuer or benefactor, or such circumstances as injustice or deprivation may be similarly interpreted but with due regard to the rest of the record.

Figures, Objects or Circumstances Omitted. If a subject omits references to objects, one may wish to infer a repressive operation. Of course, this level of inference can only be a tentative one until we have a large enough sample of norms, so that expectations regarding objects and themes introduced and/or omitted are possible.

Conception of the Environment

This concept is, of course, a complex mixture of unconscious self perception and apperceptive distortion of stimuli by memory images of the past. The more consistent a picture of the environment appears in the CAT stories, the more reason we have to consider it an important constituent of our subject's personality and a useful clue to his reactions in everyday life. Usually, two or three descriptive terms will suffice, such as succorant, hostile, exploiting or exploitable, friendly, dangerous.

Figures are Seen As . . .

Here we are interested in the way the child sees the figures around him and how he reacts to them. We know something about the quality of object relationships—symbiotic, anaclitic, oral-dependent, ambivalent, etc., at different stages of development and in different personalities. However, in a broader scheme we may descriptively speak of supportive, competitive and other relationships.

Significant Conflicts

We not only want to know the nature of the conflicts but also the defenses which the child uses against anxiety engendered by these conflicts. Here we have an excellent opportunity to study early character formation, and we may be able to derive ideas concerning prognosis.

There are those conflicts which all children experience as they grow from one phase into the next, each phase being characterized more or less by its concomitant conflict. For example, beginning at about age three, we ought not to be alarmed to find evidence of the oedipal struggle and defenses against the fantasied relationship. Also, we begin to see the seesaw of little-big, child-adult—the preparation for mastery and the frustrations because of lack of skill and mature intelligence.

Nature of Anxieties

The importance of determining the main anxieties of a child hardly needs emphasizing. Anxieties related to physical harm, punishment and the fear of lacking or losing love (disapproval) and of being deserted (loneliness, lack of support) are probably the most important. The CAT may give us excellent clues regarding puzzling manifest behavior, resulting from unconscious wishes and defenses against them.

The nature of anxiety, as with all these variables, is to be viewed in terms of age-appropriateness. This frame of reference is particularly relevant to this factor or phase, since the kind of anxiety a child is beset with tells us about the level of psychosexual development, diagnosis and prognosis. If we see a young latency child whose CAT stories reflect anxiety about his body, his helplessness, or who is still concerned with the loss of the pre-oedipal love object and desertion, we would expect many other indices of pathology, and perhaps do a careful analysis of the formal features of the CAT as well as his intelligence test. Now, if another six or seven year old gave evidence of anxiety associated with superego authority and tried to work it out in a story which stressed rules and programs, we would certainly want to pursue this, but it would be at least the kind of anxiety many children of this age experience, as part of their development.

Main Defenses

Stories should not be studied exclusively for drive content, but should, in addition, be examined for the defenses against anxieties and drives. Such a study of defenses may offer more information, in that the drives themselves may appear less clearly than the defenses against them. Also, the defensive structure may be more closely related to manifest behavior. By means of studying drives and defenses the CAT often permits an appraisal of the character structure of the subject.

Aside from a search for the main defense mechanisms, it is also valuable to study the molar aspects of the stories. For instance, some children choose obsessive defenses against a picture's disturbing content; they may produce four or five themes, each very short and descriptive, manifestly different but dynamically similar. Such a succession shows the attempt to deal with a disturbing conflict; successive stories may become more and more innocuous, showing an increase in defensive operation.

The concept of defense has to be understood in an increasingly broader sense, as has been discussed recently by Lois Murphy and her associates in connection with coping (i.e., the person's general ability and mode of meeting external and internal stimuli). With the advance in ego psychology and a focus on problems of adaptation, a study of these broad defense functions is likely to play a dominant role in the exploration of projective methods. We not only want to know the nature of the defensive maneuvers but also the success with which they are employed and (or rather) the sacrifice such maneuvers demand from the functioning personality.

The concept of perceptual vigilance may be thought of in connection with projective methods. Various studies have suggested that not only the defensive projective function of the ego is increased in stress but also its cognitive acuity may be improved at the same time.

In the study of children's stories, it must be remembered that we view the nature of pathogenicity of defenses and other structural concepts in terms of age-appropriateness. What may be quite normal at one age may be pathologic at another age. In the absence of normative data some very rough, empirical guidelines must be considered.

Severity of Superego

The relationship of the chosen punishment to the nature of the offense gives us an insight into the severity of the superego. A delinquent's hero who murders may receive no punishment other than a slight suggestion that he may have learned a lesson for later life, while a neurotic may have stories in which the hero is accidentally or intentionally killed or mangled or dies of illness following the slightest infraction or expression of aggression. On the other hand, a nonintegrated superego, sometimes too severe and sometimes too lenient, is also frequently met in neurotics. A formulation as to the circumstances under which a child's superego can be expected to be too severe, and under what other conditions it is likely to be too lenient is, of course, not only related to the difficult problem of "acting-out" but, in general, a valuable piece of information.

Integration of the Ego

This variable in its many aspects tells us about the general level of functioning; to what extent the child is able to compromise between drives and the demands of reality, on the one hand, and the commands of his superego, on the other. The adequacy of the hero in dealing with the problems the storyteller confronted him with in the CAT is an important aspect of this variable.

We are interested also in how the stories are given and must remember that ego functioning must be considered in terms of the child's age. Is the subject able to tell age-appropriate stories, which constitute a certain amount of cognizance of the stimulus, or does he leave the stimulus completely and tell a story with no manifest relation to the picture because he is too preoccupied with his own problems? Does he find rescue and salvation from the anxiety pertaining to the test by giving very stereotyped responses, or is he psychologically healthy enough and intelligent enough to be creative and give more or less original stories? Having produced a plot, can he attain a solution of the conflict in the story which is adequate and realistic, or do his thought processes become unstructured or even bizarre under the impact of the problem? Does he have the ability to go from a past background of the story to a future resolution? How does the child meet the requirements of the task he is confronted with?

These observations, together with the content variables, permit an appraisal of the subject's ego strength, thus facilitating possible classification of the patient in one of the nosologic categories.

For practical purposes a separate consideration of a variety of ego functions such as drive control, frustration tolerance, anxiety tolerance, perceptual and motor adequacy and others may be considered.

The Summary and Final Report

After all the stories have been analyzed, the main data obtained from each should be noted down in the appropriate space on page 4 of the Blank. When the summary page is studied, a repetitive pattern in the subject's responses ordinarily becomes clear.

This final report can be written in full view of the summary page. It is suggested that the form of the final report follow the sequence of the ten categories on the analysis sheet. The main themes, the second and third variables, permit a description of the *psychic structure and unconscious needs of the subject,* while the fourth and fifth variables show us his *conception of the world and significant figures* around him. Categories six, seven, eight, nine and ten may actually be used as headings for statements concerning the respective dimensions of personality.

The form of the final report will depend, of course, to a great extent on the person for whom it is intended. It is, however, strongly advised that empty phrases and erroneous inferences be avoided by the following procedures: The first half of the report may consist of general abstract statements; a second part of the report should then consist of specific documentation by excerpts from stories, from which the main abstract statements have been derived.

This arrangement is particularly useful in instances in which the psychologist reports as part of a team to psychiatrists and to social workers who may not have the time or the experience to read the stories themselves and for whom an abstracted statement will not be sufficiently meaningful.

If a diagnosis must be offered, we suggest that the following formulation be used: "The data represented in the CAT are *consistent with* the diagnosis of. . . ." This expresses our belief that the CAT is not primarily a diagnostic test and also, that preferably no diagnosis should ever be made on the basis of a single test or even any number of tests alone without integration with clinical data.

To illustrate the use of the Blank, Bellak and Adelman (1960) have presented a protocol along with complete scoring of the record blank (see Fig. 8.1).*

JAMES L.

Descriptive Data

Male, age seven years nine months, third grade, IQ 123, one sibling (brother, ten years old). The first-year teacher reported that James was overactive, had to be watched, and did not get along well with other children, since he fought a great deal. He told fantastic stories, e.g., brought in a toy and claimed his father had made it. The teacher later investigated this story and found it to be untrue. If someone said he had something, James boasted that he had two of the same thing. He constantly destroyed other children's creative play.

James' present teacher reports that his aggressive tendencies are not apparent now, but that the boy is not making use of his high IQ. He is retarded in all subjects. She has to prod him constantly to complete a job.

Not too much is known about the parents. His mother has a strong drive for social acceptance and always appears at school functions very beautifully dressed, though his family is not well off financially. It took about two years to find out that the father was a chauffeur. Mother always side-stepped this question. The boy, too, must have been affected because his father often took on any occupation (in James' fantasy) that suited the moment; for example, if the children were playing with airplanes, his father was a pilot, etc. They lived in three very small rooms with not much space for the children to play in. His parents had very little home life together because of his father's irregular hours, and there were many arguments at home because the boys were noisy when father was sleeping, etc. Because of irregular hours, the father did not have time to spend with his two boys. Mother, however, spent a lot of time with them trying to "uplift" them. When called in to school because of her child's behavior, she refused to admit that there was any problem. She blamed it on the school in general and on the teacher in particular. She had been ill for some time, possibly with rheumatic fever and anemia. There had been some rivalry between the two boys. Mother described the brother as being "slower."

---

*From Bellak, L. and Adelman, Crusa: The Children's Apperception Test (CAT). *In* A. I. Rabin and Mary R. Haworth (Eds.): *Projective Techniques with Children.* New York: Grune & Stratton, 1960, pp. 62–94. Pages 75–81 reproduced by permission of the senior author and the publisher.

Figure 8.1. Analysis Blank for case of James L.: see reproduction of 5-page form following.

SHORT FORM
BELLAK T A T and C A T BLANK
For Recording and Analyzing Thematic Apperception Test and Children's Apperception Test

Name_____James L.___________________________________Sex__M____Age__7-9__Date__May, 1959_______

Education____Third Grade______________________Occupation___Student_______________; m. (s.) w. d.
(circle one)

Referred by___________________________________Analysis by___________________________________

After having obtained the stories analyze each story by using the variables on the left of Page 2. Not every story will furnish information regarding each variable: the variables are presented as a frame of reference to help avoid overlooking some dimension.

When all ten stories have been analyzed it is easy to check each variable from left to right for all ten stories and record an integrated summary on Page 4 under the appropriate headings. That way a final picture is obtained almost immediately.

Then, keeping Page 4 folded out, the Final Report: Diagnostic Impressions and Recommendations can be written on Page 1 by reference to Page 4. Page 5 gives available space for any other notations. The stories then can be stapled inside the blank against Page 5. For further instructions see Manual for TAT Interpretation, Psychological Corporation, by Leopold Bellak or Manual for the CAT, C.P.S. Company, or *The TAT and CAT in Clinical Use*, pp. 282, Grune and Stratton, 1954, N. Y. C. by Leopold Bellak;

FINAL REPORT: Diagnostic Impressions and Recommendations

This boy shows a great deal of conflict with parental authority, particularly with mother. He feels coerced, aggressed-against and thus, feeling small, reacts with acting-out of aggression, denial of helplessness, and by making himself more important and stronger than reasonable, e.g., in story #1, 4, and 10.

There is some mild normal competitiveness with father in #2; in #7 it is accentuated with some question about the primal scene in which it may be the father indeed who comes to harm.

There is a suggestion of really felt and imagined superiority over the older brother, maybe over father, in story #3.

This boy is of superior intelligence which he uses both for self-inflation, by lying and showing off, but also constructively. His ego functioning is within neurotic limits; together with a rather unintegrated superego, his personality is consistent with a behavior disorder characterized by aggression and lying. His stories are usually well constructed, rather realistic, show good perceptual functioning and an absence of a thought disorder with an ability to be inventive and original.

	Story No. 1	Story No. 2
1. Main Theme: (diagnostic level: if descriptive and interpretative level are desired, use a scratch sheet or page 5)	Resists authority by (teasing) deception, expects punishment	Competitiveness with father, realizes own weakness, aggression against the father
2. Main hero: age____ sex____ vocation____ abilities____________ interests____ traits____ body image____________ adequacy ($\sqrt{}$,$\sqrt{}\sqrt{}$,$\sqrt{}\sqrt{}\sqrt{}$) and/or self-image____________	deceptive, resistant	Adequate but small
3. Main needs of hero: a) behavioral needs of hero (as in story): ____________	to resist, to deceive	competitive, aggressive
b) figures, objects, or circumstances *introduced*: ____________ implying need for or to: ____________	crowing, fence, showing off, suggesting need for exhibition	good perception
c) figures, objects or circumstances *omitted*: ____________ implying need for or to: ____________	reference to other chickens is omitted in this story	
4. Conception of environment (world) as: ____________	?	
5. a) Parental figures (m$\checkmark$___, f___) are seen as ____________ and subject's reaction to a is ____________ b) Contemp. figures (m___, f___) are seen as ____________ and subject's reaction to b is ____________ c) Junior figures (m___, f___) are seen as ____________ and subject's reaction to c is ____________	Father (?) seen as directive, hero reacts with evasiveness, non-compliance, and is punished Feels small	Father seen as competitor wants to be big
6. Significant conflicts: ____________	between need for resistance and compliance	wish to defeat father. Awareness of own smallness
7. Nature of anxieties: ($\sqrt{}$) of physical harm and/or punishment ____________ of disapproval ____________ of lack or loss of love ____________ of illness or injury ____________ of being deserted ____________ of deprivation ____________ of being overpowered and helpless ____________ of being devoured ____________ other ____________	fear of punishment	Fear of physical harm
8. Main defenses against conflicts and fears: ($\sqrt{}$) repression____________ reaction-formation____________ regression____________ denial____________ introjection____________ isolation____________ undoing____________ rationalization ____________ other____________	lying, showing off	Rationalization: Father would have fallen too: not so strong
9. Severity of superego as manifested by: ($\sqrt{}$) punishment for "crime":____________ immediate____________ just____________ too severe____________ delayed____________ unjust____________ too lenient____________ delayed initial response or pauses,____________ stammer____________	slightly delayed, not severe superego	
10. Integration of the ego, manifesting itself in: ($\sqrt{}$,$\sqrt{}\sqrt{}$,$\sqrt{}\sqrt{}\sqrt{}$) Hero: adequate____________ inadequate____________ outcome: happy____________ unhappy____________ realistic____________ unrealistic____________ drive control____________ thought processes as revealed by plot being: ( ) stereotyped____________ original____________ appropriate____________ complete____________ incomplete____________ inappropriate____________ ( ) syncretic____________ concrete____________ contaminated____________ Intelligence____________ Maturational level____________	fantasy adequate; outcome is realistic appropriate	good ego appropriate

5. One time there was the house of the four little bears. Two baby bears slept in the cradle and two slept in the bed but when the baby bears were asleep the mother bear and the father bear woke up. They put on their clothes and went out to fish. They caught five fish and ate four, but while they were eating, there was a knock on the door and Father bear answered, but there was no one there. The knock kept coming and father bear got so angry that he fell down and sighed and when he was sighing sawdust came in his eyes. He went up on the rooftop and saw by his surprise Woody the woodpecker pecking very hard.

(Inquiry: Who was knocking?; first response) A little girl. (Then changed to) The woodpecker. (He put the card aside and said that was the end and so I didn't question further.)

6. This is some more bears, huh? Three bears were sleeping in a cave of their own, but when they were sleeping a dog came into their home. (Points to dark shadow on the right side of the card and says that is the dog.) The dog took all the bones the bears had taken from him. Then the dog dug a hole in the bear's home and buried them there so nobody would find them and when the bears go out for a walk in the woods, they leave baby bear sleeping so I can pounce on him. Then I can get my bones at last and bring them home and bury them in the grass. Then, my master will be pleased to see me and I'll drag home the bear (baby bear) by his tail. Then, the master will give me one more bone.

7. One day the lion was after the monk because the monk knew how to jump so the lion wanted to know how to jump so he wanted to get the monk to teach him how to jump and—three more, right? And the monk refused to teach the lion how to jump. Then the monkey got away and was ready to spring on a vine, but the lion came after him and missed him and fell on his nose. Then, he got angry and said to himself: "I'll get him on the other end and catch him with my mouth." He did that, but the idea didn't work, he got so angry that his throat began to hurt. Then he went home to his folks back home and said what happened so they all went out to the monk and then all the monks were up in the trees and when the lions came by, they took their sticks and banged the lions over the head. And then the monks said to the group, "There's not gonna be no more lions for us to fool with." Then all the monkeys went on the vine and waited till the natives came by. They took their clubs and walked right by with some of their stuff on their heads. Then the king lion came out and nearly got the monkey's tail but the monkey was fast and got away and the lion jumped right down into the middle of the natives and they said, "If you don't leave the monkey alone, we'll cut off your tail and use it for a sweeping brush." But the lion didn't agree and really went after the monkey, but before he got far, the natives cut off his tail and that was the end of the ferocious lion.

8. One day at a tea party, four monkeys sat—a grandfather with one child, with earrings on his ears like the natives. A mother monkey behind him drinking tea and the father monkey too, and they were having a chatter and laughing at the baby monkey because he looked so funny—then after a while you could see a round picture of grandma monkey with her night cap on and glasses, and she almost looked like the grandma at her house and the man monkey said to the chimp: "How old are you?," so the chimp said: "First let me count on my fingers, let me see now, 1, 2, 3, 4, 5, 6, 7, 8 years old." That's all. (James would not go on with this story.)

Inquiry: Why did the baby monkey look funny?) Because he was laughing and he had his feet up.

CAT Stories

1. The rooster's gonna say, "Get some porridge from the big pot," and the chickens don't want to do it; so the chickens say to the rooster: "Go away on the fence and crow and we'll be eating our porridge." Then, the rooster comes back from crowing on the fence and the chickens didn't eat their porridge. So the rooster says: "Hurry up and eat your porridge. We're going to get some worms." And the chickies say again, "Go out on the fence and crow." (Inquiry: What will happen?) They're not gonna eat their porridge. (Inquiry: What will happen to the chicks?) They're gonna get spanked.

2. These three bears went up on the mountain with a piece of rope and the father bear wanted to see if he was the strongest between the mother and the baby, and the mother and the baby was the strongest. And baby bear was helping his mama to pull rope but the baby bear could not pull it so hard as the mama bear and the baby bear nearly fell off the mountain. If mama bear hadn't been standing up straight father bear would have fallen off the mountain too. That's a tug-of-war.

(Inquiry: What will father do?) He fell down and banged his head on a rock.

3. One time there was the King Lion named King Richard—my brother's name is Richard. He thinks he was named after King Richard—and the little mouse's name was Peepsqueak. That's what they call Jimmy (a friend) and that's what I call a mouse. "Twas the night before Christmas when all through the house not a creature was stirring but only a mouse." And Peepsqueak was the little mouse who got on King Richard's nerves so he (King R.) called a doctor to get his nerve off. And then sitting on this throne, he laughed and said, "I think I'll smoke my pipe at last." And taking his cane and pushing his throne, he moved right near the mouse's home. Then he sat waiting for the doctor to come, but the funniest thing was the doctor didn't come at all. After the mouse came out of his house, he had a little hammer and he banged on King Richard's head and that's the end.

(Inquiry: What did the mouse do that got on King Richard's nerves?) He kept on banging him on the head. (Why didn't the doctor come?) He was afraid that the lion would eat him up if he didn't cure him. (What happens to the mouse?) The lion doesn't fool around with him any more. He's afraid of him.

4. One day Mother Kangaroo and Baby Kangaroo went for a picnic. Mother Kangaroo hopped. Baby Kangaroo went on his bicycle and the baby in mother's pouch had a balloon and Mother Kangaroo bursted the balloon and she (baby in pouch) made the milk bottle tip over and spill and Mother Kangaroo's sandwiches flew. One landed on a Christmas tree top and one landed in her face and the third one on her Sunday hat. Then, they went down the hill and got ready to leave but the little baby (in the pouch) tripped her feet and she fell down and threw the basket up and all the basket dumped over and spilled. Then, the little baby on the tricycle hit a rock and bumped his bill—I mean, nose. Then he got up and having nothing to eat, he stuck his nose in a bee hive and smelled something good to eat. Just when he was reaching his little paw in, a bee came out and stinged him right on the ear and all that time the little Kangaroo (on the tricycle) spent, his mother was back home getting on her new dress and then at the end, at night time, the little Kangaroo hopped to his feet and rides the tricycle home.

(Inquiry: How did the balloon break?) Mother stepped on it. (Is the little baby on the tricycle a he or a she?) He. (What happened when everything spilled?) Mother picked him up and went home but the baby on the bicycle got left there. (What happened when he got home?) Mother spanked him.

ADDITIONAL NOTES

1) If told to do something, resists by teasing, deceptive bargaining, (repeatedly) and expects punishment. Crowing on the fence: exhibitionism here; (is a liar). The need to show off is ascribed to mother but probably holds true for narrator: Displacement of projection from hero to secondary figure in a story usually involves particularly ego-alien unacceptable drives and is called object need (O.n.) by Henry Murray.

2) Sequence: how big is father
             I am small
             I could fall too (if in need of help!)

The test report itself should usually not be confounded by relating the test materials to the interview data. However, in an additional note, it is appropriate to point out that this boy's pathology results probably to a considerable extent from mother's pretentious need to ''push'' and insist on a higher socio-economic status than the family has. She also probably encourages denial as a defense, and wishful thinking in the boy. Mother's self-centeredness and interest in being well dressed incidentally appears in the kangaroo story where she simply goes home and is concerned with dressing while the little kangaroo has its adventure with the bees, etc.

Story No. 3	Story No. 4	Story No. 5	Story No. 6	Story No. 7	Story No. 8	Story No. 9	Story No. 10	SUMMARY
Aggression against older brother	Aggression between mother and child; guilt, specifically Re: need for acquisition, mother seen as self-centered, interested in clothes	Curiosity; feels parents are eating at night. There are some noises when children are sleeping. Having to do when father being hungry, falling over.	Night time fears of being robbed and carried off	The little one is superior to the big one, the big one is angry. (Father, Brother) Big one loses, is castrated	The small one is Fanny and shows off, by being able to count.	Is there or is there not a Santa Claus. Wants tools of aggression	Aggressive, antagonistic to mother	**1-3. Unconscious structure and drives of subject (based on variable 1-3)** Is repeatedly concerned with conflict with authority—mother particularly—though also competitive and aggressive in relation to brother and father. He often feels small, aggressed against, and dominated. He meets these pressures with aggression, open antagonism/or teasing, showing off and self-inflation.
Though small, powerful and aggressive; introduced as doctor, nerves and hammer	Aggressive, orally inquisitive		Dog? Baby bear acquisitive, helpless	capable powerful	Hero is eight years old and can count	Tools, guns	Fearful, aggressive and compliant	
	aggressive		dogs, bones, master	aggression, counteraction		to get gifts tests reality	Black jack, pin	
Sees the bigger one as helpless and ill	orality, fear of aggression	eating, knocking, falling down, sawdust in eyes. Relates to fantasies about eating and noise and mishaps in relation to primary scene.	acquisition, aggression, approbation	pain in throat* peers		Hammer, gun, Santa Claus, parents	fear of aggression Need for aggression	
Implies need for self-aggrandizement				is experienced with anger, need to be big, powerful		need for reality testing, oral aggression		
	tooth for tooth	unknown things go on all the time	tooth for tooth	aggressive				**4. Conception of world:** eye for eye, tooth for tooth
Mother seen as helper —brother seen as helpless though bigger	mother is aggressive, punitive, self-centered	seen as secretive, sharing a meal		inferior, demanding, aggression	chattering, interested in child	deceptive, giving	aggressive, hurting, feeling	**5. Relationship to others:** as described in 1-3
							reactive aggression, compliance	
					?			
	aggression and guilt		aggression and acquisition—fear of it			fantasy, reality	aggression, compliance	**6. Significant conflicts:** How to meet aggression: with counter aggression, guilt occasional compliance. Meets feeling of smallness and passivity and need for counter action by wishful thinking.
			desertion approbation helplessness— devoured?	fear of being hurt (castrated)			fear of punishment, physical harm	**7. Nature of anxieties:**
Denial projection doctor is afraid	counter action; acting out, aggression	confabulation	counteraction	aggression, acting-out	performing: exhibits	denial	fantasy of power	**8. Main defenses used:** showing off, fantasy, (lying), denial, aggressive acting-out
Too lenient, unrealistic outcome, original	has a quick interaction, some punishment. Superego not integrated.		some primitivity: eye for eye non-integrated super-ego	little severity of super ego		?	uneven, black jack is sorry; unintegrated— superego	**9. Superego structure:** unintegrated superego: in many ways too weak for appropriate control, and the again primitively retaliatory, probably more so than appropriate for his age.
	good	good		unrealistic outcome		?	unrealistic powerful	**10. Integration and strength of ego:** good intelligence, inventive, perceptive and with a good structure of thought processes. Except where they are in the service of making himself bigger, then it leads to acting out and fancyful and wishful distortions.
			*The realistic detail suggests that he actually may at times experience pain in throat associated with anger.					

9. One day the baby bunny saw a big creature coming in the door, but he didn't know what kind it was and he looked at the person and it looked like Santa Claus but it wasn't Santa Claus, it was only his mother dressed up like Santa Claus. Then, he (S. C.) said: "Go to sleep or you won't get any presents." Then, after his mother dressed up like Santa Claus, she went out of the room and when he was asleep Santa Claus came in, but the baby was still awake and Santa Claus said, "Were you a good boy?" and the little bunny said: "Yes" and Santa Claus said, "What do you want?" and the bunny said: "I want a hammer and a pair of guns and a stuffed bunny just like me." So Santa Claus gave him all his presents and went into the other room with the presents. Then, at the last step, when at the head, he saw mother and daddy asleep at the head. Then, one reindeer clapped his feet and Santa Claus said "Whoa Rudolf! Rudolf! Rudolf! Stop, I'll be up there fast!"

10. One day the mother dog was washing her pup so always from now the pup didn't want to get washed. He didn't like to get washed because one day his mother scratched him like with a pen and he thought that every day mother would scratch him and he would get hurt. So every time his mother tried to wash him he ran away into the bathroom and taking the broom—the towel—he thought he could bang his mother over the head, but then he thought that wouldn't work so he took two socks and one shirt and said that the socks would be just the thing that would work. So he put one sock into the other and used it for a blackjack and hit his mother, but he didn't get away with it. He got washed that day and said: "Mother, I'm sorry I hit you and now I like to be washed every day."

Lantzourakis* and Gästrin, in Stockholm, have developed a modification of Bellak's Analysis Sheet for use in evaluating CAT protocols. Their schedule is reproduced in Figure 8.2 in Swedish, with their English translations and explanations entered beneath each heading.

They have replaced Bellak's use of "Theme" with "Picture Motive" to indicate the chief interpretive or symbolic content of the story. The heading of "Theme" is then reserved for recurrent stories, picture motives, symbols or actions.

Haworth's Analysis of Adaptive Mechanisms in CAT Responses

This schedule was developed by Haworth (1963, 1965) for use exclusively with the CAT in order to aid in the delineation of defense mechanisms and identification assessment. It is meant primarily to serve as a basis for qualitative evaluation of the stories, but it is also possible to arrive at rough quantitative "scores" for making comparisons between subjects and groups. The schedule provides a quick summary of the number and kinds of defenses employed as well as the content of items frequently used. The categories are arranged as nearly as possible on a continuum from measures indicating a high degree of control and constriction to indicators of disorganization and loosening of reality ties. In individual qualitative assessment, the total number of responses within a category and their distribution among the various subitems provide a meaningful summary picture when making personality evaluations. However, for

---

*Personal communication from Ann Lantzourakis, Stockholm, Sweden.

Figure 8.2. CAT-TAT Analysis Sheet. Ann Lantzourakis and Jan Gastrin

Tavla ar Picture number	*Bildmotiv* Picture motive (chief content)	*Utgång* Outcome (happy, realistic, etc.	*Hero* Hero (Identification figure)	*Utelämnat* (−) *Infört* (+) Omitted (−) Introduced (+)	*Affekt och relationer mellan fig.* Feelings and kind of relations between figures	*Sättatt berätta* Way of telling (story tone, choice of words, fluency, etc.)	*Teman* Themes (recurrent)	*Sekvena-analys* Sequence analysis (see Klopfer, et al., *Developments in the Rorschach Technique,* Chapter 11, "Sequence analysis")	*Prel. tolkning* Preliminary interpretation

research purposes, the quantitative measure used consists of the *number of categories* receiving "critical scores." The latter are determined by comparing the number of responses checked under each category with a pre-established cut-off point for that category. If the number of responses exceeds the cut-off point, a "critical score" is assigned to that category. Thus the highest number of critical scores would be ten, one for each category. Experimental data reported by Haworth (1963) suggest that five or more critical scores would indicate some degree of emotional disturbance, while an extremely high number (eight to ten) would indicate that the child is frantically employing many different mechanisms to bind his anxiety and that none of them are working effectively.

A sample schedule* is shown (Fig. 8.3) with the protocol of Bellak's illustrative case rescored according to this schema. (Scoring directions follow the scale itself.)

Both Bellak's and Haworth's analyses indicate considerable disturbance in this child. He scores high in seven of the ten Haworth categories with a high degree of projection and use of neurotic symbolization, as well as regressive, acting-out tendencies in opposition to parents especially. There is very little repression or indication of phobic elements. It is noteworthy that, despite so many high scores, he shows no evidence of lack of reality awareness or weakening of controls.

This same schedule has been used in a study of school children's responses to the CAT and Rorschach (Haworth, 1962); in a further comparison of those school Ss with a clinic sample (Haworth, 1963); in a comparison of animal and human forms of the CAT with school Ss (Lawton, unpublished) and in a study of clinic Ss' reactions to the animal and human sets (Haworth, unpublished).

Inter-rater scoring reliability for the schedule was found to be .88 in one study (Haworth, 1963) and 80 per cent interjudge agreement was found in a subsequent study (Lawton, unpublished). Intrascorer reliability after an interval of one year was .96 (Haworth, 1963).

A brief discussion of each of the ten categories is given with examples from children's protocols to illustrate the scoring procedures. It should be emphasized that the schedule is seen as a framework for organizing and summarizing the themes of an individual child; consequently, in clinical use, the examiner should feel free to add items that may reflect dynamics similar to those listed under any category.

A. Reaction-Formation. This category, along with the two following ones, consistently yields high scores to children with obsessive trends, although other diagnostic groups may also score high in one or another of these three areas. The following example of item A.1 (exaggerated goodness) was given by a girl:

---

*The schedule was first published in the *Journal of Projective Techniques* 27: 181–184, 1963. Pages 182–183 are reproduced with the permission of the editor.

8. They are having coffee and talking.
(Q)About how nice it is
   now that the snow is gone.
She's telling him
   to be sure to wear his rubbers,
   so he doesn't get his feet wet outdoors.
(Q) He does it
   so he won't get her mad.

The next item (A.2, oppositional, rebellion, stubbornness) may appear at first glance to be contradictory to the first. They are placed together here to tap not only the concerns of the child who outwardly manifests conforming behavior, but also the projections of the intriguing aspects of misbehavior given by the child who dares not do these things in actuality. Similar dynamics in the overly-good child were noted in a previous study (Haworth, 1962) in which children with obsessive orientations were the only ones able to recall, after a year's interval, incidents from a film in which the child character had repeatedly been secretly "naughty" and defiant to his mother when her back was turned.

Thus item A.2 would be scored for situations in which the child does something in defiance of the parent's wishes or commands, or repeatedly does what he knows he should not do. (General naughtiness, not directed so explicitly against the parent, would be scored elsewhere, e.g., C.10, or under Projection or Regression.) In the following example of a boy's A.2 response we see stubbornness and rebellion being expressed in anal terms, until the S's own guilt and anxiety mount to the point where he must describe the mother as being concerned enough to go out and look for her child; the story ends with the final resolve to be a good child.

10. About two dogs,
   mother dog
   and little dog probably got the towel muddy
   when playing outside.
Mother spanks.
He goes out and gets muddy again
   and wipes on the towel again
   and gets spanked again.
The little dog gets mad
   and runs away.
Mother gets worried,
   goes to look for him,
   finds him and brings him back home
   and gives him another spanking.
He barks, goes outside to play
   and is a good dog the rest of the day.

Figure 8.3. Analysis Schedule for case of James L.: see form reproduced on next 2 pages.

A Schedule of Adaptive Mechanisms in CAT Responses
Mary R. Haworth, Ph.D.

Name James L. ____________________ Bd: ____________ Date: ____________ Age: __7-9__

Critical Scores: Reaction-Undoing; Isolation; Deception; Symbolization; Projection-
        Introjection; Regression; Confused Identification

TOTALS   DEFENSE MECHANISMS

                   A.   *Reaction-formation* (only one check per story)
   6
 ___________   ________   1. Exaggerated goodness or cleanliness
 (A+ 1,6,7,10 2. Oppositional attitudes, rebellion, stubbornness
 B=5)   ___________   3. Story tone opposed to picture content

          B.   *Undoing and Ambivalence* (only one check per story)
          6
        ___________   1. Undoing
          2
        ___________   2. Gives alternatives; balanced phrases (asleep–awake; hot–cold, etc.)
        ___________   3. Indecision by S or story character
        ___________   4. Restates (e.g., "that_________, no this_________;" "he was going to, but_________")

          C.   *Isolation*
   7
 ___________   ___________   1. Detached attitude ("it couldn't happen," "it's a cartoon")
 (6)   ___________   2. Literal ("it doesn't show, so I can't tell.")
             ___________   3. Comments on story or picture ("That is hard"; "I told a good one.")
             ___________   4. Laughs at card, exclamations
             ___3___   5. Use of fairy-tale, comic-book, or "olden times" themes or characters
             ___________   6. Describes in detail, logical; "the end"; gives title to story
 1,3,6,7,8,9   7. Specific details, names or quotes ("four hours"; she said, "_________")
             ___________   8. Character gets lost
             ___________   9. Character runs away due to anger
             ___________   10. S aligns with parent against "naughty" child character; disapproves child's actions

          D.   *Repression and Denial*
   2
 ___________   9,10   1. Child character waits, controls self, conforms, is good, learned lesson
 (5)   ___________   2. Accepts fate, didn't want it anyway
             ___________   3. Prolonged or remote punishments
             ___________   4. "It was just a dream"
             ___________   5. Forgets, or loses something
             ___________   6. Omits figures or objects from story (on #10 must omit mention of toilet *and* tub
                          or washing)
             ___________   7. Omits usual story content
             ___________   8. No fantasy or story (describes card blandly)
             ___________   9. Refuses card

          E.   *Deception*
   4
 ___________   3,4,7   1. Child superior to adult, laughs at adult, is smarter, tricks adult, sneaks, pretends, hides
 (3) *   from, steals from, peeks at or spies on adult (only one check per story)
             ___9___   2. Adult tricks child, is not what appears to be (only one check per story)

          F.   *Symbolization*
 13
 ___________   ___________   1. Children play in bed
 (4)   ___5___   2. See parents in bed (#5)
             ___6___   3. Open window (#5, #9) ; Dig, or fall in, a hole
             ___________   4. Babies born
             4,7   5. Rope breaks (#2) ; chair or cane breaks (#3) ; balloon breaks (#4) ; tail pulled or
                          bitten (#4, 7) ; crib broken (#9)
             ___________   6. Rain, river, water, storms, cold
             ___________   7. Fire, explosions, destruction
             7,9,10   8. Sticks, knives, guns
 2,4,5,7,10   9. Cuts, stings, injuries, actual killings (other than by eating)
             ___4___   10. Oral deprivation

          G.   *Projection and Introjection*
 10
 ___________   ___7___   1. Attacker is attacked, "eat and be eaten"
 (4)   ___3___   2. Innocent one is eaten or attacked
             ___________   3. Child is active aggressor (bites, hits, throws; do not include verbal or teasing attacks)
             ___________   4. Characters blame others
             ___8___   5. Others have secrets or make fun of somebody
 3,4,5,6,7,9,10 6. S adds details, objects, characters, or oral themes
             ___________   7. Magic or magical powers

(* or 2, if both are E-2 responses)

PHOBIC, IMMATURE OR DISORGANIZED

		H.	*Fear and Anxiety*
2			1. Child hides from danger, runs away due to fear
(3)			2. Fears outside forces (wind, ghosts, hunters, wild animals, monsters)
			3. Dreams of danger
	6		4. Parent dead, goes away, or doesn't want child
	4		5. Slips of tongue by S

		I.	*Regression*
3			1. Much affect in telling story
(2)	3,6		2. Personal references
	4		3. Food spilled
			4. Bed or pants wet, water splashed
			5. Dirty, messing, smelly; person or object falls in toilet
			6. Ghosts, witches, haunted house

		J.	*Controls weak or absent*
0			1. Bones, blood ("dog bones" not applicable)
(1)			2. Poison
			3. Clang or nonsense words
			4. Perseveration of unusual content from a previous story
			5. Tangential thinking, loose associations
			6. Bizarre content

IDENTIFICATION

		K.	*Adequate, same-sex*
3	5,8		1. S identifies with same-sex parent or child character
(L=			2. Child jealous of, scolded or punished by, same-sex parent
or >K)	2		3. Child loves, or is helped by, parent of opposite sex

		L.	*Confused, or opposite-sex*
3			1. S identifies with opposite-sex parent or child character
	4,10		2. Child fears, or is scolded or punished by, opposite-sex parent
	9		3. Misrecognition by S of sex or species
			4. Slips of tongue with respect to sex of figures

This checklist has been designed primarily as an aid in the qualitative evaluation of children's CAT stories; it can also be used to furnish a rough quantitative measure for making comparisons between subjects and groups. The Schedule provides a quick summary of the number and kinds of defenses employed as well as the content of items used most frequently. The categories are arranged as nearly as possible on a continuum from indicators of high control and constriction to suggestions of disorganization and loosening of ties to reality.

Directions for Scoring: In the blank preceding each item, indicate with a check mark (or the card number, for future reference) any occurrence of such a response. A story may be "scored" in several categories and, except where indicated, a story may receive checks on more than one item under any one category.

After all stories have been scored, record the total number of checks for each category in the blank provided. The number in parentheses under each of these blanks indicates the *minimum* number of checks regarded as a "critical score" for that category.

For the Identification measure, the equivalent of a critical score is secured by comparing the relative number of checks for categories K and L. If the sum of checks for L is equal to or exceeds the sum for K, identification is considered to be "confused" and contributes one unit to the total of critical scores.

The final quantitative measure consists of the number of categories receiving critical scores (and *not* the total number of checks for all categories).

On the basis of research findings,* five or more critical scores would indicate enough disturbance to warrant clinical intervention.

*Mary R. Haworth, Ph.D., A Schedule for the Analysis of CAT Responses, *Journal of Projective Techniques & Personality Assessment*, Vol. 27, 1963, No. 2, 181-184.

While acting-out children will also give some items of the "rebellion" type (see Bellak's case), the bulk of their other items and critical scores will usually reflect openly-expressed aggressive acts such as are found under Projection and Regression.

Item A.3 (story tone opposed to picture content) occurs infrequently, but would be applicable, for example, to Card 7 if, instead of the tiger-chase, the story revolved around a happy-family event.

B. Undoing and Ambivalence. Responses scored as B.1 (Undoing) would involve a passive, or peaceful, restitutive response following a previous statement of hostility or aggression either in this same story or in the one immediately preceding it. An example would be the snake story quoted earlier in which the child speaks of the snakes scaring the family at sleep, then closes with the snake "having fun and laughing, a real, nice snake."

Item B.2 (gives alternatives or balanced phrases) reflects the S's ambivalence and indecision, as do the remaining items in this category. Carried into actual life situations, as seen in the obsessive child, such attitudes can become progressively incapacitating to the point where every contemplated action is debated from every angle until the crucial time for action has passed.

Example:

10.   Mother dog is either spanking
      or drying the little dog.
(Q) Can't tell.
(Q) Well, he got out of the bathtub just then
      or he got in trouble
      and gets spanked.
(Q) Don't know,
      I can't tell from just this picture.

Categories A and B are combined for purposes of analysis as the implied dynamics seem closely related.

C. Isolation. These items reflect intellectualization, ooververbalization, rationalization, concern with minutiae and efforts to be exact and precise. They serve to establish an objective "distance" between the stimulus and the storyteller. In the film study reported earlier (Haworth, 1962), the six children selected as obsessive on the basis of their responses to the film subsequently all scored high on the Isolation category (and five of the six Ss scored high on Reaction-Undoing).

The items used include the formal characteristics frequently noted by other investigators (Balken and Masserman, 1940; Symonds, 1948) as typical of the obsessive-neurotic approach to a storytelling task.

D. Repression and Denial. The first items are generally self-explanatory and reflect capacity to conform, to control, to learn from experience, and to accept the consequences of one's acts. Also included are items generally accepted as representing repressive mechanisms—omissions, refusals to get involved in fantasy by resorting to descriptions, and outright refusals to respond at all.

E. Deception. The responses in this category were initially noted when the CAT was used in a study (Haworth, 1962) of two groups of school children: one group were presumably neurotic while the control group were assumed to be well adjusted. It was found that half the Ss in each group gave responses of the E.1 variety in which the smaller child figure is seen as trying to trick, fool or annoy the adult. But responses to E.2, in which the adult is seen as plotting against the child, or as not really being what he appears to be on the surface, were given by half of the experimental group, but by only one-fourth of the controls.

An example of a child outwitting the adult was given by a girl as follows:

7.   Tiger and monkey.
The monkey, he liked to play
   in the banana tree.
He woke the tiger
   and the tiger got mad.
Monkey knew the tiger would eat him,
   so he rushed up a tree
   and threw all the bananas at the tiger.
The tiger slipped on them
   and lost all his stripes.
So he ran away.

In the following story the adult (lion) deliberately sets out to change his appearance or role activity in order to take undue advantage of his small victim:

3.   This is a story of a lion
   who wanted a mouse for supper.
He knew the mouse was in his corner,
   so he was pretending he was asleep.
When the mouse sneaked out
   to get some of the lion's cheese,
   the lion caught him and ate him.

A preponderance of the latter (E.2) type of item suggests considerable emotional distance between parent and child, with the adult being regarded as "two-faced" and unreliable. That such attitudes toward and about parents will seriously interfere with the identification process was demonstrated in the above-mentioned study by the fact that most of the children who scored on this item also received deviant identification scores.

F.   Symbolization. The items in this category are frequently found in the records of neurotic children and can be interpreted as any other verbal symbol according to psychoanalytic principles. Included are items suggesting concerns with primal scene fantasies, possible masturbatory and sex play, birth and impregnation fantasies, castration anxieties (mutilations, injuries), phallic symbols (sticks, guns, knives). Explosions, fires and floods may represent enuretic or masturbatory activities. The use of oral deprivation items would suggest that early affectional needs have not been met. It was obviously not possible to anticipate and include examples of all possible responses with symbolic meaning. Certainly the clinician using the schedule should feel free to include in this category anything that reflects similar dynamics.

A little girl gave this story (to Card 5), which suggests primal scene fantasies and oedipal longings:

5. Two little bears.
Mother and father went out
    and left the children at home.
Left them because
    they could get in trouble
    at the green woods dance.
Two bears hopped into bed and talked,
    Wondered why they were left alone.
They looked at the bed and said,
    "I can just see mother and father in there."
    "My mother is very sweet and pretty."
    "My father is handsome and patient."
Both say again,
    "I can just see mother and father
    sleeping in bed."

A story to Card 5 by another girl seems to refer to sex play between children in bed. (She had six brothers and sisters, and the entire family was living in a one-room house.)

5. Two little baby bears
    and mama and papa bear
    in bed with covers over their pillows.
They don't hear one word
    and are sleeping together.
(Q) The girl and boy
    nearly played all night.

They didn't wake up until noon. . .
Told their mama
    they had a real good sleep.
She said they sure did,
    because they didn't wake up until noon.

Themes of open windows, or of someone coming in the window, are usually accompanied by suggestions of dangers in entering; windows appear to be equated with bodily openings. Card 9 frequently elicits stories from boys of mother leaving the baby in the care of the older brother; a fox or other animal digs a hole up through the floor and steals the baby; rescue is accomplished by someone flushing out the hole with water. It would seem that the bedroom aspects of this card facilitate these sexual and birth fantasies.

The following story to Card 3 (by a six-year-old boy) also contains the symbolic "hole" and is otherwise replete with symbolism pertaining to castration fears, problems of origins, oedipal rivalries with the father, and fears of the intrusive aspects of sexuality which result in babies (mice).

3. That's the king.
Once upon a time
   there was this little mouse and a lion.
The little mouse got mad at the big lion
   and the lion got mad at the little mouse.
The big lion took the mouse by his paws
   and ate him.
And then the mouse's cousin came,
   and the lion ate him too.
Then the big lion fell in a trap
   which the hunters made.
   In the trap were a lot of little mice.
The hunters were elephants.
The little mice scared the elephants away
   and then the little mice killed the lion
   by shoving dirt in the hole.
And the cousin lion was scared.
Elephants are scared of mice
   because they think they can run up their trunks.
All the lions were scared of the mice
   and the mice were scared of the lions,
   and then the big elephant was scared of the mice.
So the lion was the king of the beasts
   and that's why he's setting on the throne.
There's a little crown up there.

The Rorschach further emphasized this boy's castration worries and/or fears of sex, for example: Card II. "A mad bull with two horns. They're bleeding because he stabbed people." Inferences from both projective protocols were confirmed in the subsequent therapy sessions as he worked through his fears of the dangerous aspects (to both male and female) of the male's intrusion; fears which were later generalized to include concerns about the penetrating aspects of the nursing process.

Bellak (1954) has specifically suggested that seeing the rope as being broken, on Card 2, represents castration fears; and that stories of attack or of the tail being bitten, on Card 7, suggest similar dynamics. While attack themes are frequent, and certainly suggested by the stimulus on the latter card, stories of the tail being bitten are relatively rare. (Interpretations of Card 7 need to be made with caution. It is too tempting to interpret an attack story as representing fears of castration and to also interpret a story with no attack sequence as a sign of castration fears which have been repressed. Assumptions about this particular dynamic should be made only after careful consideration of all ten cards.)

G. Projection and Introjection. Stories of attack are generally considered as representing projection of the child's own wishes against someone else and fears of reprisals from symbolic parent figures. Items 4 and 5, relating to suspiciousness, might possibly point to early manifestations of paranoid trends, particularly if present in several cards. (Little is known about the earliest danger signals for this condition; longitudinal follow-up studies of suspected cases are needed.)

Item 6 (addition of details, objects, characters, or oral themes) refers to incorporation of such new elements as integral parts of stories (rather than mere casual mention); e.g., if a hunter enters the bedroom (Card 9); or father joins the kangaroo family for a picnic (Card 4). We will want to note whether introduced elements are human (and with what personality characteristics), or inanimate (e.g., food, toys, instruments of attack). Vuyk (1953) has reported that children are more apt to project undesirable attributes of parents and children onto figures introduced into the CAT, while endowing the depicted figures with those qualities which are acceptable and nonthreatening.

Emphasis on themes of magic borders on the immature or regressive, especially if the storyteller gets "carried away" by the fantasied omnipotence. The number of such themes and their context would determine the weight given to them in qualitative evaluation of the protocol.

The next three categories grouped under the heading of the Phobic, Immature or Disorganized represent either a breakdown of established defenses or fixation at earlier, pre-oedipal levels. A preponderance of stories scoring under Regression or Weak Controls would represent the most severe pathology.

H. Fear and Anxiety. Here we find stories of feared or imminent catastrophies, vague presentiments, or dreams of a frightening nature. Slips of the tongue are also included since this phenomenon has been observed in phobic children or those who become so anxious when talking about a parent that the wrong words slip out.* An example follows:

7. Tiger and a lion. . . . I mean a monkey.
   Monkey hangs on a tree.
The lion pops out
   and scares the monkey.
Monkey might get caught by the lion,
   and the lion eats him up.
This is in the jungle.

References to parents dying or going away, or expressions suggesting that the parent no longer wants the child, also seem appropriately placed in this category. Several phobic and anxiety (sexual) indicators are represented in the following example by a nine-year-old girl:

9. Baby bunny sitting on the bed.
The mother left
   and the wolf's gonna get him.
It was a girl bunny.

---

*Slips of the tongue are also found in the records of children with aphasic tendencies.

(Q) Wolf got in there,
He was sleeping with the girl bunny.
She was frightened.
(Q) Bunny almost got out of bed,
  Girl bunny almost got out of bed,
  She almost ran into the kitchen.
She was frightened
  of that wolf in her bed
  sleeping by her, see.
(Points to dim object next to bunny).

I. Regression. Unusually marked displays of affect are uncommon in this test situation and would appear to reflect difficulty in assuming an objective attitude; in other words, the cards become too "real." Personal references also indicate lack of ability to maintain some degree of distance from the story situation, hence, represent immaturity. The following two responses by an apparently brain-damaged child are representative:

2. Big bear is pulling the rope
  from that bear
  who doesn't have anyone with him.
He wants the rope
  to tie the other person up.
They leave him while they go get food.
I'm scared of bears.

4. I'd like to ride in daddy's pouch, too.
They're going home to fix lunch.
Everyone eats and then sleeps.

Mention of spilled food, wetting, soiling, or related activities of stuffing something in the toilet, etc., are obviously regressive and suggest enuretic and anal fixations. If the category of Symbolization is also used freely, one could speculate that the current state is one of regression from a previous oedipal level. Examples of these items may range from the relatively innocuous (see example below), to stories with much reiteration of messing themes.

10. He's getting spanked,
  Done something wrong.
(Q) Messed up the bathroom.
  Just took his paw
  and swished water all over.

While mention of ghosts, witches or haunted houses could have been placed in the Fear category (and they should also be scored as Projection, G.6) their appearance often indicates a rather serious loosening of reality ties. In the following example, the witch appears to be used as a convenient means of eliminating father so the son can have mother to himself:

8. Grandmother (picture) looking at both (pairs).
Father and the witch are talking.

The witch put father in a spell.
Grandmother said,
    "Get out of here, you wicked old witch."
Then mother and son heard.
They hit the witch and she fell down.
    They called the police.
Grandmother with her face on the wall
    had a big reward.

J. Controls Weak or Absent. The first items, bones, blood and poison, are rare and indicate a severe degree of disturbance when found in CAT stories. Responses of "bones sticking out," or descriptions of bloody scenes should be regarded as danger signs of potential disintegrative processes. With regard to poison responses, Bellak (1954) indicates that they may occur in children without serious pathology and that such content represents ". . . fears of orally incorporating harmful objects related both to the mother's milk and fantasies of oral impregnation" (p. 211). The present writer has found references to poison to be so infrequent, and of such a nature when they do occur, as to regard them as extremely serious signs.

The boy who gave the following story was reacting violently to the recent addition of a stepfather into the home. He was referred for being mean and destructive and, significantly for the story content given here, would repeatedly raid the refrigerator at night. Here it is the child's body that contains and transmits poison, rather than the usual symbolism of the mother's food and sustenance being contaminated.

7. This lion, I mean this tiger
    is after this little monkey here.
If the lion goes after the monkey,
    the lion will eat up the monkey.
(Q) Then the lion will probably die
    or else hunt for more monkeys.
(Q) Probably be some poison in the monkey
    and the tiger ate the poison,
    And the lion will die from the poison.

The last four items of the category of Weak Controls all represent "cognitive slippage," loosening of thought processes, inability to maintain any distance or to exert adequate ego controls. Where loose associations or tangential ideation can be readily traced to previous cards or to known events or experiences in the child's past, a likely possibility would be mental retardation or some degree of cerebral damage. In contrast, the fantasies of a psychotic child reveal wild flights of bizarre fantasy beyond any limits of reality and reaching deep into his individualized psychotic world. Sometimes the looseness becomes more apparent as the child continues to make further comments, drifting farther afield, after he finishes the story proper. The following is one of several bizarre responses in the record of an eight-year-old childhood schizophrenic. (For his complete protocol, see Chapter XI.)

6. That's the mommie bear,
   father bear, baby bear.
Brother and sister
   are probably playing.
Mommie bear takes care . . .
   she finds food.
She can't go to the store and buy it,
   has to run and find food.
Know what king of beasts do?
Have to take a zebra and eat it.
They have to have nourishment or die.
The lion has to have blood.

(Following the above story, he launched into his current fantasy themes which were centered around the gory exploits of Dracula, Frankenstein and Wolf Man.)

K. and L. Identification. As discussed earlier, criteria for determining identifications in thematic stories are ambiguous at best. In the present schedule, identification is seen in terms of oedipal relationships, identification with the aggressor, and the role-functions (nurturance and control) of the mentioned parents. The scoring procedure consists in comparing the number of stories in which the S expresses attitudes or affects relating to the same-sex as opposed to the opposite-sex parent or child. When the latter responses equal or exceed the former, the S is considered to be confused in terms of sex-role identity.

For purposes of simplification in determining indications of identification, the following schema is proposed on the basis of the theoretical rationale given in earlier sections of this chapter.

For Boys:

	Identification is:
Perception of child figure:	
As a boy (in more definite terms than mere use of pronouns)	Same-sex
As a girl	Opposite-sex
Perception of adult figure as father and:	
As helpful, loving	Same-sex
As scolding, punishing	Same-sex
Perception of adult figure as mother and:	
As helpful, loving	Same-sex
As scolding, punishing	Opposite-sex

For Girls:

Perception of child figure:	
As a boy	(No score)
As a girl	Same-sex
Perception of adult figure as father and:	

As helpful, loving	Same-sex
As scolding, punishing	Opposite-sex
Perception of adult figure as mother and:	
As helpful, loving	Same-sex
As scolding, punishing	Same-sex

To recapitulate: Identification is determined for both boys and girls by considering the perceptions of the pictured characters with respect to the sex of the storyteller. For boys, deviant identification is represented by seeing the child character as a girl or by seeing the mother figure as punishing, rejecting or scolding. For girls, deviant identification is represented by seeing the father figure as punitive.

Identification clues are not necessarily found in every story. The ratio of positive to negative identification responses is the final determinant.

The first example represents positive identification in a girl as a result of seeing the mother as punitive and powerful:

4. On their way to a picnic,
Mother is hopping,
   baby is in the pouch
   and other baby rides his bike.
They have milk and sandwiches.
Mother kangaroo is boss
   so they behave,
(Q) Have their picnic
   and go home to bed.

Opposite-sex identification in a boy is illustrated in the next example, with the subject seeing the child character as a girl:

9. This is a little baby bed
   and a little bunny rabbit there,
A little girl with bunny rabbit hat
   in a bedroom of her own.
She's got to rest and go to sleep.
(Q-dream?) Probably dreaming about
   getting hit by an auto.
   Have to go to the hospital.
(Q-get well?) Maybe, if she doesn't get well
   she'll have to be buried
   and go up to heaven.
God will put wings on her
   and that will be nice.

CHAPTER IX

Interpretation: Part Two

An outline will be presented of factors to be considered in the interpretation and integration of all projective findings into a total picture of the child's personality. Although illustrative examples will be drawn only from the CAT, in actual clinical practice inferences from all projectives administered should be combined into a meaningful summary.

The final section of this chapter will be devoted to a presentation of a variety of responses to each of the ten CAT cards, in order to illustrate various interpretive problems, symbolic meanings and diagnostic clues.

THE INTERPRETIVE SUMMARY

Intellectual Level

Examination of word usage and reasoning ability as expressed on the CAT can supplement results from standard intelligence tests, or provide some clues when a full battery is not given. The choice of words, complexity of sentence structure, coherence of ideas and reasonableness of plots should all be evaluated in terms of age expectations. For example, what is the child's general fund of information as reflected in his descriptions? Does he recognize the animals in Card 4 as kangaroos and as from Australia? Does he speak of bears as "sleeping" or "hibernating?" Does the parent figure "spank" or "punish?" Are cause and effect explained in a logical fashion?

Indications of intellectual immaturity would include frequent use of personal references, banal descriptions of simple, everyday kinds of activities, and lack of any well-organized plot or outcome. In contrast, resorting to excessive use of detailed descriptions, specific numbers and ages, and use of direct quotes are usually indicative of an obsessive orientation, yet it is also true that it takes a rather high level of intellectual functioning to be able to produce such highly complex and detailed responses.

Often first suggestions of aphasic problems or word-finding difficulties are picked up in projective material; e.g., a child may say "clocked" when he means "closed and locked;" or that the bears were "suffocating along" when he intended to say "shuffling along;" or there may be repeated misuses of associated opposites, such as "over" for "under," "cat" for "mouse," "It's winter and it's hot—no, cold." When such responses occur frequently we should seriously consider the possibility of a central language disorder, to be confirmed by more specific testing by appropriate specialists.

Reality Contact

Loss of awareness of reality is demonstrated when a youngster mentions percepts on the first card, then perseverates the same idea on each succeeding card, regardless of the stimulus properties. In other instances, card content may be twisted and diverted to fit into the child's ongoing fantasies of the moment, with little awareness of the poor "fit." Orientation in time and space may be disturbed, or primary process thinking may predominate. Another representation of loosening of reality ties would appear to be responses describing objects in the card as being of a specific color, a phenomenon similar to "color projection" on the Rorschach.

Three stories told by a nine-year-old girl are presented to illustrate early manifestations of a weakening of control over affect and thought processes. Her response to Card 7 demonstrates an inappropriate display of affect, particularly for a girl.

7. Oooo. . . I *love* this picture (holds it to her chest)
Tiger's after the monkey,
  He eats up the monkey.
There's a string hanging from the tree,
  from one tree to another.
After he eats the monkey, the tiger says,
  "Boy, was that meal good!"
(Q-why like this picture?) Because it's a great,
  big tiger after the monkey
  and the monkey's almost falling off the tree.
  I like it because it's scary.
At home I pretend I'm a tiger or fierce lion.
(Q) Pretend I eat up different kinds of animals
  and I chase girls.

On Card 9 she runs the gamut of emotions from worry, fright and panic to a "happy dream" which is far from pleasant in content with its themes of attack and poison. Again we see expressions of inappropriate affect.

9. I don't like these so much.
The little bunny's worried
  a wolf will come in the window
  and catch him and eat him up.
He's looking out the door,
  "Mama, mama, a wolf."
He was dreaming.
Mama and father come in and say,
  "What's the matter?"
"I'm scared a wolf might come."
"Sweetheart, stop dreaming
  and have a nice dream."
They go out of the room.
He's screaming, another dream.
Mother and father say,
  "You shut up."
They leave the bunny crying and crying.
Bunny, "I think I'll go to sleep."
His dream was happy after all.
(Q-happy dream?) Kind of a funny one.
He was walking out
  and a big animal comes, and jumps,
  goes springing up,

like a poison animal came here.
The animal falls on his head,
  head over heels,
  In the night, laughing,
  and lands head over heels on his back,
  and lies flat.

Finally, on Card 10, the descriptions of anal activities and spankings from the father result in disorganization serious enough to produce repetitive use of color.

10. Father's spanking the puppy
  because he wet in the corner
  when he was supposed to go in the pot.
Is it nice to say "potty?"
Towel's hanging up
  and the puppy wiped his bottom on the towel,
  instead of being a good boy.
His poppa was very mad and spanked him.
He's sitting on a chair.
Pup's screaming,
  on his lap on his stomach.
The puppy had black eyes
  and so does the father,
The puppy had a pink mouth
  and so does the father,
The puppy had a red tongue
  and so does the father,
And he had long ears
  and so does the father.

Personal-Social Relationships

The CAT provides useful clues to the child's attitudes toward his parents, and the degree to which he feels accepted by them. Are the parents seen as nurturing and protective, or as punitive, deceptive, or unavailable when the child character is fearful and lonely? Card 8 is especially suitable for tapping the child's feelings toward adult relatives or friends of the parents.

Sibling and peer relationships are frequently revealed in Card 1 (e.g., if one child is left out or disadvantaged) and in Card 4 where the mother is shown in closest relationship to the baby. On this card, an extremely jealous child may omit mention of the baby in the pouch or indicate his desire to be the baby. Card 5 often elicits stories of the two children playing together in defiance of parental orders, a form of "ganging up" against authority figures. Sibling figures may be introduced, particularly on Card 9, to either comfort the younger child or take advantage of him.

Identification

Means of assessing identification have been presented in the previous chapter and will not be recapitulated at this point. A discussion of identification patterns is an important part of the final interpretation derived from CAT material.

Attitudes Toward Self

The more general aspects of self-concept should be considered in addition to identification *per se*. Indications of self-regard can be derived from the actions and activities of the child figures and the things done to the child by the adults. Does the child character act in a competent, self-assured manner, is he loved or rejected, helpful to others or bound up in concerns for only his own welfare? Do things turn out for, or against, him in the final analysis? Is there a feeling of mastery or of insignificance and defeat? Are children, generally, looked upon with favor by the adults, or are there indications that the parents resent the presence of children?

Emotionality

Aggression. In order to adequately interpret any aggressive response we will need to examine toward whom the aggressive acts are directed: whether the child character is viewed as the aggressor or the one being aggressed against; the intensity or subtlety of the expressed hostility; indications of masochistic pleasure; and efforts at undoing with their concomitant affects of guilt.

Some children seem so threatened by their unacceptable aggressive impulses that they will go to great lengths in attempts to minimize or "soften" the effect, but in the process the underlying affect is quite apparent. In the following story,* from a very passive, feminine, obsessively oriented boy, we can readily see his reluctance to give expression to his hostility, his recurrent maneuvers to soften or "pad" the act, and his empathy with the victim. It is highly likely that oedipal rivalries and castration fears are uppermost, with lack of ability to cope with these feelings.

7.   A lion's coming after the monkey
   for food.
The monkey climbs up the tree
   to be safe.
The lion will probably catch him
   before he gets up the tree.
Lion has his teeth in,
   paws in,
   has soft parts out
   until he gets close,
Then he jumps,
   pounces on him
   and eats him.
When he eats, then he'll go
   and look for more food.
That's *if* the monkey gets away.
Monkey looks like he's climbing up a tree,

---

*For the complete protocol, see the Obsessive-Compulsive section of Chapter XI.

But he won't have a chance.
   His fur sticks out,
   has his head turned to look at the lion,
   to make sure he doesn't eat him.

Murphy et al. (1962) discuss the case of a little girl for whom aggression was intolerable. In her response to Card 7 she has the monkey escape from the tiger but rationalizes away the aggression entirely by stating that the animals were only stuffed.

In the following example, a little girl denies the possibility of an aggressive attack, at the same time clearly indicating her method of avoiding threat; i.e., by being good, remaining overly vigilant, and not making unreasonable demands.

The lion is resting
   because he just ate a big meal
   and feels real full and good.
The mouse is watching him
   because he wants to come
   and pick up the scraps.
(Q) He knows he's there
   but he doesn't mind if he eats scraps.
   If he eats good stuff
   he would get the cat after the mouse.
(Q) The mouse is good
   and eats only scraps.

Dependence-Independence. Behavior in this dimension can be evaluated by noting whether the child character takes flight, appeals to adults for help, or stands firm in self-defense. What are the resources at his command? Must he repeatedly try to get the better of adults, or is he immobilized when deprived of their support? What is the quality of the expressed naughtiness and rebellion?

Phobic Concerns. Expressed fears and generalized anxieties should be examined. Are the fears realistic to the situation as described, or unrealistic and out of proportion to the danger? Do feared events actually take place or is there only the concern that they might happen? What dire events are seen as possible? What is the nature of the injuries, attacks or catastrophes which are feared? Are the fears specific and manageable or are the anxieties related to nebulous figures and to forces beyond human control?

Affectional Patterns. We are interested not only in assessing degrees and sources of disturbance but, even more important, areas of positive feelings and healthy strengths. We will want to know from where the child character receives affection and support, to whom he looks in times of stress, and to what extent he can trust the adult's ability to meet his needs. How much open affection is described? How much comforting is given?

Levels of Psychosexual Development

It is often possible to estimate, from the CAT responses, the child's attained level of psychosexual maturity which can then be compared with the child's current age. We would expect that a six- or seven-year-old would employ a considerable number of symbolic types of responses if oedipal problems are still current, and if defenses are becoming consolidated. But if the same age child gives few symbolic responses while strongly emphasizing themes of food and hunger or of wetting and messing, we can suspect fixation at, or regression to, pre-oedipal levels.

With respect to anal responses, is there an acting-out quality to the dirtying and splashing? Or are compulsive defenses being mobilized to ward off the threat of soiling? Both of the boys, whose responses to Card 10 are given below, were enuretic. The first boy was very hyperactive and presumed to be brain damaged:

10.   Two dogs, mother and pup.
Pup wants to get a drink.
Mother tries to keep him
    away from the stool.
    She's spanking him.
That's the mother,
    spanking the son.
She doesn't want him to go in there
    and fall in the stool
    while it's flushing.

The next boy was very intelligent, and used his day-time wetting as a threat when not getting his own way, or as a direct and obvious means of showing his defiance of his mother's authority. (His father was deceased.)* The child's therapist was repeatedly struck by the propensity of this boy for rationalizing wrongdoing in all types of symbolic play activities.

10.   Ummm, "Two Lost Pups."
Once there were two puppies
    and they had a real home
    with people.
They always had to go
    to the bathroom
    and never liked to.
So they go in the flower pots
    to water the flowers.
The mother put them out,
    'cause they kept doing that.
They ran away
    to a different home,
    and they never did find them again.

If oral themes are prominent, particularly to pictures that do not suggest orality, we will need to determine if the emphasis is on oral incorporation or oral aggression. Are the themes centered around hunger and oral deprivation and, if so, is either parent seen as the withholding agent?

---

*See Chapter XI, section on Parental Loss, for the complete protocol.

The following boy was deserted by his father at birth, had spent his first two years with his grandmother (who maintained him on strained foods), and rejoined his mother at age two. By the time of referral, at age eight and one-half, he was regarded as mean and destructive, and would raid the refrigerator continually throughout the night.

6. It's winter now.
They have a big hole
   and sleep until spring.
   All winter long, for a year.
They got food already for spring.
They won't get up until spring
   and this one's awake right here.
(Q-think about?) Probably about
   going out the first day of spring
   and get some more food
   so there'll be enough.

Oedipal fantasies may be expressed through symbolism, or take the form of castration fears (mutilations, injuries) or masturbatory concerns (rubbing, scratching, rocking, uncontrolled fires, etc.) Parental attachments and jealousies may be delineated. Primal scene fantasies may be expressed in various ways (listening, watching, peeking).

In the following example of two stories from a normal boy's record, the child's rivalry with the adult male figure is quite apparent on Card 3. He seems to be identifying both with the mouse (who continually annoys the king) and with the "person who took the queen," thus removing the culprit one degree further from the storyteller. It is then "this person" who eventually defeats the king. (The personal reference to his own father clearly confirms the oedipal hypothesis.) By Card 10, the child's longing for close affectional contact with mother comes out openly in the expression of desires to be fed and petted and, finally, to go to bed with her.

3. The king might be mad
   'cause somebody stole the queen.
The mouse crawls up on him
   and snitches at him
   and gets him all mad
   and runs back in the hole.
And the king tries to rake him out
   with his cane.
The king gets mad
   and goes to look for the queen.
But he forgets his pipe
   and the mouse took the pipe
   for his hole.
My daddy smokes a pipe and a cigar.
The person that took the queen

went back to the castle
    and made the horses run away,
And the king had to walk home.
When the person saw him,
    he ran and got on his horse.
He didn't get the queen back
    until next year.

10.   This dog's yappin'
    'cause he's hungry.
He wants to get washed,
    and mother is petting him.
The mother gets him washed
    and they have to reach to the cupboard
    to get the food,
And he wants to go out and play.
Then he plays till night
    and has supper
    and goes to bed
    and the mother does, too.

Stories of two girls are also presented to illustrate oedipal themes. The first child's mother had recently been committed to a mental hospital. In addition to the desire to have mother's "jewelry," we can infer some feeling of guilt on her part, and that she must now do penance.

10.   Mother and little boy.
He was so naughty
    that her mother had to spank him.
She did and the doggy just said, "Bow-wow."
(Q) He played with his mother's jewelry
    and broke it.
He tried to pay for it
    because he had the money,
    He really didn't.
(Q) He never played with her new things again.

Hostility to the mother is expressed more openly in the next girl's story, with the desire to eliminate the mother figure. The "daddy tiger" will not agree to this, but nevertheless pairs off with the child in the end.

7. There was a big daddy tiger.
He hadn't ate for a long time.
    He went out to find something to eat.
He spied a monkey by a tree
    taking a nap and went after it.
    He jumped on it but it got away.
That made him mad—
    All night he went without dinner.

The next morning he saw another monkey by the tree.
  That monkey didn't know how to get away.
The little monkey said,
  "You won't eat me
  because I'm just a little monkey."
The tiger said,
  "OK, but you better show me
  somebody else I can eat."
The little monkey said,
  "You can eat my mother."
Tiger: "I wouldn't do that to your mother."
Monkey: "Why don't we be friends?"
  and the tiger said he would be friends with the monkey.

The next boy's record is presented because it nicely parallels that of the first girl. In the very symbolic story, the little dog steals a bone and hides it "in his dad's bed." Here, again, the child feels guilty and repents.

10. Dog's getting spanked
  because he went to another dog's house,
  and stole the dog's bone
  and hid it in his dad's bed.
That other dog came
  and got the bone.
And dad spanked the little dog.
(Q) He learned never to take anyone's dog bone
  and hide it in a bed.

In the following story from a boy, the child figure achieves his oedipal desire to share mother's bed with even the suggestion that a "baby" resulted.

5. One night a bear sleeping in a crib.
It was raining.
  He could not get to sleep,
  He was scared of thunder and lightning.
He cries,
  His mother came and she said,
  "You may sleep down where I am
  so you can get to sleep."
One day, mother found the baby brother
  that came from her,
  She put it in the crib
  where the other baby was sleeping.
They slept until a thunder flash woke them.
Mother came and said,
  "You move your crib
  so you'll not hear the thunder and lightning."
"We will do that,"
  said the two little bears,
And they lived happily ever after.

Superego Development

Some indication of the current level of superego functioning can be gathered from the stories. For evidence of a severe, demanding superego we would ask: Is there a strong need for punishment along with suggestions of guilt and shame? Are punishments prolonged or severe in nature? Is the over-all attitude one of moralistic self-righteousness, conformity, self-punishment, or self-blame? Are there strong tendencies toward restitution?

An immature level of superego development would be manifested by absence of guilt indicators in situations where they would be appropriate; absence of punishments where ordinarily expected; denial of misdeeds; or the blaming of others. At times, conformity is expressed, but largely out of fear, or automatic "pat" types of punishments may be mentioned too readily.

In contrast to both of the above situations, an adequate level of superego will assert itself in rational, socialized behaviors, the assumption of responsibility for obedience and control, and a recognition of the demands of reality. Punishments will be realistically suited to the misdeeds. The child character may be described as "naughty" in some stories, yet thoughtful and helpful in others.

Defense Mechanisms

Finally, what means does the child have at his disposal for controlling his impulses and handling his conflicts? How rigidly is he defended or how comfortably can he modulate between prohibitions and desires? Which of the defense mechanisms are most often employed? How well are the defenses working or how frantically is the child trying first one and then another? As mentioned in previous sections of this chapter, either Bellak's or Haworth's record blanks can be of help in highlighting the particular defenses most often used by the individual child.

Adequate Adjustment

It is easy for a clinician to fall into a pattern of expecting, and finding, pathology of some degree in every child tested. But it is important to also be able to appreciate normality, as was pointed out in earlier discussions of the work of Moriarty and Murphy (see Chapter VI). Certain characteristics of CAT protocols are suggestive of a positive adjustment, adequate ego integration, and the capacity to adapt, to cope, and to maintain adequate controls. Such indicators include: seeking and appreciating nurturance; happy, successful or realistic outcomes; responsible and logical actions; realistic dreams; an expressed awareness that the threatening event could not really happen, or that the dream was "only a dream;" concentration on family activities of an "everyday" nature; a capacity for humor; and consistent identifications with adult and child figures of the same sex.

ILLUSTRATIVE EXAMPLES FOR EACH CARD

In order to emphasize the richness and variety of projective material which can be secured from the CAT, examples of different kinds of stories have been selected for each card. Purely descriptive types of responses have not been included. While isolating a story from its total context deprives it of a large area of meaning, the presentation of a variety of responses highlights the interpretive potentials of each card. (No attempt has been made to describe the children other than to indicate age, sex, and whether they were part of a school or clinic sample.)

The first examples given for each card generally picture a happy family where helpfulness, fair play and consideration for others are the rule. By contrast, the last stories in each group illustrate themes of openly expressed regressive behaviors or marked concerns with killings, and other catastrophes. In between will be found examples of childhood naughtiness, differential feelings toward the two parents, or views of parents as vigilant, punitive or scheming. Some stories reflect strong guilt feelings, efforts at restitution, or resolutions through self-punishments. Fears of the dark, unknown attackers, or desertion by parents are revealed in some of the stories.

Aggressive feelings are handled in various ways: by open retaliation, a gradual building up to an open attack by the end of the story, by passive-aggressive maneuvers (e.g., the child accidentally or seemingly unwittingly manages to annoy or hurt the adult). Often there is marked ambivalence in the face of upsetting affects. Unacceptable impulses are defended against by denial or constriction, symbolism, concern with minutiae, resorting to complicated dialogue between characters, slips of the tongue, or inability to follow a train of thought to a logical conclusion.

Finally, several of the stories illustrate the concerns of some children with reality, as they overreact to the fantasy aspects of the pictures and protest their ability to maintain contact with reality by asserting that the animals couldn't really do these things or that they are "only cartoons."

Card 1

Chicks seated around a table on which is a large bowl of food. Off to one side is a large chicken, dimly outlined.

GIRL, SEVEN YEARS, SCHOOL

Looks like chickens eating dinner,
Mother is watching.
They're eating grownup cereal
   for the first time.
Mother's thinking they're doing real well.
They'll get a treat when they finish.
Hmm, I said something wrong—
   They're *starting* to eat.
Chickens look very happy,
   because they're learning.

BOY, SEVEN YEARS, SCHOOL

There's the mother hen
   and three little babies
   eating pudding and jelly.

The mother got mad because
  she wanted them not to eat
  until their father comes home.
(Q) They waited until she went to sleep
  then they went to the kitchen,
  and got their plates and ate.

BOY, SIX YEARS, SCHOOL

Mother hen and she just got three little babies,
And they just got to the table to eat.
Mother got whiter and whiter,
  until you couldn't hardly see her.
  Almost looks like a ghost.
Then the baby chickens were afraid,
  So they jumped up and ran away.

BOY, NINE YEARS, CLINIC

They're eating chicken soup
Mother is right there—
  the shadow of that baby.
This one, this one eats soup,
That one hasn't any napkin
  so he'll spill it all over his feathers.
Table is too low,
  should say too high,
No napkin, bowl is too big.

BOY, SIX YEARS, SCHOOL

Some little birds are eating
  (Describes scene).
Maybe this rooster came and saw the food.
Maybe he took it
  but it doesn't show that, does it?

BOY, SEVEN YEARS, SCHOOL

The little birds are eating their supper
  while daddy watches
  to see that they clean up their plates.
One little bird doesn't eat his carrots.
  He's a bad boy.
  He gets spanked and has to go to bed.

GIRL, SEVEN YEARS, SCHOOL

They're eating.
The rooster could come
  and eat the food before the chickens.
Before this, the rooster made all the food.

If the rooster made all the food and ate it
  then the chickens might be hungry.
(Q) Then the chickens killed the rooster.

Boy, Eleven Years, Clinic

They're eating.
I'm not good at this (E encourages).
The mother hen made 'em some pudding for supper.
She put it on the table,
Got them to the table
  with spoons in their hands.
While she's serving,
  one gets under the table.
He has a magnet.
    There's tin on the bottom of the bowls,
    So he made the bowls go
    to the edge of the table (with the magnet).
Mother caught him
  and put him to bed without any supper.

Card 2

*One bear pulling a rope on one side while another bear and a baby bear
pull on the other side.*

Boy, Seven Years, School

Daddy bear is trying to pull the rope
  so that mother bear and baby bear
  can climb up the mountain with him.
They want to see all around them,
  and need to be way up high.
(Q) They are glad he helps them.

Boy, Seven Years, School

The bears are playing tug-of-war.
The baby is with mother
  because she's not as strong as father
  and needs him to help her.
(Q-win?) Mother and baby win sometimes
  and father wins sometimes.

Boy, Seven Years, School

The baby bear and father and mother
  are pulling the rope.
The baby's on father's side
  because mother was meaner to father and baby.
The baby almost fell
  and father almost fell, too.

(Q) Mother won
  so they fell and screamed
  and she ran away.

BOY, SIX YEARS, SCHOOL

Three bears fighting over a rope.
Papa needs it
  and mother tries to get it.
Baby's helping papa
  and mother don't got no help.
Papa gets most of the rope,
  but it breaks
  and they all fall down, down, down.
And then they tried to get up the hill
  but got exhausted since they couldn't.
So they died.
A hunter saw them and took all three
  and made fur coats out of them.

GIRL, SEVEN YEARS, SCHOOL

Raccoons got in a fight with a bear.
Raccoons found a rope
  and the bear wanted it.
Now they're having a tug-of-war.
The raccoons won.
The bear moves away and takes the rope.
Soon the raccoon found
  where the bear lived,
The raccoon cut the rope in half.
  The bear just thought it was the same.
(Q) They both won,
  only the raccoon accidentally cut the rope in half
  so both had half.

Card 3

A lion with pipe and cane, sitting in a chair; in the lower right corner a little mouse appears in a hole.

BOY, SEVEN YEARS, SCHOOL

Looks like the king of the beasts.
There's no such thing,
  so this is a cartoon.
He's waiting for someone
  because he's worried about something.
(Q) Maybe not enough food
  for the people in his kingdom
  or maybe about men who come into the jungle

and shoot animals
and bring them back for meat.

BOY, NINE YEARS, CLINIC

One time there was a lion named Golias (Goliath?)
Everytime the hunters was looking for him,
    the circus man.
The mouse helped him get loose.
    Kept nibbling, nibbling and nibbling on it,
    For a half hour
    until he got loose one night.
They caught him in a cage,
That lit. . . that little mouse.
Lion in the circus cage.
The mouse came along and got him loose.

BOY, NINE YEARS, CLINIC

Lion's can't smoke pipe,
    can't walk on two feet,
It's all wrong.
    They can't sit in a chair like humans,
    They can't even go to the bathroom like humans.
(Q-doing?) Smoking a pipe
    and thinking like a human
    but he can't do that either.
(Q-thinking?) About killing a mouse.

GIRL, SEVEN YEARS, SCHOOL

This is a story of a lion
    who wanted a mouse for supper.
He knew the mouse was in his corner
    so he was pretending he was asleep.
When the mouse sneaked out
    to get some of the lion's cheese
The lion caught him and ate him.

BOY, FIVE YEARS, SCHOOL

There's a lion in a chair
    and a mouse.
The mother runs
    and gets the mouse off the chair.
The lion went to sleep.
Mother got up in the chair
    and in his hair.
The lion woke up and said,
    "What's in my hair?"
The mouse said nothing.

Boy, Ten Years, Clinic

It's a papa lion,
  and he's old and has a pipe.
And the mouse is looking out.
And he has a cane
  and he's putting his arm on the chair.
This mouse looks out
  and is staring at something.
Mouse probably is going
to put his tail under the chair
  while he's not looking.
Then he gets up and says, "Ouch."
He jumps up and lands on the mouse.

Boy, Eight Years, School

King of the beasts
  and there's a mouse.
The lion doesn't like the mouse
  and chases it.
The mouse runs in the hole.
And the lion gets hit on the head by the hole,
  And the mouse laughs.

Boy, Eleven Years, Clinic

"The Lion and the Mouse" is the title of that.
One day, the lion became king of his country.
He went to the old shack
  where the kings live.
  It's called King's Paradise,
No crown.
He couldn't move the chair,
  the mouse is beside the chair.
The king ate all of the food of the mice.
One of them said,
  "The only furniture left is the chair,
  because we ate it all."
The king's in the chair.
  The mice ate the chair up.
The king fell on the floor
  with his cane and pipe,
  But the chair was all ate up.

Card 4

A kangaroo with a bonnet on her head, carrying a basket with a milk bottle; in her pouch is a baby kangaroo with a balloon; on a bicycle, a larger kangaroo child.

Boy, Five Years, School

Once there was a kangaroo
  and a little kangaroo.
They hopped along and went to a picnic,
  ate their lunch and came home.
Mother blew a balloon up for the baby.
The other baby wanted to play on the tricycle.
They ate their lunch.
He went to play with his friends
  and told them of the fun he had on the picnic.

Boy, Seven Years, Clinic

A kangaroo, the mother went to the store.
Brother kangaroo had his pajamas on
  and went to the store with her.
Mother turned around and got mad,
  because he didn't supposed to come.

Boy, Eleven Years, Clinic

Baby kangaroo rammed into mother kangaroo,
  and another baby in the pouch.
He'll go flying
  when the baby kangaroo hits her.
They're going on
  a picnic.

Girl, Seven Years, School

Once upon a time there was a mother kangaroo
  who had lots of trouble with her little kangaroos,
  one aged three, one two.
She even had to carry the two-year-old
  in her you know what.
Three is a stinker, too.
  He follows her all over on his bike.
They just bother her and bother her.

Girl, Seven Years, School

Once there were two baby kangaroos
  and a mother kangaroo.
and the baby kangaroos went to school
  and the mother wanted
  to get them to school on time.
One day they fiddled around a lot
  and she had to pull them to school.
And when she got to school
  she remembered it was Saturday
  so she took them home.

The next day she did the same thing
   and remembered it was Sunday
   and she took them home.
Monday she thought it was Sunday
   so she stayed home.
(Can't think of anything else.)

GIRL, SEVEN YEARS, SCHOOL

Kangaroos are going on a picnic.
All at once they see
   that a house is on fire.
They don't know whose house it is
   but they hurry and call the fire department.
Fire department comes
   and puts out the fire
And they go on to the picnic.
(Q) Guess some kid played with matches
   and a fire came.

Card 5

A darkened room with a large bed in the background; a crib in the fore-ground in which are two baby bears.

BOY, SEVEN YEARS, SCHOOL

Mama and papa bear
   and baby bear were in bed.
Mama bear and papa bear woke up
   and it was Christmas.
They snuck back to bed.
The baby bear saw them
   put presents under the tree.
He went to the basement
   and peeked at the presents.

GIRL, SEVEN YEARS, SCHOOL

Bears are playing in bed,
   They are tickling each other
   and giggling.
Mother comes and says,
   "You quit that and go to sleep."
The bears quit and go to sleep.

GIRL, FIVE YEARS, SCHOOL

Once there was a baby,
   he slept in a crib.
   He was jabbering and jumping around.
Father woke up and said,

"What's the matter with you?"
"I want my bottle."
"Drink that up and go to bed!"
Baby kept on jumping.
Soon mother woke up and said,
    "Go to bed, tomorrow is a busy day."
Baby went to bed
    and he wouldn't do it for the father.

GIRL, SEVEN YEARS, SCHOOL

There's a stuffed bear in the crib.
It looks like a baby's crib.
Looks like two people in bed.
The mother will probably have a baby.
    Man's probably happy.
The woman hurts.
He's sleeping.

BOY, SEVEN YEARS, SCHOOL

Here's the baby bear sleeping.
Mother and father covered their heads
    because they're scared in the night.
It's snowing out
    and they're afraid of the snow.
The babies are thinking
    mother and father are running away
    and they watch to see that they don't get up.

BOY, FIVE YEARS, SCHOOL

There's nobody in bed.
    They decided to go out.
Ghosts came in.
Baby said,
    "No one in the house but me."
But there was—the ghost.
"Get out, ghost!"
Then father came
    and the ghost was gone,
That's the end of this story.

GIRL, FIVE YEARS, SCHOOL

Once upon a time the bears
    were gone for a long time.
Went back and found
    their babies' heads cut off.
They went to the sheriff.
There was a man with green eyes,
    black slacks,

black hair and black shoes.
His name was John.
John had asked for food from them (the babies).
They slapped him
and he had to kill them.
He didn't get food from his family
because he was from Kansas.

Card 6

A darkened cave with two dimly outlined bear figures in the background; a baby bear lying in the foreground.

BOY, EIGHT YEARS, SCHOOL

Papa and mommie bear
and baby bear are sleeping
But baby bear wakes up
and looks outside.
He's cold,
so he goes up by mommie and papa
and gets warm.

BOY, SIX YEARS, CLINIC

What's this?
Bears are camouflaged.
Here we go,
sleep, sleep, sleep. (Singsong manner).
Here we are in our cave,
happily camouflaged.
(Q) Baby cub and big teddy bear.

GIRL, NINE YEARS, CLINIC

Three bears laying down,
And baby bear woke up.
And papa bear said,
"You'd better go to sleep, baby bear,
or I will never catch you any fish."
I said,
"No, I don't want no fish."
Mother bear said,
"You'd better go to sleep
or daddy won't get no candy for you."
They was living in a brick house.

BOY, SIX YEARS, SCHOOL

Baby awake,
wants to see if mama and daddy
are still there.
(Q) Maybe a hunter could come and get them.

Girl, Five Years, School

Once upon a time there were some wild bears.
They lived in a hole
  where the trees were.
  Three bears.
They thought a tree was a bear,
  scared them every night.
  They dreamed about it.
Judy came calling,
  She tasted their breakfast food,
  "This one is too cold" etc.
  (Told Goldilocks story through bears finding her in bed. . . . . .)
Judy ran out of the room and ran home.
And she never went back
  unless her mother said she could,
One day she went away,
It was burned up.

Boy, Eight Years, Clinic

There's a mother bear and a papa bear
  sleeping out in a cave.
Papa and mama bear
  were thinking of something.
The wise owl said,
  "I thought of something."
They got up fast.
The owl said,
  "Give them (the babies) to the kangaroos."
"No, they're not kangaroos,
  we'll not give them to them."
The wise owl hit them on the head
  with a piece of pipe.
Poor old wise owl.

Card 7

*A tiger with bared fangs and claws, leaping at a monkey which is also
leaping through the air.*

Boy, Seven Years, School

Monkey is being chased by the lion.
He catches it and eats it.
The monkey tried to climb the tree
  but slipped.
The lion is pleased with himself.

Girl, Seven Years, School

This is a story of a tiger,

who is trying to catch a monkey
 for his supper.
The monkey is smart
 and likes to tease the tiger.
 He almost lets him catch him
 before he jumps up into the tree.
The monkey giggles
 and the tiger gets mad.
(Q) He goes to look for another monkey to eat.

BOY, SEVEN YEARS, SCHOOL

There's a big lion
 after a monkey.
Monkey's going to get up in the tree
 because the lion wants to eat him up.
She falls down a hill
 and the monkey gets away.
A big stone rolls down
 and runs over her (the lion).
But a stone hits the tree
 and the little monkey gets killed, too.

GIRL, FIVE YEARS, SCHOOL

Oh, there was a monkey named "Ziggy."
Lion came and growled and said,
 "I'm going to eat you up!"
Lion had sharp teeth and a big nose.
He said,
 "Why don't I ever eat monkeys up,
 I think I'll eat this one."
He didn't like to.
 "Please can I eat you."
"No, you may not."
"I'll give you a diamond ring."
"No, cause you're too dangerous."
The monkey climbed all over
 and jumped on the lion.

GIRL, NINE YEARS, CLINIC

The little monkey is afraid of the tiger.
Monkey ran up and looked at him,
 Monkey's afraid of him.
(Q-happen?) It's gonna be dead.
Tiger won't catch him.
Look, what happened!
His spots are coming off.
 (Points to dots on ground, then put her finger on tiger's mouth, then laid

her hand on card so that edge of her palm was between tiger and monkey)
The monkey grabs bananas
   and throws at him.

BOY, NINE YEARS, CLINIC

The tiger's trying
   to get the mother monkey.
There's a crocodile right there, see?
He's going to step on it
   if he's not careful.
   A poison crocodile.
Step on it and he's dead.
   Then the monkey will be safe.
And he's staying dead forever.

STORIES TOLD TO CARD 7 BY SWEDISH CHILDREN*

This is a tiger
   who is making a long jump
   and tries to take a monkey.
The monkey is so frightened
   that he jumps up a tree
   and the tiger becomes so baffled.
"Just take care when you will come down,"
   said the tiger.
"If I ever am coming down,"
   said the monkey.
Then the tiger went away,
   and the monkey contentedly sat
   eating a coconut.

A tiger was hunting a monkey
   at a river,
   but the monkey climbed a tree,
   so the tiger could not reach him.
So the tiger fell in the river
   at a rock
   and he drowned.
Then the monkey climbed down again,
   and ran to his mommy.
But the tiger's mommy and daddy
   were sad
   because the tiger was lost.

Once upon a time there was a tiger,
   and his name was "Sharp Tooth."

---

*Appreciation is extended to Ann Lantzourakis, of Stockholm, for providing these
examples and giving permission for their use.

And he wanted very much a mouthful.
So he caught sight
  of a monkey in a tree.
He thought,
  "It will be nice
  to have some monkey's steak."
The monkey tried to twirl around
  but the tiger pulled him down
  by his tail.
Then he killed it by biting
  and ate it.

Once upon a time there was a lion
  and he liked to eat a monkey
  and he climbed the tree.
And then he became sad
  and he went to the people
  and nobody of the people were at home.
So he went to a town
  and there it was beautiful,
  and there were so many people
  and he ate all the people.
You get so uneasy
  when there are so many people.
He ate them all,
  No, one was left, who said:
  "Now the lion is walking
  in the town."

Card 8

Two adult monkeys sitting on a sofa drinking from tea cups. One adult monkey in foreground sitting on a hassock talking to a baby monkey.

Boy, Seven Years, School

The monkeys are having a tea party.
Little monkey is with father.
He's telling him to be a good boy
  and not to talk when grownups talk.
They are saying he's a good boy,
  He behaves good.

Girl, Seven Years, School

Little monkey had a great big bear.
Great big bear
  had a mother and father.
They were living pleasantly in their new house.
They went to grandmother's house

  and took her picture.
That day she had a heart attack
  and died.
They all felt sad
  so they hung up her picture.

GIRL, NINE YEARS, CLINIC

The papa said,
  "Mother, we're drinking coffee" (low voice).
Sister said,
  "You'd better go to bed."
See what they did,
  They're in their underwear (giggles).
  That one ain't (points to picture of a monkey).

GIRL, SEVEN YEARS, SCHOOL

Monkeys don't like each other.
They try to get together,
  One invited the other to a party.
They're whispering
  how they don't like each other.
They've got something to drink
  and the others don't notice.
Little one says,
  "Can I have something to drink?"
Mother scolds him for asking,
  finally she asks.
They got two glasses of water
  and threw it in their faces.
They went outdoors
  and never came back.

GIRL, SEVEN YEARS, SCHOOL

Once there was a mother, baby,
  daddy and grandma monkey.
Mother and daddy and grandma
  scolded the baby monkey for nothing
  and said bad things about him.
One day when grandma was there
  they sent baby to his room.
He decided he'd go out the window.
  He jumped out the window
  and landed on a traffic light,
  and made the traffic light
  go all different colors
  like it isn't supposed to,

And the cars got in a big jam.
And the mother and daddy and grandma
  had to go to jail,
    because they were mean to the baby monkey
    and made the baby go out the window.

GIRL, FIVE YEARS, SCHOOL

Once upon a time happy monkeys
  made people laugh,
  talked secrets.
The other father visited
  and the father got mad.
"What's up with the secrets?"
  Father and baby weren't in on it.
"I'll marry this man," says mama.
So father had to get married again.
  They went to a new church.
Got a beautiful home,
  borrowed money to buy it.
They went to the park
  after moved into the house.
    "Nice park."
    "It's pretty."
They went home and to bed,
  woke up and ate.
Mother said, "Time to eat, honey,
  Have scrambled eggs,
  milk and orange juice."
The orange juice was poison.
"Who did it?"
The baby got sick and died.
They got another child,
  he died again.
Got another child.
  Father never died.
Other child lived for a long time,
  became a teenager and married.
Had another one.
Father died, he was old.
She had a child.
  Her husband got dead
  and she has a child.
She wondered:
  maybe husband not dead really.
She went to bed and dreamed about it.
  She got up.

Card 9

A darkened room seen through an open door from a lighted room. In the darkened one there is a child's bed in which a rabbit sits up looking through the door.

GIRL, SEVEN YEARS, SCHOOL

A bunny rabbit girl.
She got scolded
  for not drinking her milk.
They put her in bed
  because she didn't drink her milk.
She wondered why she didn't drink it.
(Q) She dreamed she wished she had drunk it.

GIRL, SEVEN YEARS, SCHOOL

This one's about a sleeping monkey.
He's in bed
  but is waked up.
It's dark and
  he's scared a hunter might come get him.
He falls asleep
  and wakes up in the morning OK.
He laughs at himself
  for being scared of nothing.

BOY, SEVEN YEARS, SCHOOL

Baby bunny is sleeping in a little bed.
She saw door opening,
  and he stood up and put his ears up.
Thought someone was coming
  in the house to get him.
The bed is starting to break
  because one foot is off
  and it makes the bed crooked.
The wind comes and he covers his head.
  Then he puts his head up
  because he still thinks someone
  will get in the house and break everything.
(Q) He goes to sleep after awhile.

GIRL, FIVE YEARS, SCHOOL

There was a little rabbit
  sleeping in bed.
He heard something out of his bank.
He scrambled out of bed,
  "Mother, I hear something

rattling in the piggy bank,
   like a window breaking."
"Could be a burglar."
"I'm going to set an alarm."
"Let's check in your piggy bank."
"Mother, my two dollar bill is gone!"
"We'll get you another one at the bank."
She got him one,
   and hid it from him (the burglar).

BOY, EIGHT YEARS, CLINIC

About a little rabbit
And he saw this old house
   with a crib in it.
   He slept in it.
He didn't know these men
   were moving a lady in (into the house).
The man came
   and the baby hid under the bed.
The man said,
   "Oh, little rabbit"
   and picked him up.
The rabbit bit him.
The man didn't like it
   so the rabbit hid under the covers.
   The rabbit got in the moving van
   and got away.

GIRL, SIX YEARS, SCHOOL

Baby bunny and no one else.
The door opens.
A hunter came in
   and shot the rabbit and that's all.
(Q) Mother and father came back
   and he's dead.
Mother shouldn't have left him alone.

Card 10

A baby dog lying across the knees of an adult dog; both figures with a minimum of expressive features. The figures are set in the foreground of a bathroom.

BOY, EIGHT YEARS, SCHOOL

Mother dog is spanking the puppy.
He got water all over the floor
   when he got out of the bathtub.

He isn't careful
  so when he plays
  he splashes water all over.
(Q) She spanked him,
  he yelled,
  and then she sent him to bed.

GIRL, SIX YEARS, SCHOOL

He's getting a spanking from mother
  because he hurt someone.
Hit them when playing,
(Q) Don't know why, that's all.

BOY, SIX YEARS, SCHOOL

Father puppy gives the baby puppy
  a spanking for being naughty.
He went outdoors.
  He played in the mud and got dirty.
He had to go to bed
  without any supper.

BOY, EIGHT YEARS, CLINIC

Mommie—I mean father—papa dog
  is going to spank the boy dog.
Cause boy dog nearly flushed the toilet,
  I mean, took a bath
  and he never. . . . (blocked)
(Q) He never dried hisself ,
  or that's the only thing I know.
(Q) So daddy—mommy—probably spanked him.

BOY, SEVEN YEARS, SCHOOL

One day, two dogs lived in a house.
One was bad because he went in the yard
  when he had to go to the bathroom.
Mother got mad,
  she not like that,
  she spanks.
But every time he goes to the bathroom in the yard.
Mother comes and puts him in the bathroom
  so he could go the rest.
One day mother said,
  "You'll not go outside if you do that again."
One day he went to bed wet—
  almost wet the bed,

but went right to the bathroom
and went there.
Mother was proud
cause she didn't like for him
to go in the yard.
And he went to the bathroom happily ever after.

Boy, Six Years, School

Doggies in bathroom
and they're going to drink water.
Get spanked for playing in water,
flushing the toilet
and drinking water from the toilet.
I don't like toilet water, do you?

C H A P T E R   X

Diagnostic Studies

A number of studies will be reviewed which have utilized the CAT as one of the major instruments for assessing the personality correlates of specific diagnostic entities. The first section covers studies of physical problems, then follow reports of articulatory disorders, mental retardation, cerebral palsy, childhood schizophrenia, various degrees of emotional disturbance, and finally, studies of children who have suffered parental loss.

PHYSICAL PROBLEMS

Diabetes

The diabetic child has been studied by Bennett and Johannsen (1954a). The medical, social and psychological aspects of the illness were examined to determine their effects on personality. Subjects were 58 diabetic children between the ages of 7 yrs. 10 mos. and 9 yrs. 11 mos. who were attending a diabetic camp. Measures used included ratings of behavioral data by camp counselors and psychological assistants; a questionnaire (concerning the home environment) administered to both parent and child; psychological tests, including the CAT, Rorschach, MPT, Rosenzweig Picture-Frustration Test, and the Draw-a-Man. Unfortunately, no control group was used for the CAT data.

Before discussing the specific CAT findings, the general conclusions of the study should be reviewed. It was concluded, on the basis of the measures used, that diabetes does have a very real impact on the child's personality and produces some very specific effects. For instance, those children who had had diabetes for the longest periods of time felt the most restricted, suggesting that the child does not "get used to" his disability. Those who developed diabetes at the youngest levels, and those most severely afflicted, showed the greatest personality reactions of dependency and cravings for affection, although appearing socially mature and independent on the surface. With respect to parental attitudes, when the parents emphasized general restrictions, the child reported feeling restricted and showed traits of inhibition, withdrawal and passivity. The stronger the parents' beliefs in restrictions only in diabetic matters, the better adjusted the child appeared to be.

CAT responses were scored for the presence of 35 themes and tendencies, such as: conflict; frustration; insecurity; anxiety; feelings of incompetence; hostility; depression; aggressive, dependent and withdrawing behaviors; extent of perceived adult hostility; environmental restrictiveness, protectiveness or rejection.

Some of the significant findings specifically attributed to the CAT are given below (all comparisons are with those Ss at the opposite extreme of the continuum under discussion):

Those Ss who have had diabetes the longest have more active and more withdrawing fantasy heroes and fewer heroes who are punished. Those who developed diabetes later in life have fewer fantasy heroes who aggressively

182

attack the environment. Children with the highest insulin dosages, the highest glucose content, and the most insulin reactions all given fantasy heroes who feel and act dependent.

Subjects whose parents have the most restrictive general philosophy have fewer fantasy heroes, and give fewer stories utilizing the whole picture, while those whose parents believe most in diabetic restrictions give fewer heroes who are frustrated. Children who feel most restricted have fewer fantasy heroes and more of their heroes feel depressed.

In a comparison of sexes, girls give fewer fantasy heroes than do boys, but more of their heroes engage in conflict, feel and act dependent, and are pictured in hostile environments.

Physical Disability

Katzenstein (157) used the CAT (and also the DAP, Pigem Test, Symonds Picture-Story Test and Staabs Sceno-test) in some of her evaluations of children with polio and other physical disabilities. She presents excerpts from several cases to demonstrate the manner in which the child's reaction to his disability is reflected in his test responses. For example, a boy of five years, four months, had been wearing a leg brace for almost a year. His drawing of a boy shows an extreme degree of shading over the leg area, from trunk to feet, as if to conceal his defect. The CAT-S was also administered to him and he was particularly interested in the picture of a kangaroo whose leg is in a bandage or cast, tail bandaged and using crutches. The author reports it was very difficult to distract the child's attention from this picture to the remaining cards.

Physical Anomalies

Macedo de Queiroz and Reichnardt Epps (1962) report on the psychological study of 14 subjects with gonadal or phenotypic sexual abnormalities. There were nine cases of Turner's syndrome and five pseudohermaphrodites. One of the latter was genotypically feminine but with masculine secondary sexual characteristics while the other four were masculine with feminine or ambiguous secondary characteristics. Ages ranged from nine to 44 years. Clinical, medical and endrocrine studies were made as well as psychological evaluations using the Rorschach, TAT, CAT, MMPI and intelligence tests.

The projectives were analyzed for the presence of male and female traits. More specifically, for the CAT and TAT, attention was given to determining whether the Ss identified with the masculine or the feminine figures. No information is given as to which Ss were given the CAT, as opposed to the TAT; presumably this was determined by the ages of the Ss.

In the group with Turner's syndrome, the most outstanding feature was mental deficiency, with six of the nine cases falling within MA levels of six to eight years. CAs for these six ranged from 12 to 25 years. In the pseudohermaphrodite cases, mental levels were generally comparable to CAs and neurotic traits were the prominent feature in the psychological findings.

Gibson (1958) was interested in the reactions of young children to surgery and hospitalization. He used the CAT, DAP and Blacky as personality measures in a study of 29 five-to-eight-year-old children with congenital anomalies (obstructions of the alimentary tract) which had required surgery in the first four months of life. The control group consisted of children with no physical handicaps or prior hospitalizations. The projective material was analyzed by means of numerous items grouped under ten variables, such as anxiety, defense mechanisms, reactions to frustration, oral and anal comments, references to surgery and hospitalization. Very few of the individual items yielded significant differences and no over-all differences between groups were reported.

ARTICULATION PROBLEMS

Kagan and Kaufman (1954) explored the possible relationships between functional speech disorders and emotional problems as revealed in CAT responses. Their sample consisted of 40 first-grade children (25 boys and 15 girls) with normal speech, matched by sex, age and IQ to 40 children diagnosed as "severe functional articulation cases" by a speech therapist. Functional disorders included errors of omission, substitutions, and additions of speech sounds, all presumed to have no known organic basis.

The CAT stories were analyzed for: (1) number of words per protocol on the hypothesis that speech handicapped children would be more reticent to engage in verbal activities; (2) the number and character of oral themes, with the assumption that the child with speech problems may be expressing early anxieties and conflicts from the oral stage via oral-speech mechanisms; (3) themes expressing the child's hostility directed toward parental figures; and (4) themes expressing the child's perception of parental hostility directed toward the child figure, on the hypothesis that emotional conflicts related to parent-child tensions may be expressed through the speech process.

Their findings were as follows:

(1) *Number of words.* Significantly more of the experimental group fell below the median figure (52.9) for mean words per story. The over-all means per story for the girls' articulation group (46.6) and the boys' group (50.9) were both considerably below the respective figures for the control group (69.6 and 63.4, respectively).

(2) *Oral themes.* When comparing themes of oral aggression as opposed to socially accepted oral acts (such as eating, smoking) the articulation group gave significantly more of the oral aggressive types of responses, than did the control group.

(3) *Themes of hostility toward parent figures.* There were no significant differences between groups on this measure.

(4) *Perception of parent hostility directed toward child.* Significantly more of such themes were given by the articulation group.

The authors interpret their findings as suggesting that articulation cases may come from punitive homes, or homes where the child fears punishment if he expresses his aggression; or the child may be satisfying his need for punishment, by persisting in a behavior that is not approved (i.e., making articulatory errors).

FitzSimons (1958) also studied children with nonorganic articulatory problems, and was concerned with the developmental, educational and psychosocial factors that might contribute to the speech difficulty. There were 70 first-grade children in each of the experimental and control groups, matched for age, IQ, sex and school locale. There were 40 boys and 30 girls in each group.

Data were secured by interview with the mother, the Vineland Social Maturity Scale, Metropolitan Reading Readiness Tests at the beginning of the school year and Metropolitan Achievement Tests at the close of the year, the Kuhlmann-Anderson Group Test of Intelligence, the CAT, and a teacher rating scale for the evaluation of oral participation in class.

Interview information secured from the mothers revealed that significantly more of the experimental group had experienced abnormal birth conditions, delays in locomotor and communicative skills, early weaning and toilet training, and more childhood diseases before age three. As compared to the normals, the articulation group had a greater incidence of conduct and habit disorders; lower reading readiness and achievement test scores; lower report card grades in language, reading and work habits; and lower "oral participation" scores. There were no differences in the Vineland Scale.

The CAT protocols were analyzed for the mean number of words and for the following dynamics: aggression, conflict between autonomy and compliance, fears and anxieties, hostility directed toward parent figures, orality, perception of parents as authoritarian, sibling rivalry, and type of story outcome. There were no differences in story length. The normal Ss gave more stories with positive outcomes, while the articulation group gave significantly more themes of aggression, fears and anxieties, and perceptions of the parents as authoritarian. None of the other dimensions reached significance.

FitzSimons interprets her results as suggesting a relationship between nonorganic articulation disorders and psychological factors, and that the speech problem "may be satisfying a need for the reduction of internal tension." She points to the importance of treating the psychological aspects as well as the symptom itself.

MENTAL RETARDATION

Only two studies could be found which were specifically concerned with the reactions of retarded children to the CAT. Butler (1961) administered the test to 50 institutionalized Ss, ranging in CA from 9 yrs. 7 mos. to 18 yrs. 7 mos. and in MA from 3 yrs. 6 mos. to 9 yrs. 10 mos., with a mean MA of 5 yrs. 2 mos. IQ's ranged from 30-77. The chief purpose of the study was to compare the S's responses to the animal and human forms of the test, using the Washington State version of the cards, and generally similar methods of analysis, i.e., reaction time, total time, and words per card. In addition, the author used omissions and additions of characters, rejections, self references, expressions of feelings and of conflict, and number of stories with definite outcomes. No significant differences were found between the two forms of the test.

Butler (1961) summarizes his impressions of the usefulness of any story-telling technique with a retarded sample as follows:

These data may be compared with the data from young, normal, and disturbed S's in the Mainord and Marcuse study (1954) and the data from school children of higher ages presented by Furuya (1957). The retarded S's stories were most often simply enumerative of what was on the card. They took no longer to respond initially but took longer on any given card and eventually produced fewer words per card or protocol; this fact is probably related to their poorer expressive ability in relation to S's of normal intelligence . . . . Finally, the finding that such a small percentage of the stories have ascertainable expressions of feeling and conflict and are, at the same time, almost exclusively enumerative, generally questions the usefulness of thematic techniques, as presently interpreted, with S's of the intelligence level of this sample (p. 622).

Budoff (1963) also reports on the comparative usefulness of animal versus human forms of the CAT with retarded Ss. On the basis of Rorschach findings that the lower intellectual levels give more animal responses, he reasoned that richer and longer stories might be expected from retarded Ss when compared to controls. He used 12 borderline retarded Ss in first grade (mean MA= 4 yrs. 5 mos.; IQ range=70-78) and a control group of 11 first-grade Ss of dull-normal to low-average intelligence (mean MA=5 yrs. 8 mos.; IQ range=87-91). By his own admission, all Ss were performing at a very low level, particularly in verbal areas. Consequently marked differences on the CAT task could hardly be expected and indeed were not demonstrated.

Protocols were analyzed for word count and mean Transcendence scores. The analysis of variance for word count yielded a significant difference in the direction of longer stories to the human set for the retarded group, while the controls showed no difference between forms. Little meaningful information could be derived from the Transcendence scores since 39 per cent of the responses given by the retarded Ss and 29 per cent of the stories given by the controls were so meager and/or descriptive that they could not be scored. In fact, the main significant variable for both analyses proved to be the nature of the picture situations, with Cards 4, 7, and 8 eliciting longer stories and higher Transcendences scores than Cards 3, 5, and 9 irrespective of animal or human characters or IQ level of Ss.

Budoff points out that Cards 4, 7, and 8 portray the figures as clearly inter-acting with each other in an activity involving all characters. In contrast, the three cards (Cards 3, 5, and 9) eliciting the least response either show the main character in isolation or depict no common focus of activity. Budoff suggests that for retarded and low-average children, and possibly also for very young normals, pictures should be designed with more overt implications of activity.

Boulanger-Balleyguier (1960) makes some comments on her clinical findings relative to the CAT when used with retarded children. She found a large number of omissions; strong perseverative trends despite the nature of the specific stimulus presented; characters might be indicated but neither named nor described; and few of the typical normative responses characteristic of the child's chronological age level.

CEREBRAL PALSY

Holden (1956) compared CAT responses of a small number of cerebral palsied children with a group of normal Ss of the same mental ages. The sample consisted of eight cerebral palsied children (ages 5 yrs. 7 mos. to 12 yrs. 11 mos.) with a mean MA of 7 years and an average IQ of 73.1. The seven control Ss (ages 6 yrs. 2 mos. to 7 yrs. 8 mos.) had a mean MA of 7 years 5 months and average IQ of 101.5. Data were analyzed according to the percentage of descriptions versus thema (additional story, feelings, affect or endings), and by the number of descriptions given by each S.

The cerebral palsy group gave significantly more descriptions (p<.01); there were 61 per cent descriptions (and only 39 per cent themas) as compared to the control group with 28 per cent descriptions (and 72 per cent themas). Considering the proportion of descriptions to each card, this figure for the cerebral palsied group ranged from 38 to 100 per cent; the range of descriptions for the control group was 10 to 50 per cent. The average number of descriptive stories per child was 6.0 for the cerebral palsied and 2.8 for the controls.

It was also observed that the experimental group tended to use irrelevant details and to get involved in the enumeration of small details, thus manifesting the stimulus-bound quality frequently noted in studies of the brain damaged. This behavior was not found in any of the control Ss. As Holden (1956) points out, "The brain-injured child's performance is qualitatively different from the nonbrain-injured, and is on a lower more primitive level despite similarities of mental age. . . . They appear relatively unable to adopt an abstract attitude to 'tell a story,' are stimulus-bound, and rigidly continue with the concrete attitude giving descriptions to the cards" (p. 7).

CHILDHOOD SCHIZOPHRENIA

Gurevitz and Klapper (1951) administered the CAT to ten schizophrenic children and to 18 cerebral palsied children within the age range of five to 12 years. All IQ's were within the normal range. The cerebral palsied group consisted of mild to moderate spastic hemiplegia with no serious sensory or speech involvement.

Dimensions used for the analysis were organized under the following headings: formal characteristics, general quality of content, structure of content, figures of projection, general mood, affective elements.

The results were presented largely as qaulitative findings. In describing the schizophrenic children's reactions, the authors say: "Hostility and anxiety were predominant in the responses of this group of children; this could be observed in the content of the stories, the nature of their outcomes, the qualities attributed to the characters, and in the interpersonal relationships, particularly those involving child and adult" (Gurevitz and Klapper, 1951, p. 57). The schizophrenic children's stories were often bizarre, perseverative or confabulated although there may have been an initial close adherence to the stimulus. They tended to dramatize responses, engage in conversations with the characters in the picture and give proper names to the animals. Father figures were frequently noted but usually seen as hostile in nature. The child figures were also seen as anxious and hostile and little relatedness was shown to either child or mother figures.

The responses of the cerebral palsied group were characterized by literal descriptions with little spontaneous elaboration or distortion. Mother figures were the most often mentioned and were seen both positively and negatively, i.e., as dominating, accepting, protecting, depriving or hostile. The typical child figures were usually of the same sex and viewed as moderately apprehensive and anxious, and somewhat hostile and deprived, but also with some affectional elements. There was very little relatedness expressed to either the father or sibling figures. The general emotional tone of these S's responses was lacking in affect, both with respect to qualities of the characters and to the child's own lack of involvement in the storytelling process.

As part of a study of aggressive and anxious children, Boulanger-Balleyguier (1960) reports some clinical observations of six- and seven-year-old psychotic children. She found many signs of disturbance in their CAT protocols, with false perceptions, few popular responses, frequent omissions of figures, and a large number of "cruel details" and stories of mishaps and deaths.

MUSCULAR TENSION

Plutchik (1954) was interested in studying the relationship betwen muscular tension and expressions of fantasy, on the theory that residual tension which is not released in activity will persist and may find eventual release in fantasy activity. She studied nine boys and nine girls of nursery school age (four years) using teacher and parent ratings of tension and of fantasy activities, and ratings of fantasy on CAT stories. Items rated as indicative of muscular tension included such things as: heavy breathing, stuttering, vomiting, tremors, restlessness, tics, bed wetting, and poor motor coordination. Fantasy items on the rating scales included: making up stories, creative block play, imaginary companions, playing alone and talking to self.

CAT stories were rated (on a ten-point scale) for: introduction of objects, actions described which were not illustrated, use of adjectives to describe objects or characters, and story length. The following correlations were reported:

Teacher's rating of fantasy versus parent's rating of fantasy	.853
Teacher's rating of tension versus parent's rating of tension	.503
Teacher's rating of tension versus teacher's rating of fantasy	.891
Teacher's rating of tension versus CAT fantasy	.725
Teacher's rating of fantasy versus CAT fantasy	.798

One could certainly argue that some of the items considered as indicators of "muscular tension" are, instead, means of reducing tensions (i.e., bed wetting, grinding teeth, restlessness, etc.). It might have been more parsimonious to have hypothesized a relationship between fantasy measures and disturbances revealed in deviant motor expressions rather than inserting the second-order cause and effect theory of tension reduction. In any case, substantial correlations were found between the motor behaviors checked and the fantasies revealed on the CAT or observed in the school situation.

EMOTIONAL DISTURBANCE

The disturbances included in this section range from judgments of poor adjustment by teachers to actual clinic referrals. So far as can be determined none of the Ss included in these studies were considered to be psychotic.

The first study was concerned with the adjustment patterns of nursery school children. Raff (1951) asked teachers of each of four nursery groups to select those five children considered to be the best adjusted socially and those five children deemed to be worst adjusted. These 20 worst and 20 best-adjusted children were then administered the CAT. Complete protocols were rated for the presence or absence of fantasy, movement, constructiveness, energy, control, and hostility toward parent figures. Ratings were also made for specific versus free-floating anxiety and for indications of maturity versus immaturity.

The 16 most extreme cases (on the basis of teacher ratings) were then studied more intensively. In the well-adjusted group (eight Ss) each area was scored in the positive direction by more than half the Ss, and there was a low incidence of hostility expressed toward parents. In contrast, the socially maladjusted group gave very few positive responses, especially in the areas of fantasy, constructiveness, control and maturity, but they were also low on hostility toward parents.

De Sousa (1952) administered the CAT to 15 children who had been referred to the school psychologist as behavior problems and to 15 children who were rated by their teachers as being well adjusted. Equal numbers of cases were selected at each age level from six through ten years. Stories were analyzed for content and structural details. Content items included: characteristics of the hero; his attitude toward important figures in his world and their attitude toward him; introduction of objects, figures and external circumstances. Structural details referred to such things as coherence, mood, type of ending, evidences of blocking and indecision, self-references, treatment of details, and amount of verbalization.

Numerous differences were found between groups. The maladjusted children more often saw the identification figure as inferior and rejected (or as ambivalent as to whether accepted or rejected); more often identified with the character seen as aggressive; saw the environment as more threatening; and more frequently expressed antagonism to the mother figure. There were no differences between groups in the amount of antagonism expressed toward the father or in the attitudes of parents and siblings toward the hero.

Significant differences were noted between groups in the introduction of objects, figures or circumstances, with greater occurrence in the maladjusted group of: punishment, violence, accidents, aggression, friends, enemies, injustice, deception, stealing, pursuers and weapons. There were no differences in the frequency of introduction of themes of food, deprivations or benefactors.

Significant findings relating to the structure of the stories included more incoherent stories, more depressed and fewer happy stories, more blocking, indecision, unusual detail treatment and distortions in the maladjusted group. There was no significant difference in the number of words, although the maladjusted group had a higher mean figure. For both groups, Cards 8 and 9 elicited the most verbalization, while Cards 1 and 2 elicited the least.

For one further method of comparison, three clinicians were asked to divide the 30 protocols into equal groups of presumed well- and poorly-adjusted and arrived at a significant discrimination between groups.

De Sousa (1952) summarizes his findings as follows:

In general, the maladjusted child tends to view his world as threatening to him. This attitude is not reflected in his portrayal of parental or sibling attitudes toward him, but occurs in his repeated introduction of punishment, death, accidents, enemies and violence against a melancholy backdrop of depression, tragedy, rejection, and inferiority. In his fantasies, he reacts to these threats with vigorous rebellion and attempts to dispel them with aggressive behavior. He introduces injustice, deception, stealing and weapons to deal with them and aggressive acts, violence, and death are directed toward those with whom he is in conflict. His general approach in fantasy suggests that he is constantly on the defensive against a world in which he is inferior and rejected and from which he expects no compassion (p. 53).

Mainard and Marcuse (1954), as reported in more detail in Chapter IV, administered six animal cards and six equivalent human cards to 28 children (ages 5 yrs 4 mos. to 8 yrs. 5 mos.) who were either on the therapy waiting list of a psychiatric clinic or residents of a home for emotionally disturbed children. While the main focus of this study was a comparison of the stories elicited by the human versus the animal form, the data were also compared with that previously secured from a normal population, using the same cards and the same method of analysis. They report that the disturbed group took slightly longer to respond to each card, while their total response time and mean number of words per card were considerably less than the normal group Unfortunately, no comparative analysis of dynamic factors was reported.

Simon (1954) administered the CAT to 49 Viennese children between the ages of 2.8 and 6.9 years. Of the group, 21 were manifesting some difficulties in that 11 were attending a kindergarten for neurotic children, four were under treatment at a child guidance clinic and six were enrolled in a kindergarten for the physically handicapped. The control group consisted of 28 normal children. Some of her findings demonstrating differences between the two groups were as follows: Of the 19 cases showing good awareness of reality, 17 were in the control group; while of the ten cases with very poor reality testing, eight were in the disturbed group. The four children showing the most extreme passivity were all in the control group. In terms of sex-role identity, of the 21 children attending the normal kindergarten, 12 showed some degree of confusion (four, markedly so); of the 15 neurotic or clinic cases, eight showed some confusion in identification (five to an extreme degree).

Simon (1954) summarizes her findings on group differences as follows: "The principal distinguishing signs between the two groups seem to be that the better-adjusted children show a more realistic appreciation of the apprehended perils, show relatively greater confidence in the protective quality of their parents, and take a more optimistic view of the ultimate outcome of the conflicts" (p. 219).

Boulanger-Balleyguier (1960) has published a monograph reporting a CAT study of six- and seven-year-old normal and disturbed children. From a pool of 126 clinic referrals she selected those Ss in this age group whose most prominent behavioral reactions were either aggression or anxiety. These were contrasted with 39 normal children (mean IQ=109.4). There were 30 Ss in the Aggressive group (mean IQ=99.3) and 18 in the Anxious group (mean IQ=108.2). The Aggressives are described as destructive, impulsive, antisocial, independent of adults and lacking in self-control. The Anxious children were passive-resistant, exhibited excessive self-control, were timid, withdrawn, fearful, dependent (especially toward mother), had immature habit patterns, and compensated for their few friends by reading and daydreaming. Some interesting differences in family histories were found: children from both clinical groups had experienced absences (of six months or more) from the home, especially before the age of three; there were significantly more "only" children in the clinical groups than in the normal group. The Aggressive Ss had a more disrupted family life than the Anxious, with more broken homes, more fathers completely absent, and more mothers who worked or were physically ill. In contrast, more mothers of the Anxious group were described as emotionally disturbed, with a high proportion showing tendencies toward anxiety and depression.

The CAT protocols were first examined for differences in formal structure. There were no differences between groups in the number of omissions and no significant differences in number of false perceptions, although the Anxious tended to give more than the Normals, with the Aggressives giving the fewest. There was a tendency for the Normals to give more popular responses than the clinical groups; the difference for girls was significant. The Anxious group gave many more additions and fabulations than the Aggressives or Normals, confirming the theory that withdrawn, fearful children have a more intense fantasy life and create more imaginary characters.

Perseverations were infrequent for all groups, but were given more often by the disturbed children. Themes perseverated centered around daily activities for the Normals, but around conflict and morbid aspects for the more disturbed Ss. Cruel details were also rare, but were given twice as often by the Anxious as by the Aggressives or Normals. Cruel details were those which involved detailed descriptions of the way the harm was done, with a mixture of pleasure and horror on the part of the storyteller. A few of the highly disturbed Ss gave a large number of responses of this type.

Boulanger-Balleyguier has proposed an anxiety index consisting of: additions, fabulations, and cruel details.

In an analysis of the story content, the descriptions of the hero were examined. Significantly more Anxious than Aggressive Ss saw the figures as human, with the Aggressives more often speaking of the figures in terms of the animal represented. The Anxious were differentiated significantly from both the Aggressives and Normals in seeing more figures specifically as boys or girls. The author questions whether the naming of the sex of child characters is thus an indication of identification of the S or a sign of anxious attempts at affirmation of an identification which may in reality be confused.

In terms of the hero's activities, the Anxious mentioned more aggressive and dependent activities than the other two groups, suggesting that the aggressive stories of the Anxious child indicate projection of aggressive tendencies or, more likely, repressed desires for freedom and for revenge where the environment does not permit the child to overtly rebel. On the other hand, the greater incidence of dependency stories would be reflecting the child's overt character. The Anxious group tended to mention more oral and anal activities, while Normals, especially girls, tended to emphasize orderliness and cleanliness.

The Anxious attributed significantly more aggressive activities to the mother than did the Normals, while Normals gave significantly more dominating activities to the mother than did the Aggressives. The Anxious children generally saw the parents as hostile, with parental authority representing a perpetual threat of enforced obedience. The mother was seen as more dominating by the Normals than by either of the disturbed groups but her authority engendered less conflict and was better accepted; in contrast, the Aggressive Ss described an environment lacking in authority figures.

Both disturbed groups mentioned more misfortunes and deaths than did the Normals but the entire incidence was too small to determine statistical significance. The Aggressives gave more themes of misfortunes and the Anxious gave more death themes.

In terms of resolution of conflicts, the Aggressives saw a large number of successes for the hero and few for the mother; they also presented the largest number of unresolved conflicts. The Anxious gave significantly more success to mother (when compared to the Aggressives) and to the father (in comparison with Normals). The Normals attributed significantly more successes to characters other than hero or parents (when compared to the disturbed groups).

To summarize: The Normal child's stories reflect better perception of the stimulus and his thought processes seem in better harmony with that of the adult world than is true for the disturbed groupings. There are fewer frightening and morbid aspects in his stories; mother is ascribed an important and dominating role which is accepted as the normal perogative of the adult who is responsible for the daily aspects of family living. The Normals seem less egocentric than the disturbed Ss.

The stories of the Aggressives remain fairly objective, with meager imaginative features, and no more aggressiveness in their stories than in those of the Normals. But, like the Anxious, these children show signs of emotional immaturity, are egocentric, less capable of sharing others' points of view, and conscience formation seems retarded. There is no firm authority; parents are seen as negligent and unconcerned with the child's welfare.

The Anxious move further from the stimulus than the other two groups, giving free reign to the imagination, projecting their own image of the world which is often centered around morbid and depressing themes. The greater emphasis on the sex of the figures reflects the S's anxiety concerning his own identification which must be so strongly affirmed. The hero is egocentrically described as engaged in much aggressive activity, while the other characters, especially the mother, are in perpetual conflict, with the parents usually emerging successful.

Beller and Haeberle (1959) used six CAT cards in a study of dependency motivation in emotionally disturbed preschool children. The investigators were interested in determining the relationship of phantasy to the strength of dependency motivation (e.g., frequently and persistently seeking help from an adult) and dependency *conflict* (e.g., high on *both* dependent and independent striving).

Two experimental situations were designed to precede the CAT administration. In the dependency situation, a toy was exposed out of the child's reach to see if he would seek the adult's help. Following this, a similar situation was presented in the context of structured doll play. Three CAT cards (Cards 1, 4 and 9), chosen to elicit dependent phantasies, were then administered. In the experimental aggressive situation, toys could be reached only after knocking over obstacles; this was followed by a similar doll play situation and then by three CAT cards (Cards 3, 7 and 10) chosen to elicit aggressive phantasies.

It was found that highly dependent children introduced family figures and help-seeking themes to Card 9 significantly more often than did low-dependent Ss. In contrast, children high on dependency conflict introduced more threatening figures to all three dependency cards. With respect to Card 1, more high (than low) dependent Ss introduced themes of direct gratification of oral needs while children high on dependency conflict gave more aggressive and punishment phantasies to this card than did Ss who had low dependency conflict.

Following the aggressive experiment, the high dependent Ss gave stories to the aggressive cards which denied or belittled the aggressive role of parental figures. Children with high dependency conflict, on the other hand, gave significantly more aggressive themes to dependency cards, while children low in dependency conflict gave more aggressive responses to the aggressive cards.

To summarize the findings, children high in dependency motivation give more dependent phantasies, more themes of direct need gratification, and tend to deny the threatening or aggressive aspects of parental figures. Children who have high dependency conflict give more phantasies of threat, pain and punishment in situations suggestive of dependency and at the same time tend to magnify the aggressive role of parents. Those Ss with high dependency conflict are thus displaying an inappropriateness and lack of adequate differentiation between dependent and aggressive stimuli.

Haworth (1963) compared CATs of school Ss with those of Ss referred to a psychological clinic, using her Analysis Schedule to evaluate the responses. In a previous study (Haworth, 1962), 15 presumably normal school Ss had been compared with 15 matched school cases who had given prior deviant responses to a film test. The mean of critical scores on the CAT for the experimental group was 4.73, for the control group 1.26, and for the combined school sample, 3.00. Fifteen clinic cases were then matched (for sex and school grade) to the school sample. The mean number of critical scores for the clinic group was found to be 6.73. In the school sample, only eight Ss (all experimental) had five or more critical scores and 15 Ss had three or more. By contrast, no child in the clinic group had fewer than four critical scores, while 14 of the 15 cases had five or more scores.

Table 10.1 compares the frequency of critical scores for the two school groupings and the clinic sample.

Table 10.1 Frequency of Critical Scores for Each Category of the CAT Schedule†

		School Control N = 15	Control versus Exper.	School Exper. N = 15	Exper. versus Clinic	Clinic N = 15	Clinic versus Control
1.	Reaction & undoing	1	****	9		10	****
2.	Isolation	2	****	11		12	****
3.	Repression & denial	4		8		11	**
4.	Deception	4		7		2	
5.	Symbolization	1	*	6		8	***
6.	Projection & introjection	3		7		8	
7.	Fear & anxiety	2		6		8	*
8.	Regression	0		2	****	10	****
9.	Weak controls	0	*	4	****	14	****
10.	Identification	2	****	11		11	****

     * .05 level of significance.
    ** .025 level of significance.
   *** .01 level of significance.
  **** .005 level of significance.

†Reproduced, with the permission of the publisher, from the *Journal of Projective Techniques* 27:181–184, 1963.

The clinic group differed significantly from the school experimental group only in those two categories which suggest the most pathology, namely Regression and Weak Controls. The only two categories where no differences were found between any of the groupings were Deception and Projection-Introjection. Presumably these categories can be considered to represent typical responses for children of this age group, regardless of the presence or absence of emotional problems.

A search of the literature has revealed two Japanese studies of disturbed children in which the CAT was the major instrument used.* In a study by Marui (1957):

CAT responses by two groups of five- and six-year-old children were compared; 34 children in reformatories and 50 children from a kindergarten. Bellack's pictures were used with minor modification. Results were as follows: the institutionalized children rarely projected parents and emotional parents-child relation in their

---

*Unfortunately, the only information available on these two studies is from the abstracts appearing in *Psychological Abstracts* 34: 4129, 6037, 1960. The abstracts are reproduced with the permission of the Managing Editor, American Psychological Association.

response, their need responses were limited to food and play, their stories were picture dominant and poorly structured and were neither happy nor unhappy but emotionally neutral. It was concluded that CAT is a useful tool to investigate need, anxiety, and conflict in children (*Psychol. Abstr.* 34: 6037, 1960).

A brief summary of Kanehira's (1958) study is as follows:

CAT records of 30 problem children in the clinic of Tokyo Central Child Welfare Center are discussed in relation to their backgrounds. It was found that those who have more affection for parents tend to make stories including parent-child interaction and do not neglect the parents, whereas those who have less affection tend to make stories without parent-child interaction and neglect the parents. Those who have democratic and permissive parents tend to make stories of protective parents with happy results, whereas those who have authoritarian and restrictive parents tend to make stories of rejective parents with unhappy endings (*Psychol. Abstr.* 34: 4129, 1960).

PARENTAL LOSS

The emotional problems of orphanage children were studied by Stevenson (1952) using the CAT. Subjects were 24 children (12 boys and 12 girls) eight and nine years of age who had spent at least their first five years at home, then had subsequently been sent to an orphanage in Halifax due to the death or separation of parents. All were of at least average intelligence. An equal number of controls from intact homes were matched for age, sex, IQ, and socioeconomic level.

The findings are reported under the following headings:

(1) *Adequacy feelings.* Twice as many orphanage children feel generally inadequate, and the difference is especially noted among girls.

(2) *Aggression.* Orphanage children show less aggression, seemingly due more to repression than because of less hostility. In situations where the child character is the target of aggressive acts, the orphanage children more often submit passively or give themes of flight, with no fantasied protector to whom they can look for help.

(3) *Guilt.* Guilt reactions for any reason, but especially for aggressive actions, are highest in the orphanage group.

(4) *Sex typing.* This is less well established among the orphanage children, who are more uncertain as to the sex of the heroes. Orphanage girls use more male heroes than the control girls.

(5) *Sibling rivalry.* Stories of rivalry appear much less often in the orphaned group, but when they do occur, there is less aggression and more withdrawal.

(6) *Anxiety.* Anxiety is high in both groups, but the orphanage Ss show a larger number of more intense fears. For this group, fear of deprivation and of disapproval far outweigh fear of punishment or of physical harm.

(7) *Attitudes toward parents.* "The children of the control group are, on the whole, influenced by reality in their attitudes to their parents; in the orphanage the reverse is true. While a minority express a preference for the parent who is active and responsible, two-thirds reject the attentive parent for one who is dead or has deserted them, building up a fantasy picture of

that parent which makes acceptance of the remaining one still more difficult" (Stevenson, 1952, p. 181).

In summarizing her data, Stevenson (1952) states: "The contrast with the control group is greatest in two areas: the controls give as well as ask for affection; and they attempt more active solutions to their problems. Where unwholesome defenses appear they are more like neurotic symptoms, especially compulsions, in contrast to the schizoid withdrawal of so many of the orphanage group" (pp. 181-182).

In a study of the projective responses of children who had lost a parent before the age of six, Haworth (1964) found that specific types of items were given more frequently by parentally deprived children than by children from intact families. Projective data, largely from the Rorschach, CAT and TAT, were secured from 95 children who had lost one or both parents and from 87 control cases. The parentally deprived Ss were selected from the files of two different clinics and from residents of children's homes (who had not been clinic referred). Controls for the clinic Ss were children from continuously intact families but who had also been referred to a clinic for emotional problems. School Ss served as controls for the nonclinic children with loss.

An index of 20 "loss" items was prepared and used in the analysis. Some of the items were specific for the Rorschach, but the following types of responses could be found in the CAT (or the other verbal techniques employed):

(a) Responses referring to damage to a ship or a mountain.

(b) Responses referring to temperature contrasts (e.g., hot and cold, on the same card); color projection (seeing chromatic color on the black and white cards); percepts of spaces filled to bursting (e.g., "basement filled with honey," "balloon popping").

(c) Responses directly reflecting parental loss or felt desertion, including mention of haunted houses, ghost towns, empty rooms or no place to stay. (Whereas normal children may often speak of a *child* character as running away, 29 per cent of the parentally deprived children spoke of the *parent* going away and not returning, as contrasted with only 9 per cent of children from intact families.)

(d) Responses referring to successive attacks (e.g., a tiger eating a monkey with a hunter killing the tiger); two figures fighting over a third; magical change of form or species. (The "attack" items may be stimulated by the child's experiences of being passed from parent to parent or foster family, etc., or by knowledge that the parents are fighting over his custody.)

(e) Responses of death, bones, blood, anatomy and ghosts.

The extent of use of the "loss" responses was analyzed in relation to deprived children versus children from intact families; and, within the loss group, data were analyzed with respect to any sex differences, sex of "lost" parent in relation to sex of child, and any differences between clinic referred and nonclinic Ss (residents of children's homes) with parental loss.

The mean number of loss responses for the total loss group was significantly higher than for the combined control groups. There were no significant differences between clinic referred and nonclinic Ss who had lost a parent. Apparently, loss of both parents results in more disturbance than the loss of only one parent (irrespective of the sex of the lost parent), and losing both parents, including the death of one of them, yielded the highest number of loss reactions. Although the tone of the loss items reflects considerable aggression and activity, boys with loss did not differ from girls in the number utilized, and girls with loss exceeded boys from intact families.

It was felt that the content of the responses utilized so frequently by these parentally deprived children—dealing with themes of damage, contrasts, separation, successive attacks and death—reflects a marked degree of depression and premature preoccupation with questions of hostility, ambivalence, sexuality, origins and death.

SUMMARY

The CAT has been used in the psychological assessment of a variety of clinical disorders, ranging from physical disabilities to psychoses. Many different evaluative criteria have been employed, with varying degrees of statistical sophistication. In most of the studies, control groups have been used or Ss selected from the extremes of a continuum. The demonstrable and meaningful differences reported provide evidence for the usefulness of the CAT as a projective and diagnostic instrument.

CHAPTER XI

Diagnostic Protocols

Illustrative protocols of various diagnostic entities will be presented more or less on a continuum of fantasy production from representative examples of the constricted, barren records of retardates, through the rich fantasy life revealed in neurotic records to final representations of the psychotic process.

RETARDATION

Girl, CA=12 years 2 months (WISC Full Scale IQ below 46; Verbal=56).

This girl's general behavior and reactions were on a primitive immature level. Note, in her stories, the extensive use of descriptions of the basic activity represented in each picture. Additional inquiry yielded little in the way of additional material. Imaginative and fantasy skills are totally lacking.

1. They're eating,
   going to get ready to eat.
(Q) Going to eat now.

2. This bear and this bear and this bear,
Trying to pull this bear (single) up.
(Q) Don't know (rubs head as if it aches,
   pulls strands of hair).

3. Well, he's just settin' down,
Watching something.
(Q) Don't know.

4. Mother and little one
   going for a picnic.
And the other one
   riding bicycle.
(Q) Go home.

5. There's two bears
   going take their naps.
(Q) Probably get up.

6. They're sleeping.
(Q) Don't know.

7. Well, lion,
   he's gonna get that monkey.
(Q) Don't know.

8. Those two talking,
   whispering about something.
(Q-others?) Don't know.
(Q-next?) Then going home.

9. He just got through
    taking his nap.
(Q) Play.

10. He's feeding the dog.
No, he's gonna spank the dog.
(Q-why?) Don't know.
(Q-next?) Probably cry.

Analysis Schedule: Repression and Denial

Girl, CA=10 years 10 months (WISC Full Scale IQ=72; Verbal=72;
Performance=78).

Although this child's mental level is considerably higher than the first case
presented, her stories are also largely bland and descriptive. There are more
qualifications and mention of more details, but no integration into concepts
over and above those pictured on the cards. The general activities mentioned
are of a simple, everyday type and no objects or characters are introduced.

1. Chickens are eating
    some kind of food.
Mother is in back of table.
(Q) Not eating yet,
Mother has come to fix the dishes
    and put the food in bowls.
2. Playing tug-of-war.
Bears have a rope
    and playing tug-of-war.
Mother bear and the baby bear
    is going to win.
3. Lion is sitting in a chair
    and he's hanging on to a cane
    and smoking a pipe.
There's a mouse down on the floor,
King of beasts.
(Q) He might get kicked out,
    the lion.
4. They're in the woods—kangaroos.
Next to oldest is riding a tricycle.
Mother is carrying a baby,
    has a hat and purse on.
Back there is a house.
Baby is carrying a balloon.
5. At night—bears are asleep.
Two baby bears sleeping in the bed.
Mother—
    don't see anybody on big bed.
It's dark in there
    and they're asleep.

6. Bears are sleeping,
   Mama and Papa bear is inside sleeping.
   Baby bear is right by them—awake.
   Can't get to sleep.
(Q) The light—
   it's morning and in winter
   and they hibernate.
   He hasn't gone to sleep yet.

7. Lion is jumping at monkey
   and monkey is screaming.
It's in the morning,
   and the lion is hungry
   and then he's jumping out of the tree.
(Q) Monkey runs up the tree.

8. The mama bear—no, monkeys,
A picture on the wall
   and mother and father is talking and drinking
   and sister and baby are by him talking.
In a house and going to drink some coffee
   and go to bed.
   Dark outside.

9. Well—the rabbits in bed.
Looks like he's sick.
It's in the morning.
   It's going to get up,
   and the door's open
   and the window's open—top and bottom.
(Q) He looks like he's sad.
(Q) It's a her—a girl.
(Q) I suppose her mother
   keeps on telling her to get back in bed.

10. Mama is spanking the little dog—
   the child in the bathroom.
Toilet and towel and bathtub.
Sitting in chair
   spanking the dog.
(Q) He must be naughty.
(Q) Water all over the floor.

Analysis Schedule: No critical scores.

CEREBRAL PALSY

Boy, CA=7 years 10 months (Stanford-Binet IQ=102).
   This boy was a spastic diplegic of average intelligence who had been
adopted in infancy. Speech was labored, with many false starts and unfinished

phrases. While his record is more detailed and imaginative than many cerebral palsy protocols, it is nevertheless very much bound to the stimulus and concerned with covering all the details in the pictures. Themes of injury are prominent, as on Cards 3 and 9, reflecting his own feelings of motor helplessness and vulnerability, which are brought out even more openly in the additional inquiry to Card 10 where he expresses fears of falling into the toilet. On Card 5 the examiner has also tried to assess his feelings toward his handicap, in the additional inquiry, and he handles this quite realistically.

1. Well, they're a . . birds, I think,
    and they're sitting around the table
    and there's bowls and . . this big .
    and where they put this stuff in the big bowl here
    and there is a table and chairs and a . .
And I can see a rooster
    over here in the corner.
(Q) I think it is that . . .
    once upon a time . .
(Q) Bir . birds or chickens or the other
    are . . are . were eating . .
    and were gettin ready to eat
    and they're sittin there gettin ready,
And . . their mother's comin over . .
    comin over here in the corner
    to see rooster and that's why.
(Q) So the mother comes over
    and dishes out the stuff
    and they start to eat.
(Q) He's out maybe crowing.
(Q) Went out and played.

2. The bears, two big bears and a little bear
    out pulling on a rope.
(Q) And I think the one bear wouldn't go
    and it . . and it . on the rock . you know
    right by the edge and I think that . .
The little bear and the big bear fall off the edge
    because this bear over here lets go of the rope
    and they're pulling
    and they go off the edge and down to . .
(Q) Father (Q) and this is the mother.
(Q) Because she was . . she wanted to
(Q) They went down.
(Q) They just a . . might have fallen
    into some water or somethin.
(Q) They went . . . they got out of the water
    and a . . went back home.
(Q) They didn't . . . they told her to go out

and never come back again.
(Q) Terrible.

3.   This is a . . you know out of the jungle
     they always have to have a King of the jungle.
Well this is the King of the jungle and a . .
He's sitting here and he's worried
     and he's chained
     and he's a real old lion
     and his cane is sitting by the edge of his chair
     and he's holding his car keys . .
     worried about something.
(Q) Worried about the forest . .
     that somebody might . that some of the animals might get hurt.
(Q) Maybe by coming out in the road . .
     like a squirrel might come out in the road
     and get run over . .
(Q) A lot of times it does . . .
     Like sometimes dogs get around the floor
     so you know how many times a dog gets run over.
(Q) Once mine almost did though.
     Well he . . he . . his chains popped,
     you know, how the chains break sometime.
He went down where the place for the boats were,
     he went down there
     and the people were talking about . . the dog
     and you know they were talking about
     and they . . . and they happen to look over . . . and they . .
And Twinkle was my dog's name
     so they rushed down there and got her
     and brought her back home
     and stuck the thing around so the a . .
     was around the pole and the pole here . .
He was riding around the pole
     and took back around the chain.

4.   I think this is . What are they?
Kanga . Kanga . . Kanga Kangaroos,
A mother and she's bringing a picnic basket,
     her baby in her pocket,
     and her . . her . . another baby in the pocket
     is about one-year-old probably,
     and the one in the bike is about three
     and the . . . the . . . and the young she is dragging is.
She is hopping along
     with her hat and her purse
     and they're going down to the woods,

Anyways the baby's got a balloon
   and he's riding a bike
   and they're going down to the woods to have a picnic.
(Q) He feels that . . he thinks he's lucky.
(Q) Because he . . his mother can take him
   and he has to peddle to go.
(Q) Because he can't peddle or nothing yet.

5.   (Q-Tell me about that)
I think there are two little teddy bears sleeping
and a . . . and their mother and father are out
   maybe fixing lunch or dinner or something
and they're laying down in their pen sleeping,
and there is a lamp and a bed,
   a window, and a curtain, and a shade,
   and a table in there
   and they are sleeping in there.
And when their mother and dad
   get through with supper,
   they're going to come in too . . .
Well they will bring her in
   and they tell, you know,
   "Come out and eat".
(Q-What were they doing while they were waiting?)
   Laying, sleeping.
(Q-What was the little boy dreaming about?)
About he going to be a grown-up
   and be a big bear.
(Q-What's he going to do when he grows up to be a big bear?)
   He's going to have a family
   and some children and everything.
(Q-Suppose one of his children has cerebral palsy, how will he feel about
that?)
   Terrible.
(Q-Why?) Then he . .
   he'd have to wear something to help it walk.
(Q-How would the little boy feel about this?)
   He wouldn't like it either.
(Q-Why?) Cause . . . then . .
   he couldn't walk enough . .
   he'd have to have something
   on his leg all the time.

6.   These, I think, are some bears again
   and they are in a cave
   and the mother and father are laying down
   and this little baby.

(Q) Well, .a. . . he's thinking about something.
(Q) Well, . . how he's going to . .
  what's he going to be when he grows up.
(Q) I think a father bear.
(Q) Care for his family probably.
(Q) By he'll care for his family
  and get them food, all that, . .
  and nice things to do.

7. This is the jungle.
  There is a monkey, a tree,
  and a big tiger,
  and it's running after the monkey,
And he's climbing that tree in the jungle
  and—and the tiger's after the monkey and . .
I think he's mad at the monkey for some reason.
(Q) Because I either think
  he took some of his food or did something.
(Q) A . . boy. It's a man really.
(Q) Because it goes up the tree
  and it don't come down until the tiger goes away.

8. Well, . . . there's a mother and a father . . in the picture . . .
And I think there's some people come over to visit
  and this one . . man over here
  is pointing to the boy for some reason
  and he's, she whispers in his ear.
And . . . and he's drinking coffee
  and I think he says we're going to . . .
Monkeys . . the two monkeys on the davenport
  are the owners.
And the other two are just visiting him
  and telling the monkey something.
(Q) I think that . . that . .
  want to play or something like that.
(Q) It's when they don't have anybody
  to visit with or nothing.

9. Well, . . . this is a . . . is a .
  little baby bunny in his room . .
  and he's sitting up.
And the curtains and a . . .
  mirror, lamp, table . . .
  in his pen and he's in his room.
And the mother and father
  are probably gone away
  and probably a baby sitter's there and a . . .
(Q) Thinking about what

he's going to be when he grows up.
(Q) Mother bunny.
(Q) Ya, mother bunny.
(Q) Yes, he's worried.
(Q) That they might get run over
   or something like that.

10.   There is a mother dog
   and I think the dog has done something wrong
   and she is going to spank him.
She is sitting in his chair,
   and there's the bathroom, and the towel,
   and the toilet and everything.
(Q-What did the dog do wrong?)
   He might have went outside
   when his mother told him not to.
(Q-Why did he do that?)
   Because he wanted to.
(Q-Let's suppose this is a little doggy who wets his pants. What would his
mother do?)
   Would have to clean them out and everything.
(Q-Would she make him do it?) Yes.
(Q-What would he think about that?)
   He wouldn't like it.
(Q-Why not?) Because he don't like
   to get his hands in that.
   He'd be in all that.
(Q-Why did he wet his pants?)
   Because he didn't want to go to the bathroom.
(Q-Is because he doesn't want to go to the bathroom because he doesn't want
to touch himself. Is that why?)
   I think he's afraid
   he'll go down the toilet.
(Q-Why is he afraid?)
   Because he might go down the toilet
   and his mother wouldn't know it
   and she would flush him down the toilet.
   Analysis Schedule: Isolation
                        Projection and Introjection
                        Fear and Anxiety
                        Confused Identification

BRAIN DAMAGE

Boy, CA=7 years 8 months (WISC Full Scale IQ=99; Verbal=110;
Performance=87).

This child was diagnosed as "chronic brain syndrome associated with a
convulsive disorder." At the age of five, he had suffered a head injury when

a nail penetrated near the edge of his left eye. Grand mal seizures began one year later, following an attack of chicken pox.

Word-finding difficulties are particularly apparent throughout the CAT protocol, especially on Cards 1, 2, 4, and 9. He was restless throughout testing. When pushed for more details he would become vague and almost incoherent, e.g., during the additional "dream" inquiry to Card 5. Oral-dependent needs are prominent throughout this record.

1. Three little chickens
    and mother rooster, I mean mother hen.
One of the chickens
    doesn't have a napkin on
    like the rest of them should.
Mother chicken's going to
    give them some food.

2. Three bears having a tug-of-war.
    Two against one.
Mother bear, I mean papa bear
    and baby bear going to win.

3. Lion sitting in chair
    with cane and pipe.
Mouse and he. . . (yawns and becomes vague)
    He's going to come out
    and look at the lion.
(Q) The lion will see him and take him.
(Q) Eat him.

4. Mother kangaroo pulling
    'nother giraffe, I mean kangaroo.
Going on picnic.
Baby kangaroo has a balloon
Mother kangaroo and other kangaroo
    has bicycle and a purse.
(Q) Wolf might come and eat 'em up.
(Q) Don't know.
We going to do all of them?

5. Two little baby bears
    and they're sleeping.
    One of them's sleeping.
It's in the night
    and they're in bedroom.
(Q) (Yawns) The bear that's not asleep
    might get out
    and go outdoors
    and go in some people's house
    and get some of their food

and bring it back.
(Q-dream?) Maybe a policeman or something.
(Q-police do?) Policeman naughty policeman.
(Q-why?) Don't know.

6. Two bears sleeping, hibernating rather.
Little bear just came in to sleep.
Big bears are already asleep.
  They're in a cave.
(Q-why little one late?) Because he was
  out picking berries.
  'Cause he didn't have any food.
(Q-didn't big bears give?)
  No, just one big one.
Hope this is the last.

7. Tiger's going after the monkey.
Monkey will climb tree
  and throw a coconut down
  and hit the tiger on the head.
He's going to swing
  from one of the branches.
(Q) The tiger might wake up
  and climb the tree
  and get the monkey and eat him.
Hope there's no more.

8. These two monkeys,
  two of them were talking,
All four talking to each other.
(Q-talk about?) Don't know (closes eyes, yawns, restless).

9. Little rabbit's in bed, sick.
It's Peter Rabbit,
  and Moppy, Floppy.
Moppy and Cotton Tail were good.
But Peter was bad.
Because he went right straight to
  Mr. McGeorge's . . . Gregor's garden
And his mother told him not to.
His mother said that
  his father had an accident,
  got caught by Mr. McGeorger
  and Mrs. McGregor made him into rabbit pie.
(Loud yawn).

10. Little puppy, playing together,
  playing in bathroom.
No, the mother dog

is giving baby dog a spanking.
(Q) Because he ran off.
(Q) Baby dog doesn't run off anymore.

Analysis Schedule: Projection and Introjection
               Fear and Anxiety

BEHAVIOR DISORDER, ACTING-OUT

Boy, CA=7 years 8 months (Stanford-Binet IQ=92).

The referral problem was exclusion from school because of extremely aggressive physical attacks on peers. He used much profanity and adopted an insolent, superior attitude toward teachers and other adults. When he could not be in control of a situation he would soon lose interest, become careless, or refuse to cooperate altogether. The examining psychologist reported: "He seems basically to be a typical acting-out child, operating in a very immediate, immature and impulsive fashion. . . It was difficult to hold this boy's attention to projective tasks. His approach is literal, with no use of fantasy or imagination." His overriding concern was to get through the task as quickly as possible. On Card 1 of the CAT he demonstrates his typical behavior pattern of changing the "rules of the game" to suit his own ends. His chief defenses, as reflected in the CAT, are isolation and denial. There was almost no identification with any of the stimulus figures.

1. Getting ready to eat.
(Q) Go back in the nest.
(Q) Go to sleep.
(Q) Nothing else.
Are we going to go through all of those?
No, I can't do that.
I know how to do it quicker.
Take half like this (taking four cards)
    and lay them out for a story.

2. The name is "Three Bears,"
    I know that.
(Q) Having a tug-of-war, with a rope.
Somebody put ink on
    to look like this.
(Q-win?) Don't know.
(Q-who are they?) Father (single figure),
    mother and baby (pair).
(Q-win?) Don't know (long pause).
    Papa might win.
I don't want to go through all them, OK?

3. Don't know what happens.
Lion sitting on chair.
(Q-thinking?) Don't know,
    Because it ain't real.

Let's don't do them all,
  too hard for me.

4. There's a kangaroo.
Mr. and Mrs. Kangaroo going on a picnic.
Nobody going on a picnic,
  Mrs. Kangaroo is,
  not father, probably working.

5. Don't know who's lying in bed.
(Q-happen?) Don't know what's going to happen.
I can see a lump on the bed,
  because somebody might be in it.
(Q-dream?) Ain't dreaming about nothing.

6. Just three more to go,
I'm glad (yawns),
There's papa and mama bear
  going, "ug, ug, ug,"
  because they're all tired out.
They're sleepy and say,
  "Lets go to bed," and say,
  "Who's eating my porridge?"
The little bear gobbled it all up.

7. Don't know. That's Tarzan.
Lion's chasing the monkey.
Monkey's trying to get away.
How come monkey's scream so much?

8. I hate monkeys.
Don't like to tell stories about them.
They're drinking coffee,
  having a little party.
(Q-who comes?) Everybody's there,
  That's all I can say.

9. Little bunny. . . .
  Going to sleep in his bed.
He likes it there,
  He's smiling.

10. I think the little dog's saying,
  "Where, oh where, did my little dog go?"
He's thinking that.
(Q) One's going to the bathroom.
Other one's going to bed,
  Going to bathroom first.

    Analysis Schedule: Isolation
                Repression and Denial

CHARACTER DISORDER

Boy, CA=9 years 0 months (WISC Full Scale=108; Verbal=108; Performance=107).

This boy is the third child in a sibship of six and, interestingly enough in view of some of the CAT responses (e.g., Cards 3 and 9), was the only one of the children who was not enuretic. He was referred for silly actions in school and highly aggressive behavior toward his sibs, such as wrapping a rope around a younger child's neck. He would frequently dress in girl's clothes and said he wanted to become a priest.

His CAT responses reveal competitiveness and a self-centered, managerial orientation. Child characters are seen repeatedly as stronger and more capable than the parents (Cards 5 and 7). There is much dependence on magic (Cards 5 and 7). Good things rarely happen and children are generally in the way. There is much peroccupation with birth fantasies (Cards 3, 4 and 9) although two of these stories could also be interpreted as reflecting enuretic concerns. It is notable that the mother figure is rarely mentioned after Card 1 except in a derogatory fashion (Card 8) or in terms of her having "gone away" (Card 9). Where other children usually mention mother figures (Cards 5, 6, and 10) it is only the father whom he talks about.

1. Looks like mother got em to eat.
    Eat noodle soup with chicken,
    Not chicken, because they're chickens,
    with vinegar.
Mother chicken takes them out and buys some more.
One chicken spilled some of his,
The big bowl spilled and the chicken said,
    "At least I got *some*,"
    cause it spilled into his.

2. Playing tug-of-war,
    little brother and big brother
    against the medium-sized brother.
Big brother is pulling the most;
    He ain't even trying.
Little brother is standing behind,
    they win.

3. There's the king.
A bee always comes in his house,
    He tries to get it out.
He calls his servants, and he said,
    "Get out of the house
    and fill the house with water."
Lion said it wouldn't work,
    "It would kill my mouse."
So he sent for another servant,
    He said, "Get out of the house,"

That didn't work.
He sent for another servant,
    a dog professor,
    he said "Get out of the house, take the mouse,
    turn the lights out."
It worked.
The king gave him $100,
    graduated him and that's all.

4.   The kangaroo always put the baby in the pocket.
     The medium-size one is on the bike.
One day the kangaroo couldn't open the pocket,
    she was worried.
When she was sleeping,
    she found the zipper was moving inside.
    It was the little kangaroo.
She said, "Do you know why the zipper wouldn't work?
    She (the baby) was holding on tight
    so it wouldn't work."

5.   One day it was snowy and all rainy.
They couldn't go in bed,
    too cold in bed.
    Put their toys in bed
    and the bed was freezing.
One said, "I see some lumps in this bed,
    think I know what made it."
He put the light on,
    there was papa lying down.
Baby spanked the papa
    and turned the snowswitch off
    and the cold switch off.
And everybody came and played,
    and they lived happily ever after.

6.   Papa bear and baby bear
     sleeping for a long winter's nap.
     Dreamed about Santa Claus.
Baby bear woke up and said,
    "Gee, pop, don't we get our surprises yet?
    No toys in here
    and it's almost spring."

7.   Once a lion was always strong
     and scared all the monkeys and animals.
One day he tried to scare,
    but not enough courage.
He said to the owl,
    "Give me courage, you nasty owl."

The owl said, "You don't need me,
  you had some before.
  Put on your magic shoes and get courage."
The lion said to the owl,
  "Thank you for giving me courage."
The owl said "There's not courage in magic,
  It's in the dirty old boots.
  You have the courage, why do you come to me?"

8. Once a monkey,
  dad, mom, grandmother and boy monkey.
The dad and mom were talking.
The grandpa talked to the little boy monkey,
  "Don't listen to them, listen to me;
  The picture on the wall is grandma monkey,
  it's not a picture.
  That's herself looking through a hole in the wall
  for fourteen years."
One day she said to the grandpa monkey,
  "Don't you dare say that to your son."
And that's the end of the happy monkeys.
(Q) She doesn't want anyone to say,
  "Don't listen to your mom."

9. Once there was a rabbit—
  three rabbits, son, baby, mom.
Mama had to go away.
So the brother took care of the baby.
  It was good until the baby cried.
He went in the room
  and said "Shut up!"
He put on his hat and danced.
The brother laughed and went away,
  Walked and thinking about what mama said
  about taking care of baby brother.
The fox and a weasel had a hole in the fort,
  The weasel snatched the baby.
The brother rabbit came back
  and found the baby gone.
He kept on walking,
  took one more step
  and fell in a hole.
He saw the weasel and the baby in a sack,
  he was about to cook him.
The brother rabbit saved the baby rabbit.
  Went back up the hole,
  got the hose,
  and squirted water

until the baby came out into the air.
The baby rabbit started to laugh,
   so the brother rabbit squirted him too,
   and put the baby rabbit to bed for a whole hour.

10. Once a little dog wanted to see all the animals,
   So his father took him to the zoo.
He saw the giraffe and a turtle.
The manager said,
   "Get out, you nasty dogs."
So he went to the skunk cage,
   and took the chain off.
The zoo man caught him
   and put him in the zoo.
The father dog got him out to see the big raccoon.

   Analysis Schedule: Reaction-formation and Undoing
                         Isolation
                         Deception
                         Symbolization
                         Projection and Introjection
                         Regression

NEUROTIC ACTING-OUT

Boy, CA=9 years 5 months (WISC Full Scale IQ=120; Verbal=101; Performance=138).

This boy was described on referral as being destructive, hard to control, cruel to animals and other youngsters and as having no respect for authority. At school he would urinate on other children and throw their wraps in the toilet. Excerpts from the psychologist's report are as follows: "He is a fearful and anxious child with unresolved oedipal conflicts and castration fears. He overreacts to fears of attack from adults by striking out first. . . . Also prominent is his feeling of being neglected and ostracized by adults when he has misbehaved. . . . He sees both parents as punitive and rejecting, especially his mother, and expresses derogatory feelings toward females in return. Reality contact is good. He is aware of acceptable standards and that his behavior does not always measure up. As yet he has not settled on any consistent pattern of coping with his anxiety but tries various maneuvers (such as intellectualization, rationalization, projection and denial) but none of these are very successful. Consequently he appears inconsistent and unpredictable. His basic conflicts revolve around authority figures, leaving little interest or energy for establishing any close relationships with peers."

1. Some chickens eating some worms.
Looks like they're pounding spoons
   on the table.
Mother's right beside them
   in case one of them
   steps out of line.

(Q) Nobody, but she just might
  if somebody did.
(Q) She'd hit or peck them on the head.

2. Bears playing tug-of-war.
One bear looks unhappy
  because the others are winning.
Little bear came to help the big one.
(Q-who are they?) Don't know their names.
  Better call him Clyde (big one with little).
(Q-win?) Clyde and the little bear.
(Q-other one do?) Be pretty mad.
  Maybe he'll hit,
  or go off and start pouting.

3. Grandfather lion sitting in a big chair.
  Holding a pipe,
  looks digusted.
Mouse is looking at him,
  wondering what he's doing that for.
Lion just sits there.
That's all I can see in the picture,
  so I'll not make anything up.
  Last time (to Card 2) I made something up.
(E encourages to make up something)
I don't want to,
  better tell the truth.
(E encourages) Lion came up
  and popped the mouse,
  hit him one.
The mouse just lay there,
  He died.
  The end.
The lion just sat there.

4. Mother kangaroo, baby,
  two baby kangaroos.
Mother is in a hurry to go to the store
  and get back home.
One little kangaroo is on a tricycle,
  the other in the mother's pouch.
The mother can just barely keep up
  with the little one.
The little one can just barely keep up
  with the mother, I mean.
The mother kangaroo stumbles over a rock,
  falls, and breaks the milk.
  Has to go way back to the store.

5. Ooo, a couple of bears asleep (whispers).

There's little baby bears in crib,
  two of them.
They're talking to themselves,
  "When mama and daddy go to sleep,
  we'll go out and get some honey."
And they did
  and got a spanking, that's all.
  Cause mother and daddy bear were tired.

6. More bears!
Well, mother and father bear in a cave.
Little baby bear's creeping out
  to get something to eat
  because they're hibernating.
He'll come back and go to sleep,
  because it's cold weather.
(Q-dream?) Oh, about what they'll do
  when they wake up.
They don't want to wake up
  because hunters will get them.
Anyway just be hungry.
Bears are always hungry,
  just like pigs.

7. Ugh (long pause).
Well, there's a lion or a tiger.
Lion's going to get the monkey.
The monkey hurries up a tree,
  but the lion catches him
  and eats him.
Lion says, "My, a good dinner,
  if I could only have a good dinner everyday."
Monkey in his tummy says,
  "I hope you don't!"
What do you do with these stories?
Do you put them in your files?
My stuff's not that good.
(Asked about ages, etc., of other children seen in clinic.)

8. Gosh, look at that picture
  (indicates grandmother monkey's picture)
  It looks funny.
Monkeys are drinking coffee
  and kinda have . . . well. . .
  telling tall tales, maybe.
Father monkey tells a story
  to the little monkey,
  and he's listening.
I bet that little monkey

doesn't like that grandma on the wall.
It doesn't look good.
(Q) I don't think she should wear glasses
  and she needs her face prettied up.
That's all.
That was a dumb story.

9. Ooo . . . rabbits. .
  We used to have some.
Little baby rabbit's in bed.
Mother and dad are in their room sleeping.
He gets up.
  Runs and gets something
  in Mr. McGregor's garden,
  and gets caught.
His dad found him,
  gave him a spanking
  and put him back to bed.
I shouldn't talk so fast (E was having trouble getting this all written down)
I think that's why I'm in here.

10. A dog over here.
Looks like the dad is giving him a spanking,
  for doing something wrong.
Puppy dog is wowing and yelling.
Then he put him down
  and wouldn't have nothing to do with him.
Then that little dog
  wouldn't do nuttin' wrong any more.
  Nothing wrong any more.
(Q-do?) Probably was chasing a cat,
  and mother cat gave big daddy dog heck
  so he has to spank the little dog.
(Q-mother cat say?) 'Your little puppy
  better not gang up on my little cat again,
  or you'll see the last of it."
That's all.

> *Analysis Schedule:* Reaction-formation and Undoing
>   Isolation
>   Deception
>   Projection and Introjection
>   Regression

PSYCHONEUROTIC REACTION

Boy, CA=4 years 8 months.
  This record is presented to illustrate the extensive fantasy which is sometimes obtained from a very young child. He was attending a nursery school
for normal children. No case history or behavioral data were available.

Some of the prominent features of his stories, e.g., the personal references, are to be expected at the younger ages, but the pervasive and recurrent themes of introjection, self-destruction, and helplessness in averting disasters (at times accompanied by inappropriate affect) are certaining not age-typical and suggest considerable disturbance. There is a strong emphasis on orality, usually with negative overtones, and cannibalistic, incorporative fantasies. The numerous references to being enclosed (e.g., inside a tree, or a box, or an electric plug) suggest concerns and questions about pregnancy and birth. There is a marked emphasis on, and anxiety connected with, reality testing: characters repeatedly are fooled, misled, or misperceive reality; things are not what they appear to be. The child must doubly attempt to reassure himself that his productions are only fantasy by using the distancing device of stuffed toy monkeys at home who are telling these stories to him as he relates them to the examiner.

1. Hen and baby chickies.
(Q) You know, I have a couple of monkeys at home
    who tell me all of my stories.
Funny about chickens.
Once when the mother hen told the babies
    that she thought they should eat themselves up.
How could chickens eat themselves up?
They're eating, which I think is funny—
    holding spoons in their wings.
(Q-mother hen?) I imagine she has a separate table
    bigger than they do
    'cause she's bigger.

2. They're bears—pulling a rope.
This story I know.
The monkey told me
    that the mother bear told the little bear
    to get in between her finger nails.
(Q-whose?) The mother bear's finger nails.
(Q) Looks like the three bears.
    Daddy and mommy and baby.
    They're pulling a rope.
(Q-why?) I suppose to see who's the strongest,
    to see who can break it.
(Who do you suppose will break it? Question repeated three times before
he answered. At first he kept repeating "to see who's the strongest.")
    Daddy, 'cause he's the strongest.

3. That's a lion.
I got to think about him.
    I know I got a lot of stories up in my head.
    This is a funny one.
The lion is eating his meal
    and has his tail on the table.

He didn't know,
  he thought it was his spoon
  and here it was his tail
  and he picked it up
  and put it in his soup
  and put it in his mouth.
(Q-Is this story about this lion?)
  Yes, but, of course, you never know
  if it's the same one as in the picture.

4. Little baby riding in mother's pocket
  and 'nother one riding on a bicycle.
The monkey said
  that the tree said to the kangaroo,
  "Do you think you can live inside me
  and I'll eat you up
  and you'll eat me up?"
The kangaroo said
  the first part he could do
  but "how could I eat you up
  when you already ate me up?"
This is a crazy story.
(Q-who are these kangarooes?) Mommy—
  This little fellow is the one the tree spoke to.

5. Ah. I can't make out the animals.
These little fellows the monkey said,
  the mother said, the baby bear said,
  he got put in a box
  when he was right outside the door
  and got carried right back in the house.
The mother said,
  "Why didn't you get my things?"
"I was halfway out the door
  and got put in a box
  and carried right back in."
She said the first part. (Points to lump in large bed.)

6. That's bears in a hole in a tree.
They're hibernating, it looks like.
  That means sleeping in the winter.
The monkey told the story
  about how the mother told the babes
  to get inside one of the electric plugs
  and "What will you do to us?" they said.
"I would plug the toaster up inside you."
"How could you?"
"Just like that."

Mothers really do silly things.
  Not the kids.

7. That's a tiger, isn't it?
The story of it is—
  The monkey said the lion went toward the fire
  and the tiger thought it was food for him
  and started to eat it
  and burned his mouth.
That was crazy.

8. These are monkeys now.
You know my monkeys tell me these stories.
  I really make them up myself
  but I pretend the monkeys tell me.
  They couldn't really
  'cause they're stuffed animals.
You know I have a bunny at home, too
  and he tells me stories
  but he doesn't know as many as the monkeys
  'cause they've been all over the world.
  They've been to China.
  I've only been to England.
The monkey went outside
  and went toward a tree
  and thought it was his house.
So when he got inside
  he found it wasn't his house.
So he went outside to find it
  and accidently jumped into a stream
  and that was the end of it.
(Q-Who are these monkeys?) I don't know.
(Q-who's the mommy?) I don't know.
  (He had a worried, fearful expression on his face while being questioned.)

9. That's a bunny and his bed.
The story is the monkey said,
  once upon a time the bunny went out
  and . . . something.
He thought the hole in the ground
  was his house for his cage.
He went down to see if there was a door,
  and he didn't see any
  so he went out into the woods
  and got caught in a trap
  and that was all.
That's the joke
  at least a little bit of a joke.

10. That's dogs, isn't it?
The dogs saw a fireplace
  from their hole
  and wanted to go to the toilet.
They thought that was the door
  and went to it
  and then they got burned.
That's the joke.

    Analysis Schedule: Reaction-formation and Undoing
                 Isolation
                 Repression and Denial
                 Symbolization
                 Projection and Introjection
                 Regression
                 Weak controls
                 Confused Identification

Boy, CA=8 years 2 months (WISC Full Scale IQ=121; Verbal=105; Performance=135).

Despite his high intelligence, this boy was failing in school. At home, he had been subjected to rigid discipline and high expectations for mannerliness, cleanliness, etc. He was overly good, very conscientious, and liked to play girls' games with his two older sisters. He had recently been having nightmares of being deserted or of his house catching on fire.

His CAT stories were extremely long and involved, with careful attention being paid to every aspect and detail. Only four stories are reproduced here, but they serve to illustrate his strong oedipal feelings. The marked masturbatory reference at the close of Card 2 suggests he may be resorting to self-stimulation to compensate for the friends he would like to have but can't reach out for. In Cards 4 and 9 we find preoccupations with the birth process, attachment to mother, further masturbatory symbolism and strong guilt feelings. On Card 10 he fantasies rebellion and in so doing plays out a symbolic oedipal theme which terminates in regression to the anal level.

This record is an almost classical example of the neurotic child's preoccupations with oedipal, primal scene, and birth themes, along with indications of masturbatory impulses, strong guilt feelings and castration fears.

2. Once there was a bear
  who was very lonely.
  He wanted to play with somebody.
He mostly liked tug-of-war.
One day there came two bears,
  they were lonely too.
  They wanted to play tug-of-war, too.
One day the bear was very lonely
  and came to the two bears,
  "Please let me play tug-of-war with you."

They said, "We don't know,
  maybe next day."
He said, "Huh, I don't like them,
  I'll not play with them."
Next day, he took the rope
  and went to the house
  where the two bears lived,
And said, "Come out,
  you said you'd play with me today."
They said, "We don't remember that,
  us telling you that we could play with you.
  Wait until the next day."
Next day, he said, "Come out, please."
They said, "OK."
He said, "Wait, I have to get the rope."
  But he crawled into bed.
The others waited all day.
Next day he said, "Where were you?"
Finally, they played tug-of-war
  and they struggled and struggled.
One day they played again.
The rope kept sliding out
  of his two little hands,
  The rope went back and back
  And the bear found himself back in bed.

4. Once there was a kangaroo.
  She was a very happy kangaroo.
But one day she felt something,
  She wondered what was that.
She knew she was a mother.
She went to the doctor
  and knew she would have a baby.
Next day, the baby was out.
Next day, she said,
  "What shall I do?"
She couldn't go to mass
  with the baby hollering.
  She left the baby.
Sunday morning was her birthday.
  Presents were under the table.
She went away on the trike
  and caught up with mother.
Mother said,
  "You found your present, go home."
Baby said,
  "No, I want to go to mass with you."

One day she felt another thing.
She went to the doctor again,
  "What's the matter with me?"
The doctor said, "Don't worry,
  you're going to have another baby" (Laughed).
Next day the baby was out.
They went to the carnival.
Next day was Sunday,
  "Oh, oh, two babies in a row,
  Guess I'll go
  and take both of them."
The mother didn't know
  the baby had a balloon with her.
  Didn't know it was full of gas.
The balloon got out of her hand,
  flew around to the candle at the altar.
  All of a sudden, the balloon popped.
The altar boy told the priest,
  "Must have been a robbery."
The priest went on with the mass.
  After the mass, the priest saw no sign of a body.
Next day he found a body,
  he pushed him.
  He woke up,
"I thought you was dead."
"No, just sleeping."
The end.

9. Oh, a baby rabbit,
  all about rabbit babies.
  Once there was a rabbit.
Mother said to the brother,
  "I'm going to get something,
  take good care of her."
The baby started to cry.
The brother started to ack (act) up.
"How about the stuff mother has in the closet?"
  He got the stuff,
  and made a play with the baby.
A sly fox looked in the room and saw the baby.
He said, "They'll just do for my appetite."
There's a hole under the rug.
  They didn't know under the rug was a hole.
When the boy went outside,
  he didn't know the fox
  was drilling a hole.
The fox put a sack over the baby.
When the brother came back in the house,

he looked for the baby.
He fell in the tunnel,
  and saw the sly fox with the baby.
  He ran and ran but couldn't catch up.
  He didn't know—
  he knew he had the—his brother.
Then he said, "I'll catch up no matter what."
  He caught up because
  the fox was about to bake his son.
He said, "You won't get him."
The fox hurried and ran.
He heard water,
  "I'll run the other way."
  He knew the sack wouldn't float,
  Out came the water with him—his brother.
He pushed the fox down
  and drowned him.
He took out the boards
  and put new boards in.
He told his mother, "I'll repay you."
Mother opened the hole,
  saw the sack and the water,
  She said, "That's a good supply of water."
That was a pretty long story.

10. Once there was a dog,
He was a very naughty dog.
  "I'll sneak outside,
  I don't care what my mother says."
He forgot his mother told him
  he couldn't go out for the rest of the week.
  The week wasn't done.
He didn't stay in the house,
  he ran away.
"Nobody will catch me."
He ran and ran.
On the way he found something,
  "A pretty good hat for me."
He didn't know the king of the jungle
  had lost his cap.
"I could be king of the dogs."
He went home,
  Mother wasn't there.
  He hid under the stool.
His mother needed to go.
  Before she sat down
  she found something in it.
She said, "Here is the king of the jungle's hat."

The king of the jungle said,
  "Thanks, I'll pay you by the paddle."
The little dog came home.
  He looked in the stool
  and couldn't find the hat.
Mother said, "Where have you been?
  You'll have to stay in the house
  for one more week."

OBSESSIVE-COMPULSIVE REACTION

The following two records illustrate the typical reaction patterns of the obsessively oriented child, with intellectualization, rationalization, isolation of affect, much concern with details and minutiae, and long, involved direct quotations for the characters in the stories. These children frequently give titles to each story. Often they are unable to make up their own minds, or those of their characters, resulting in vacillation, indecision, ambivalence and uncertainty. There is usually much balancing of phrases, consideration of several alternatives, and the use of undoing to cover aggressive outbursts. They become intrigued with the fantasied naughtiness of the child characters who can defy the parents, and may present stories of the child character running away in order to get the parents to show some concern. The protocols of these children are usually exceptionally long.

Boy, CA=9 years 0 months (WISC Full Scale=108; Verbal=101; Performance=114).

This boy is the third of six children, with the youngest three being children of his mother's second marriage. All siblings are girls. He plays doctor with his sisters and tries to get them to undress. He is beset with fears of the dark, of elevators, of losing his lunch box, that the driver of any car in which he is riding will not be careful, or that he may get lost on his way to school. He is aware that his peers regard him as a "sissy."

The CAT record is replete with overqualifications and balancing of opposites. Card 7 elicits a notable example of a passive-aggressive maneuver, in that the lion is careful to keep his claws and fangs concealed until the moment of attack. Note how he also must consider all possibilities and alternatives, together with a suggestion of incipient paranoid patterns of vigilance, suspicion and distrust of other's motives. Mother is shown as being disgusted with her children (Card 8), which he must undo on Card 9 by proclaiming "what a nice mother he has." The anxiety is not wholly allayed so he resorts to more compulsive routines and details, exact time interval notations, etc. On Card 10 he dares to fantasy messiness and dirt, with repeated infractions of the rules, until the mother figure becomes concerned, goes to search for him, and the child finally decides to be "a good boy for the rest of the day."

1. There's some baby chickens,
   eating something.
The mother chicken is standing behind them.
Nope, better make that roosters.

(indicates all figures)
Combs on their head,
Eating some spinach.
Their tablecloth is white
  with red lines going around.
Table's made out of wood,
  chairs are wood,
  napkins.
  On the spinach bowl,
  there's flowers.
(Q) Going to eat it.
(Q-then?) Digest it.

2. Looks like three bears
  having a tug-of-war.
A rope in their hands,
  on the end a knot on each side.
Looks like father bear and baby bear
against the mother.
The rope's almost tearing.
Have black nose,
  Other one's eyes look like popped out, (single)
  Other bear's eyes looking in the middle.
  Baby bear's eyes looking on the ground.
They're tugging hard
  On a hill.
(Q-win?) The two bears.
(Q) The two bears will go falling
  when she lets go of the rope.

3. Looks like a lion,
  has a cane, and a pipe.
The mouse is looking out the thing.
The floor has flowers on it.
He's sitting on his tail,
  his eyes are shifty.
Looks like he's going to smoke his pipe.
Mouse looks like he's going to run out.
(Q) I think the lion chases the mouse.
There's five things on his foot (pads).
He's sitting on a big chair.
(Q-happen to the mouse?) He's probably going to eat it.

4. A kangaroo and two babies,
  one on trike,
  other in the pouch.
They're heading for the forest.
In back of the forest,
  I see a house.

Have hat on, basket,
  balloon in hand, purse,
  and big, long tails.
(Q) Going to eat the stuff
  mother gots in the basket.
On the house there's a chimney
  and two things sticking out.
On the bicycle, there's a red line
  on his tire.
Two trees.
Mother kangaroo's heading for home,
  then got babies out
  and put them on the table.
Got food out,
  they eat the milk, bread, bananas.
When they're done
  they come running back again
  and get some more,
  and running back.
On both pictures
  there's an "E" and a "4" and an "E" turned backwards.
  ("E's" refer to brackets around the card number)
Gray clouds in the sky.
The fir trees look like winter,
  the other trees have no leaves.

5. About a baby bear,
  He's in a room with a bed.
Looks like two bears
  and they're wrestling (indicates crib).
In night time, it's winter,
  going to sleep in bed now.
  Sleeping on a pillow in a crib.
That's all I can see,
  besides a tiny door,
  right down there.
(Q-next?) Looks like more snow
  will come down.
They're hibernating.
(Q-dream?) They're in a room.
A big bed they're dreaming about,
  and there's a light on a dresser,
  and a roof over their heads.
  That's what they're dreaming about.

6. This looks like baby bear
  and father bear and mother bear,

sleeping in a tree.
    Leaves inside.
Looks like baby bear's ready to get out.
Mother bear's asleep.
Baby bear looks like he's going
    to get up and go out
    to get some food.
Sleeping in a tree,
    three bears.
That's all I can see.

7.   A lion's coming after the monkey
    for food.
The monkey climbs up the tree
    to be safe.
The lion will probably catch him
    before he gets up in the tree.
Lion has his teeth in,
    paws in,
    has soft parts out,
    until he gets close.
Then he jumps,
    pounces on him
    and eats him.
When he eats, then he'll go
    and look for more food.
That's *if* the monkey gets away.
Monkey looks like he's climbing up a tree.
But he won't have a chance.
    His fur sticks out,
    has his head turned to look at the lion,
    to make sure he doesn't eat him.

8.   Looks like a bunch of monkeys (smiles).
Probably having a coffee break.
Looks like one of the monkeys has children,
    telling them to sit down.
Two sitting on the davenport
    talking to each other.
On the wall is a grandma ape.
One monkey's telling the other
    'What a mean kid you've got!"
The other one says,
    "Don't you think I know it."
One said, "he's nice,"
    One said "he's mean,"
    The other says, "I know."

It keeps on until one comes up and says,
  "Is that all you can say. . .
  'Don't I know it'?"

9. Looks like a rabbit sitting up in bed,
  probably thinking about something.
Probably thinking about
  what a nice mother he has.
Probably dreaming,
  has a window in there.
It's probably morning,
  he gets up,
  puts clothes on,
  brushes teeth,
  washes,
  puts his shoes and sox on.
Then he gets breakfast,
  and plays, if it's Saturday.
He'll play with Jerry Brown and me,
  then go back for lunch,
  eat cabbage and carrot soup.
Then back out to play
  with me and Jerry Brown.
Then one-half hour later
  he'll have breakfast,
  I mean dinner.
Then outside again,
  then come in to sleep.

10. About two dogs,
  mother dog and little dog, probably.
He got the towel muddy
  when playing outside.
Mother spanks.
He goes out
  and gets muddy again,
  and wipes on the towel again,
And gets spanked again.
The dog gets mad
  and runs away.
Mother gets worried,
  goes to look for him.
She finds him, brings him back home,
  and gives him another spanking.
He barks, goes outside to play
  and will be a good dog,
  for the rest of the day.

Analysis Schedule: Reaction-formation and Undoing
                    Isolation
                    Deception
                    Symbolization
                    Regression
                    Confused Identification

Girl, CA=8 years 3 months (Above average intelligence).

The next record was obtained in a school sample, with little case history material available. From the teacher's report, the child was always extremely careful to be sure she was doing the right things, overly concerned with details, and generally a "model" student. The father was reported to be very rigid, domineering and overcontrolling.

With respect to the CAT, the parallels with the previous clinic case are remarkable. In both protocols, the child characters are frequently naughty, verbally aggressive, and engage in oppositional behavior directed against the parents. There is much concern with fair play, exact measures of time and distance, and fantasies of escape. Both storytellers handle the aggressive aspects of Card 7 by masking the attacker's intentions and attempting to deny the actual fact of destruction of the monkey (*"if* the monkey gets away," and only eating the monkey's bananas!). Both show concern with the necessity to be on guard and visually vigilant; children are not liked by the adults on both Card 8 stories; and in Card 10, both have the child track mud into the house, avoid any mention of toileting procedures, and imply that the dirtying and messing happens repeatedly and annoys the parents.

1. Looks like there's three little baby chickens
    and then here's three little tiny bowls
    and a big bowl in the middle.
They're waiting for supper
    and here's their mother coming
    and this big bowl.
It seems like they're looking in it.
Might have something they like
    and they're anxious to eat it
    to see how it tastes.

2. Looks like these bears
    are playing this game, tug-of-war.
One bear has very big eyes
    cause he sees the other bear
    has the little one in back of him pulling.
He thinks it's unfair
    cause the other bear is even bigger, too.
Still it looks like he's going
    to fall over backwards,
    cause they're on a cliff.
The little one may fall off, too,

cause he looks like he's going down hill.
All are scared and out of breath.
This guy falls over the cliff,
 and the little bear and big bear win.

3. This lion,
 I guess he was smoking a pipe.
He's in the chair.
This mouse always gets chased
 but this time the lion's waiting
 for the mouse to come out farther.
The mouse is trying to see
 if he's tired
 and maybe won't chase him.
The lion's trying
 to make the mouse think he's tired
 and won't get him.
(Q) I think the mouse was smart enough to stay in.

4. This one's kinda hard.
This one is a mother kangaroo
 and a baby
 and another little bigger one.
They're going off to a party in the woods.
Mother's holding onto her hat.
 She's jumping so fast
 it wants to fall off.
She goes fast
 cause the little kangaroo
 is riding so fast,
 he's only one-half inch behind her.
(Q) Kinda anxious to get there
 cause they're hungry.

5. This looks like nighttime
 and two little bears
 are supposed to be asleep,
 but are still awake playing.
It's very dark
 but they don't think
 mother and father are still in there.
But the bed is lumpy,
 so mother and father are still in there.
They're hiding because
 they are naughty bears.
They sneak out
 and get a cookie.
But this time
 mother and father hear them plan
 and don't let them do it.

6. It's wintertime
    and of course bears are hibernating,
    except the little bear.
He has his eyes open
    and is looking out in the snow
    while mother and father sleep,
And he sees a rabbit.
He's ready to jump out,
    only if he does this
    he'll land in deep snow
    and he won't be able
    to find his way back in.
(Q) Guess he has to walk through the snow
    until he finds a cave for himself.
Mother and father wake up in the spring
    and find him gone.
They never find him
    cause he hears them
    and thinks it's mountain lions
    who could beat him,
    so he goes in the trees and hides.
They never find him.
(Q) After he finds out he is lost,
    he follows tracks
    and he finds them
    when they're catching fish.

7. I've got to look at this pretty well. . . .
There's this great big lion
    who's been hunting for food all day
And she's hungry.
This monkey was looking for food, too.
The lion saw him
    and hid till the monkey came.
The monkey jumped to the vine
    and got up high.
The lion hid behind a rock
    and waited
    until the monkey came back down.
The monkey was pretty smart
    and climbed back up in the tree.
The lion missed lots of times
    but one time he found the monkey's home
    and ate all the monkey's bananas.

8. I guess there's this mother monkey
    having friends over.
While they talk and drink coffee,
    little monkey comes in

and starts fumbling around
  and asking for a drink.
He gets tired and goes to the visitors.
He tells her how nice her flowers are.
He pesters and interrupts
  and mother tells him
  not to do it.
The lady whispers to her husband
  that she doesn't like the little monkey
  cause he keeps interrupting.
He goes to get food
  like his mother said,
And he got grapes
  like he liked,
  not bananas
  like they liked,
So he had to go out
  by himself to play.

9. It's a windy night
  and little rabbit's in bed.
And they left the door open
  and the door kept
  banging open and shut.
So the rabbit got scared.
He got his clothes
And when mother and dad came home
  they found him gone.
So they went to look for him.
They spanked him
  and put him back to bed.
Then in the morning
  he was another bad boy,
  cause he stole cookies
  and then couldn't eat his breakfast.
So they spanked him again.

10. This is about the same thing.
He was bad
  cause he got mud on his paws
  and tracked up the rug and furniture.
(Q) He forgot to wash his feet
  all the time.
Mother and dad got tired,
  so they spanked him.

      Analysis Schedule: Reaction-formation and Undoing
                                  Isolation
                                    Repression and Denial

> Deception
> Symbolization
> Fear and Anxiety

PARENTAL LOSS

Boy, CA=7 years 3 months (WISC Full Scale IQ=118; Verbal=129; Performance=103).

This boy's protocol is a good example of obsessive preoccupations, but also illustrates his still intense reactions to the sudden death of his father (from a heart attack) one year earlier. (In terms of the 20 items of the parental loss index, there were nine on his CAT in addition to items also on the Rorschach.) When referred he was not doing well in school, despite his superior verbal skills. He had regressed since his father's death, playing alone, using a bottle, taking dolls to school and being very dependent on his mother. He frequently wet his pants when he could not have his own way, and would also threaten to do so if crossed. In play therapy, he would have adult characters disobey laws or drive shrewd bargains, and usually find some way for them to rationalize such behavior. Excerpts from the psychological examination contain the following:

He is struggling with a great deal of anxiety and hostility and the consequent guilt. The anxiety is so great that it hampers the full use of his high intelligence in integrative tasks. He has adopted a pseudomaturity, with intellectualization, isolation and repression as his chief means of defense. There are many indications of an obsessive-compulsive character structure. When the defenses can no longer contain the anxiety, he regresses to quite immature behavior.

His projective material is richly symbolic . . . . as he attempts to deny his hostility or turn it back onto himself. The passive-aggressive orientation is clearly expressed in his Rorschach percept of a "mad dog licking himself" (Card II). Two cards (Rorschach IV and V) reveal his concerns around his father's death, implying fulfilled death wishes toward his father, with fears of reprisal, and guilt over his lack of real grief or feeling of loss. . . . In the inquiry he became quite disorganized and immature, pretending to shoot at the "ghost" (percept on Card IV) by jabbing his fingers at the "eyes," *"heart"* and "mouth," then he continued this behavior to the "seagull" (Card V), saying he was "choking it to death." He then launched into a discussion of the events surrounding his own father's death. . . . Later, on the CAT, he seems to reflect his fears of retaliation as the lion (Card 3) "chokes the mouse to death."

Also prominent in the CAT is a fear of abandonment and the feeling that one must be good and conform to be retained in the home. This feeling could well be related to the fact that there is an older adopted brother in the family, which may be reinforcing fears that, since his own family is beginning to break up, he also may be passed on to someone else. This kind of story on several cards then leads to a new theme on the two final cards suggesting strong identification with his older brother and possibly some sex play between the two. Both are punished for an enuretic episode and run away from home together. Again, he becomes anxious and disorganized with slips of the tongue and incoherence.

The only interpersonal relationships described involve hostile affect: characters are mad at each other, and mothers are restrictive, punitive and rejecting unless the child is "good." He is afraid to actively disobey his mother but will play tricks on her (Cards 4 and 5) and be secretive about his activities. In his story to Card 8, which involves repeated rejections by parental figures, the child finally "cracks his mother's picture"—a depersonalized passive-aggressive mode of expression for his hostility.

Note the imputing of feminine gender to the small figure on Card 2, and the confusion in sexual identity expressed when talking about the card (8) he liked best.

1.   Don't think I can, oh yes,
The rooster went out to pick wheat,
   "Who will help me make some bread?"
(Then patterned rest of story after *The Little Red Hen,* with pig, wolf, cow, etc., saying "I won't.")
"Who will help me cook it?"
   (All) "I won't," etc.
"Who will help me eat it?"
   (All) "I will."
The rooster said,
   "You didn't help cook the bread
   so you can't have it."
And the chickens ate by themselves.

2.   Once upon a time
   a bear played tug-of-war.
He had nobody to play with,
   so he went to mama and papa bear
   and she asked him and her
   if they would play
   tug-of-war with her.
And she said, "Sure,"
And the mama slipped off
   and they pulled and drug her up.

3.   Once this big lion
   never did like mouses.
One day the mouse came out.
The lion was scared,
   smoked his pipe,
   put the pipe on the mouse's head.
The lion choked him to death
   and was never afraid of mouses again.

4.   That's one I can't tell a story about.
(*E* encourages) Once there was a kangaroo
   and had a baby kangaroo
   who liked to play with balloons,

One day his favorite balloon popped.
And the son had to go to the store
  to get another balloon.
He fooled the kangaroo
  and went right behind.
He goes to the store
  to get a balloon for the baby.
He want back and got ten cents,
Then he went to the circus
  and got four balloons.
  Only supposed to get one.
So he left three at home
  and brought one
  to the baby kangaroo.

5. Ugh, boy!
Well, this little bear. . .
And the doctor was supposed to come.
  He had a cold.
He got out of bed
  and wandered around the house.
  He hid in a closet.
Doctor came and he wasn't there.
Mother walked five miles
  to find him,
  but couldn't find him.
They looked under the bed,
  in the lampshade,
  under the covers.
The doctor said,
  "Do you have an old closet?"
They looked there and found him.
Ten miles she walked.
How many are we supposed to tell?
(*E*-Ten altogether)
Five more then.

6. Once this bear couldn't find a cave
  to hibernate with the baby.
So they try to dig a hole in the ground,
  Couldn't dig.
They found a dog and said,
  "Come with me
  and find somebody to dig a cave."
The dog said,
  "We can do it by ourselves."
So they dug five miles down,
  started over,

made a cave for mama and papa bear
  to sleep in,
  and baby too.

7. Once this tiger liked the monkey
  and the monkey didn't like him.
So the tiger hunted for a gorilla,
  too big for him.
He went on to another place.
There was cliff.
  The monkey tried to get to the other side,
  five feet down.
The tiger fell
  and the tiger killed himself.
The monkey dropped a coconut,
  chatter, chatter. . . .
(Here he mumbled and talked too fast to record.)
He had all the animals in the jungle on him,
  didn't like it.
He called mother monkey to help.
She killed most of the animals.
  One she couldn't kill.
Papa came and killed it.
  They went away,
  and never saw the animals again.
Can you make titles to these?
This is "The Monkey and Tiger that Wanted to Eat."
(Then he went back and gave titles to all the previous cards:)
  Card 6: "The Bear Cave"
  Card 5: "Poor Bear"
  Card 4: "Kangaroo Fooler"
  Card 3: "King Lion"
  Card 2: "Bear Tug"
  Card 1: "Eating Breakfast"

8. Once upon. . . I'll give a title first:
"Monkey that had a Home After All."
Once monkey never had a home.
So he went trying
  to find other homes.
He met a great big monkey and said,
  "Hi, Mom and Pop."
They said
  "Get away, little guy."
He knocked on another door,
  "Can I have a home with you?"
"Yes, if you be good."
So he found a home
  and he was good.

At the last thing,
  when going to move out,
  he cracked his mother's picture.
They made him find a new home
  and build one by himself.

9. "Peter Rabbit got Lost."
Once there was a rabbit named Peter,
  there was his mother and father and him.
She went to town.
He—she—he told his mother—I mean brother—
  to take care of him.
(Talked too fast to record all)
A wolf came and dug underground
  and took him.
Burned up. . .
  In a gunny sack.
Mother came back,
  "Why weren't you here
  to take care of him?"
Brother said,
  "I wanted to get food."
Mother said,
  "Next time when I say
  'Take care of him',
  You better do that.
  Next time if I say,
  'Get food'
  You get food."
I sure can tell good stories.
Think when I grow up
  I'll be a storyteller.

10. Ummm, "Two Lost Pups."
Once there were two puppies
  and they had a real home
  with people.
They always had to go
  to the bathroom
  and never liked to.
So they go in the flower pots
  to water the flowers.
The mother put them out,
  'cause they kept doing that.
They ran away
  to a different home,
  and they never did find them again.

(*E* Which picture did you like best?)
(Child chose Card 8)

Because he kept being good
  and at last got bad.
That was a silly thing to do,
  to get bad at the last.
Look at him—her earrings on.
It should be a her
  but it's a him.

> *Analysis Schedule:* Reaction-formation and Undoing
> Isolation
> Deception
> Symbolization
> Projection and Introjection
> Fear and Anxiety
> Confused Identification

BORDERLINE PSYCHOTIC

Engel (1963) defines the "borderline" category of psychotic disturbance as denoting ". . .shifting, changing, alternating ego states which bring about bewilderingly rapid changes in overt behavior not only when the child is with different adults, but also with the same adult within an hour" (p. 426). She goes on to describe these children as having a vivid fantasy life, a tenuous hold on reality, polarities and contrasts in their concepts (big-little, good-bad, etc.), basic fears of annihilation and concern with themes of survival, a pervasive sense of helplessness, and frequently using distancing devices.

Boy, CA=9 years 4 months (WISC Full Scale IQ=102; Verbal=109; Performance=94).

At the time of referral and testing, this boy was preoccupied with gorillas and grizzlies, in fact he had just completed reading the encyclopedia through the "G" volume. (The CAT cards thus fit easily into his present interests.) Excerpts from the psychological report describe aspects of his projective material:

When presented with highly structured tasks (intelligence testing) he is in contact with reality much of the time, although his thoughts frequently wander to seemingly unrelated associations, but definitely pulled from a massive store of inner and ongoing fantasy. There is more regression and loss of control on the projective tasks, extreme anxiety becomes evident, and percepts are concerned with disintegration and decay. Also prominent are fantasies revolving around gorillas and grizzly bears and their powerful, threatening aspects. He feels orally deprived at very deep levels. Females are not mentioned at all or seen as empty, rejecting and frightening. . . . He seems to be making a desperate attempt to maintain contact with reality by compulsive maneuvers and isolation techniques.

Several responses could be interpreted as fantasies of impregnation with frightening and dangerous overtones. His final response on the Rorschach (Card X) was "A blue bat (blue center area, D2) flying around in a cave (portion enclosed by long red forms, D9); there's a little seed (orange, D3). Some kind of a . . . *yike.* . a monster (gray figure, D8) crawling on top and dropping the seed." The CAT immediately followed the Rorschach and his response to Card 1 carries over the percept of seeds, more particularly a search in which seeds are found, and these are father's seeds. Then on Card 6 (which pictures bears so important to this child) he mentions the cave, which may have triggered off memories of the two previously mentioned responses. He tells of a bear running away from his cave and deciding "to tell everybody about his wonderful discovery." He then gives a title to the story: "Finding Out," which confirms the above impressions and suggests that much of his interest in reference books may also be part of this search.

1. (He first told the traditional story of *The Little Red Hen,* then *E* asked him to "now tell a different story.")
"The Story of How the Little Birds Ate."
One cold winter
   all the birds were hungry,
   nothing to eat at this one place.
They looked and looked.
They found out about seeds,
Found a bunch
   the father had,
Cooked them and had lunch.
That's a short story.
(Q) Then they sang a merry tune.

2. What kind of a bear is that? (large on right)
I think that's playing tug-of-war.
Once there was a real strong bear
   who wanted some guys—
   Baby bear and another bear to pull
   to see if could pull them over,
   so played it.
All of a sudden,
   one strong bear pulled them both over.
He had won;
   he was the strongest bear.
   His name was Grizzly.
So that's how the strong bears named Grizzly
   got their names.
   The grizzly is the strongest.
   That's the story of Mr. Grizzly.

3. (laughs) "The Lion and the Mouse."
Once there was a lion,
   the king of the jungle,
   and this very little mouse.
He caught it,
   thought it would be good to eat.
He said,
   "Please, kind lion, let me go.

I'll help you someday."
The lion said,
   "OK, but get in your mousehole
   before I change my mind."
They saw a roast turkey (a trap?).
   The rope slipped from a branch
   onto the lion's neck.
A hunter took the lion to a circus.
The mouse saw it.
   He shot a hole big enough
   for the lion to drop out.
   And he quickly ran away.
The story of the lion and the mouse.

4. Those are kangaroos.
This is the story of Hurry, the Kangaroo.
Once at home,
   went out to eat,
Some careless people dropped a match.
It burned all of the forest
   except a little bit.
They looked around,
   all burned except a few trees.
At last they found something to eat.
The story of Hurdy Murdy.

5. Is this a kitten or a bear?
I think it's the story of the three bears,
   but we know that too well.
Once two little bears.
Nothing to eat there but honey.
   They looked all around,
   saw some meat.
   Tasted everything
   but nothing tasted good.
   Everything tasted worse
   than honey and fish.
So that's what they lived on.
The story of cubby banter bear and panda baby.

6. Is this a bear?
The story of how the little bear
   got away from the wolf.
The little bear wanted a cave.
   Made one hole,
   saw the wolf coming to get him.
So he ran away
   so the wolf never found him.
So the bear decided to tell everybody

about his wonderful discovery.
So that's the story of "Finding Out."
I give them all funny names.

7.   The story of Dummy the Monkey.
Once there was a monkey
   who was walking all around.
Thought of the greatest fight of all.
He saw a tiger,
   they fought and fought but couldn't win.
He ran away from the tiger,
   he went so fast
   the monkey was all scratched up,
   Finally, he came to a sad ending.
The monkey was so weak
   he couldn't fight anymore.
He ended up in the lion's stomach.

8.   (laughed) Are these gorillas?
The story of the gorilla family.
Once some gorillas and had a baby.
   They thought it was good to have them.
He was jumping for joy.
   Then he found out it wasn't too happy.
They told him
   as soon as he was old enough
   he would have to go on his own.
So he went off on his own.
Others came for tea and got some.
That's the story of Henry McGilla.

9.   It looks like a bunny.
This is a story of the Haunted House.
One time a ghost
   looked like a white rabbit.
   He found a haunted house.
People came in
   and thought it was a good home.
But when they heard scary chatters
   they went away.
Nobody came there again.
He was happy because he was the only one
   that wanted to live there.
   So he stayed, and ate lots of lunch.
So that's the story of the ghost.

10.   What's that?
   Why is he over the other dog's knee?
Once there was a dog.

He was always trying to be bad,
  bothering other animals.
And his father was getting
  real, real mad.
So he taught him a lesson not to do it,
  And he remembered it.
  Looks like he's spanking.
(Q-what do bad?) Hurting other animals,
Dig up and tear up Mrs. Pig's flowers
  and killing Mrs. Cow's grass.
  All kinds of bad things.
  Taking away all the water from them
  and stealing.
That's the story of Puppy Bad-O
  who turned out to be Puppy Good-O.

    Analysis Schedule: Isolation
                  Repression and Denial
                  Deception
                  Symbolization
                  Projection and Introjection
                  Fear and Anxiety
                  Regression

CHILDHOOD SCHIZOPHRENIA

The records of seriously disturbed children contain increased amounts of magical thinking, omnipotence, oral features and bizarreness. There is a lack of structure or cohesiveness to the stories, and characters are continually in danger of losing control. Loose associations, tangential thinking, and poor reality contact are prominent features. In the most severe cases, the child's autistic fantasies are so intrusive that all semblance of any relationship of story to picture is obscured; one element in the first card, or in the previous test, may determine the theme and content for all remaining cards.

Boy, CA=8 years 11 months (Diagnosed as childhood schizophrenia, with some indications of possible organic component).

At time of testing, this boy's main preoccupations were centering around comic book or TV characters, such as Superman, Bat Man, Zorro, or Frankenstein. He had brought a comic book with him and persistently kept trying to substitute it for the CAT cards. Nevertheless his first four stories remain fairly close to the stimuli, then he becomes sidetracked back to his comics and thoughts of the devil. The projected search for food on Card 6 starts him off on a theme of imminent danger from starvation, and from there he launched into more side excursions into comic-book land.

Note on four cards (Cards 4, 5, 8 and 9) this child's protests concerning the impossibility of animals assuming human characteristics, and his assertions that they are not "real" animals, but only stuffed. We have observed this phenomenon in previously discussed, and less disturbed cases, throughout this

volume, always emphasizing that such protestations suggest fears of losing
contact and strong needs to seek reassurance that fantasy is only fantasy and
could not replace reality. The increased, almost persistent, use of the device
by this child, would seem to indicate a frantic need to reassure himself that
some of the fantastic images floating by are, in fact, just that. We are re-
minded of Woltmann's (1951) observations that psychotic children would
become upset by puppet shows and need to go behind stage for reassurance
that the characters and story were only make-believe.

1. That's a chicken.
    They're eating.
That's a rooster.
(Wanted to show *E* his comic book, also pictures he had drawn of Bat Man,
Dracula, etc.)

2. This is a bear pulling.
    That's a bear,
    three bears pulling ropes.
(Q) One bear slips off. . .
(Distracted by toys on *E*'s shelf.)
(Q) He might break his leg (single.)

3. That's a lion,
    King of the beasts.
A little mouse,
    mouse is smaller,
    lion is bigger.
(Q) Big lion's trying to . . . try . . . try . . .
    to eat that little monkey.
No, he's trying to sit down.
(Q-next?) Roar for his crown.

4. That's a kangaroo and Mrs. Kangaroo,
Never heard of kangaroos
    riding a bike.
But they jump and hop.
Bet they're going on a picnic.
(Resumes his comic book and discusses further drawing he plans, with:
    His suit's black, have to color the pants blue, belt red).
(Q) I bet that kangaroo
    wants his mommie to hop,
And so she hops and hops and hops,
    That's what kangaroos do.
Bet that's a devil,
    foot in yard.
Devil's a evil thing.

5. This is a bedroom.
Somebody's sleeping in the bed,
    probably the mother.

Hey, never heard of
  two little baby bears in bed.
One bear crawled in
  and the other bear crawled in.
(Q) Mother will wake up and say,
  "Who crawled in my baby bed?"
The baby got out,
  and the little bears
  crawled in again.

6. That's mother bear,
  father bear, baby bear.
Brother and sister
  are probably playing.
Mommie bear takes care. . . .
  she finds food.
She can't go to the store and buy it,
  has to run and find food.
Know what king of beasts do?
Have to take zebra and eat it,
They have to have nourishment or die.
The lion has to have blood.
(Then launched into long, involved stories of Dracula, Frankenstein and
  Wolf Man.)

7. This is a tiger,
  trying to get that little monkey.
Bet he's going to get it,
  because the little monkey's
  going to fall.
He's going to get that bad little monkey
  who was bothering his babies.
  He was chasing.
Tiger got him.
Tiger slipped on the little monkey
  and fell down in the deep river,
  with that little monkey,
  and splashed in the water.
If a timber wolf got after me,
  I'd kick him in the water,
  because timber wolves can't swim, can they?
(More stories about Fox Man, Dracula, etc.)

8. That's a monkey. . . 'nuther. . . . 'nuther.
  Toy monkeys.
Whoever heard of monkeys? (points to picture)
Monkeys aren't real,
  they are real,

There's not such a thing
  as a mummy.
Only Wolf Man in the story.
(Q) All silly monkeys,
  a whole box of them.
That monkey ain't talking.
  He doesn't say, "Who."
  He doesn't know how.
He's just a stuffed, stuffed,
  stuffed toy monkey.

9. This is a rabbit, sleeping.
A stuffed rabbit.
  sleeping upstairs, is it?
This is a house.
(Q-happen next?) Nothing.
I bet that toy rabbit's
  going to get torn up
  by the baby or something.

10. A puppy getting washed.
This is a puppy all dirty (points to adult).
Then he's clean.
This puppy's kinda dirty,
  This puppy clean.
  Dirty ears, but clean.
Doesn't have ears washed yet.
I bet his ears are brown.

> *Analysis Schedule:* Isolation
> Symbolization
> Projection and Introjection
> Regression
> Weak controls

Girl, CA=8 years 11 months (IQ=122, Diagnosed as childhood schizophrenia).

One major feature of this girl's symptomatology was her vividly enacted fantasies of being a wolf, accompanied by growling and crawling on all fours. The CAT protocol was secured after ten months of intensive inpatient treatment. She is immediately concerned (on Card 1) with the incongruity of animals assuming human attributes, doubtless, in this case at least, reflecting her own animal versus human identification problems. She continues these protestations on six succeeding cards (2, 3, 4, 8, 9, and 10). It is also interesting that the card which upsets her the most (Card 3) has as it's main character a lion, the one animal in this series that probably most resembles a wolf. Her reaction is to turn the card over and then to crawl under the table, probably not only to "escape" from the picture, but also as if the scene has triggered off a re-enactment of her animal role.

Her concern (on Card 7) that all things must eat to survive, is reminiscent of the previous S's similar response to Card 6, and highlights the deep oral fears so characteristic of schizophrenic children. No parent figures are mentioned until Card 10, where the puppy "takes his father's bone and buries it," suggesting some oedipal interests.

1. This is not a beauty!
Is no color on it,
   it is plain black and white.
(Q) Three chickens and a hen.
(Q) Eating breakfast.
(Q) They do like it.
(Q) This one I like,
   looks bigger than the others.
(Q) They have spoon, bowls, tablecloth.
Ask me now what is wrong about this picture!
(Q) Well, chickens are not supposed
   to have spoons, bowls and tablecloth.

2. Will you know what is wrong about this one?
Everything!
First, bears are not supposed
   to play tug-of-war.
They are not supposed
   to have a rope.
(Q) Don't know.

3. Lions are not supposed
   to sit on a chair,
   to have a cane, a pipe,
   to be in a building.
(Q) I don't like
   the way he is looking about me.
(Q) He will be turned down,
   that he cannot look at me.
   (She turns the card over.)
(Q) His eyes!
   (She hides herself under the table.)
(Q) That's all.

4. Kangaroos are not supposed
   to have hats, a balloon or a bike.
They are supposed
   to jump
   and not to ride on bikes.
Besides, the track
   has only one wheel.
(Q) That's all.

5. Why am I looking at this picture?
(Q) Teddy bears in a crib.

(Q) Why have I to look at them?
(Q) They are dreaming of honey.
(Q) Don't know.

6. Bears.
They got to sleep.
The little one
   is going to sneak out.
Will see the snow.
(Q) That's all.

7. Ooooh! Tiger! and monkey!
Tries to climb up the tree,
   but it is too late.
(Q) The tiger will get it.
(Q) Kill it.
(Q) Because everything got to eat.
(Q) Here are vines.
How come his tail here?

8. Ooooh! Everything is wrong
   in this picture.
Just look at it!
Monkeys are not supposed
   to have a couch,
   and cups, and pictures (etc.)
(Q) This one is telling
   the young one such thing.
(Q) Don't know.
(Q) Maybe to behave.

9. Mmmmmm! Bunny in bed.
It is mixed up!
(Q) How can I answer such things?

10. Oh boy! Dogs are not supposed
   to give a spanking,
   to have a toilet.
(Q) He was bad.
(Q) He took his father's bone
   and buried it.
(Q) In the yard somewhere.
(Q) Don't know, that's all.

    Analysis Schedule: Isolation
                       Repression and Denial
                       Regression
                       Confused Identification

Boy, CA=13 years 5 months (Childhood schizophrenia of long-standing).

This final record is a good example of the constricted, almost single-word responses given by those in whom the disease process has been present for a long time. These reactions are similar to the Rorschach responses of schizophrenic children, as discussed by Halpern (1954), in which content is repetitive, unelaborated and poorly perceived. Halpern points out that the first response may or may not be related to the stimulus, and the child subsequently "plays with the concept" in a perseverative fashion when presented with subsequent cards.

The only activities described by this boy are eating, playing and sleeping, with less and less relationship to the actual activities portrayed on the cards.

1. Ducks
(Q) Eating.
(Q) Don't know.

2. Bears.
(Q) Playing.
   (Pats head, laughs.)

3. A lion
(Q) Don't know.

4. Making Easter baskets.

5. Playing.
(Q) Sleeping.
(Q) Play.

6. Playing.

7. Lion.
(Q) Playing.

8. Playing.
(Q) Playing.
(Q) Play rockus.

9. (This card was not administered)

10. Playing.
She's sleeping.
Is this the toilet?
(Q) Going to take a bath.

Analysis Schedule: Repression and Denial
Weak controls

CHAPTER XII

Multiple Testing

Two types of comparative use of the CAT will be discussed in this chapter: (1) longitudinal studies in which the CAT has been administered at repeated intervals; and (2) situations where the CAT has been administered as part of a test battery and comparisons made between kinds of data secured from the various tests employed. Reviews of research studies in each area will be supplemented with clinical reports.

LONGITUDINAL STUDIES

Repeated administrations of the same test need to take into consideration the time interval between tests. If the interval is too short, the subject may remember and repeat his previous responses, or he may become bored and not respond at all. Where intervals are fairly long (i.e., one or two years or more), the particular dynamics revealed at one time may be influenced by the development level of the child and so may not be observable at a later date. Furthermore, the particular defenses employed will be expected to vary within the same child as he grows and matures in all areas.

As a preliminary to discussion of specific longitudinal uses of the CAT, a consideration of studies by Kagan and Moss (1959) and Kagan (1959) will provide some background. Kagan and Moss (1959) studied a sample of 86 children who had been administered the TAT at the mean ages of 8-9, 11-6, and 14-6. Protocols were scored for achievement fantasy. They found that the proportion of Ss using achievement themes tended to increase with age. Phi coefficients indicated that the presence of achievement fantasy on the first administration was significantly associated with its subsequent occurrence on the second and third administrations, thus suggesting more than chance stability for this particular motive during childhood and adolescence.

Kagan (1959), using the longitudinal TAT data on these same 86 children, scored the protocols for the presence of the following needs or press: n-Dependence, n-Nurturance, n-Achievement, n-Physical Aggression, n-Indirect Aggression, n-Indirect Aggression to Parents, p-Physical Aggression, p-Indirect Aggression. Kagan was interested in the stability of TAT content over time in relation to the degree of ambiguity in the fantasy stimulus, reasoning that ". . . absence of a certain motive in a theme told to a [structured] stimulus suggests that content is apt to be a more valid measure of conflict than absence of this content to an ambiguous stimulus" (Kagan, 1959, p. 266).

The data he presents are concerned with the extent of *presence* of motives, rather than their absence, on specific cards. He found that only two of the content dimensions were in fact stable over time, these being Physical Aggression by the hero, and n-Achievement. Significant phi coefficients were found for n-Achievement from the first to the second administrations and for n-Physical Aggression from the first to the second, and from the second to the third administrations. These two themes occurred with highest frequencies on specific cards which suggested these contents (Cards 1 and 17BM for *n*-Achievement and 3BM for *n*-Physical Aggression). The simplest explanation for this finding would seem to be that Ss are more apt to tell the same type of story or use similar themes when the content of the card is specifically structured to suggest that theme.

There is only one published longitudinal study using the CAT. Nolan (1959) administered the test to 25 Ss at ages 5-10, 6-10, 8-10, 9-10 and 10-10. Protocols were scored for *n*-Achievement, *n*-Affiliation, and *n*-Power. Nolan was interested in assessing the relative stability of these needs through repeated administrations and also any fluctuations with age and sex.

Results indicated that all three motives showed an increase with age. There were no significant sex differences although there was a tendency for boys to exceed girls on *n*-Achievement at each age level. For all Ss, there was a significant difference from age 6-10 to 8-10 on all three motives, with an additional significant increase in Affiliation scores from ages 9-10 to 10-10 and for Power from 5-10 to 6-10. Nolan concluded that the eighth year seems crucial in personality development as indicated by the increased use of all themes in the interval from 6-10 to 8-10, but he also points out the unfortunate omission of testing at age 7-10, thus preventing further delineation as to the more precise time of increase. It should also be noted that he reports a large number of individual differences in scores from one age level to the next, and actual reversals in some scores for some children, thus suggesting that development in individual cases may be irregular and nonuniform.

A ten year longitudinal CAT study[*] is currently underway at the Institute of Human Development, Florida State University. Data are being analyzed on 268 protocols from children tested at successive intervals from ages three through 11 years. A preliminary paper by Witherspoon and Rochester (unpublished) has analyzed apperceptive responses for the percentage of use of different dynamics at each level for the group as a whole. Tentative findings suggest that identification with mother is consistently given with high frequency while identification with father tends to decrease with age. Aggression shows a definite decrease with age, especially for boys whose initial usage is quite high. The category of acceptance by adults increases with age for both sexes while orality is maintained at moderate levels at all ages. The remaining dynamics under study—fears, oedipal, toileting, cleanliness, sibling rivalry, and sexuality—were given infrequently at any age. Future plans for this project involve an analysis of the extent to which these dynamics are employed over time by individual children. This is the kind of longitudinal information which is greatly needed.

LONGITUDINAL CLINICAL DATA

Ainsworth and Boston (1952) and Wheeler (1955-56) have presented an extensive longitudinal case history report of a child who had been separated

---

[*]Dr. Ralph L. Witherspoon is directing the project, assisted by Dr. Eugene Byrd, Dr. Marjorie Stith, Dr. James White, Jr., and Mrs. Aileen Rochester. Doctoral dissertations, reported in greater detail in this volume, by Drs. Robert Nolan and Marvin Rosenblatt, have also been part of the overall study.

from his parents from age one to age four while in a TB sanatorium and also for several shorter returns to the hospital at intervals. At the time of the Ainsworth-Boston report three Rorschachs had been administered and two CATs, the latter with a six-month interval between tests. The first CAT was administered at age six, at the time of one of the shorter hospitalizations. The protocol revealed hostility toward, and rejection of, mother figures; more positive feelings toward father; and confusion of sex roles. Six months later, after returning home, a second CAT showed marked withdrawal in all areas, no recognition of characters as family members, but instead, only marked aggression and insecurity and with no figures of identification. The approach on both protocols was largely one of enumeration and description, but there were some fantasy aspects. The authors hypothesize that ". . . this further withdrawal from relationships is a result of the third cluster of hospitalization experiences. . . It is as though the phantasies that sustained him through the hospital experience [at the time of the first CAT] broke down after return home, leaving him no alternative to the rejection of all hope for satisfactions from his parents or other people" (Ainsworth and Boston, 1952, p. 185).

In the actual family situation, the boy had shown a similar change, with no affection being expressed toward any family member. The authors emphasize that congruence was found between the child's behavior and theoretical inferences as to expectations on the basis of the early deprivation, and the interpretive hypotheses from the projective data.

In discussing the value of retests, the authors (Ainsworth and Boston, 1952) state:

The interpretation of differing performances upon retesting with the same instrument presents certain difficult problems revolving about the questions of change versus continuity. If there are changes from one test to the next, is this because there has been a change in the personality? If so, does it seem related to major events in the life of the subject? Or, particularly in the case of a young child, can the changes be attributed to a developmental process? Or have differing test situations and circumstances evoked different responses? Or is it merely that different samples taken of the functioning of the personality reflect somewhat different facets? . . . .

In this study the most helpful feature of the retests would seem to be the continuity of certain of the concepts and of certain features of the general approach from one test to the others. Not only does this continuity tend to confirm interpretative hypotheses which first were presented rather tentatively . . . but also the repetition of concepts with differing degrees of expansion of explanation was of considerable assistance in the interpretation of the content of his responses. Roddy gave no sign of recollecting his responses from previous tests, or even of having seen the cards before. Therefore, the continuity of the concepts, particularly of those which are not commonly evoked by the stimulus material with other subjects, points to significant "constants" which Roddy himself brings to his perception of the world (p. 189).

In an appendix to the study, the two CAT protocols are presented side by side and the three Rorschachs are presented in similar format.

Wheeler (1955-56) reports on an additional follow-up administration of the

Rorschach and CAT to this same child after a two and one-half year interval. He was then nine years two months of age and there had been no further hospitalizations. At this time, in the home situation, he still favored his father over other family members and often became quite aggressive, demanding and stubborn with his mother. The third CAT is presented by Wheeler in conjunction with the previous two for comparative purposes. In the third protocol there was a marked lack of interaction between the characters, and preoccupation with appendages. Emphasis is on the father figures, especially the size differential between adult and child. Oral aggressive overtones are also prominent. Where characters are described as interacting, the main themes are of fighting or scolding, while on cards which specifically allow for tenderness or affection (Cards 1, 4, 5, 6, 8, and 9) he omits any description of interrelationships between characters. Throughout the test, he thus shows poor capacity for object relationships or deep emotional experiences. At this time the child was diagnosed as presenting both a long-standing neurotic reaction and a character disorder.

Bellak and Adelman (1960)* have published the following clinical study of a child to whom a second CAT had been administered after an interval of 19 months.

Following are side-by-side the responses of a boy who at the time of first testing was 6 years 10 months, and at the time of the second testing 8 years 5 months. The boy was originally referred to the school psychologist because he was found extremely immature, showed off constantly, wanted to be different and to get attention, made silly noises, pushed other children and was found to be frequently inattentive. At the time of first testing his Stanford-Binet IQ was 124. He behaved in a very uneven fashion, shouted at the psychologist, wouldn't sit down, and engaged in some baby talk. The reason for his second test was that he was a classroom disturbance; he didn't conform, tripped and hit children and looked unhappy. He had few friends. His academic work was considered good, and the teacher thought he probably had an IQ of about 140.

Stories

Age: 6 years 10 months	Age: 8 years 5 months
1. What are these chickens? This chicken was eating badly and spilling and making work for the big chicken and the big chicken has to spank them and send them back to their grandfather.	1. I wonder what it is. I know! The hen and the naughty little people, when the fox fell in the river! There were three and they were bad and they didn't want to help and they spilled crumbs. And one day the fox came and ate the mother hen up and then he fell asleep and they put rocks in him and he drowned. (Mother hen

---

*From Bellak, L., and Adelman, Crusa: The Children's Apperception Test (CAT). *In* A. I. Rabin and Mary R. Haworth (Eds.): *Projective Techniques with Children.* New York: Grune & Stratton, 1960, pp. 62–94. Pages 83–85 reproduced with the permission of the senior author and the publisher.

was out when they put rocks in?)
Which would you rather have, four
days of rain, fog or snow? (Which
would you?) Snow, then we could
have snowball fights. Which would
you rather have, three days hot or
three days cold? (You?) Cold because
I don't like short-sleeved shirts. (Want
to look at the next one?) O.K.

3. You wouldn't be able to get near
that would you? Would he eat a mouse?
(Do you think so?) Yes, I think so but
I don't know if the lion will find him
or not. He's waiting for someone to
come along that isn't looking what he's
doing and he'll eat him.

3. (Timothy voluntarily picked up
card 3, looked at it and said:) No, I
don't want that, I feel like scaling it
out of the window. A lion pooing on
his chair. Somebody stole something
of his and he was thinking what to do
and there was a little mouse there and
he bit his tail and the lion put dynamite in the hole and blew him up.
Which would you rather have, calm or
a hurricane? (Calm, and you?) I
don't know, hurricane, maybe.

5. I guess it's the night time and
someone must be away and it's just
getting black and I don't know what
this is, I'll call this smoke and there is
a fire outside and when they come
back they find their house is all burned
down. That would make you cry,
wouldn't it?

5. The mother bear and the daddy
bear were out and two little bears
came in and slept in this crib. And it
was dark and after they slept they
woke up and ran out the back door
and when mother and father came
home it was dark and they didn't
know what was wrong and they never
found 'em. Now, I have 32-38, here
comes the kind of flag you have for
39-46. I like a fast wind that blows
trees down, do you? (Not very much.)
(Timothy picked up the next card.)

6. What is those, those swimming?
Oh, a bear in his cave and the baby
bear is with him. What eats bears, can
you think of anything? (Can you?)
No.

6. What's this! There's three bears
and they have no house and they slept
in a cave and one night someone put
some mud over it and when they woke
up they had to claw their way out.
And the next night the same thing
happened and the next night the little
bear didn't go to sleep and he saw a
man there. And the next day he told
his mother and daddy and that night
they ate the man up. 65, next is, no
55-65, no that isn't right. I'm the best
in numbers in my class. (Timothy continued to write and say aloud, wind

speeds to above 75.) Which would you rather have, above 75 with 10 below zero and cloudy or 8 to 12 with 70 and clear? (I'll take 10 below) Once it was zero and I ran all around, I am just about done, now I want to play a game with you.

Brief Analysis

In both Card 1 stories, the children eat badly, are naughty and antagonize the big chicken who punishes them and sends them away. In the second testing an aggressive animal is introduced, a fox, who eats up the mother and is, in turn, drowned for his misdeeds, whereupon the child reverted to an obsessive preoccupation with the weather which went all through the testing. In the story to picture 3, in the first session, he is anxiously concerned with the idea that one has to be careful or else one is devoured. In the second session, he wants to do away with the card altogether by scaling it out the window. There is much more evidence of violence and anal regression here with the lion "pooing" on his chair. The aggressive orality now relates specifically to the castrating notion of biting off the tail. There is also the suggestive evidence of explosive emotional tension in connection with the dynamite and the wish for a hurricane. In story 5, in the first testing, the reference to smoke and fire suggests a great deal of aggressive urethral sexual preoccupation, as does the reference to crying. This would be most suggestive of a history of enuresis (which we were unable to check on) but is certainly consistent with his aggressive behavior, including the aggressive need to show off. The second testing gives a much less clear-cut story except that the little bears run out when the parents come home and are never discovered. This is followed by some reference to figures and the discussion again of violent weather, in this case a fast wind.

Story 6, in the first session, introduces water, supporting the notion expressed in story 5, and again a preoccupation with oral incorporation. The second story 6 has to do with being walled up with mud and watchful night time observations. This is suggestive of insomnia perhaps associated with oral incorporation fantasies; and then again the preoccupation with numbers, windspeeds and the weather; his restlessness is also indicated by the reference to running.

An examination of the test material suggests not only the marked pathology consistent with the clinical report of aggression and showing off but also that the process is worsening. Judging by the leaving of the stimulus, the inappropriate material and very poor drive control, this boy is probably on the way towards a psychotic condition. Obsessive preoccupation and acting-out have so far served as brakes on the ego disintegration. A school psychiatrist who saw the child suspected that he might be schizophrenic (pp. 83–85).

Unfortunately, no studies could be found where the CAT was used as a means of measuring progress in therapy, with longitudinal type data being secured before, during and after therapeutic intervention. This should be a very fruitful area for research not only in terms of the projective instrument itself but also for the evaluation of therapy as well.

COMPARISONS OF CAT WITH OTHER PROJECTIVE TESTS

Studies reporting the use of the CAT as part of a test battery have usually

employed the Rorschach, with drawings, and sentence or story completions
often included. In discussing the selection and usefulness of various tests in
the psychological evaluation of children, Halpern (1957) points out:

> In examining a child it is customary to give a number of tests rather than just
> one. Among these are generally an intelligence test, possibly school achievement
> tests, drawings of human figures, and one or more of the projective tests. The use
> of several tests is important since each one gives different information about the
> personality of the child, highlights different facets of behavior, and probes differ-
> ent levels of the personality. Thus, the intelligence test gives a picture of the
> child's intellectual strengths and weaknesses. The Rorschach, on the other hand,
> points up the degree of emotional control he has atttained, the effect of his emo-
> tional reactions on his intellectual functioning, the personality resources at his
> disposal, and the use he is making of them. The apperception tests reveal the
> sources of the child's specific disturbances. Sometimes the quality of the produc-
> tions on the Rorschach or the Children's Apperception Test indicates that the
> child's potentialities are much better than his formal IQ suggests, but that because
> of his emotional difficulties he is not applying his assets fully and constructively.
> Conversely, there are those who can perform with considerable efficiency when tasks
> are laid out and planned for them as on the intelligence test but who become
> strikingly inadequate when called on to organize things on their own. Knowing
> such facts about a child can be helpful in deciding how a child's problem can
> be best handled, the need for psychotherapy as against a "let well enough alone"
> policy, the type of school he should attend, and so on (p. 775).

We would not expect to find similar content or themes on the Rorschach
and on the CAT, or that necessarily the same dynamics would be revealed to
the same extent on each test, since the stimulus properties of the two tests
differ as well as the nature of the response task and the levels of personality
that are probed. We might even find quite different responses to different
tasks, from the same child, yet we could also anticipate that there would be
some over-all indications of either disturbance or "normality" regardless of
the test used.

Magnusson (1960), in Sweden, administered a battery of projective tests
to 12 sets of identical twins, ages nine and one-half to ten and one-half. Tests
used were the Rorschach, CAT, Bender Gestalt and Draw-a-Man. For analysis
of data, one child from each twin pair was randomly assigned to one of two
groups. Two judges evaluated the Rorschachs and two different judges evaluated the CATs using ratings along a seven-point scale for selected variables.
Seven of the 11 Rorschach variables were identical with seven of the 11 CAT
variables. Interrater reliabilities on each dimension were all positive and fairly
high, ranging from .17 to .80.

Intraclass coefficients are presented for each judge on each dimension of
the Rorschach and CAT. On the Rorschach, the two judges each found fairly
modest positive correlations for members of twin pairs on measures of Emotional Maturity, Intelligence, and Control; while two dimensions—Aggression
and Inner Conflicts—yielded almost no correlation by either judge, suggesting
differences between pair members on these latter variables. For the CAT,
Intelligence was the only dimension to receive a high positive correlation between pair members by both judges. The correlations for the remaining vari-

ables on both tests varied greatly between examiners, e.g., on the Rorschach, Reality Adjustment resulted in a correlation of .44 for one judge and .00 for the other judge; Dependency on the CAT yielded r's of —.58 and .61. In fact, Dependency, as measured by either the Rorschach or the CAT yielded the largest discrepancies in between-twin r's, the lowest r's in interrater comparisons, and the only negative r's in interjudge ratings between the Rorschach and CAT. Such findings seemingly indicate that one member of the twin pairs is usually more dependent than the other.

Measures of "general adjustment" on each test were arrived at by having one judge rank-order the Rorschach protocols in each twin group, and two judges work together to rank-order the CATs. The Rorschach r was .36, while that for the CAT was —.22, suggesting that variables as tapped by the Rorschach were more similar between pair members than were those for the CAT.

In contrast to the above findings, r's for Terman-Merrill IQs of twin pairs were .88; for Pascal-Suttell scores on the Bender-Gestalt, .92; and for the DAM raw scores, .80. Finally, comparisons of the over-all ratings of general adjustment derived from each of the four tests showed correlations with the CAT of .35 for the Rorschach; .38 for the Bender-Gestalt; and only .03 for the DAM.

As pointed out in a previous discussion of this study in Chapter VI, the CATs were administered when the Ss were ten and one-half years of age. The variability and inconclusiveness of the CAT findings may in part be a function of the children having passed the upper age limits for the appropriateness of this test.

Boulanger-Balleyguier (1961) has made a comparative study of the Rorschachs and CATs administered to 155 French children between the ages of three and eight years. Fifty of the Ss had been referred for psychiatric consultation, and the remaining 105 were nursery and primary school children. For the analysis, the sample was divided into two groups by age: three to five years (N = 76), and six to eight years (N = 79). Relationships were sought between CAT dimensions (such as popular responses, additions, omissions) and the usual Rorschach determinants.

For the group as a whole, the most outstanding correlation (.52) was found between the number of characters mentioned on the CAT and the number of responses (R) on the Rorschach. Both dimensions can be seen as measures of productivity, with the inference that children will respond in a consistent fashion irrespective of the test used.

For the younger group, fairly high and significant r's (from .34 to .55) were obtained between the number of popular responses on the CAT and each of these Rorschach dimensions: P, A per cent, $F+$ per cent. Omissions on the CAT correlated negatively with $F+$ per cent, and number of activities attributed to secondary CAT characters correlated positively with R. In essence the positive relationships found in this age group represent those dimensions on each test that are considered as measuring reality orientation and capacity to react to situations in conformity to one's age group. It is also interesting that there was correspondence between the measures of precision of perception on the two tests, i.e., few omissions and high $F+$ per cent.

Relationships between CAT findings and Rorschach movement and color responses were found only in the older group, since few very young children give movement or *FC* on the Rorschach. Boulanger-Balleyguier views the positive correlations between movement responses and both the percentage of human characters seen on the CAT (.53) and CAT additions (.46) as indicating similar dynamics, since creative imagination and interiorization of thought processes would be involved in giving human characteristics to the pictured animals. There was a fairly low, but positive, correlation (.32) between the percentage of hero's interpersonal relationships seen on the CAT and sum of color. The color dimension becomes significant only as greater proportions of *FC*s are given, so that the measures from both tests are reflecting aspects of the emotional relationships with others.

Contrary to expectations, there was no correlation, in either age group, between the percentage of human characters mentioned on the CAT and *H* per cent on the Rorschach. Evidently the factors that would lead a child to report humans are not the same for the two tests, since, as also mentioned above, the human characterizations on the CAT were found to be associated with Rorschach movement and color responses, rather than with human content *per se*.

The incidence of pathological signs on both tests was evaluated for four subgroups: Anxious (N = 9); Withdrawn (N = 17); Aggressive (N = 26); Well adjusted (N = 34). The most striking findings were that the Anxious gave the highest percentages of cruel details, and false perceptions on the CAT, and *Do*, Refusals and *Clob* on the Rorschach. The Aggressives give high proportions of deaths to heroes and others, and cruel details on the CAT, high *Clob* on the Rorschach and the fewest Anatomy responses of any grouping. The Withdrawn gave the highest percentages of any group on two Rorschach variables: Shock and Anatomy. The normals were not high on any dimension of either test, and tended to respond more like the Withdrawn rather than resembling either of the other two groups.

It is thus shown that both the Anxious and the Aggressive groups give a high percentage of cruel details (CAT) and *Clob* (Rorschach), suggesting these signs as indicators of serious disturbance, particularly since these two kinds of responses were extremely rare among the other two groupings.

Boulanger-Balleyguier (1961) concludes her study by offering two possible reasons for the modest correlations and other differences noted between responses to the two tests: intraindividual variations in the Ss themselves, and difficulty in finding variables for comparison which have the same dynamic significance from test to test.

As part of a validation study of a projective film technique, Haworth (1962) administered a battery of individual projectives to two groups of school children. The experimental group (N = 15) was selected on the basis of certain deviant responses to the film which had been administered eight to 12 months previously. The control group (*N* = 15) was matched for sex and school grade and had given no deviant film responses. The Rorschach, CAT, Despert Fables and DAP were administered to each child individually. Judges were told that half the group of 30 Ss had scored high either on the film's Obsessive Index or

Table 12.1 Selection of Deviant Cases by Three Judges*

		Judge A	Judge B	Judge C
Obsessive	1	+	+	+
	2	+	+	+
	3	+	+	+
	4	+	+	+
	5	+	+	+
	6		+	+
Guilt-Anxiety	1	+	+	+
	2	+	+	+
	3	+	+	
	4	+		
	5		+	+
	6		+	+
	7		+	+
	8		+	+
	9		+	
Totals		9	14	12
Controls	1	+		
	2	+		
	3	+		+
	4	+		
	5	+		
	6	+		
	7		+	+
	8			+
	9			
	10			
	11			
	12			
	13			
	14			
	15			
Totals		6	1	3

*Reproduced, with the permission of the publisher, from the *Journal of Projective Techniques* 26: 47–60, 1962.

on both the Guilt and Anxiety measures. They were instructed to select, from inspection of the individual projective protocols, those 15 Ss presumed to comprise the experimental group. The first two judges (A and B) were free to use any method of selection they wished to devise. As shown in Table 12.1, judge A correctly identified nine of the 15 experimental Ss (which was no better than chance) and judge B selected 14 of the 15 ($p = .005$, Fisher's exact probability). These two judges agreed on only eight of their selections (non-significant).

Judge B, while making her selections, had developed certain indices for each test (including the Schedule of Adaptive Mechanisms, Haworth, 1963). This process had yielded 15 "deviant" Rorschachs, 15 CAT's, 17 DAP's and 16 Fables. The final task of selecting 15 presumed experimental cases involved a progressive selection from cases scoring high on all four measures, to those high on Rorschach and CAT, and finally those scoring high one one or the other major test and one minor test. As mentioned above, 14 of the 15 cases so chosen proved to be correct. Inspection of these results indicated that the criteria developed for the DAP and Fables would not have selected any better than chance. Consequently, only the Rorschach and CAT protocols were given to judge C with instructions to score them according to the same objective criteria used by judge B.

As shown in the last column of Table 12.1, judge C was able to select 12 of the experimental cases ($p = .005$) and agreed with judge B on these 12 cases as being disturbed and on 12 cases as being controls. These two judges also agreed on a misselection of one control case as being disturbed and on the misselection of one experimental case as being a control. It is interesting to note that the obsessive cases were the most uniformly selected by all judges. Of the seven cases where all three judges agreed, five were obsessive (out of a total of six obsessive cases).

Table 12.2 indicates the extent of agreement between judges B and C when applying the objective criteria to the Rorschach and the CAT. Both judges agreed on the selection of 11 cases with the Rorschach and on 11 cases using the CAT. Nine cases were scored high by both judges for both tests. Three more cases were scored high by both judges on one test and one judge on the other test, thus attesting to considerable consistency in the ability of both tests to pinpoint disturbances of the types being evaluated in this study, i.e., obsessive orientations and guilty, anxious (probably hysterical) tendencies.

The author (Haworth, 1962) concludes: "The results of the present study suggest that children do tend to give consistent responses, reflecting the potency of dynamic dimensions, irrespective of the projective medium employed. The dynamic origins of these responses are highlighted by the fact that such consistencies are observable over the time span of 8-12 months between the original projections to the film and the subsequent responses to the individual test battery" (pp. 58-59).

In Haworth's (1964) study of parental loss, reported more fully in Chapter X, the Rorschach and CAT (or TAT) were the main projectives examined. Of the children with loss, 26 had been given both the Rorschach and the CAT, as had 44 of the controls. Three of the 20 response items could only be scored on the Rorschach. Counting the number of times the Rorschach and the CAT contributed to the remaining 17 items, revealed no differences between the two tests for either group, as shown in Table 12.3.

Again, the findings suggest that either test will reveal problem areas, or that both are effective in tapping personality dynamics to an equivalent degree. Even more important, from the standpoint of projective testing, is the implication that children will respond in consistent fashion in various media.

Simson (1955, 1962) administered a variation of the HTP in conjunction with the CAT to 28 German girls, ages eight to ten. Ss were first instructed to draw a house, then a man, then a woman, and then anything they wished. Following the drawing task, Simson's human form of the CAT was administered. Finally, Ss were asked to tell stories to each of their drawings. (In a

Table 12.2 Selection of Deviant Rorschach and CAT
Protocols when using Objective Criteria*

		Rorschach		CAT	
		Judge B	Judge C	Judge B	Judge C
Obsessive	1	+	+	+	+
	2	+	+	+	+
	3	+		+	+
	4	+	+	+	+
	5	+	+	+	+
	6	+	+		
Guilt-Anxiety	1	+	+	+	+
	2	+	+	+	+
	3	+		+	
	4				
	5	+		+	+
	6	+	+	+	+
	7	+	+	+	+
	8	+	+	+	+
	9	+	+	+	
Totals		14	11	13	11
Controls	1			+	+
	2				
	3				+
	4				
	5				
	6			+	+
	7	+	+		
	8				+
	9		+		
	10				
	11				
	12				
	13				
	14				
	15				
Totals		1	2	2	4

*Reproduced with the permission of the publisher, from the *Journal of Projective Techniques* 26: 47–60, 1962.

pilot study, the children were asked to tell stories immediately after drawing, but this procedure was not found to be as productive.) Simson felt that the task of telling stories to the drawings would be facilitated by the prior storytelling to the projective pictures and that by combining CAT and drawings, greater freedom and more spontaneous productions would result. He reasoned that not all problem areas would be tapped for an individual child in a standard set of pictures and that the inclusion of drawings might uncover additional dynamic areas. His clinical observations confirmed this impression in that important themes often appeared in stories told to the drawings which either were not touched upon at all in the CAT or were referred to only fleetingly.

Table 12.3 Mean Number of Loss Items Contributed by Rorschach and CAT

	N	Rorschach	CAT	P
Loss group	26	3.31	2.62	ns
Control group	44	1.06	1.18	ns

Dhondiyal (1961-62), working in India, was specifically interested in the projective aspects of children's spontaneous paintings and drawings. Art products of eight clinic Ss were compared with those of a school class of 44 children, ages seven to 11. A total of 482 drawings (including the children's spontaneous comments) were studied and interpreted by "scoring" various items grouped under categories such as: identification figure, emotional climate, intelligence, orientation to the environment, ego integration, superego manifestations and symbolism. Five children (four "abnormal" and one gifted) were studied more intensively, with added data from the CAT, Bender Gestalt, and clinician's or teacher's reports. An example is given of the "scoring" of ten drawings by one child, with illustrations of each. One table for each of the five intensive cases compares the extent to which various personality traits were revealed in the drawings, the CAT, the Bender Gestalt, and observations of clinician or teacher.

It was the author's conclusion that art products were markedly superior to the other measures in extensiveness of bases for personality appraisal, but also that most of the aspects revealed in the drawings were confirmed in one or another of the other instruments. Art revealed all the personality traits found in the CAT, but failed to reflect the sensory-motor patterning and perceptual organization which were demonstrated in the Bender Gestalt.

MOTHERS' CATS VERSUS CHILDREN'S PSYCHOLOGICAL EVALUATIONS

Van Cauvenberghe (1960) has employed a unique variation of testing with the CAT by administering it to the mothers of preschool age children. She was interested in assessing the mother's personality, her expectations of, and relationships to, the child viewed in the light of the child's development and social adaptation. The sample was composed of 30 young French mothers and their children drawn equally from three socio-economic groups, and ten mother-child pairs from a hospital population.

In presenting the CAT to the mothers they were told that the pictures had been drawn for children and they were then asked to invent stories such as they would tell to their children. TATs were also administered to some of the mothers after an interval of 18 months. A careful anamnesis was obtained on each child from interviews with the mothers. The children were given an intelligence test, and the Düss Fables, and asked to draw their family and other figure drawings. (Unfortunately, the CAT was not administered to the children.) Observations were also made of mother-child interactions.

Results indicated that the CAT is an appropriate instrument for use with parents, revealing the mother's personality, typical modes of reaction, defense mechanisms, and attitudes toward the child. (The TAT yielded comparable data in terms of story structure and manner of adaptation.) The CAT used in this way provides a projective test of family relationships as viewed by the mother, and insights into the mother's conception of the maternal role. The mother's position in relation to the authority-paternal role was revealed, e.g., on Card 3. In the 50 per cent of cases where the mothers saw the lion as strong, the King, etc., their children were on the whole active, independent and happy. The children of the 25 per cent of mothers who saw the lion as old, but nevertheless strong and feared, also reacted as the former group of children. The remaining 25 per cent of mothers saw the lion as old and weak, and their children were passive and the most anxious, on the basis of the anamnesis and the children's tests.

Norms for mothers' responses to each card are presented; e.g., on Card 1, all gave themes of nourishment, and described the depicted situation more in terms of what was shown, while they tended to tell stories on the remaining cards of situations that "should be." On Card 2, children were most often described as being with the mother, in fact, on most child-parent cards, the adult was seen as the mother figure. On Card 3, the mouse was seen by only 65 per cent of the mothers, and was omitted in all cases where the mother was known to be disturbed. All cards, except Cards 3 and 7, evoked family situations, and especially revealed mother-child relationships.

Some tentative conclusions were drawn from the social class distributions: the lower middle-class mothers were the most rigid and anxious; middle-class mothers told the most stories with educational intents; working-class mothers were the most natural, spontaneous, imaginative and sentimental in their storytelling.

Specific areas of disturbance in the children or the mothers were analyzed for any relationships with the mothers' stories. For those children who had shown difficulties in weaning or with enuresis, there was no relationship with the mothers' CATs, character structure or methods of training. In 93 per cent of the cases where the child had experienced difficulties on entering school, there was a direct relationship with the mother's disturbance as revealed by strong anxiety on the CAT. Finally, in all cases where the mother's protocols revealed psychological disturbances, the child's history and test results demonstrated emotional difficulties.

CLINICAL EXAMPLES OF BETWEEN-TEST DATA

The previously discussed reports of Ainsworth and Boston (1952) and Wheeler (1955-56), on the same little boy tested at different stages in his development, represent the only known published material in which responses to the CAT and other projective tests have been presented and compared. Taken together, these two studies present protocols of four Rorschachs and three CATs administered over four years' time. Wheeler's study presented clinical interpretations of the last Rorschach and CAT after summarizing the previous testings as having shown substantial agreement between tests. He points out the two outstanding features of the final CAT as being an inability to interrelate the characters and preoccupation with phallic characteristics. Counterparts of these responses were observed in the Rorschach in terms of the absence of human figures or movement responses, fragmentation of figures, and attention to small details, especially projections. He also notes that two features were revealed on the CAT that could not be deduced from the Rorschach: material pertaining to the perception of the father figure, and the further delineation of emotional tendencies, specifically revealing the presence of oral aggressive and destructive impulses and the lack of any capacity for tender feelings.

Sandler,* in an unpublished paper, has collected and interpreted the CAT and Rorschach responses of a little girl, aged seven years seven months, of high average intelligence. The girl was an only child in an Orthodox Jewish home. The mother reported considerable feeding difficulties throughout childhood, and the child was still eating very little. Toilet training had never been completed, since daytime accidents still occurred at school or at play with other children. The mother was an extremely conscientious housekeeper and maintained orthodox customs and practices despite her husband's objections that the family stood out as "different" in the neighborhood. The mother reported she must constantly be "after" the child to wash, study, practice or eat. During the joint interview, the mother displayed similar attitudes toward the child, being openly critical, correcting her many times, and answering questions put to the child.

The CAT stories and Sandler's clinical notes follow:

1. I see something faint.
    It's a rooster.
One day three chickens were eating breakfast.
    This is too hot for one chicken
    and too cold for the other chicken.
    But this little chicken's porridge was just right.
They were all jealous of the little chicken.
Mother said,
    "You two go away and
    I'll fix you some more porridge."
The mother went away
    and the little chicken finished his porridge.
Then a great big rooster came
    and ate the little chicken all up.
Then mother came back
    and the other chickens told her what happened.
She cried.
But the little chick
    inside the rooster's stomach
    was still alive
  because the rooster had swallowed him whole.
He had a little spoon
    and he carved a hole in his stomach
    and went off home.

---

*The author is indebted to Dr. Louise Sandler for permission to use the protocols and her diagnostic impressions of this case from an unpublished manuscript, "An Evaluation of the Children's Apperception Test in Clinical Practice: A Case Study."

Then mother saw him
   and picked him up and kissed him.
And she never cooked porridge
   that was too hot or too cold again.
   Just porridge that was just right.
(Q-which chicken in the picture got eaten up?)
The chicken without the bib got eaten up.

Clinical Notes. This story shows a typical children's "morality fable." However, the mother is the punished one and must learn to do the right thing. The child sees herself as capable of being prepared against unpleasant and threatening surprises. Does this child desire to control her mother by covert threats to herself? Note that the "bibless" child is eaten. Why did he not have a bib? Is it neglect of mother or, perhaps, the rebellion of the child?

2. Once upon a time there lived three bears.
They never knew what games were.
   When somebody asked them to play games
   they did not know how.
They didn't have any friends.
Baby had an idea.
   They would take a rope
   and watch the other animals play games.
They saw some animals
   play games with a rope.
   They started to play the same thing.
When the animals saw it they liked them.
   And now they got friends.

Clinical Notes. Here it appears that the child wants social acceptance for herself and her family. What are the "games" which the child feels she must teach her parents to play? She cannot (in this story) go off and play by herself but it appears that she needs family participation or sanction. Again, she teaches the grown-ups the most acceptable way to behave. Is this criticism of the parents who "don't know the ropes?" . . . This may be the child's view of the orthodoxy of the home which prevents her from taking part in the activities of the neighbor children.

3. One time there was a lion.
   A very strange lion. (long pause)
Oh, I know a good one.
He liked to eat mice,
   And I do not know why.
One day, he found a little mouse.
The mouse said, "Let me go and some day
   I might do a good deed for you."
The lion laughed and said,
   "If you promise,"
   And he let the mouse go.
Then the mouse said,
   "Thanks, sucker."
The lion got very mad.
One day a man went

into the jungle shooting.
He saw the lion and said,
  "Let's shoot him."
They started to shoot
  but they didn't like to shoot a lion.
  So they caught him in a net and went off.
The mouse saw him and said,
  "I'll get you out of this some way."
He gnawed the rope
  and set the lion free.
They were friends from then on. (long pause)
I said "sucker"
  because I saw it in a cartoon.
  A mouse said sucker.

Clinical Notes. Once again, this child moralizes to the authority figure. It appears, however, that she would have preferred to vanquish the authority entirely but could not reconcile the impulse with her apparent need to prohibit such impulses. Thus far, it seems that this child is very concerned with increasing her own importance in her own eyes. It is significant that she felt compelled to explain the reason for her use of the word "sucker." Is it because of her need to impress the tester favorably?

As to her handling of the father figure, we see that by the use of a well-known children's fable, she managed to turn the mouse into the powerful one. With the lion made powerless, she can be friends with him.

4. One day—a bright sunny day.
Mrs. Kangaroo bounced by Mr. Kangaroo's house.
She said,
  "I'll make a race with you."
Mr. Kangaroo said,
  "I do not know how to hop.
  I can ride a bike,
  but I cannot hop."
She said,
  "I'll have a race anyway."
Next day, Mr. Kangaroo rode his bike
  and rode and rode,
  until the race was over
  and finally he won.
So then Mrs. Kangaroo didn't talk about
  how fast she could run anymore.

Clinical Notes. Only one child is mentioned in this story and that child is seen as challenged by the mother figure. Once again, the child teaches the mother a lesson—in this case, not to brag.

All the stories indicate that the child feels very much on the defensive with her parents. She sees them as challenging her and she appears to have the attitude that she had better "keep them in line."

5. One night there was a great storm.
Mother and father

and the two twins were asleep.
One bear was Hoppy
  and the other bear was Floppy.
Floppy said,
  "Hoppy, I want to run away.
  It is too cold in this house.
  But the fence is too high."
So she took a knife and said,
  "Knife, break fence."
The knife said "No."
She saw a stick
  but the stick said "No."
(This is repeated with a "scissors" and a "hammer").
So she went to a cloud and said.
  "Make it foggy."
The cloud said it would
  if she would get an angel
  to "sit on me."
So she got an angel.
  So the cloud made the sky foggy.
  So the knife cut the fence.
And that is how the little
  bear ran away from home.

Clinical Notes. This story follows another well-known children's fable. She uses a known fable in story 3 as well, but not in stories 1, 2, and 4.

In the story, the child rather directly states her desire to escape the stimulus. In fact, she leaves the stimulus almost immediately in her transition to a story of how she escapes the "cold" house.

She paid a good deal of attention to the details of this story as she remembers it. It should be noted that when her memory of the story failed her, she unhesitatingly went on with her own "clouds," "fog," and "angels." There is no doubt that this child has a rich store of fantasy which serves her special needs. Perhaps one could venture to say that any anxiety-producing situation causes her to turn from reality to her ego-supportive fantasies.

6. They are hibernating.
Once upon a time
  Poppa Bear, Mamma Bear and Baby Bear. . . . .
Little bear was very sleepy.
When spring came
  he was still sleeping.
Mamma and daddy went to the water
  to eat lily pads.
A bird came and sang a happy song
  but the little bear did not wake up.
When he did wake up,
  he wondered where mama and daddy were.
He thought that Spring is here
  and mama and daddy were awake.
He ran to the lily-patch.

There was mama and daddy.
That's how he learned his lesson.
(Q-"What was the lesson he learned?")
He learned not to sleep too long.

Clinical Notes. Again, a moral is expressed but in this story it is the child who learns not to be caught unaware ("not to sleep too long"). It appears that the child is expressing her fear of not being ready for her parents' movements and actions. It was previously noted (in stories 1, 2, and 3 in particular) that this child sees herself as very capable, alert and ready to meet situations. In this story, she recovers quickly (finds her parents) but is determined that this type of inactivity (sleeping too long) will not be indulged in again; she won't "be caught napping." The need to control the course of events is apparent.

7. Oh, oh! Once upon a time
    there was a little baboon.
One day he met a lion.
The lion didn't like him.
    He said he would try
    to make a plan to eat the baboon up.
But he couldn't find anything.
So he roared and scared the little baboon.
He thought,
    "I will go across the river
    and then he will follow me."
He said,
    "Little baboon, it is too bad
    that you do not know how to swim.
    I am going to the other side of the river."
But the baboon climbed on the lion's back
    and went across with him.
The lion didn't know
    he was on top of hm.
So he learned not to play tricks
    on the little baboon.

Clinical Notes. By manipulation of another familiar children's fable, she again manages to have the strong figure (tiger-lion) lose to the weaker figure (baboon-monkey). The tiger is taught that the smart monkey cannot be bested. There appears to be little doubt that when the child is threatened (anxiety-arousing situation), one of her defenses is flight into fantasy. She handles her hostility by attempting to exalt her ego. It is as though she is saying: "You can not hurt me because I am superior to you and I know it." The question arises as to why she repeatedly employs such a strong defensive attitude. It would appear that hostility takes this form of expression because it gives her a relatively "safe" way of expressing her aggression. Superego development is clearly evidenced but it is apparent that she must use a good deal of energy to prevent direct expression of her aggressive impulses.

8. There are four baboons . . .
    I don't know the story for this one.
Mother baboon is saying,

"What an awful wild cat
  we have for a son."
Aunt Baboon had to scold him.
He talked back to Aunt Baboon.
Aunt Baboon asked,
  "Do you want ice-cream?"
Baby said, "Why should I?
  I don't like you
  and I don't like anything you have."
Aunt Baboon said,
  "You should go to bed without any dinner."
So he learned his lesson after all.
(Q-"Why did he say he didn't want ice-cream?")
Well, he was angry but he wouldn't show it.

Clinical Notes. The apparent hostility shown in this story is in sharp contrast to the seemingly justified (defensive) position she assumed in her previous stories. It is doubtful that this child permits herself to strike out in this fashion very often. She has probably learned that she cannot let her parents know how she feels. She would customarily use the more oblique expressions of resentment: enuresis? It is interesting that she is sorry that she showed her anger (the "wild cat") not because it was not right to say what she did to her Aunt but because of the danger of expressing herself in this way. It is "Aunt Baboon" who is the target of her anger. Probably, the child's defenses cannot permit her to direct the outburst at the mother-figure. However, in this story the child shows the anger which threatens her defenses and control.

9. First, there was a baby bunny.
He lived in a great big house in fairy land.
  It is on a little cloud.
He did not like to go to sleep
  when his mother told him to.
So mother said he could be up
  as long as he wanted to.
She went to sleep.
He went to bed
  and read some books in bed.
But his toys were asleep
  and everyone was asleep
  so he went to bed.

Clinical Notes. In this story we can see the child's vivid imagination at work. It is significant that this calm story is located in "fairyland." Here the mother is passive, obliging and compliant. It should be recalled that in Story 6, the child was concerned about sleeping while her parents were awake. Again, in this story she is ready to sleep only when she is certain that there is nothing that she is missing. This suggests the possibility of a sleeping disturbance.

10. I don't know a good one . . . .
A mother is giving her baby
  a spanking in the bathroom.
Maybe, I know . . .
Once upon a time, a little puppy

loved to play in water.
One day mother said,
   "Go to bed."
She told him to wash his feet and hands,
   his neck and face.
And he got the water
   all over the bathroom.
He went to the toilet
   and put so much paper into the toilet
   that it overflowed.
Mother came up to tuck him into bed
   and couldn't find him.
She looked all over
   and found him in the bathroom
   in his bathing suit
   playing in the water.
She was very angry
   and she sent him to bed
   without his ice-cream and cookies.
And he never did it again . . .
And the water bills besides.

Clinical Notes. In this story regressive trends emerge. That this regression takes place in response to a picture evoking images of excretory functions is particularly interesting. Perhaps this child is recalling her own earlier experiencs with toilet training. Her obvious enjoyment of water play and the manner in which she emphasizes water in her story suggests the possibility of enuresis. Hostile and rather fearful feelings towards the mother clearly show in the story. However, guilt is expressed at the end of the story and, once again, as in story 8, she learns that it is best not to express her aggression.

The Rorschach record is presented below:

Response	*Inquiry*
I. ∨ Skeleton face like the one a boy brought to school— I touched it and it felt gooey.	Here are the eyes, nose and brain up here (touches). It is gooey here. It looks like wet glue.
Here is a bridge and a house with windows. Like a nice scene.	Well, the bridge is here (outline of blot). It is over water down here. The house is standing on it with its window here (water is white of card).
II. ∨ Something just blew up. It crashed and it looks like fire coming out (mmm, a hard one).	Well, it looks like smoke was crashing and it was coming out and the fire is coming out here. (Space and bottom red).
∨ Here's a head—People dancing together. Here's the body, other hands and these are feet.	It looks like that and these are red hands here.
III. ∧ That's simple. Looks like men trying to lift something.	The position of the men.

∧ These would be lamps here. Hanging lamps.

∨ Two men lifting up their feet. They are rushing in a hurry.

They look like they're rushing . . . these things (indicates shadow between heads).

∨ These would be sea-horses.

(Side red details) The shape is like sea horses.
Add: One of the men's bowties fell off when they were rushing. It looks like a bowtie.

IV. ∧ This is a giant doing this with his feet (illustrates).

This part doesn't belong (indicates lower extension). He's laying down.

∨ This is a man with his head looking down between his legs. I saw an acrobat doing that. He has a crown on his head here.

V. ∨ It is a butterfly with its legs out. The feelers are over here.

∧ Here is a rabbit dressed up in gowns coming out.

It is tip-toeing and its gowns are all around it.

VI. ∨ It is a skull of a back of a person.

The spine is here. Here is the hip bone and a leftover arm.

∧ Oh, a monster with eyes, nose and feet. Fire is coming out of its neck.

It looks like it—It's the shape of fire, isn't it?

VII. ∧ I like this one. There are two girls turning their backs to each other with pony tails going up. Their tongues are sticking out.

∨ There are two little bunnies looking back.

VIII. ∧ I like this one. It has all different colors . . . Mmm, nice. There are two rats climbing up a Christmas tree.

This part looks like a colored Christmas tree.

< Here is a rainbow with two animals on the sides pushing it. Like this (illustrates).

IX. ∨ It looks like a waterfall.

Maybe its like scenery with a person looking both ways. Well, not exactly scenery but colors around him. Different colored water around him.

∧ Behind here it looks like a
mountain with water crashing
up to it.

X. ∨ There are two foxes crashing
down on each other and other
animals are looking. Here is a
sea horse on top.

Well, they are sliding down and the
heads are down here. Here are kangaroos, and bugs and spiders. Here is a
seahorse. They are shaped like animals.

∧ This way it looks like a design
I made in school.

There are different pretty colors and
its even on both sides.

Excerpts are presented from the examiner's analysis of the Rorschach:

The responses show the high degree of fantasy activity in which this child engages in her attempts to resolve the problems she faces in her world. She sees herself as a person who must "tip-toe" about in careful fashion if she is to protect herself (Card V). It is this sensitivity to herself in relation to those about her that is to a large extent responsible for her withdrawal. She sees her family as restrictive or pressuring (response 2, Card VIII) and she is finding it a difficult task to conform to their demands upon her. She apparently knows that she cannot succeed in overt expressions of her dissatisfaction and feels the need to adapt herself (FC is just beginning to emerge) to those who are so important to her. Her adjustive efforts are mature for her age (Fc and FK) but are ineffective in the face of her excessive amount of conflict ($m = 3 + 1$). Feeling as though she would explode (as on Card II) appears to express a desire on her part to alter a world in which she is not too happy.

Conflict with her mother (Card VII) is one of this child's major problems. At the same time, there appears to be a strong identification with the mother ("two girls") ("two bunnies") that would suggest the influence of the superego involvement (feelings of guilt) in her relations to her mother.

The content of the responses is not too deviant. Although there are a number of morbid responses in her protocol (skeleton, skull, monster), these are not atypical at her age. She shows a healthy interest in people (H responses), and reality is well perceived (good form responses). However, she appears to find it most difficult to deal with more exciting affects (Cards IX, X) in an objective fashion.

The quality of her many movement responses indicates the extent to which this child has internalized (identified with) adult concepts and attitudes. . . . . The child's dissatisfaction with her environment is expressed by her in direct fashion (card reversals). It is further apparent in her tendency to avoid the practical or conforming demands of life (low D per cent) which challenge her emotional controls. . . . Her emotional development definitely appears to be lagging when compared with her intellectual development. In her desire to adjust to an environment in which she finds little security, she is exerting control over emotional involvement with the outside world and her emotions are turned back on herself. However, it is apparent that her anxiety has invaded her fantasy life and she is unable successfully to maintain equilibrium. . . .

In summary, the main themes, fantasies and conflicts as revealed in both the CAT and the Rorschach were tabulated by Sandler as follows:

<table>
<tr><td>CAT</td><td>Rorschach</td></tr>
<tr><td>1. Mother seen as challenging, competitive, punishing.</td><td>Conflict with mother.</td></tr>
<tr><td>2. Guarded and suspicious type of sensitivity to situations.</td><td>Adjustive attempts by means of sensitive appraisal of situations $(Fc=1+1)$ and introspection $(FK=2)$.</td></tr>
<tr><td>3. Fantasies of a wish-fulfilling nature; fantasies of omnipotence.</td><td>Highly introversive $(M:$ sum $C=7:2)$.</td></tr>
<tr><td>4. Need for preparedness; defensive attitudes apparent.</td><td>Guarded, insecure (content of response to Card V: "bunny on tip-toe;" "butterfly with feelers").</td></tr>
<tr><td>5. Conflicts between superego and aggression, autonomy, and reacts with withdrawal into fantasies (see 3, above).</td><td>Excess amount of unrelieved tension or aggressivity $(m=3+2)$.</td></tr>
<tr><td>6. Assumes maturity of adult in fantasies as method of defense. Stories 8 and 10 (the child in a child's role) show uncontrolled and regressive emotional response.</td><td>Intellectual maturity and control are on higher level than emotional maturity and control (content and form level of M responses are superior to C responses: $Fc=0+2$; $C'=0+1$; $CF=2+2$).</td></tr>
</table>

When pathology approaches psychotic proportions, both Rorschach and CAT are very likely to reflect the illness. In fact, if one or the other test does not contain marked distortions, the assumption can be made that there are still islands of intact functioning. The following protocols were given by another girl of seven years, who was referred to a clinic because of immaturity, inability to concentrate or to remember any but religious information. "She talks but it doesn't make any sense." At play, she would either pretend to be a dog or play like a boy. The psychologist found much fear of being hurt, not only on the CAT but in replies to the intelligence test (Stanford-Binet, form L-M) as well, e.g.,

Year VI. Differences: "A dog could kill the baby bird;" "glass can fall and hurt you, wood doesn't hurt anything, if it fell on your leg it would kill you."

Year VII. Similarities: "A ship sails and a car drives instead. Have to be careful with your car so nobody gets killed."

Thought processes were often found to be quite loose, with a flow of irrelevant ideas; identification problems (animal versus human) were marked; fears of destruction were pervasive—all pointing to an incipient psychotic process. The Rorschach was administered first:

Rorschach

Free Association	Inquiry
I. Eagle.	(W)—Has little bits of wings.
Bird.	(Upper half of card) Birds meet eagles and birds live with eagles. Baby birds. Reminds me of a dead eagle—and it's

That's all.

II. Somebody playing chop suey.

Reminds me of somebody drinking out of a straw hat.

A lion people.

III. It reminds me of an alligator.

Butterfly.

Reminds me of a wolf—wolf people, people that eat all kinds of animals.

IV. Looks like something that flies in the air, can't tell.

Looks like a mess. Somebody made a mess out of it.

V. A little baby butterfly, can't fly.

That's all.

VI. A cat, a lion cat.

(Did somebody paint a picture for you?)

VII. A hand.

An ear.

---

just laying there and has no head, it's dead.

(W) Have hands together. (Q) A girl and a boy, looks like twin girl and boy. (Q) The nose—it doesn't look the same, just the necks (pointed to her own neck).

(Hat is lower D1) (Dd 25) looks like a straw. Looks like black cats—got two straws. (Q) persons.

(D1) Has a jaw.

I'll tell you something. There is Jesus, the Holy Spirit. I can't remember the other one. The church, he built it.

(D7) Looks like it's in the water.

(D3) Looks like it's flying.
Add:
A butterfly has got two things—if it had a head, it would look like a live one. Must have eaten it. Some people eat butterflies—even dogs and sometimes butterflies like dogs.

(D11) Has a back—straight down with one hand. Other hand on the other side.

(W) Has two wings.

(W) Has all messy stuff, like it has dots in it.

(W) It always have little things up there. (Q) It can fly if it was alive—it's just laying there.

(W) Has whiskers. (Q) Has hair around its neck. (Q) Because he has hair right here.

(W) Pointing like this (took both hands, made fists with thumbs out and pointed them).

Saw that on another card.

A bunny.

(D4) Has a round thing that looks like a bunny.

A ship.

That was on another card.

A telescope.

That was on the other one.

VIII. An ink pad.

(W) Has paints shall I name the colors for you? pink, blue-green, etc.

And different color butterflies.

(D2) Butterflies have two wings.

Wolf.

(D8) Has a round thing on it, a line.

A world.

(W) Because a world has different colors on it.

(Wanted to straighten cards.)

IX. Inside of bones.

(W) Bones have all colors in it—if you eat all colors of candy.

A heart
and blood.

(Ds8) Has the color of it.
It always looks like something, it looks reddish and some times it looks like an apple colored.

That's all.

X. A river

(W) River has a mess underneath.
(Q) Sometimes they're shaped like that. Sometimes it stands up like that (raised card up and down) and sometimes it has waves.

and a rat.

A rat always has a little round thing that they sneak out with and get the cheese.

The CAT is in many ways more bizarre, with repetitive themes of death or killings in nearly every story. When scored on the Schedule of Adaptive Mechanisms (Haworth, 1963), the critical scores clustered toward the pathological end of the continuum: Symbolization, Projection, Fear and Anxiety, Regression, and Weak Controls. There were very few scorable responses in the other areas, suggesting little in the way of healthy resources or defensive potential remaining. Note, in story 8, the concern of this child with reality-irreality aspects: "A play puppet monkey."

Cat

1. They were—one is a mother
   with three baby chickens
   eating their cereal—
   but one wasn't there.
So baby birds went looking for him.
Mother chicken crying, but came to him

with the other baby birds.
They got all the dishes,
  gathered it up,
  and they got their stew.
When done, got down
  and went to bed and took a nap.
When they got up,
  the mother chicken was gone.
They looked and looked for her.
When she came,
  they all spanked mother chicken.
Mother chicken got mad
  and sent them to bed.
Mother chicken got mad and said,
  "You get to bed and stay there
  and don't come out."
The chickens went into the living room and made a mess.
Got a spanking
  and went back into the bedroom.
(Q-How feel?) Bad.

2. Mother bear and father bear
  and baby bear pulling.
  Playing tug-of-war.
Baby helped father,
Fell on the bricks
  and all died,
  but one didn't.
The baby got the mother
  and tied her up.
Father not dead.
  Took him home,
  but he fell in the river.
He was dead.
Baby bear was dead, too.

3. One day, there was a big, ole mean lion.
He ate a mouse.
  Lion eat all the mouse.
  All the mouse left.
Hunters kill the lion.
  Took him to bear hunts,
  then to the zoo.
The trainer put his head in the mouth.
The lion bit the man
  and the man died.
Lion got mad
  and they killed him.

4. They lived, a family of kangaroos.
Baby in the pouch.
Little girl riding a trike.
Mother is hopping to the store.
  She hopped and hopped and hopped.
Almost got in the fire.
Steeplehouse almost gone.
Got things out,
  and they all died in the fire.
  Only one didn't die.
One baby was walking to the forest.
  Saw Yogi Bear.
Yogi Bear was mean
  and killed the baby.

5. One baby was playing with his cousin.
One day his father woke up.
  Father sneaked out of the house.
Got in trouble.
  Got in trouble
  and all sent back to bed.
A rug was under the bed.
  Baby slipped under bed and died.
Mother and father died, too.
(Here she wanted to straighten all the cards.)

6. I know this one.
One baby cub was sleeping
  with his mother and daddy.
Daddy got up
  and killed the baby.
The mother got up
  and killed the father
  and she died.
(Q-Why?) Were real mean.
Didn't like each other
  and were blind—
  their eyes were blind.

7. All the monkeys went away.
A sterocious lion came.
Monkey was frightened
    and he got away.
Lion charged after the monkey
  and killed baby monkey.
Lion was killed by hunters.
Tarzan could save them.
  Tarzan killed the lion.

8. I like that.
They were little—one daddy,
   a sister, mother, and one brother.
Then they played a joke on the father.
   All played a joke.
All killed each other.
They had a play puppet monkey,
   and he wasn't dead.

9. Were one baby rabbit and one brother.
   Saying something to his baby brother.
One thing—the baby laughed
   like the sister did,
   and he cried
   and he runned away.
Thinking about that,
   the mother was sad.
A wolf got the baby.
   The baby cries
"Junior, where are you?"
   Went down hill
   and killed that old fox.
Went back to bed and was safe.

10. One time there lived a father dog
    spanking a boy dog
    for playing in the stool.
The boy cried
   and the father sent him to bed.
He said, "You naughty dog,
   get back in your bed."
Well, that was all.
(Q-Feel?) Read mad—
One time he got up
   and killed the father dog
   and he died.

Occasionally, one sudden and isolated, but bizarre, response will appear on both the Rorschach and CAT. For example, a first grade boy in one of the author's school samples responded to Card III of the Rorschach with:

It's two teenagers and love coming out of them. They look alike but they must be different.

Looks like they're dancing. It's a boy and a girl (Q-Love?) The red spots. Every time you love someone you feel love coming right out of you and it's red.

Later in the session, he gave the following response to Card 8 of the CAT:

8. Once four monkeys were happy,
But a strange man came

with a shotgun.
He shot the mother—no, a teenager,
  and couldn't shoot the others.
  They ran real fast.
The teenager was—
  No, the man was mad at her
  to make sure she was dead.
(Q) They went on a date
  and she stopped him
  because he said mean things.
(Q) Police put him in jail
  and then in the electric chair.

No further information was available on this child, but one can readily speculate that aspects of male-female relationships were prominent in his fantasies at that time. In the Rorschach response, positive (but precociously erotic) aspects of love are uppermost; the teenager concept, on the subsequent CAT, becomes frought with danger, attack and ultimate death for both parties.

Along the lines of the present discussion, we should recall the case presented in Chapter VIII of the little girl who had been treated for pinworms and who saw worms and snakes on both tests, with level of response markedly deteriorating at these times.

The CAT and Rorschach do not always complement each other in such dramatic fashion as demonstrated in the preceding cases. The next child, a boy of six and one-half years, had been relinquished by his parents three years previously. His Rorschach, administered first, suggests serious underlying pathology, with poor form level, bizarre and gory responses, color projection and color naming.

Rorschach

Free Association	*Inquiry*
I. A boat.	Part of it (lower half). (Q) Two boats.
Or a face.	Two eyes, his nose and this is his mouth; (Q) Face of a monster; they got some bones and these things; (Q) These are rocks on the face.
II. A cat face, some eyes and a nose.	Eyes (D2), nose (S), mouth that's leaking (D3); (Q) What something drips; looks like blood; (Q) Eyes and mouth are like a cat's face; Look like cows and they're kissing.
III. A lion's face.	Eyebrows (D2), that's his nose (D3), mouth. Know what these look like? Ants (D1) This is a bow tie (D3).
IV. Some bones.	Lots of bones, (Q) a skeleton of a cat. —Now it looks like something flying, these are the wings and that's the feet.

V. A butterfly.	That's their two feet, two wings, head.
A rabbit.	But if dose wings were off, it would look like a bunny rabbit then.
VI. Some fire.	It's red—a little bit. Add: That's a cat's rug.
VII. Some cats.	Two, one here and one over here. (Q) They were ready to go but they were the same cats (meant a reflection).
VIII. Some different colors, I see pink, orange, blue and grey, purple and brown.	What are these crawling up there?
IX. Some horses.	(D3)
And some dogs.	(D1)
And a man	Lady and man (D4-pink). Lady on one side, man on the other.
and a lady.	
X. I see two spiders.	(D1)
I see some worms.	(D4) water worms.
I see some alligators.	(D7)
And a lion.	I didn't say "lion" in this picture.

The CAT of this same child contains little that is bizarre; stories are generally closely tied to elements in the stimulus cards, and there are no loose associations. The outstanding themes are death (including that of the "daddy monkey" on Card 7), oral deprivation, sensitivity to cold, fear of storms and lack of support or gratification from parent figures, all reflecting still acute reactions to the real losses which he has experienced.

Cat

1. That chicken and that big chicken
   got a big bowl.
(Q) They aren't eating.
(Q) They're—they don't got no food.
(Q) But the mother's going to eat
   all of the food herself.
(Q) I'm all finished.

2. Bears are playing tackle
   and mother ran on this side
   and the dad and the baby on this side.
Daddy bear's going to win.
(Q) They're going to break the rope
   and then they're going to

    fall off the mountain.
(Q) They'll get dead.
I'm finished.

3. A lion's smoking a pipe
   and there's a little mouse hole
   with a mouse in it.
The lion's sitting right in the king's chair.
(Q-mouse?) He's looking right at the lion.

4. They're riding on the street,
   those kangaroos.
There are Indians back there.
Daddy's carrying the baby
   and the boy kangaroo's riding the bicycle.
(Q-Indians?) They are far, far away.

5. Three little bears
   and the baby ain't scared,
   but the mommy and daddy are scared
   from the rain and the lightning.

6. These are about bears in the winter.
Do you know where they were sleeping?
   In their hole.
When winter started they were asleep,
   but the baby wasn't asleep by the leaves.
(Q) It was real cold
   and the cold woke him up.

7. The lion jumped real high
   and he wanted to kill the lion.
You know what he did?
He killed a daddy monkey.

8. There was a picture of a grandpa mommy
   and there was a little boy and dad
   and they were talking to each other.
There was a girl
   and there was a man,
   and they were drinking a cup of coffee.

9. The rabbit was in bed
   and part of it was broken;
And the door was open
And it was real cold.

10. The daddy was ready to take the baby to bed—
   No, to the toilet.
Then he wanted him to go to the bathroom.
(Q) He's pulling him in.

In comparing the findings from the Rorschach and the CAT, it would seem that the CAT in this case reflects the child's actual situation and his more or less conscious feelings in reaction to the loss of his parents; while the Rorschach points to the effects of the loss in terms of weakened ego structure and the potential for serious disintegration in emotional situations.

SUMMARY

Studies have been reviewed in which the CAT was either administered at intervals or compared with other tests in a battery. Only one published CAT study has been conducted on a longitudinal basis and only a limited number of variables were under investigation. There is certainly a need for more studies using the instrument in repeated testings over time, for the study of developmental trends and for assessing therapeutic progress.

The CAT has been compared with the Rorschach in two studies of normal versus disturbed children, and compared with drawings in two studies. It was used as part of a battery in a study of twins and of children who had lost a parent. All experimenters report substantial consistencies in diagnostic information derived from the various tests, although differences in the eliciting power of CAT, Rorschach and drawings are also demonstrated. It is probably not so much a question of more or less data, as of different kinds of information to be derived from different tests, which would be logically expected in view of the diversity in the projective stimuli. Different dimensions and different levels of personality can be expected to be tapped by the various instruments.

One further study involved administration of the CAT to mothers of young children. An elaboration of this procedure to include dual administration to mother-child pairs should yield interesting results in terms of the perception of roles between the generations.

Illustrative clinical examples have been presented from published reports and unpublished data. Personality changes over time were demonstrated in the longitudinal case reports. Where the CAT was part of a battery, similar themes were often in evidence regardless of the test used, while other instances were presented to demonstrate different results from test to test; as, for example, when the Rorschach seemed to reflect the effects on basic personality of the situational stress revealed in the CAT.

Again, more studies are needed, with larger and more clearly defined samples, to highlight those areas of difference and of potential usefulness of the respective tests.

CHAPTER XIII

The CAT-H (Human Form)

PURPOSE AND DESCRIPTION OF TEST

As of 1965, a human form of the CAT has been made available under Bellak's aegis. The new CAT-H (Bellak and Bellak, 1965; Bellak and Hurvich, 1965) will serve both research and clinical purposes. Comparative research can now be done with a standard human form readily accessible and produced under the direction of the author of the original test. The clinician now has two forms of a children's test from which to choose, with the possibilities of using both, if differential responses appear likely; of switching to a second form if the first one presented is not proving to be productive; and of substituting an "alternate" form if retesting becomes necessary within a short span of time. Bellak sees the two forms as offering a needed degree of flexibility to the clinician rather than one form being a replacement of, or competing with, the other form of the test.

The current form of the CAT-H (see Fig. 13.1) is the result of several revisions made during the process of clinical and research trials. Naturally, every effort was made to produce card pairs as similar as possible—not an easy task when transposing from animals and their wild life habitats to humans in a civilized setting. Facial characteristics and clothing need to be as ambiguous as possible with respect to sex for both child and adult figures. The situations portrayed in several cards are especially difficult to translate from animal to human terms. Card 7 poses almost unsurmountable obstacles which may, in large measure, be contributing to the different results obtained with the two forms. Similarly, something may well be changed, or lost entirely, when the human mother in Card 4 cannot be shown in as close a symbiotic relationship with her baby as in the kangaroo scene. The emotional impact of Card 6 (cave) is not easily converted to human surroundings. In Card 3, the lion can be changed into a father figure of questionable similarity, but the role relationships between the lion and mouse are lost completely in the transposition. For example, observations made by one of the research workers,* while testing with one of the earlier versions of the CAT-H, serve to highlight the different dynamics elicited by the two forms:

On Card 3, the mouse and lion being of different species make the animal version much more flexible in that:
The lion is hungry and eats the mouse;
The mouse pleads for his life (either successfully or unsuccessfully);
The lion and mouse become friends;
The mouse pulls the lion's tail or does something else to the lion to annoy him;
The lion chases the mouse, but the mouse *can* escape;
The mouse serves the lion in some fashion;

---

*The author is indebted to Mary Austin for these observations. The child figure on the earlier version of the card being used at that time was shown wearing suspenders, yielding a strong pull toward "boy" responses.

The lion takes care of the mouse, feeds him, etc.

In addition there is also some possibility of assuming "natural enmity" between the two, whereas in the human version it is father (uncle, grandfather) and son. The "natural" (acceptable) relationship between them is loving, and the defensive or guilty child must be more open to express hostility (either father to son, or son toward father). Father may become annoyed because the boy is interrupting his thoughts, but the boy does not usually do something *to* the father to produce anger. If father is hungry, he's waiting for dinner—not entertaining any notion of dining on the son! It is not likely that the son will escape hostility or punishment through cleverness. Also, the lion can be angry at the mouse for no reason; if the man is angry at the boy, it is usually because the boy is bad or is a "pest."

Although the earlier versions have been redone to make the clothing and hair treatment still less sex-typed, nevertheless, most of the above observations relate to the human condition, regardless of specific sex attributes.

Three cards posed little problem in the way of conversion: Card 5 (bedroom scene), Card 9 (with one figure in bed), and Card 10 (bathroom scene). Of medium difficulty were the three cards (Cards 1, 2, and 8) which depict three or more characters.

SCORING AND INTERPRETATION

Scoring procedures have not been developed specifically for the new form. It would appear that either Bellak's Short Form Blank for the TAT and CAT, or Haworth's Analysis Schedule can be used.

The latter schedule was used in the two research studies with the CAT-H reported in Chapter IV, and the next section, but it is not possible as yet to assess the extent to which the schedule is, or is not, suitable for the human form. While the instrument was constructed for use with the animal version, very few of the items relate specifically to the animal characteristics of the cards. It is possible, however, that other items may need to be added to make the schedule equally appropriate for the human form.

There should obviously be no difficulty in using Bellak's blank, since it was devised for use both with human pictures (TAT) and animal (CAT).

RESEARCH

Two studies have been completed with the CAT-H, namely, Lawton, (unpublished) with a school sample of 52 kindergarten and second graders, and Haworth (unpublished) with 22 clinic patients, aged six to ten years. Most of the results have been reported in Chapter IV, since comparisons were made with the animal CAT, but they will be summarized briefly here. In both studies, responses were evaluated by means of the Analysis Schedule which yields critical scores in any of ten possible categories of defense mechanisms.

Both studies showed a trend for more Projection-Introjection to be used on the animal form. With normal Ss, Repression was also used somewhat more on the animal than on the human form. On the remaining eight variables, and for both studies, there were no differences between forms.

In terms of intra-subject comparisons, except for a few instances, there was no consistent patterning whereby one could predict that the frequent use of a

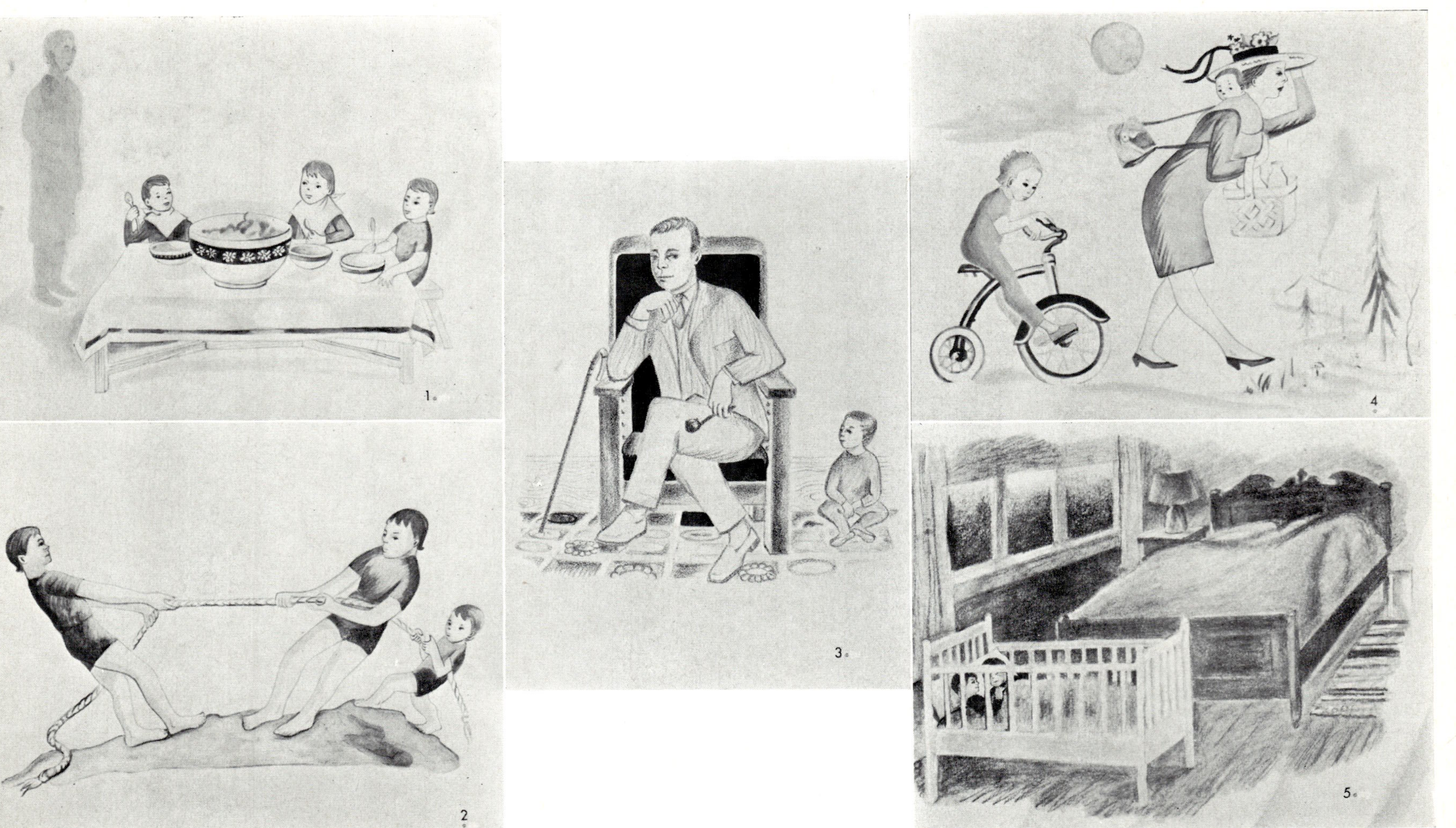

Figure 13.1. The CAT-H (see also facing page). (Reproduced with permission of L. Bellak.)

6.

7.

9.

8.

10.

defense mechanism on one form would be duplicated on the other version. As noted in Chapter IV, normal children did tend to use Isolation, Projection-Introjection and Reaction-Undoing on both forms, while clinic cases tended to give duplicate usage to Confused Identification, Projection-Introjection, and Weak Controls. For both samples, close to 55 per cent of the total number of critical scores represented parallel responses to the two forms, and 45 per cent of the scores were "single" instances, appearing on only one form for any individual subject.

The general patterning seems thus to be one of differential pulling power between the two tests, rather than either marked similarities or straightforward differences between them. Hammer (1958), in commenting on earlier comparative studies of animal and human stimuli for use with children, suggests that the *discrepancy* between a child's responses to animal and human pictures would provide sources of information about the child's conflicts and defenses. Further research may well confirm this point of view.

In contrast to the lack of agreement between forms in eliciting various defense mechanisms, there was remarkable concordance in the general themes given to equivalent cards in the two sets. Both Lawton and Haworth have tabulated specific card by card comparisons in terms of the "common" responses most often given to each card. These are presented in Table 13.1.

CLINICAL USE OF THE CAT-H

Complete protocols of animal and human CATs will be presented for two clinic cases. In the first case, the child received four critical scores on each form, although the actual categories varied between forms. The second case is presented as an example of marked discrepancy between the two forms, in this instance favoring the human set (with four dimensions) over the animal (with one dimension). Illustrative excerpts from two other records will also be discussed.

1.   Boy, CA = 7-0. WISC Full Scale IQ = 110.

The CAT-H was administered during an outpatient evaluation, and the CAT-A was presented three months later on admission to inpatient care. The diagnosis was that of a severe adjustment reaction of childhood, with disruptive behavior, inability to conform at school, negativism and extreme lack of cooperation in all areas.

CAT-H	*CAT-A*
1. Eating breakfast,	1. Uh, a light bird (looks on back of card).
They might be eating oatmeal.	
There's three ready to eat the oatmeal.	Three (chickens).
Yummee, One says, "Yummee."	What's that? (Points to large bird.)
The second one says, "Yummee."	O yeh, chick's feeding her little babies.
The third one says, "Yummee."	(Tries to stand card up against a book.)
(Q-next?) "Let's get our clothes on, and go outside and play hopscotch."	Now, three little chickens eating breakfast, or lunch, yeh, lunch.
They made three hopscotch.	Getting ready for nice, nice worms.
(Talks slowly as if dictating.)	Yummee.

Table 13.1. Comparability of Themes Given to the CAT-A and CAT-H
by Normal and Clinic Subjects

	Normals (Lawton)		Clinic (Haworth)	
Card	Same on both forms	Differ between forms [a]	Same on both forms	Differ between forms [a]
1.	Oral gratification	A. *Adult is mother*	1. Oral gratification Adult is mother	H. Oral deprivation
2.	Game Pair is winner	A. More fighting H. Child with peer	2. Game Pair is winner	A. Child with mother or father H. Child with peer
3.		A. Child attacked A. *Adult-power* H. Adult-old	3. Child attacked	A. *Adult-power* H. Adult-old A. *Child teases adult*
4.	Picnic or to store	A. If disaster H. If child hits adult	4. Picnic or to store	
5.	Sleep Parents in bed		5. Sleep or play Parents in bed	
6.	Sleep		6. Sleep	
7.	Attack and escape	A. If become friends	7. Attack and escape	
8.	Scoldings Mention picture Secrets	A. *Male adults*	8. Scoldings	H. Mention picture A. *Male adults*
9.	Sleep Attack Loneliness		9. Sleep	H. Loneliness
10.	Other naughtiness	H. Toilet naughtiness A. Learn lesson	10. Toilet naughtiness	H. Learn lesson
	Punished by same-sex parent		Punished by same- or opposite-sex parent	

(a) Italicized findings represent exclusive use by one form of the test.

2. They're fightin' over the rope.
(Long pause, looks confused)
(Q) "Let's go, we. . . no, not we. . ."
(Q) "Let's get to push her out in the
water."
So they get the jump rope.
"If she keeps it, it'll hang on a tree,

Get grind up for tiny chickens.
Mommy eats whole worms,
one big one eats whole worms.
Must like 'em better.

2. Fighting over a jump rope.
(Q—win?) (Points to pair, calls each
a "bear".)
These guys are going to win,
going to measure (runs finger along
rope and from ear to ear of bears).
He's a little below his ear,

and we'll pull it down
and she can't hold so good."
(Names the single and small figure
with his sisters' names, the large
figure on the right is given his
brother's name).

3. Father is sittin' down.
Little kid is sittin' on the floor.
They have a room colored white,
painted white, not colored.
Do you have a hook stick, what is this?
(*E*—Cane?)
Yes, a cane and a rug.
Do you smoke a chimney,
What's this? A pipe (laughs at
error)

4. "Ouch," goes the lady,
"Why did you run over my foot
with your bicycle?"
I gotta think.
"Let's get outa here, baby,
so he won't run over me."
(Q) The kid goes fast,
and we go fast.
"We better go faster than the bicycle.
If he don't go as fast as us
he won't make it good.
He'll be slow."

5. "Good night, baby."
No, make it this way,
"Good night, - - - - (his younger
brother)
Good night - - - - (his younger
sister)
Are you going to go to sleep
before Daddy comes up
and spanks us?
Because—(self) and—(sister) **get up**
and get us up.
Ooo, that window gets lots of wind,
and it's open.
Let's go downstairs to get **Mamma**
and Daddy
to come up and close it."

so he's bigger and stronger
and got a little buddy.
He (single) doesn't got no buddies.
If they let go,
they'll fall backwards . . .
get hurt.

3. Don't know any to this one.
Got a mouse,
a mouse house.
(Q) Don't see nothing, no good,
don't get it,
don't get a story on this one.

4. Going to town,
don't get time to see these.
Yeh, going to town.
Going to get some groceries,
and go home and eat.

5. Two little dolls sleeping,
babies, I mean.
This be brother and this be sister,
This be me and my big sister,
little, bigger than other sister
(in big bed).
(Q—next?) That's all, just talk,
just talk and get so sleepy,
go to bed, nightie-night.
(Q—dream?) They dreamed about
there was a well that . . .
and it's always got some junk
in it . . .
A sister (cistern) . . . like sisters that
have a hose.
I've been dreaming about it.
It gets all cleaned out
and water's in it.
I run by and fall in.
That's what I like to dream.
It scares me . . . wakes me up.
(Note: His father is a plumber.)

6. This tent is. . . .
   I rolled out of my tent.
How'll I get back.
Kids pushed me out,
Ouch. . . . Here we go.
Down, down, down we go. . . .Up,
   Oh no, down again.
(Q) How would I get up,
Which way would I get on them?
Ouch (other one falls).
On no, not me down here.
How would I go out?
Ouch, which way would I get up?

7. Is this a giant?
"Let's get out of here, Hansel,
He's going to cook us . . . . NOW!
Let's get out fast,
   before he cooks us."
I can't think of any more.
(Q—get away?) Uh huh.
The giant falls down
   and we go up.
We go away and he falls down.
How would he get us?
   But we're running.
He's falling down.
He could get us by hitting sticks.
"Ouch, ouch, ouch," the giant says.
Is that the last one?

8. Boy, you go and get your clothes on
   while I go and talk
   to the other ladies.
Lady, you go and get lipstick
   and get all pretty
   while I talk to this girl—lady."
I'm tired talking, how many more?

6. Can't get a way with this,
   I don't get this one.
Once three little piggies . . .
   whatever they are . . .
Made a little cave.
Had to go over a great, big bump.
Is this a bump? (Points to large figure.)
Had to go over two bumps . . . bears.
Had to go around the bears,
   round the bump,
   round the bear and
   over the bump,
And go hunting in their cave.
And the three little pigs
   had a nice time in it,
Until the bears came
   and ate 'em all up.
Is this all?

7. A tiger tracing (chasing) after a
   monkey.
(Long pause as he looks at card.)
(Q) Monkey climbs up,
   the tiger gets halfway up,
Then falls down and dies.

8. (Snaps at card with finger, long
   pause.)
Can't make up a story.
How do they walk on their hands?
   Feets look like hands.
   Do them hands get weared out?
(Q) They are doing some talking,
   these two are talking,
   and so are these two.
All talking about something.
Always talking about somebody,
   sneaking with their feets (points
   to one on couch)
So he walks up (gestures with fingers
   to indicate feet moving)
   to try to get her coffee to drink.

9. Night.
"What way do we go to sleep?"
Let's just close our eyes,
    to get to sleep, - - - - (younger sister)
"I can't," said - - - - (younger sister)
"What way would I go to do it?"

9. Little rabbit going to sleep
    and having fun,
    and rabbit staying up
Cause he wants to look for wolves.
    So he doesn't get ate up.
(Q—wolf come?) No, wolf gets killed,
    with an ice pick.
He came in the window . . .
    put head in.
It (ice pick) went through his head.
    The ice pick was fixed,
    so if lift the window
    it comes down.
It went through,
    and came out his eyes.
It came out both eyes.
    Sticked eyes,
    So be really killed.

10. "Quit holding your potty,
    Do you gotta got to the bathroom?"
"No."
"Then quit holding your potty."
"Ouch, ouch."
Smack, he's getting a spanking.
(Q—why?) Keeps holding his potty,
    but he doesn't have to go.
(Q—what next?) Same thing and he
    gets it again,
    holds his potty again.
"What way to get out of this?
    I'll quit it,
    go to the bathroom,
    and be all done."

10. Little doggie taking a bath.
    He's going to try to learn
    how to swim.
Like his mother does.
So he can go out
    in water deep.
(Q) Swims out.

Analysis Schedule: Isolation
    Symbolization
    Regression
    Confused Identification

Analysis Schedule: Symbolization
    Projection
    Weak Controls
    Confused Identification

Card 10 of the human set elicits a quite unabashed toileting story, while on the animal form it is Cards 5 and 9 which are most productive. Card 5, as in the earlier human picture, produced associations with his siblings, but in the second protocol such associations lead on to themes connected with father, flooding and drowning, and fearful dreams. Card 9 is a remarkable instance of classical oedipal castration fantasies.

2. Girl, CA = 9-8. WISC Full Scale IQ = 97.

This child had been relinquished by her parents and adopted at age three. She was referred for gorging her food, body scratching, persistent masturbation and exposing herself when outdoors. There was case history material to suggest that she may have been a victim of sexual molestations in early childhood. The animal CAT was administered first, followed two and one-half weeks later by the CAT-H.

CAT-A	*CAT-H*

CAT-A

1. Little chicks are eating
Mother is coming to feed them.
  They're having porridge.
  Like the three bears.

2. This is three bears
  and they're pulling a rope.
They're up on a big rock.
(Q—win?) Papa bear.

3. I see a little mouse
  right down here.
The lion is smoking a pipe.
  He's got a cane.
That's all.

4. Once upon a time
  a mother kangaroo
  went out for groceries,
  and she's coming home.

CAT-H

1. Once upon a time they lived on a
  farm.
Mother made some porridge,
  They're having porridge for lunch.
Know what happened? Too hot.
Went out for a walk.
One little girl, Goldilocks,
  ate all the porridge.
When this one, Donny (far right) came
  home
He said, "Somebody's been sitting in
  my chair."
Billy said, "Somebody's been sitting in
  my chair."
And this one, John, said,
  "Some one's been sitting in my
  chair
  And broke it all up."

2. Once upon a time, there lived some
  Boy Scouts,
  taking some exercises.
Little one's Billy,
  big one's John.
  and the other one (far left) is
  Danny.
Taking their exercise.
Little Billy fell back on the rock.
  Big John fell backwards.
The chief came.
Big Danny didn't fall backwards,
  he fell frontwards.

3. Once upon a time in this family,
  Having company for baby Sally's
  birthday.
Next morning he came again
  and Sally got a spanking.
He said, "Baby Sally,
  why did you break up my pipe?"
She said, "I was just having some fun."
(Q—he do?) He was a robber.

4. Once upon a time,
  four lived in this family.
A snowy day.
The man had to carry home

Baby kangaroo got a balloon and a
   bike.
They see some toadstools.
I see some milk and cheese and meat.

5. Once upon a time,
      there lived four bears.
Mother and father covered their whole
      self,
      Even their heads.
Baby bear was playing in bed.

6. The same; Once upon a time
      there lived four bears.
Now they're sleeping in a hole.
Papa bear woke up
      and then baby bear woke up.
And they said,
      "Let's go out for a walk."
Then mother bear and other baby
      bear woke up.
They found out
      Papa and other baby bear
      were gone.
(Q—happen?) Mother bear and baby
      bear came
      and looked for them.
Mother bear spanked other baby bear
      because she woke up first
      with Papa bear.

7. Once upon a time, there lived a
      monkey named Cheetah.
A big tiger came along
      and was after him.
(Q) Tiger's going to chew him up.

8. Once upon a time, there lived some
      monkeys in a house.

some bread and milk and cheese
   for his wife.
When her husband came home,
      he was carrying a rabbit,
And their home was right around the
      corner,
      and a snowy night.
That evening a robber came
      and stole all their clothes
      and their baby girl.

5. Four lived in this family.
      Two baby boys, no . . . .
      One boy and one girl.
Mother and father slept together.
It was Hallowe'en night
      and a goblin came in
      and took everything they got.
Mother and father said,
      "Arrest those things,
      arrest that man."
"Don't take off (all?) our clothes
      cause they're not for you."

6. Once upon a time three lived
      in a cabin house;
      that means a tent.
One night some animals came
      and tore down their tent
      and they were all scratched up.
One was awake in the night
      and got up.
      and shot every single animal.

7. One day a little boy,
      Jack in the Beanstalk,
He went up to the giant's palace,
      and the giant caught him,
      and says, "Oh, baby."
(Q) Nothing.

8. Once upon a time there lived six
      in a family.

Mother monkey has some flowers in
   her hand.
Brother is going to spank little brother.
Mother and father are drinking coffee.

It was Christmas night.
Little Johnny didn't know what to do—
   He sneaked out of bed.
     Sneaked out the window, and got
     out. (Long pause).
Grandmother's picture is hanging up in
   the dining room (sighs).
Christmas day out tonight,
   and they had a wonderful night.

9. Once upon a time there lived Alice
   in Wonderland.
There was a rabbit
   that got a broken leg.
   He had a beautiful house.
When he was all well,
   he chased Alice again,
And she got a broken arm
   so she couldn't play.
(Q—how break?) Bumped into a great
   big thing.

9. Once only one lived in this house.
He was sick because
   his mother and father were dead.
The telephone rang,
   and he couldn't get out of bed,
   cause—cause he was sick.
(Q—how end?) He got married then
   and lived happy ever after.

10. Once upon a time there lived
   Blacky and mother.
One day, Blacky was taking a shower
   when he shouldn't.
Mother came in
   and took him on her knee
   and spanked him.

10. Once upon a time, there lived two
   in a family.
Mother was going to give baby a
   shower but she missed.
He jumped into the shower (laughed).
Then after they were married
   happy ever after,
   and then that week
   she got a new baby.

Analysis Schedule:
   Projection-Introjection

Analysis Schedule:
   Isolation
   Symbolization
   Projection-Introjection
   Fear-Anxiety

In this example we see that the animal stories are rather bland and relatively unproductive, except for the oedipal situation alluded to in Card 6, and the story to Card 9 suggestive of a sexual attack. In marked contrast, on the subsequent CAT-H, her past traumatic experiences and current reaction patterns begin to be revealed quite clearly by Card 3 with an intruder-robber accosting a girl-child. The robber theme is continued on the next card, where he steals not only clothes but a baby girl. Anxiety amounts on Card 5 with reworking of the robber-clothes theme, resulting in two slips of the tongue ("things" for "men", and "off" for "all" when speaking of clothes). On Card 6, scratching appears in relation to an animal attack amidst destruction of the home (tent) and death to the intruders. Card 7, as would be expected by the nature of the stimulus, elicits another attack story. Card 9 contains a theme of parental death (desertion?) and immobilization of the child. Yet, along with so much disaster, the two final stories involve resolution by marriages which are "happy ever after."

The above stories, and the two excerpts to follow, suggest that when children have experienced frightening, traumatic episodes, particularly in relation to other persons (in each of these cases, an adult) then perhaps the human form of the CAT may serve to bring out more of the child's anxieties and fears with respect to those specific events. Certainly many other clinical examples have been presented throughout this volume to illustrate ways in which the animal form has pinpointed known problems in the child's past. The suggestion being made here is that, for some children and some situations, the human form may be more effective in eliciting reactions to specific stress.

The following three pairs of stories from a young girl again illustrate reactions to known real-life situations, with references to them appearing much more dramatically with the human form.

3.   Girl, CA $=$ 8-0, Above average intelligence.

This child's mother was alcoholic and reportedly would leave the girl and her siblings alone in the house. Three of the stories to the CAT-H (administered two weeks after the CAT) reflect her reactions to drink and desertions. The complete CAT-H protocol scored high on seven defense mechanisms while the animal form only produced one high score.

CAT-A	*CAT-H*
1. Can this be make believe?	1. The man had some children.
(Long pause) They're eating.	Most of the time
The rooster could come	they have oatmeal for breakfast.
and eat the food	They're ready to eat.
before the chickens.	It didn't taste right,
Before, the rooster	so they drank water.
made all the food.	It still had an aftertaste.
If the rooster made all the food	They got drunk on wine.
and ate it,	Father didn't know;
then the chickens	They acted funny
might be hungry.	and went to bed.
(Q) I don't know much about it.	They sleep-walk,
(Q) The chickens killed the rooster.	go out into the road.
	A car was coming
	and they all got killed.
2. The raccoons got in a fight	2. Two men, and they. . . .
with the bear.	One man decided
The raccoons found a rope,	he wanted to get married.
and the bear wanted it.	He did, and had a child.
Now they're having a tug-of-war.	A cow was on one end of the rope.
The raccoon won.	Both pulled so hard it breaks.
The bear moves away	He sells the rope
and takes the rope.	without the cow on it,
Soon, the raccoon found out	And tries to milk the rope
where the bear lived.	with no cow on it.
The raccoon cut the rope in half.	The man shot the other man.

The bear just thought it was the same.
(Q) They both won.
 Only the raccoon accidentally
 cut the rope in half,
 so they both had half.

5. Four bears live in a house.
When the people go out,
 they (the bears) come in.
Papa and mama put the baby
 in the crib,
 They're sleeping.
The people come home
 and find the bears.
They take the two baby bears
 to the zoo.
Mother bear comes,
 and follows them to the zoo.
They caught mother and father bear
 and put them with the babies.

The sheriff came
 and took the baby
 to the orphanage.

5. Mother couldn't leave baby alone,
 but had to this time.
She put them to bed.
When they were asleep,
 she left.
She left a tape recorder.
He heard it when he woke,
 he went back to sleep.
The tape recorder ran out.
Mother came home.
Baby slept all day,
 because woke up.

The final pair of stories contrasts responses to Card 3, in which the story to the human form pinpoints some of the possible sources of this child's speech hesitancies, word finding difficulties, slurring of words, and general impaired verbal fluency. Much of the family interaction in the home focussed around the boy's speech, all to no avail.

4. Boy, CA = 8-6, Superior intelligence.[*]

CAT-A

3. Once there was a tiger
 who wished he had his crown back.
 He knew he was King of the beasts.
He went out for a walk,
 One time . . . then . . .
 one time on his walk
 he found a crown on the ground.
He said, "I remember I put it there."
 So he picked it up.
He saw a mouse and said,
 "I'm King of the Beasts,
 so I don't have to
 be afraid of a mouse,
 Come, I won't eat you up."
The mouse said, "Don't eat me,
 One day I might save you."
The mouse found the lion in a trap
 (retold most of traditional tale).
The mouse nibbled and said,

CAT-H

3. Once there was a man.
Well, there's this little boy with him.
The little boy always
 wanted to hear a story,
 but the father wouldn't.
 But he always kept asking.
He told him to sit near him.
 He just sat there
 with a mumble on his face.
The boy began to say something
 and the father told him
 to keep quiet.
The father kept on trying
 to say something
 but the boy kept interrupting him.
(Much more in mumbling tones, *E*
 unable to record it all)
The father didn't want the boy to
know

---

[*]This boy's complete CAT-A protocol is presented in the section on neurotic reactions in Chapter XI.

"There, you can go now."
The lion said,
    "Mouse, you don't have to leave.
    You can live with me.
    I'll give you a little house.
    I'm getting very lonely sometimes."
The end.

that he didn't know the story.
The boy kept interrupting him.

Whereas the first (animal) story tended to see father as forgetful and basically passive, despite his kingly accouterments, the CAT-H story portrays the father as aloof, withholding and rejecting. It seems highly likely that this second story reflects the everyday events centered around conversation and speech. We may well ask if this boy is not allowed to interrupt adult conversations, is not listened to when he does attempt to speak, and is scolded for "mumbling?"

Closer examination of the stories does reveal the same basic character structure assigned to the weak father figure in both instances. On the animal form, the king of the beasts knows his title but feels inadequate even in front of a mouse until he regains the outward symbol of his power; even then he must reassure himself that he is stronger than the child. On the human form, the father is perceived as again "putting up a front" in that he was really trying to keep the boy from realizing that he (the father) did not know the story in the first place.

SUMMARY

The CAT-H now provides a standard alternate form of the test for research and clinical use. Nevertheless, the inherent difficulties in providing similar and equivalent forms, when using humans as contrasted to animals, must be kept in mind both in the clinic and when evaluating comparative research findings. The hypothesis of a differential "pull" for the two forms best summarizes the studies to date with the CAT-H.

Clinical data has been presented to illustrate situations in which the protocol pairs were comparatively similar and markedly dissimilar. It was suggested that, where the child's real-life situation has been chronically or acutely traumatic or where the chief source of difficulty lies in parent (or adult)- child relationships, then the human form may more clearly elicit the feelings, anxieties, or hostilities connected with these persons or situations. A corollary assumption might be that the animal form may elicit those dynamics representing a broader spectrum and at deeper layers of personality.

Further investigations with both forms are needed to determine whether either form does actually surpass the other, either in clarifying basic personality dimensions or in eliciting modes of reaction to, or methods of defending against, situational stress.

The CAT Supplement (CAT-S)

The CAT Supplement (CAT-S) was developed by the Bellaks (1952) to provide pictures that might elicit the child's reactions to specific situations, current stresses, or problems not necessarily common to all children (See Fig. 14.1).

The cards were designed in such a way (stiff cardboard with a plywood core, cut-out format, washable) that they could be used as a play technique with very young children or children too disturbed to be able to engage in a formal storytelling process. The test originators suggest, in the latter instances, laying all the cards on the table and letting the child select, handle, rearrange, or talk about them spontaneously.

DESCRIPTION OF THE TEST

The cards are described in the manual (Bellak and Bellak, 1957) as follows:[*]

1. This picture shows four mice-children on a slide. One is just sliding down, one about to start the slide, and two are climbing up the ladder. Numbers one and three suggest males; two and four suggest females (skirts, bows in hair).

A play situation, this picture permits expression of fears of physical activity, of physical harm, and problems in social (play) activities with other children generally, and with the opposite sex specifically. The children may be seen as happy, as fighting, as pushing, frightened, etc.

2. A classroom situation with three little monkeys, two sitting at typical school desks, one standing with a book in hand, and one of the seated monkeys holding his tail.[†]

This picture lends itself to a projection of problems with the teacher, schoolmates, and other classroom situations (learning, reciting, etc.). It leaves ample play for ascription of various characteristics to the unseen teacher, and a number of predicaments of the pupil reciting as well as possibilities for wishes to show off knowledge, to relate fears of inadequacy, stagefright, etc. The monkey holding his tail in his hand may give rise to stories concerning masturbation.

3. This picture shows children "playing house." Father mouse, with eyeglasses much too big for him and obviously belonging to an adult, is receiving a beverage from "Mother mouse" while toys and a baby doll in a carriage are dispersed about them.

Here, children may have a chance to relate their wishful fantasies about being grown up and doing what seems to them desirable and possibly forbidden. The apperceived, imagined relationships in the family will be clearly depicted. Because this picture encourages particular identification with adults, it is more likely to prompt wishful fantasy rather than biographical data. Thus, it is especially necessary to conduct an inquiry at the end of the test to determine—as much as possible—the level from which this story comes.

---

[*]Reproduced from the manual with permission from the authors.

[†]The situation is frequently not recognized as pertaining to a classroom by preschool children.

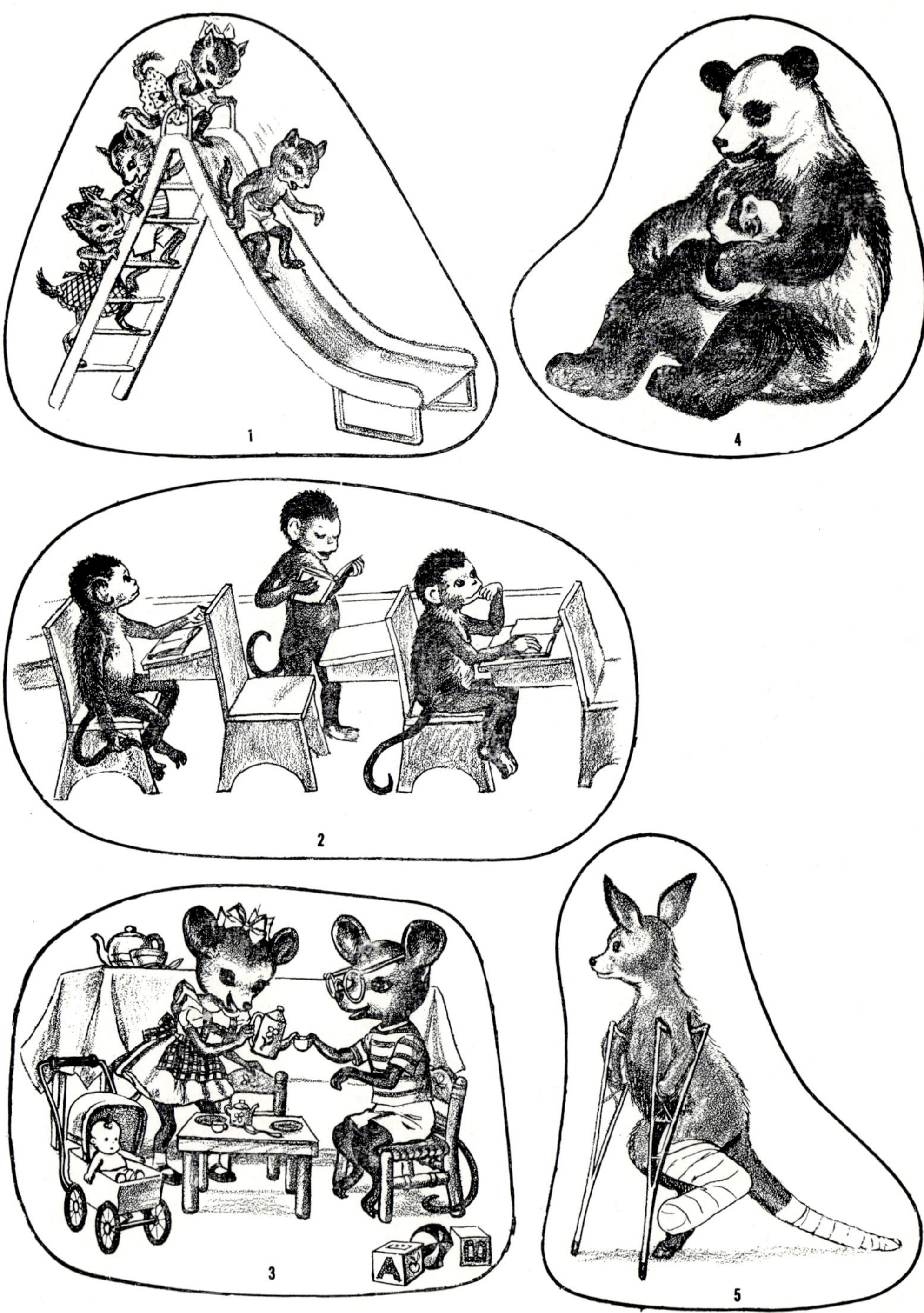

Figure 14.1. The CAT-S (see also facing page). (Reproduced with permission of L. Bellak.)

4. A big bear sits crouched forward, holding a baby bear on its lap and in its arms.

This picture may elicit themes of wishes of oral nature, sentiments against infant siblings, regressive tendencies, etc. Light will also be shed upon the conflict between remaining (and wanting) to be dependent and independent, as well as the general relationship to parents.

5. This picture depicts a kangaroo on crutches and with a bandaged tail and foot.

It prompts stories of fear of injury and castration. It may elicit feelings about a physical handicap or a feeling of general inadequacy, as well as illuminating for us something about the subject's body image (see #7). Social rejection related to physical handicap may also be touched upon.

6. A group of four foxes—two male and two female—are in a race with the goal in sight and one male closest to it.

Competitiveness to siblings and playmates and the accompanying feelings may be dealt with here, as well as notions of success or failure.

7. A cat stands before a mirror looking at its image.

This should elicit ideas of body image—as Schilder described it: "The image of the human body means the picture of our own body which we form in our mind . . . the way in which the body appears to ourselves." Picture #7 may tell us the ideas the growing child has about himself and his body, the shortcomings, pride. The tail may have phallic significance in the card particularly, and children may express their notions about some people being "so plain" and some "so fancy," as well as their ideas concerning sexual differences, exhibitionism, etc.

8. A rabbit doctor is examining a rabbit child with a stethoscope; some bottles of medicine are visible in the background.

Here we may be told stories of fears and traumata connected with physical illness, operations, doctors, and hospitals. An impending or past tonsillectomy or such, may be clearly revealed in its more or less traumatic and more or less specific meaning for the individual child. We may also obtain biographical or fantasy detail concerning illness of a family member.

9. A grown deer is taking a shower and is half hidden by a shower curtain. A small deer is looking towards the larger figure. An enema bag hangs against the wall.

Here we hope to learn more about the subject's ideas of sexual differences, nudity, voyeurism, the family practices in bathroom habits; whether or not a child is being overstimulated, what disturbances there may be in this area; the child's handling of the situation, if any. The enema bag may give us biographical data concerning his feelings about enemas as well as stories illuminating any masturbation practices in connection with the scene.

10. An obviously pregnant cat, standing upright, with large belly, and apron askew: it is designed to bring out ideas about where a baby comes from and fantasies and/or fear about this. It should be particularly useful with children who are in the process of expecting a sibling or who have recently had one and seem to have special problems with it. (Ideas about the necklace, e.g., its being torn, may well refer to notions about the body.) (pp. 3–4).

The Bellaks (1957) also suggest that single (or several) CAT-S pictures may be added to the regular CAT administration, especially in cases where it is known that the S is, or may be, having problems in any of the specific areas depicted on the CAT-S cards. They state:

For instance, CAT-S picture #5 may be given to children with a temporary or permanent physical disability or with a history of disability. It might permit one to learn about the psychological effects of this somatic problem upon the specific child. Or, children with any kind of psychosomatic disorder or hypochondriasis might project these onto the stimulus. Picture #10 may permit us to learn what fantasies a boy or girl may have about the mother's pregnancy. If, e.g., a child is brought to a clinic with a number of behavioral problems, and the history shows that the mother is currently pregnant or delivered relatively recently, then this picture may permit one to learn about the possible specific relations between the behavior problems and the fantasies concerning the family event.

In short, the CAT Supplement may be used in specific situations for the purpose of eliciting specific themes—as seem indicated (p. 2).

Katzenstein (1957), in Brazil, has reported a clinical case study in which figure drawings and picture No. 5 of the CAT-S (kangaroo with bandages and crutches) yielded complementary information from a boy of five and one-half. Eight months previous to testing, it had been discovered that the capsule of the superior articulation of the femur was absent, and braces had been prescribed. The child's figure drawing was notable for the strong, heavy black shading covering the figure from waist to feet, completely hiding the legs. When shown the CAT-S, he was particularly drawn to picture No. 5 and it was difficult to get him to respond to the other pictures.

Boulanger-Balleyguier (1957) has commented that the standard CAT cards depict far more parental figures and activities than figures which could be seen as brothers and sisters, consequently little information can be gathered with respect to peer and sibling relationships in CAT stories. In contrast, she points out, several of the CAT-S cards represent situations which could suggest interactions with siblings and/or age-mates.

SCORING AND INTERPRETATION

Bellak has pointed out that the Short Form TAT-CAT Blank is also appropriate for use with the CAT-S. As an aid in gathering normative data, Brower and Bellak (1954) have prepared a tabulating scheme for the CAT-S which provides a check list for each card for the categories of: Figures (age, sex, identity, etc.), Objects and Details, Problems and Outcomes, Outcome Quality, Figures and Objects Introduced, Portrayal of Figures, and of the Outside World.

NORMATIVE RESEARCH

Very little research has been reported on this instrument. Fear (1951)* administered the supplement to 40 children, ages six and seven. Only the first nine cards were available at that time. Tabulations were made of the frequency of themes, attitudes expressed, outcomes, figures and objects omitted or introduced, total story time and total words per picture. The most frequent themes were those descriptive of the pictures, while those themes which departed from the picture stimuli more often seemed to reveal the child's problems and deeper dynamics. One-third of the Ss introduced themes not repre-

---

*This study was a bachelor's thesis under the supervision of L. J. Stone.

sented by the pictures. Sex differences were noted, with girls giving more themes, departing more from the stimuli, and introducing more figures. In terms of outcomes, there were more happy or successful, than unhappy or failure, endings. About one-fourth of the stories did not have outcomes.

Picture No. 2 elicited the largest number of introduced figures. One-fourth of the Ss introduced a mother figure to each picture; half of the children did not introduce any additional figures into their stories.

Further card by card findings from the Fear study are summarized by Bellak and Bellak (1957) as follows:

To picture #1, 31 of the 40 children respond with stories directly concerning the stimulus situation (of a playground with slide). Eleven of this total sample speak of gayety, while ten mention apprehensiveness.

To picture #2, 38 responded with stories of a schoolroom. The two who do not, we shall return to speak of in greater detail. Twenty-five children introduced a teacher into the story (none being present in the picture).

To picture #3, only 23 children plainly refer to playing house, while 17 introduce themes of their own (27 and 28, respectively, identify the male and female figures in the picture correctly); recognition of the stimulus increases with age.

To picture #4, 27 responded strictly to the presented stimulus, while 27 introduced or added stimuli of their own.

To picture #5, 30 children responded with characterization of the kangaroo as hurt, while ten speak of it as sick.

To #6, 21 children speak of the race as dangerous, 12 feel happy, and 13 are apprehensive.

In #7, 23 children refer to the mirror manifestly; the seven year olds of both sexes do so about twice as much as the six year olds.

To #8, 21 speak of the child as sick, 22 children introduce the mother as a figure.

To #9, more girls speak of washing and dressing than do boys, and more so at age seven than at age six. Thirty-three children, in all, speak of it manifestly as a bathroom scene.

Thus, such data, when based upon large enough numbers, may permit us to deal with a record in terms of how it meets certain norms and will help us identify a deviation (also such a normative scheme may be useful to demonstrate developmental trends).

For instance, if more than half of our sample introduce the mother in picture #8, it would not be reasonable to infer from such an introduction in any individual record, a clinically significantly greater dependence upon the mother than in most children of this age. On the other hand, if 38 out of 40 children speak of #2 card as a schoolroom situation, any child who does not do so merits special attention. Surely enough, the records of our two deviants (as mentioned earlier) are very informative, e.g.: one of them says this:

"Three little monkeys were reading very good. Suddenly a fourth one came in. It said, 'Oh, they are reading. What dopes they are. They never knew how to fight teachers.' The teacher said, 'You must not disturb them.' They fought and fought with the teacher and she said, 'You must go to the cellar and be drowned.' They cried and cried. The three little monkeys had finished their books. She said, 'You bad, bad children. You must come to be drowned.' So she drowned them (the bad ones). The good monkeys finished another book in a minute. Another and another, seconds and minutes, halves of seconds, fourths of seconds.

Finally they read all the books in the world and she said, 'What wonderful children you are.' "

Although implicitly this story refers to a school situation, it does not do so explicitly. At any rate, even without norms, a clinician would have considered this story as indicative of special problems of aggression and fear, and compliance (p. 8).

CLINICAL USE OF THE CAT-S

The CAT-S appears to be particularly well adapted for use with young children and retarded Ss with mental ages below five or six years. In all the examples presented in this section, the cards were presented singly, but in random order, or three or four cards were placed on the table at one time and the child determined the order of responding.

The first case is that of a boy five years one month of age, with a mental age of four years seven months (IQ = 89). Verbal comprehension was close to age level, although his speech patterns and word pronunciations were rather immature. His CAT-S stories were descriptive and generally nonproductive.

3. Teaparty.
   Bear and pup, and school.
(Q-story?) Once a time, kid and baby,
   Drinking coffee.

5. Fox, crippled foot and tail,
   walk around in cast.

4. Bear and wittle (little) bear,
   Nice funny one.
(Q-story?) Once a time, two bears,
   One's a daddy bear,
   Bitsy bear.

2. Monkeys in school,
   Reading.

6. Foxes in neighborhood,
   Running.
(Q) Don't know, running.
That's a funny one (on left)
   His pants.

7. Cat thinks his hair is pretty.
(Q-next?) Go party.

8. Rabbits, he's the doctor,
   A funny one.
(Q) Cause, a rabbit doctor.
(Q) Go home.

9. Deer taking a bath.
   That's funny . . . taking a bath.
(Q) Go play.

1. Side (slide), that's a side.
Kids playing on side,
   That's a funny one.
(Q) Side down, weeee.

10. That's the cat mummy,
   such a funny.
(Q) Cause, to take care the children.
(Q) Bring em home and fix yunch (lunch).

The next little girl (age six years eleven months) had an MA of five years and an IQ of 72. She was extremely hyperactive, very verbal, and overreactive to all stimuli, showing the typical reactions of a brain-damaged child. Emotionally, she was immature, impulsive and highly anxious. There was marked strabismus and eye-hand coordination was poor. Note the perseverations of content.

8. Looks like going to have hurt.

4. Looks like teddy bear's being mad.

2. These kids read a book,
   at own desk.
What is teacher mind?
Is that a teacher? (center standing figure)
They're all finking (thinking)
   what a teacher say to do.
Think a thousand of people
   are learning.

6. All kinds running to go home,
My, oh my, lots of things happen.

5. He's going . . . . his back hurts.
He's going somewhere to learn.
(Q) Learn school.

9. He's putting his shoes on.
Somebody hop in there,
   Get hurt in bathtub.

1. All outside,
   Slide on slide.

10. He had big trouble,
   big trouble.
Mother fought (thought) kids
   coming in house.

3. Teaparty.

7. Mother said,
   "Get in your house (scolding voice)
   It's raining."

The next two children were each functioning at a three-year level. The first boy (age three years six months), of average intelligence, was referred because of an adjustment reaction to situational stress in the family setting. There was some question as to whether reality orientation was still intact. In these stories it can be seen that he is generally aware of the reality aspects, except for missing the implications of injury in picture No. 5 (kangaroo on crutches). The numerous personal references would be considered quite typical for so young a child.

2. Two monks, so they're going to school.
When done going,
   they send them home.

5. So this one goes hopping.
Goes to a home
   and knocks on the door,
   and door's unlocked
   and he wakes them up.
(Q) He bangs,
   he whistles like a dog.

4. This is a dog.
Looks like a bear,
   with little baby bear.
So then all the old bunch of bears
Went for a walk.
Here comes Goldilocks,
   Her eats porridge and milk.
When they come back,
   it's all gone.

10. A cat . . . what doing?
This cat goes running off.
Got bracelet (necklace) like a mom.

7. There's another cat.
So he looks in there and sees him.

9. This one combing hair
   and this one is putting his shoes on.
   I mean, combing his neck.
Saw it at a deer thing,
   whole bunch of deer,
   licked me on my hand
   when I gave them corn.
Decided to go shopping
   when I got home.
Shopped for suitcase and clothes
   for vacation here. (Reference to inpatient care.)
Deer don't really talk.

1. Them cats are going down the slide,
   Going up the big ladder.
8. That's a daddy,
   and a boy one.
This one has ear,
   and this one shaving him.
3. Some more bears,
   boy and mother and baby.
No story to it,
Blocks and ball.
6. What's running? Foxes.
(Q) Maybe bear getting them.
Daddy, mother, daddy one.

The next boy was five years eleven months of age but functioning at a 32 month level (IQ = 45). There are many instances of perseverations, misperceptions, uncertainties as to what he sees, or the objects seen suggest others usually associated with them (e.g., swing-slide). Here again, the personal references are consistent with his mental age but, in this case, their content suggests a view of the world as potentially threatening. At one point (picture No. 7) his response deteriorates into combining the cards as play objects in a very primitive fashion.

2. Three monkeys at desk in school.
That monkey won't bite me.
(Q) That's monkey's kids.
How come in a cage?

8. The monkey doing, sitting down.
Is that a cat?

6. (Refused)

9. Monkey going to go in.
(Q) Up on a cage.

5. That monkey won't hurt me.
My dad has one like that (points to crutch, but father does not use one.)

3. Is that the monkey that's feeding?
(Q) Going play coffee.

7. (Laughs) Mirror.
(Points to pregnancy card, No. 10)
Here's the monkey that's following somebody.
(Lays No. 10 at right angles to No. 7)

1. That monkey following somebody.
(Q) They're sliding.
   Here's that monkey that's sliding.
Where's the swing?

4. A monkey.

For examples of CAT-S stories from somewhat older children, the reader is referred to Bellak (1954) where selected stories are presented from six- and seven-year-old normal Ss. One final case, also from Bellak (1954), is that of a ten-year-old girl who was in psychotherapy.*

The following two stories were told by a ten-year-old girl who was in psychotherapy for nausea and vomiting apparently related to unconscious pregnancy fantasies. She was also suffering from a great many fears.

Story #5: I can't think of what kind of an animal this is supposed to be. I know the name of it but I can't remember it. Anyway, the animal broke its leg and it was very hard for it to get about. It can't go any place because of the broken leg and it's always left behind. He doesn't mind; he feels that when his leg is better he'll get along just as well as anyone else.

Story #8: The little rabbit is sick. The doctor is examining it. He tells the rabbit he's got the grippe and he has to stay in bed. The rabbit doesn't want to stay in bed; he wants to go out and play. He does go out and play and as a result of that he gets very sick and has to stay in bed for a month. As a result of that, he gets a heart condition and has to be very careful and can't run around like all the other rabbits.

In story 5 she tells in essence her own feelings of bodily inadequacy. She responds with a typical defense of denial, minimizing the emotional implications. Her associations, however, showed her real concern when she told of a man she knew who had had his leg cut off (apparently because of gangrene) and of another man who had both legs cut off in an accident.

Story 8 also shows her fear of illness and the phobic limitations she imposes on herself (having to be very careful) (p. 238).

SUMMARY

The CAT-S has been devised as a supplement to the standard CAT cards. It appears to fulfill several purposes: eliciting children's reactions to specific, stressful situations (such as illness, injury, mother's pregnancy) and providing stimuli for the evaluation of attitudes and responses toward peers and siblings. It may also be more suitable than the regular set for presentation to very young children.

Administration differs from the CAT in that the cards may not only be presented sequentially, but laid out all at once or presented a few at a time, more as a play technique. A child lacking in verbal skills may thus at least be able to indicate preferences or arrange the cards in relation to each other. Selected CAT-S cards may also be added to a standard CAT administration. Scoring and interpretation are handled as in any other projective technique.

There has been very little research interest in this instrument, and only one study has been reported. Examples have been presented of protocols from very young children, those of low mental ages, and one older, disturbed child.

---

*Reproduced from Bellak, L.: *The TAT and CAT in Clinical Use,* 1954; with permission of the author and the publisher, Grune & Stratton, Inc.

REFERENCES *

*Ainsworth, Mary D., and Boston, Mary: Psychodiagnostic assessments of a child after prolonged separation in early childhood. *Brit. J. med. Psychol.* 25: 169–201, 1952.

Amen, Elizabeth W.: Individual differences in apperceptive reaction: a study of responses of pre-school children to pictures. *Genet. Psychol. Monogr.* 23: 319–385, 1941.

Ames, Louise B., Learned, Janet, Métraux, Ruth W., and Walker, R. N.: *Child Rorschach Responses: Developmental Trends from Two to Ten Years.* New York: Hoeber, 1952.

Andrew, Gwen, Hartwell, S. W., Hutt, M. L., and Walton, R. E.: *The Michigan Picture Test.* Chicago: Science Research Associates, 1953.

*Armstrong, Mary Ann: Children's responses to animal and human figures in thematic pictures. *J. consult. Psychol.* 18: 67–70, 1954.

Balken, Eva, and Vander Veer, A. H.: Clinical application of the Thematic Apperception Test to neurotic children. *Amer. J. Orthopsychiat.* 14: 421–440, 1944.

*Bell, J. E.: The Children's Apperception Test. *In* O. K. Buros (Ed.): *The Fourth Mental Measurements Yearbook.* Highland Park, N. J.: Gryphon Press, 1953, pp. 168–169.

Bellak, L.: The concept of projection: an experimental investigation and study of the concept. *Psychiatry.* 7: 353–370, 1944.

*—: *The Thematic Apperception Test and the Children's Apperception Test in Clinical Use.* New York: Grune & Stratton, 1954.

*—: *Short Form: Bellak TAT and CAT Blank.* New York: C. P. S. Co., 1955.

*—, and Adelman, Crusa: The Children's Apperception Test (CAT). *In* A. I. Rabin and Mary R. Haworth (Eds.): *Projective Techniques with Children.* New York: Grune & Stratton, 1960, pp. 62–94.

*—, and Bellak, Sonya, S.: *Children's Apperception Test.* New York: C. P. S. Co., 1949.

*—, and —: An introductory note on the Children's Apperception Test (CAT). *J. proj. Tech.* 14: 173–180, 1950.

*—, and —: *The Children's Apperception Test—Supplement* (CAT-S). New York: C. P. S. Co., 1952.

*—, and —: *Manual for the Supplement to the Children's Apperception Test—*(CAT-S). New York: C. P. S. Co., 1957.

*—, and —: *Children's Apperception Test Manual,* 4th ed. New York: C. P. S. Co., 1961.

*—, and —: *The CAT-H.* New York: C. P. S. Co., 1965.

*—, and Hurvich, M. S.: *Manual for the CAT-H.* (Human modification of the C.A.T.) New York: C. P. S. Co., 1965.

*Beller, E. K., and Haeberle, Ann W.: Motivation and conflict in relation to phantasy responses of young children. Paper read at meeting of the Society for Research in Child Development, Bethesda, Maryland, March, 1959.

Bender, Lauretta: A Visual Motor Gestalt Test and its clinical use. *Res. Monogr. Amer. Orthopsychiat. Ass.,* No. 3, 1938.

—, and Rapoport, J.: Animal drawings of children. *Amer. J. Orthopsychiat.* 14: 521–527, 1944.

*Bennett, E. M., and Johannsen, Dorothea E.: Psychodynamics of the diabetic child. *Psychol. Monogr.* 68: No. 11 (Whole No. 382), 1954. (a)

*—, and —: Some psychodynamic aspects of felt parental alliance in young children. J. *abnorm. soc. Psychol.* 49: 463–464, 1954. (b)

*Biersdorf, Kathryn R., and Marcuse, F. L.: Responses of children to human and animal pictures. *J. proj. Tech.* 17: 455–459, 1953.

Bills, R. E.: Animal pictures for obtaining childrens' projections. *J. clin. Psychol.* 6: 291–293, 1950.

—, Leiman, C. J., and Thomas, R. W.: A study of the validity of the TAT and a set of animal pictures. *J. clin. Psychol.* 6: 293–295, 1950.

Blatt, S. J., Engel, Mary, and Mirmow, Esther L.: When inquiry fails. *J. proj. Tech.* 25: 32–37, 1961.

---

*Bibliographic items referring wholly or largely to the CAT are indicated by an asterisk.

Blum, G. S.: A study of the psychoanalytic theory of psychosexual development. *Genet. Psychol. Monogr.* 39: 3–99, 1949.

—, and Hunt, H. F.: The validity of the Blacky Pictures. *Psychol. Bull.* 49: 238–250, 1952.

*Bolgar, Hedda: Symposium: Validity aspects of multiple projective techniques in child research. Paper read at meeting of the American Psychological Association, Chicago, Sept. 1956.

*Booth, L. J.: A normative comparison of the responses of Latin-American and Anglo-American children to the Children's Apperception Test. Unpublished doctoral dissertation, Texas Tech. Coll., Lubbock, Texas, 1953.

Borstelmann, L. J.: Sex of experimenter and sex-typed behavior of young children. *Child Develpm.* 32: 519–524, 1961.

*Boulanger-Balleyguier, Geneviève: Étude sur le C.A.T.: influence du stimulus sur les récits d'enfants de 3 à 8 ans. *Rev. Psychol. Appliquée* 7: 1–28, 1957. (a)

*—: Résultats d'une application du C.A.T. à des enfants normaux et anormaux. *Psychol. Franç.* 2: 92–94, 1957. (b)

*—: La personnalité des enfants normaux et caractériels a travers le test d'apperception C.A.T. *Monogr. Franç. Psychol.* No. 4, 1960.

*—: Comparison des résultats donnés au C.A.T. et au Rorschach par de jeunes enfants. *Rev. Psychol. Franç.* 6: 55–63, 1961.

Boyd, Nancy, and Mandler, G.: Children's responses to human and animal stories and pictures. *J. consult. Psychol.* 19: 367–371, 1955.

Bridges, Katharine M. B.: A genetic theory of the emotions. *J. genet. Psychol.* 37: 514–527, 1930.

*Brower, Judith F., and Bellak, L.: Tabulating scheme for CAT-S. *In* L. Bellak: *The TAT and CAT in Clinical Use.* New York: Grune & Stratton, 1954, pp. 255–268.

Brown, D. G.: Sex-role preference in young children. *Psychol. Monogr.* 70: No. 14 (Whole No. 421), 1956.

—: Masculinity-femininity development in children. *J. consult. Psychol.* 21: 197–202, 1957.

*Budoff, M.: The relative utility of animal and human figures in a picture-story test for young children. *J. proj. Tech.* 24: 347–352, 1960.

*—: Animal versus human figures in a picture story test for young, mentally backward children. *Amer. J. ment. Defic.* 68: 245–250, 1963.

*Butler, R. L.: Responses of institutionalized mentally retarded children to human and to animal pictures. *Amer. J. ment. Defic.* 65: 620–622, 1961.

Buss, A. H., and Durkee, Ann: The association of animals with familial figures. *J. proj. Tech.* 21: 366–371, 1957.

*Byrd, E., and Witherspoon, R. L.: Responses of preschool children to the Children's Apperception Test. *Child Develpm.* 25: 35–44, 1954.

*Cain, A. C.: A supplementary dream technique with the Children's Apperception Test. *J. clin. Psychol.* 17: 181–184, 1961.

Caplan, H.: Some interview techniques in child psychiatry. *J. Pediat.* 38: 128–140, 1951.

Child, I. L., Potter, E. H., and Levine, Estelle M.: Children's textbooks and personality development: an exploration in the social psychology of education. *Psychol. Monogr.* 60: (No. 3). Pp. 1–7, 43–53, 1946.

*Chowdhury, Uma: *An Indian Adaptation of the Children's Apperception Test.* Delhi, India: Manasayan, 1960.

Coleman, W.: The Thematic Apperception Test. I. Effect of recent experience. II. Some quantitative observations. *J. clin. Psychol.* 3: 257–264, 1947.

Cook, R.: Identification and ego defensiveness in thematic apperception. *J. proj. Tech.* 17: 312–319, 1953.

Dennis, W.: Performance of Near Eastern children on the Draw-a-Man Test. *Child Develpm.* 28: 427–430, 1957.

*DeSousa, Therese L.: A comparison of the responses of adjusted and maladjusted children on a thematic apperception test. Unpublished master's thesis, Loyola Univer., Chicago, 1952.

*Dhondiyal, S.: Art as a projective technique for deviant children. *U. Rajasthan Stud. Educ.* 5: 60–126, 1961–62.

*Duhm, Erna: Erfahrungen mit dem CAT. *Diagnostica* 1: 14–15, 1955.

*Earle, Margaret J.: *Rakau Children: from Six to Thirteen Years.* Wellington, New Zealand: Victoria Univer. Publ. Psychol., No. 11, 1958. (Monographs on Maori Social Life and Personality, No. 4.)

Eiserer, P. E.: The relative effectiveness of motion and still pictures as stimuli for eliciting fantasy stories about adolescent-parent relationships. *Genet. Psychol. Monogr.* 39: 205–278, 1949.

Emmerich, W.: Parental identification in young children. *Genet. Psychol. Monogr.* 60: 257–308, 1959.

Engel, Mary: Some parameters of the psychological evaluation of children. *Arch. gen. Psychiat.* 2: 593–605, 1960.

—: On the psychological testing of borderline children. *Arch. gen. Psychiat.* 8: 426–434, 1963.

*Ephrussi, R.: Autonomie et dépendance chez l'enfant, étudiées par la planche du kangourou. *Enfance* 4: 401–405, 1955.

*Fear, Clara: A study of a projective technique: The Children's Apperception Test Supplement. Unpublished bachelor's thesis, Vassar Coll., 1951.

Feifel, H., and Lorge, I.: Qualitative differences in the vocabulary responses of children. *J. educ. Psychol.* 41: 1–18, 1950.

Fine, R. A scoring scheme and manual for the TAT and other verbal projective technique. *J. Proj. Tech.* 19: 306–316, 1955.

*FitzSimons, Ruth: Developmental, psychosocial, and educational factors in children with nonorganic articulation problems. *Child Develpm.* 29: 481–489, 1958.

Flavell, J. H.: *The Developmental Psychology of Jean Piaget.* Princeton, N. J.: D. Van Nostrand, 1963.

Frank, L. K.: *Projective Methods.* Springfield, Ill.: Charles C Thomas, 1948.

Freud, Anna: *The Ego and the Mechanisms of Defence.* New York: International Universities Press, 1946.

Freud, S.: Analysis of a phobia in a five-year-old boy (1909). In: *Collected Papers,* Vol. III. New York: Basic Books, 1959, pp. 149–289.

—: *Totem and Taboo* (1913). New York: W. W. Norton, 1952.

—: From the history of an infantile neurosis (1918). In: *Collected Papers,* Vol. III. New York: Basic Books, 1959, pp. 473–605.

*Furuya, Kenji: Responses of school-children to human and animal pictures. *J. proj. Tech.* 21: 248–252, 1957.

*Genn, M. M.: Review of the CAT. *Quart. J. child Behav.* 2: 469–470, 1950.

Gesell, A., and Ilg, Frances L.: *The Child from Five to Ten.* New York: Harper and Bros., 1946.

Gewirtz, J. L.: Three determinants of attention-seeking in young children. *Monogr. Soc. Res. Child Develpm.* 19: No. 2 (Serial No. 59), 1954.

Gibby, R. G., Stotsky, B. A., and Miller, D. R.: Influence of the preceding test on the Rorschach protocol. *J. consult. Psychol.* 18: 463–464, 1954.

*Gibson, R. M.: An exploratory study of the effects of surgery and hospitalization in early infancy on personality development. Unpublished doctoral dissertation, Univer. of Michigan, 1958.

*Ginsparg, H. T.: A study of the Children's Apperception Test. Unpublished doctoral dissertation, Washington Univer., 1957.

Goldberg, Ilsa: Use of remedial reading tutoring as a method of psychotherapy for schizophrenic children with reading disabilities. *Quart. J. child Behav.* 4: 273–280, 1952.

Goldfarb, W.: The animal symbol in the Rorschach test and an animal association test. *Rorschach Res. Exch.* 9: 8–22, 1945.

Goldfried, M. R.: The connotative meaning of some animal symbols for college students. *J. proj. Tech.* 27: 60–67, 1963.

—, and Kissel, S.: Age as a variable in the connotative perceptions of some animal symbols. *J. proj. Tech. & Pers. Assess.* 27: 171–180, 1963.

Granick, S., and Scheflen, Norma A.: Approaches to reliability of projective tests with special reference to the Blacky Pictures Test. *J. consult. Psychol.* 22: 137–141, 1958.

Griffiths, Ruth: *A Study of Imagination in Early Childhood and Its Function in Mental Development.* London: K. Paul, Trench, & Trubner, 1935.

*Gurevitz, S., and Kapper, Zelda S.: Techniques for and evaluation of the responses of schizophrenic and cerebral palsied children to the Children's Apperception Test (C. A. T.). *Quart. J. child Behav.* 3: 38–65, 1951.

*Halpern, Florence: Projective tests in the personality investigation of children. *J. Pediat.* 38: 770–775, 1951.

—: *A Clinical Approach to Children's Rorschachs.* New York: Grune & Stratton, 1953.

Hammer, E. F.: *The Clinical Application of Projective Drawings.* Springfield, Ill.: Charles C Thomas, 1958.

*Haworth, Mary R.: Responses of children to a group projective film and to the Rorschach, CAT, Despert Fables and D-A-P. *J. proj. Tech.* 26: 47–60, 1962.

*—: A schedule for the analysis of CAT responses. *J. proj. Tech. & Pers. Assess.* 27: 181–184, 1963.

*—: Parental loss in children as reflected in projective responses. *J. proj. Tech. & Pers. Assess.* 28: 31–45, 1964.

*—: *A Schedule of Adaptive Mechanisms in CAT Responses.* New York: C. P. S. Co., 1965.

*—: CAT versus CAT-H with a clinic sample. (Unpublished.) Univer. of Nebraska.

—, and Rabin, A. I.: Miscellaneous techniques. *In* A. I. Rabin, and Mary R. Haworth (Eds.): *Projective Techniques with Children.* New York: Grune & Stratton, 1960, pp. 314–330.

—, and Woltmann, A. G.: *Rock-A-Bye, Baby: A Group Projective Test for Children.* (Manual and film.) University Park, Pa.: Psychological Cinema Register, 1959.

Heiman, M.: The relationship between man and dog. *Psychoanal. Quart.* 25: 568–585, 1956.

Hemmendinger, L.: Perceptual organization and development as reflected in the structure of Rorschach test responses. *J. proj. Tech.* 17: 162–170, 1953.

Henry, W. E.: *The Analysis of Fantasy: The Thematic Apperception Technique in the Study of Personality.* New York: John Wiley, 1956.

*Herman, H.: Review of the CAT. *Amer. J. Psychiat.* 108: 317–318, 1951.

Hilgard, E. R.: Impulsive versus realistic thinking: an examination of the distinction between primary and secondary processes in thought. *Psychol. Bull.* 59: 477–488, 1962.

*Holden, R. H.: The Children's Apperception Test with cerebral palsied and normal children. *Child Develpm.* 27: 3–8, 1956.

*Holt, R. R.: Review: The CAT and manual. *J. proj. Tech.* 14: 198–200, 1950.

*—: The TAT Newsletter (Special C. A. T. issue). *J. proj. Tech.* 15: 537–544, 1951.

Inhelder, Bärbel: Some aspects of Piaget's genetic approach to cognition. *In* W. Kessen and Clementina Kuhlman: *Thought in the Young Child. Monogr. Soc. Res. Child Develpm.* 27: No. 2 (Serial No. 83), pp. 19–34, 1962.

*Jackson, R. W.: A comparative study of the TAT and CAT with children. Unpublished master's thesis, West Virginia Univer., 1955.

Jelliffe, S. E., and Brink, Louise: The role of animals in the unconscious. *Psychoanal. Rev.* 4: 253–271, 1917.

Jensen, A. R.: The reliability of projective techniques: review of the literature. *Acta Psychol., Amst.* 16: 108–136, 1959.

Jones, R. M.: The Negation TAT: a projective method for eliciting repressed thought content. *J. proj. Tech.* 20: 297–303, 1956.

*Kaake, Norma E.: The relationship between intelligence level and responses to the Children's Apperception Test. Unpublished master's thesis, Cornell Univer., 1951.

Kagan, J.: The measurement of overt aggression from fantasy. *J. abnorm. soc. Psychol.* 52: 390–393, 1956.

—: The stability of TAT fantasy and stimulus ambiguity. *J. consult. Psychol.* 23: 266–

271, 1959.

—: Thematic apperceptive techniques with children. *In* A. I. Rabin and Mary R. Haworth (Eds.): *Projective Techniques with Children.* New York: Grune & Stratton, 1960, pp. 105–129.

—, and Moss, H. A.: Stability and validity of achievement fantasy. *J. abnorm. soc. Psychol.,* 58: 357–364, 1959.

*Kagan, Marion G., and Kaufman, Marilyn A.: A preliminary investigation of some relationships between functional articulation disorders and responses to the Children's Apperception Test. Unpublished master's thesis, Boston Univer., 1954.

*Kanehira, Teruko. Diagnosis of parent-child relationship by CAT. *Jap. J. Case Stud.* 3: 49–63, 1958. (*Psychol. Abstr.* 34: 4129, 1960.)

*Katzenstein, Betti: Estudos individuais e orientação psico-pedagógica de crianças acometidas de poliomielite. (Case-studies and psycho-pedagogical guidance of children attacked by poliomyelitis.) *Rev. Psicol. norm. e patol.* 3: 77–85, 1957.

*Kenny, D. T.: The Children's Apperception Test. *In* O. K. Buros (Ed.): *The Fifth Mental Measurements Yearbook.* Highland Park, N. J.: Gryphon Press, 1959, pp. 126–127.

King, F. W., and King, Dorothy C.: The projective assessment of the female's sexual identification, with special reference to the Blacky Pictures. *J. proj. Tech. & Pers. Assess.* 28: 293–299, 1964.

*Koch, Helen L.: The relation of certain family constellation characteristics and the attitudes of children toward adults. *Child Develpm.* 26: 13–40, 1955.

*—: The relation of certain formal attributes of siblings to attitudes held toward each other and toward their parents. *Monogr. Soc. Res. Child Develpm.* 25: No. 4 (Serial No. 78), 1960.

*—: Twins and others. Presidential address to the Division of Developmental Psychology, Amer. Psychol. Assoc., St. Louis, Mo., Aug. 1962.

*—: A study of twins born at different levels of maturity. *Child Develpm.* 35: 1265–1282, 1964.

*Lawton, Marcia J.: Animal and human CATs with a school sample. (Unpublished). Univer. of Nebraska.

Ledwith, Nettie H.: *Rorschach Responses of Elementary School Children.* Pittsburgh, Pa.: University of Pittsburgh Press, 1960.

*Lehmann, I. J.: Responses of kindergarten children to the Children's Apperception Test. *J. clin. Psychol.* 15: 60–63, 1959.

Lesser, G. S.: The relationship between overt and fantasy aggression as a function of maternal response to aggression. *J. abnorm. soc. Psychol.* 55: 218–221, 1957.

Leventhal, T., Slepian, H. J., Gluck, M. R., and Rosenblatt, B. P.: The utilization of the psychologist-patient relationship in diagnostic testing. *J. proj. Tech.* 26: 66–79, 1962.

Levy, S., and Levy, R. A.: Symbolism in animal drawings. *In* E. F. Hammer (Ed.): *The Clinical Application of Projective Drawings.* Springfield, Ill.: Charles C Thomas, 1958, pp. 311–343.

*Light, B. H.: Comparative study of a series of TAT and CAT cards. *J. clin. Psychol.* 10: 179–181, 1954.

Lindzey, G.: Thematic Apperception Test: interpretive assumptions and related empirical evidence. *Psychol. Bull.* 49: 1–25, 1952.

*Lumpkin, W. T.: A sociometric and projective study of interpersonal relations among certain pupils at the Oglethorpe Elementary School. Unpublished master's thesis, Atlanta Univer., 1952.

*Lyles, W. K.: The effects of examiner attitudes on the projective test responses of children. Unpublished doctoral dissertation, New York Univer. (School of Educ.), 1958.

*Macedo de Queiroz, Aydil, and Reichnardt Epps, D.: Uma contribuição às características psicológicas da intersexualidade humana. *Rev. Psicol. norm. e patol.* 9: 3–20, 1963.

Macfarlane, Jean W., and Tuddenham, R. D.: Problems in the validation of projective techniques. *In* H. H. Anderson and Gladys L. Anderson (Eds.): *An Introduction to*

Projective Techniques. New York: Prentice-Hall, 1951, pp. 26–54.

*Magnusson, D.: Some personality tests applied on identical twins. *Scand. J. Psychol.* 1: 55–61, 1960.

*Mainord, Florence R., and Marcuse, F. L.: Responses of disturbed children to human and to animal pictures. *J. proj. Tech.* 18: 475–477, 1954.

*Marui, Sumiko: C. A. T. ni kansuru ichi kenkyu: yogoshisetsu shuyoji to kateiji no hanno ni arawareta sai ni tsuite. (A study on the CAT: A comparison of the children in reformatories with home children on their responses.) *Bunka* 21: 133–141, 1957. (*Psychol. Abstr.* 34: 6037, 1960.)

Masling, J.: The influence of situational and interpersonal variables in projective testing. *Psychol. Bull.* 57: 65–85, 1960.

Menninger, K. A.: Totemic aspects of contemporary attitudes toward animals. *In* G. B. Wilbur and W. Muensterberger (Eds.): *Psychoanalysis and Culture.* New York: International Universities Press, 1951.

*Millar, Mary Aileen: A study of common stories told by nursery school children on the Children's Apperception Test. Unpublished master's thesis, Univer. of Alberta, 1952.

*Moriarty, Alice E., and Murphy, Lois B.: Coping maneuvers as observed in or inferred from CAT responses. (Unpublished.) Menninger Foundation, 1960. (a)

*—, and —: Observations of patterns in perception related to basic motivations of children. (Unpublished.) Menninger Foundation, 1960. (b)

*—, and —: Rivalry in the family as seen through the CAT. (Unpublished.) Menninger Foundation, 1960. (c)

*Muller, P.: *Le CAT: Recherches sur le Dynamisme Enfantin.* Bern: Hans Huber, 1958.

Murphy, Lois B. et al.: *The Widening World of Childhood: Paths Toward Mastery.* New York: Basic Books, 1962.

Murstein, B. I.: A conceptual model of projective techniques applied to stimulus variations with thematic techniques. *J. consult. Psychol.* 23: 3–14, 1959.

—: *Theory and Research in Projective Techniques (Emphasizing the TAT).* New York: John Wiley, 1963.

—, and Pryer, R. S.: The concept of projection: a review. *Psychol. Bull.* 56: 353–374, 1959.

*—: The Children's Apperception Test. *In* O. K. Buros (Ed.): *The Sixth Mental Measurements Yearbook.* Highland Park, N. J.: Gryphon Press, 1965.

Mussen, P., and Distler, L.: Masculinity, identification, and father-son relationships *J. abnorm. soc. Psychol.* 59: 350–356, 1959.

—, and —: Child-rearing antecedents of masculine identification in kindergarten boys. *Child Develpm.* 31: 89–100, 1960.

—, and Rutherford, E.: Parent-child relations and parental personality in relation to young children's sex-role preferences. *Child Develpm.* 34: 589–607, 1963.

*Nolan, R. D.: A longitudinal comparison of motives in children's fantasy stories as revealed by the Children's Apperception Test. Unpublished doctoral dissertation, Florida State Univer., 1959.

*Olim, E. G., Hess, R. D., and Shipman, Virginia C.: Relationship between mothers' language styles and cognitive styles of urban preschool children. Paper read at meeting of the Society for Research in Child Development, Minneapolis, March, 1965.

Olney, E. E., and Cushing, H. M.: A brief report of the responses of pre-school children to commercially available pictorial material. *Child Develpm.* 6: 52–55, 1935.

*Ōuchi, Gosuke: C. A. T. ni kansuru kenkyu: II. T. A. T. tono hikaku. (A study on CAT. II. A comparison with TAT.) *Bunka* 21: 194–207, 264–265, 1957. (*Psychol. Abstr.* 34: 6042, 1960).

Papania, N.: A qualitative analysis of the vocabulary responses of institutionalized, mentally retarded children. *J. clin. Psychol.* 10: 361–365, 1954.

Parsons, T.: Family structure and the socialization of the child. *In* T. Parsons, R. F. Bales, and associates (Eds.): *Family, Socialization and Interaction Process.* Glencoe, Ill.: Free Press, 1955.

*Peters, Alice, and Bellak, L.: Tabulation scheme for CAT. *In* L. Bellak: *The TAT* *and CAT in Clinical Use.* New York: Grune & Stratton, 1954, pp. 242–254.

Phillips, L., and Smith, J. G.: *Rorschach Interpretation: Advanced Technique.* New York: Grune & Stratton, 1953.

Piaget, J.: *The Child's Conception of the World.* New York: Harcourt Brace, 1929.

—: *The Language and Thought of the Child* (1923). New York: Humanities Press, 1951.

—: *The Origins of Intelligence in the Child* (1926). New York: International Universities Press, 1952.

—: Three lectures: I. The stages of the intellectual development of the child. *Bull. Menninger Clinic* 26: 120–128, 1962.

Pitcher, Evelyn G., and Prelinger, E.: *Children Tell Stories: An Analysis of Fantasy.* New York: International Universities Press, 1963.

*Plutchik, Lillian: The relationship between muscular tension and expressions of fantasy in nursery school children. Unpublished master's thesis, Univer. of Wisconsin, 1954.

*Rabin, A. I.: The Children's Apperception Test. *In* O. K. Buros (Ed.): *The Fifth Mental Measurements Yearbook.* Highland Park, N. J.: Gryphon Press, 1959, p. 127.

*Raff, Eleanore: Some intra-psychic patterns of nursery-school children judged by their teachers to be socially the best or worst adjusted in their group. Unpublished master's thesis, Univer. of Chicago, 1951.

*Rooney, Kathryn: The productivity of young children in response to human and animal pictures. Unpublished master's thesis, State Coll. of Washington, 1952.

*Rosenblatt, M. S.: The development of norms for the Children's Apperception Test. Unpublished doctoral dissertation, Florida State Univer., 1958.

Rosenzweig, S.: Apperceptive norms for the Thematic Apperception Test: I. The problem of norms in projective methods. *J. Pers.* 17: 475–482, 1949.

—, Fleming, E. E., and Rosenzweig, Louise: The Children's Form of the Rosenzweig Picture-Frustration Study. *J. Psychol.* 26: 141–191, 1948.

—, and Mirmow, E. L.: The validation of trends in the Children's Form of the Picture-Frustration Study. *J. Pers.* 18: 306–314, 1950.

—, and Rosenzweig, Louise: Aggression in problem children and normals as evaluated by the Rosenzweig Picture-Frustration Study. *J. abnorm. soc. Psychol.* 47: 683–687, 1952.

*Sandler, Louise: An evaluation of the Children's Apperception Test in clinical practice: a case study. (Unpublished.) Bryn Mawr Coll.

Sanford, R. N., Adkins, M. M., Miller, R. B., and Cobb, E. A.: Physique, personality and scholarship: a cooperative study of school children. *Monogr. Soc. Res. Child Develpm.* 8: No. 1 (Serial No. 34), 1943.

Schwartz, A. A., and Rosenberg, I. H.: Observations on the significance of animal drawings. *Amer J. Orthopsychiat.* 25: 729–746, 1955.

*Shaffer, L. F.: Review of the CAT. *J. consult. Psychol.* 14: 161, 1950.

*Shneidman, E. S.: The TAT newsletter (CAT issue No. 2). *J. proj. Tech.* 17: 499–502, 1953.

*Sidler, Martha: Tierpantomimik durch Kinder. *Schweiz. Z. Psychol. Anwend.* 15: 196–209, 1956.

*Simon, Maria D.: Der Children's Apperception Test bei gesunden und gestörten Kindern. *Z. Diagnost. Psychol.* 11: 195–219, 1954.

*Simson, E.: A modification of the Children's Apperception Test. Unpublished master's thesis, New York Univer., 1952.

*—: Untersuchungen über idiographische Testmethoden für Kinder mit besonderer Berücksichtigung des Children's Apperception Test. Unpublished doctoral dissertation, Ruprecht-Karl Universität, Heidelberg, 1955.

*—: Vergleich von CAT und einer inhaltsanalogen Mensch-Bilderserie *Sonderdruck aus Diagnostica* 2: 54–62, 1959.

*—: Der CAT-Z, eine standardisierte Testkombination. *Praxis Kinderpsychol. Kinderpsychiat.* 11: 125–128, 1962.

Spiegelman, M., Terwilliger, C., and Fearing, F.: The content of comics: goals and means to goals of comic strip characters. *J. soc. Psychol.* 37: 189–203, 1953.

Stevenson, H. W.: Social reinforcement with children as a function of CA, sex of E, and sex of S. *J. abnorm. soc. Psychol.* 63: 147–154, 1961.

—: Piaget, behavior theory, and intelligence. *In* W. Kessen and Clementina Kuhlman: *Thought in the Young Child. Monogr. Soc. Res. Child Develpm.* 27: No. 2 (Serial No. 83), pp. 113–126, 1962.

*Stevenson, Margaret: Some emotional problems of orphanage children. *Canad. J. Psychol.* 6: 179–182, 1952.

*Stone, L. J.: The Children's Apperception Test *In* O. K. Buros (Ed.): *The Fourth Mental Measurements Yearbook.* Highland Park, N. J.: Gryphon Press, 1953, pp. 169–170.

Symonds, P. M.: *Adolescent Fantasy: An Investigation of the Picture-Story Method of Personality Study.* New York: Columbia Univer. Press, 1949.

Templin, Mildred C.: *Certain Language Skills in Children: Their Development and Interrelationships.* Minneapolis: University of Minnesota Press, 1957.

Thetford, W. N., Molish, H. B., and Beck, S. J.: Developmental aspects of personality structure in normal children. *J. proj. Tech.* 15: 58–78, 1951.

Tomkins, S. S.: *The Thematic Apperception Test.* New York: Grune & Stratton, 1947.

*Toppelstein, S.: Apperceptive norms for the Children's Apperception Test. Unpublished master's thesis, Ohio Univer., 1952.

Van de Castle, R. L.: Effect of test order upon Rorschach human content. *J. consult. Psychol.* 28: 286–288, 1964.

*Van Cauvenberghe, Paulette: L'utilisation du CAT chez l'adulte pour l'étude des relations de la mère et de l'enfant. Paris: Mimeographed monograph, 1960.

Vernon, M. D.: The relation of cognition and phantasy in children. Part II. *Brit. J. Psychol.* 31: 1–21, 1940.

*Vuyk, Rita: Projektionsphänomene bei Kindern. *Schweiz. Z. Psychol. Anwend.* 12: 124–134, 1953.

*—: *Plaatjes als Hulpmiddel bij het Kinderpsychologisch Onderzoek.* Leiden: H. E. Stenfert Kroese N. V., 1954.

Watson, R. I.: *Psychology of the Child.* New York: John Wiley, 1959.

Weisskopf, Edith: A transcendence index as a proposed measure in the TAT. *J. Psychol.* 29: 379–390, 1950.

*Weisskopf-Joelson, Edith and Foster, Helen C.: An experimental study of the effect of stimulus variation upon projection. *J. proj. Tech.* 26: 366–370, 1962.

*—, and Lynn, D. B.: The effect of variations in ambiguity on projection in the Children's Apperception Test. *J. consult. Psychol.* 17: 67–70, 1953.

Werner, H.: *Comparative Psychology of Mental Development* (Rev. ed.). New York: Follett, 1948.

*Wheeler, W. M.: Psychodiagnostic assessments of a child after prolonged separation in early childhood. II. *Brit J. med. Psychol.* 28–29: 248–257, 1955–56.

*Wirt, R. D.: The Children's Apperception Test. *In* O. K. Buros (Ed.): *The Sixth Mental Measurements Yearbook.* Highland Park, N. J.: Gryphon Press, 1965.

*Witherspoon, R. L., and Rochester, Aileen: Developmental characteristics and the dynamics of responses given to the CAT. (Unpublished.) Florida State Univer.

Wohlwill, J. F.: From perception to inference: a dimension of cognitive development. *In* W. Kessen and Clementina Kuhlman: *Thought in the Young Child. Monogr. Soc. Res. Child Develpm.* 27: No. 2 (Serial No. 83), pp. 87–107, 1962.

Wolff, P. H.: The developmental psychologies of Jean Piaget and psychoanalysis. *Psychological Issues.* 2: No. 1 (Monogr. No. 5), 1960.

—: Developmental and motivational concepts in Piaget's sensorimotor theory of intelligence. *J. Amer. Acad. Child Psychiat.* 2: 225–243, 1963.

*Woltmann, A. G.: Review of the CAT. *Amer. J. Orthopsychiat.* 20: 844–845, 1950.

—: The use of puppetry as a projective method in therapy. *In* H. H. Anderson and Gladys L. Anderson (Eds.): *An Introduction to Projective Techniques.* New York: Prentice-Hall, 1951, pp. 606–638.

Index of Names

Adelman, Crusa, 123, 128, 252, 308
Adkins, M. M., 314
Ainsworth, Mary D., 24–26, 250, 251, 262, 308
Amen, Elizabeth W., 63, 308
Ames, Louise B., 38, 63, 308
Andrew, Gwen, 63, 308
Armstrong, Mary Ann, 42–44, 46, 70, 73, 122, 308
Austin, Mary, 282

Balken, Eva, 56, 63, 143, 308
Beck, S. J., 38, 315
Bell, J. E., 308
Bellak, L., 1, 2, 6, 7, 10, 13, 19–21, 31, 33, 41, 43, 52, 62, 66, 68, 69, 89, 107, 108, 117, 122, 123, 128, 139, 146, 149, 252, 282, 283, 297, 300–302, 307–309, 313
Bellak, Sonya S., 1, 41, 43, 282, 297, 300, 302, 308
Beller, E. K., 193, 308
Bender, Lauretta, 38, 60, 308
Bennett, E. M., 79, 182, 308
Biersdorf, Kathryn R., 27, 42–44, 73, 308
Bills, R. E., 41, 308
Blatt, S. J., 12, 16, 308
Blum, G. S., 33, 309
Bolgar, Hedda, 7, 16, 17, 309
Booth, L. J., 14, 67, 71, 72, 83, 84, 309
Borstelmann, L. J., 17, 309
Boston, Mary, 24–26, 250–251, 262, 308
Boulanger-Balleyguier, Geneviève, 24, 30–32, 67, 74, 76–80, 88, 186, 188, 191, 193, 256–257, 301, 309
Boyd, Nancy, 36, 39, 309
Bridges, Katharine M. B., 58, 309
Brink, Louise, 35, 311

Brower, Judith F., 301, 309
Brown, D. G., 120, 309
Budoff, M., 28, 33, 42, 43, 45, 46, 49, 50, 122, 186, 309
Buss, A. H., 36, 309
Butler, R. L., 27, 49, 50, 185, 186, 309
Byrd, E., 22, 26, 67–69, 73, 118, 250, 309

Cain, A. C., 13, 309
Caplan, H., 34, 36, 309
Child, I. L., 36, 39, 309
Chowdhury, Uma, 7, 10, 83, 85, 86, 309
Cobb, E. A., 314
Coleman, W., 63, 64, 309
Cook, R., 32, 309
Cushing, H. M., 36, 313

Dennis, W., 66, 309
DeSousa, Therese L., 14, 24, 189, 190, 309
Despert, Louise, 65
Dhondiyal, S., 261, 310
Distler, L., 119, 313
Duhm, Erna, 310
Durkee, Ann, 36, 309

Earle, Margaret J., 83, 86–88, 310
Eiserer, P. E., 117, 310
Emmerich, W., 119, 310
Engel, Mary, 12, 15, 16, 238, 308, 310
Ephrussi, R., 80, 310

Fear, Clara, 301, 310
Fearing, F., 36, 314
Feifel, H., 56, 310
Fine, R., 122, 310
FitzSimons, Ruth, 24, 185, 310
Flavell, J. H., 53, 55, 57, 310
Fleming, E. E., 64, 314
Foster, Helen C., 32, 42, 43, 45, 46, 69, 122, 315
Frank, L. K., 19, 21, 25, 310

Freud, Anna, 59, 60, 119, 310
Freud, S., 1, 19, 34, 310
Furuya, Kenji, 42, 43, 45, 46, 186, 310

Gästrin, Jan, 137, 138
Genn, M. M., 310
Gesell, A., 60, 310
Gewirtz, J. L., 17, 310
Gibby, R. G., 15, 310
Gibson, R. M., 183, 310
Ginsparg, H. T., 27, 67, 70–73, 80, 91, 310
Gluck, M. R., 16, 312
Goldberg, Ilsa, 36, 310
Goldfarb, W., 36, 310
Goldfried, M. R., 37, 310
Granick, S., 26, 311
Griffiths, Ruth, 63, 311
Guha, B. S., 7, 10
Gurevitz, S., 24, 187, 311

Haeberle, Ann W., 193, 308
Halpern, Florence, 61, 114, 248, 255, 311
Hammer, E. F., 38, 286, 311
Hartwell, S. W., 63, 308
Haworth, Mary R., 22, 24, 27, 28, 47, 48, 50–52, 80, 89, 109, 120, 137, 139, 141–144, 193–194, 196, 257–259, 274, 283, 286, 287, 311
Heiman, M., 35, 311
Hemmendinger, L., 60, 311
Henry, W. E., 20, 122, 311
Herman, H., 311
Hess, R. D., 83, 85, 313
Hilgard, E. R., 311
Holden, R. H., 24, 187, 311
Holt, R. R., 14, 311
Hunt, H. F., 33, 63, 309
Hurvich, M. S., 282, 308
Hutt, M. L., 63, 308

Ilg, Frances L., 60, 310
Inhelder, Bärbel, 53, 311

Jackson, R. W., 27, 42–44, 311

Jelliffe, S. E., 35, 311
Jensen, A. R., 24, 311
Johannsen, Dorothea E., 79, 182, 308
Jones, R. M., 14, 311

Kaake, Norma E., 80–81, 118, 311
Kagan, J., 29, 116, 117, 249, 311, 312
Kagan, Marion G., 24, 184, 312
Kanehira, Teruko, 195, 312
Katzenstein, Betti, 183, 301, 312
Kaufman, Marilyn A., 24, 184, 312
Kenny, D. T., 7, 312
King, Dorothy C., 120, 121, 312
King, F. W., 120, 121, 312
Kissel, S., 37, 310
Klapper, Zelda S., 24, 187, 311
Koch, Helen L., 26, 73, 81, 82, 312
Kris, E., 1

Lamont, Violet, 1
Lantzourakis, Ann, 137, 138
Lawton, Marcia J., 28, 42, 43, 45, 46, 50, 51, 80, 139, 283, 286, 287, 312
Learned, Janet, 38, 308
Ledwith, Nettie, H., 38, 312
Lehmann, I. J., 67–69, 83, 84, 312
Leiman, C. J., 41, 308
Lesser, G. S., 117, 312
Leventhal, T., 16, 312
Levine, Estelle M., 36, 39, 309
Levy, R. A., 36, 38, 312
Levy, S., 36, 38, 312
Light, B. H., 27, 42–44, 46, 312
Lindzey, G., 20, 29, 116, 312
Lorge, I., 56, 310
Lumpkin, W. T., 83, 312
Lyles, W. K., 15, 312
Lynn, D. B., 27, 30, 122, 315

Macedo de Queiroz, Aydil, 183, 312
Macfarlane, Jean W., 21, 312
Magnusson, D., 22, 28, 82–83, 255, 313
Mainord, Florence R., 47, 48, 186, 190, 313
Mandler, G., 36, 39, 309
Marcuse, F. L., 27, 42–44, 47, 48, 73, 186, 190, 308, 313
Marui, Sumiko, 7, 8, 194, 313
Masling, J., 15, 313
Masserman, J., 143
Menninger, K. A., 34, 313
Métraux, Ruth W., 38, 308
Millar, Mary Aileen, 31, 67, 69, 70, 77, 79, 313
Miller, D. R., 15, 310
Miller, R. B., 314
Mirmow, Esther L., 12, 16, 64, 308, 314
Molish, H. B., 38, 315
Moriarty, Alice E., 17, 74–76, 79, 80, 88, 161, 313
Moss, H. A., 249, 312
Muller, P., 26, 73, 313
Murphy, Lois B., 17, 74–76, 79, 80, 88, 156, 161, 313
Murray, H., 2, 25
Murstein, B. I., 19, 33, 41, 52, 313
Mussen, P., 119, 313

Nolan, R. D., 25, 26, 28, 72, 73, 250, 313

Olim, E. G., 83, 85, 313
Olney, E. E., 36, 313
Ōuchi, Gosuke, 41, 313

Papania, N., 56, 313
Parsons, T., 119, 313
Peters, Alice, 66, 313
Phillips, L., 38, 314
Piaget, J., 53–55, 57–59, 63, 314
Pitcher, Evelyn G., 37, 38, 64, 65, 314
Plutchik, Lillian, 188, 314
Potter, E. H., 36, 39, 309

Prelinger, E., 37, 38, 64, 65, 314
Pryer, R. S., 19, 313

Rabin, A. I., 120, 311, 314
Raff, Eleanore, 24, 89, 189, 314
Rapoport, J., 38, 308
Reichnardt Epps, D., 183, 312
Rochester, Aileen, 250, 315
Rooney, Kathryn, 314
Rosenberg, I. H., 36, 38, 314
Rosenblatt, B. P., 16, 312
Rosenblatt, M. S., 27, 67, 70–73, 250, 314
Rosenzweig, Louise, 60, 64, 314
Rosenzweig, S., 60, 62, 64, 314
Rutherford, E., 119, 313

Sandler, Louise, 263–272, 314
Sanford, R. N., 63, 65, 117, 314
Scheflen, Norma A., 26, 311
Schwartz, A. A., 36, 38, 314
Shaffer, L. F., 314
Shipman, Virginia C., 83, 85, 313
Shneidman, E. S., 80, 314
Sidler, Martha, 14, 314
Simon, Maria D., 24, 78, 79, 190, 191, 314
Simson, E., 42–46, 51, 259, 260, 314
Slepian, H. J., 16, 312
Smith, J. G., 38, 314
Spiegelman, M., 36, 314
Stevenson, H. W., 17, 55, 315
Stevenson, Margaret, 24, 195, 196, 315
Stone, L. J., 7, 301, 315
Stotsky, B. A., 15, 310
Symonds, P. M., 65, 117, 122, 143, 315

Templin, Mildred C., 60, 315
Terwilliger, C., 36, 314
Thetford, W. N., 38, 315

Thomas, R. W., 41, 308
Tomkins, S. S., 25, 315
Toppelstein, S., 46, 66, 67, 70–72, 315
Tuddenham, R. D., 21, 312

Van de Castle, R. L., 15, 315
Van Cauvenberghe, Paulette, 261, 262, 315
Vander Veer, A. H., 56, 63, 308

Vernon, M. D., 56, 57, 63, 315
Vuyk, Rita, 20, 80, 147, 315

Walker, R. N., 38, 308
Walton, R. E., 63, 308
Watson, R. I., 58, 315
Weisskopf, Edith (see Weisskopf-Joelson)
Weisskopf-Joelson, Edith, 27, 30, 32, 42, 43, 45, 46, 69, 122, 315

Werner, H., 34, 53–55, 58–60, 63, 315
Wheeler, W. M., 24, 250, 251, 262, 315
Wirt, R. D., 30, 315
Witherspoon, R. L., 22, 26, 67–69, 73, 118, 250, 309, 315
Wohlwill, J. F., 315
Wolff, P. H., 315
Woltmann, A. G., 243, 311, 315

Index of Subjects

Abstraction, 56, 85
Additions, 31, 43, 72, 77–78, 124–125, 147, 191
Adjustment, positive, 61, 74, 76, 78. 161–162, 191, 192
Adopted children, 110–111, 233
Affect, inappropriate, 113, 153–154, 217
Affectional patterns, 156, 196
Age levels
    in development (see Developmental levels)
    in projective stories, 59, 63–64. 67–73
Age norms in CAT
    latency period, 70–73
    preschool period, 67–70
Aggression and aggressive responses, 2, 3, 22, 29, 51, 68, 79, 87, 109–110, 116–117, 155–156, 185, 191–193. 195, 234, 250, 257, 293
Ambiguity (see Stimulus ambiguity)
Ambivalence, 143, 197, 224
Anal themes, 50, 148, 154, 157, 220. 224, 229 (see also Toileting themes)
Analysis of Adaptive Mechanisms (Analysis Schedule), 27, 47, 50–51, 89, 137–151, 258–259, 274, 283
    reliability of, 27–28, 139
Animal symbolism, 35–37
Animal versus human stimuli, 33. 39, 41–52
Animals
    in child's life, 34
    in children's drawings, 38
    in children's stories, 35, 37
    in myths, 34–35
    in primitive cultures, 33–34

Animism, 58
Anxiety, 6, 29, 87–88, 109, 125, 147–148, 187, 191–193, 195, 213, 233, 238, 257–259
Apperceptive distortion, 19
Apperceptive method, 2
Articulatory problems, 75, 184–185
Austria, 78, 190–191

Behavior disorder, acting out, 14, 143, 208
    protocol, 208–209
Bellak's TAT and CAT Blank (Short Form), 27, 89, 122–134, 283, 301
Bender Gestalt, 15, 22, 82, 255–256, 261
Birth fantasies, 3, 144, 197, 210, 217, 220
Bizarre responses, 74, 114, 149, 187, 242, 274, 277, 278
Blacky Pictures, 27, 33, 38, 120, 184
Borderline psychosis, 238–239
    protocol, 238–242
Brain damage, 148, 149, 205–206, 303
    protocol, CAT, 205–208
    protocol, CAT-S, 304
Brazil, 301

Canada, 84, 195–196
Case history information, 23–24, 109–116
Castration fears, 3, 6, 144–146, 158, 213, 290
CAT (Children's Apperception Test)
    administration, 12–13
        to mothers, 261–262
        variations of, 13–14, 43
    card descriptions, 3–6
    evaluative comments, 6

history of, 1
nature and purpose, 1
typical responses to each card, 3–6, 70,
    72, 75–76, 79–80, 89–106, 162–181
CAT compared with other projective tech-
    niques, 254–261
    Bender Gestalt, 255–256, 261
    Despert Fables, 257–259
    Draw-a-Man, 255–256
    Draw-a-Person, 257–259
    drawings, 259–261
    Rorschach, 255–259, 263–281
CAT-H (Children's Apperception Test—
    Human), 43, 47, 282–296
    clinical use, 286–296
    comparison with CAT, 286–296
    research, 283–286
    scoring and interpretation, 283
CAT-S (Children's Apperception Test—
    Supplement), 183, 297–307
    clinical use, 303–307
    description of test, 297–301
    research, 301–303
    scoring and interpretation, 301
Cerebral palsy, 187–188, 201
    protocol, 201–205
Character disorder, 14, 210
    protocol, 210–213
Childhood schizophrenia, 36, 149–150, 187–
    188, 242, 245, 247–248, 252–254
    protocols, 242–248, 252–254
Color projection, 153–154, 278
Common themes, 66–67 (see also Popular
    responses)
Concrete Operations (Piaget), 55
Conflicts, 20, 125
Controls, weak, 51, 149–150, 153, 194
Coping maneuvers, 18, 76, 126, 161
Coping Project (Menninger Foundation),
    18, 74, 76
Countertransference reactions, 16
Cross-sectional studies, 2
Cultural-free aspects, 2, 7, 66, 77, 85–86

Death themes, 65, 79, 111–112, 147, 188,
    192, 196–197, 233, 272, 279, 293
Deception, 144, 194
Defense mechanisms, 7, 18, 19, 21, 58, 59–
    60, 126, 161
Defenses, 2, 3, 14, 16, 32, 125–126
Denial, 18, 74, 143
Dependence-independence, 156, 192, 193
Description, 67–68, 71, 187, 198 (see also
    Enumeration)

Descriptive studies, 74–79
Despert Fables (Düss Fables), 22, 38, 257–
    259, 261
Developmental aspects, 26, 53–61
    in emotional development, 58–60
    in mental development, 53–56
    in thought and language, 56–58
Diabetic children, 182–183
Diagnostic studies, 182–197
Draw-a-Man Test (DAM), 22, 82, 182, 255–
    256
Draw-a-Person Test (DAP), 15, 22, 183,
    184, 257–259
Drawings, 259–261, 301
Dream technique, 13–14

Ego, 20, 21, 127
Emotional development (see Developmental
    aspects)
Emotional disturbance, 47–50, 57, 189–195,
    262
Enumeration and description, 56, 67–68, 71,
    80–81
Enuresis, enuretic symbols, 144, 210, 233,
    262
Examiner
    attitudes, 15
    influence of, 15–17
    sex, 15, 17
Expressive behavior, 2, 7

Fears, 2, 3, 6, 22, 68, 79, 109, 147–148, 156
Figure drawings (see DAM, DAP)
Film, as a group projective technique, 22,
    23, 257
Fixations, 59
Formal Operations (Piaget), 55
French, 12, 26, 74, 76–78, 191–193, 256–
    257, 261–262

German, 12, 259–260
Guilt feelings, 63, 195, 220, 233

Hero, 123–124
Hierarchization (Werner), 55, 61
Humor, 18, 161

Iconicity, 32
Id, 59
Identification, 3, 7, 26, 32, 117–121, 150–
    151, 154–155, 192
    with aggressor, 119
    with animals, 1, 33–35, 41, 80–81
    confused, 51, 150–151

with opposite-sex, 119–121, 150–151, 234
   with parents, 69, 71, 250
   with same-sex, 119–121, 150–151, 161
Impregnation fantasies, 238
Impulses, 20, 21
Independence, 3, 59
India, 7, 85–86
Intellectual levels, 80–82, 152 (*see also* Mental retardation)
Interpretation of projectives, 107–121
Interpretive responses, 63, 67–68, 71, 80–81
Interpretive schema, 122–151
Interpretive summary, 127–128, 152–161
Introjection, 35, 146–147, 217
IQ correlations, 77–78, 81, 85
Isolation (cognitive), 51, 143, 224
IT Scale, 120
Italian, 12

Japanese, 7, 194–195

Latency, 70–73, 76, 126
Latin-American, 84–85
Little Hans (Freud), 1, 34
Longitudinal studies, 24, 249–254
   clinical data, 250–254
   need for, 2, 250, 254
   protocols, 252–254

Magic and magical thinking, 18, 35, 57–58, 65, 147, 210, 242
Manifest versus latent levels, 1, 21, 116–117
Maori culture, 86–88
Masturbatory themes, 2, 3, 6, 144, 158, 220
Mental development, 53–56
Mental retardation, 13, 50, 56, 80–81, 183, 185–186, 198, 199, 303
   protocols, CAT, 198–200
   protocols, CAT-S, 304, 306
Multiple examiners, 17
Multiple testing, 249–281 (*see also* Test battery)
Muscular tension, 188–189

Needs, 27, 41, 71, 73, 81, 249–250
   n-Achievement, 73, 249–250
   n-Affiliation, 250
   n-Physical aggression, 249–250
   n-Power, 250
Negative affects, 20, 38, 39
Negro children, 3, 14
Netherlands, 20
Normal samples, 41–47, 62–88
   protocols from, 89–106

Normative studies with CAT, 41–47, 67–88
Norms, determination of, 62–67
Obsessive reactions, 23, 57, 139–143, 224, 229, 257–259
   protocols, 224–233
Oedipal themes, 2, 22, 43, 50, 69, 71, 146, 157–160, 213, 220, 246, 290, 293
Omissions, 31, 32, 43, 77, 79–80, 125, 186, 191
Oppositional tendencies, 50, 140, 224, 229
Oral deprivation themes, 19, 47, 144, 238, 242, 246, 279
Orality, 2, 3, 6, 18, 19, 22, 35, 68, 74, 79, 147, 157–158, 184–185, 217, 242, 250
Outcomes, 72, 79, 127, 161, 185
Overt versus fantasy behavior, 29, 116–117

Parent-child relationships, 16, 17, 26, 36, 74, 79, 81–82, 87, 184–185
Parent figures, attitude toward, 2, 3, 6, 20, 51, 154, 187–188, 192, 195–196, 210, 213, 234, 296
Parental loss, 195–197, 233–234, 259, 278–281
   protocols, 233–238, 279–280
Passive-aggressive maneuvers, 224, 229, 233–234
Peer relationships, 20, 87, 154, 301
   lack of, 213
Perceptual difficulties, 30–32, 80, 306
Perceptual distortions, 32, 74
Perseveration, 152, 186, 187, 191, 248, 304, 306
Personal references, 57, 148, 217, 305, 306
Phobias (*see* Fears)
Physical anomalies, 183–184
Physical disabilities, 183
Picture-Story Test (Symonds), 1, 2, 122, 183
Poison themes, 149
Popular responses, 30, 62, 77, 191
Pre-operational stage (Piaget), 55
Primal scene fantasies, 2, 6, 43, 144, 158, 220
Primary process, 14, 57, 59, 63, 152
Projection, 18, 35, 46–47, 51, 146–147, 194, 283, 286
   theories of, 19–21
   types of, 19
Protocols, CAT
   clinic cases, 108, 112, 113, 114–115, 153–154, 198–200, 205–216, 220–229, 233–248, 252–254, 274–277, 279–280, 286–293, 295–296

compared with CAT-H, 286–296
normal samples, 89–106, 135–137, 158–159, 216–220, 229–232, 263–269, 294–295
Protocols, CAT-H, 286–296
Protocols, CAT-S, 303–307
Psychoneurotic reactions, 190–191, 213, 216–217, 220
protocols, 213–224
Psychosexual development, 58–59, 156–160
Psychotherapy, 2, 254, 307
Punishment themes, 3, 6, 39, 59, 69, 74, 161

Reaction-formation, 51, 139–143
Reaction time, 43, 46, 109
Reality awareness, lack of, 79, 148–149, 152–154, 190, 238, 242–243
Reality, concern about, 162, 217, 238, 242, 245, 274
Recording of stories, 12, 13, 46
Recurrent themes, 20, 107
Refusals, 75, 109, 143
Regression and regressive trends, 6, 16, 18, 58, 59, 148–149, 194, 238
Reliability, 21, 24–28
scoring reliability, 27–28, 139
test-retest, 25–27
Reports, psychological, 127–128, 152
Repression, 32, 51, 60, 109, 143, 283
Resistance, 18
Responses for each card
card 1, 162–164
card 2, 164–165
card 3, 165–167
card 4, 167–169
card 5, 169–171
card 6, 171–172
card 7, 172–175
card 8, 175–177
card 9, 178–179
card 10, 179–181
Retarded subjects (see Mental retardation)
Role of parent, 119–120
Role-playing, 14
Rorschach, 2, 6, 15, 16, 22, 23, 34, 38, 60–61, 82–83, 88, 146, 182, 183, 196, 233, 238, 248, 251–252, 255–259, 262, 269–281
protocols, 114, 269–271, 272–274, 278–279
Rosenzweig Picture-Frustration Study, 64, 182

Schizophrenic children (see Childhood schizophrenia)
Secondary process, 59
Self-concept, 114, 155
Sensory-motor stage (Piaget), 53–54
Sequence analysis, 107–109
Sex differences, 17, 37, 64–65, 73–74
Sexual preoccupations, 113–116, 145, 197, 233, 293
Sibling rivalry themes, 2, 3, 22, 195
Siblings, 20, 78, 87, 112, 154, 290, 301
Sibship patterns, studies of, 81–83
Slips of the tongue, 112, 147, 233, 293
Sociocultural studies, 65–66, 83–88
Socioeconomic levels, 84–85, 262
Sociometric studies, 83
Spanish, 12
Stimulus properties, 29–40
ambiguity, 29–32, 249–250
color, 32, 42
Story dynamics, 68, 71
Story length, 46, 67, 71 (see also Word count)
Sublimation, 18, 60
Superego, 59–60, 126–127, 161
Sweden, 82, 137, 174–175, 255–256
Symbolization, 144–146
Syncretic thought, 57–58

TAT (Thematic Apperception Test), 1, 2, 15, 19, 27, 41, 88, 117, 183, 196, 249–250, 261
Tabulation schemes
for CAT, 66
for CAT-S, 301
Test battery, 14–15, 254–261
sequence of tests, 14
Testing situation, 17–18
Thought and language, 56–58
Thought processes, loosening of, 112, 114, 127, 149, 153, 238, 242, 272
Time measurements, 66
Toileting themes, 2, 19, 22, 68, 74, 148, 290 (see also Anal themes)
Transcendence Index, 27, 30, 46, 50, 73, 122, 186
Twin studies, 22, 82–83, 255–256

Undoing, 113, 143

Validity, 21–24

WISC, 71, 81
Word count, 43–46, 66, 184
Word-finding difficulties, 12, 206, 295